DATE DUE	RETURNED
MAR 2 8 2011	MAR 3 1 2011
MAR 1 7 2012	MAR 2 8 20

BRAND NEW CHINA

BRAND
NEW
CHINA

Advertising, Media,
and Commercial Culture

JING WANG

HARVARD UNIVERSITY PRESS

Cambridge, Massachusetts

London, England

2008

Library of Congress Cataloging-in-Publication Data

Wang, Jing, 1950 July 5–
Brand new China : advertising, media, and
commercial culture / Jing Wang.
p.   cm.
Includes bibliographical references and index.
ISBN-13: 978-0-674-02680-3 (cloth : alk. paper)
ISBN-10: 0-674-02680-2 (cloth : alk. paper)
1. Advertising—China.   2. Marketing—China.
3. Brand name products—China.   I. Title.
HF5813.C5W37   2007
659.10951—dc22   2007027501

To
Bruce Oltchick

Contents

Preface

My interest in writing a book about contemporary Chinese advertising began in the late 1990s. While putting together another project, I stumbled upon a fascinating phenomenon in the history of Chinese popular culture: the colorful outburst of corporate logos in the urban centers of south and north China around 1988. It was then merely a decade since the return of commercial advertising after the Cultural Revolution, and television commercials as well as print advertising still carried socialist baggage.

Imagine a health-drink manufacturer who suddenly discovers the cash value of visual symbols. The relationship between "invisible assets" and a figurative image becomes clear, which in turn triggers a sharp visual turn of the corporate culture. The health-drink maker was Apollo *(Taiyang shen),* based in Guangdong province. In 1988 the company adopted a corporate identity management system, imported from Japan, which emphasized a firm's philosophy of management, organizational strategies, and visual identity. In China, it was the concept of visual identity that initially attracted the most attention.

Apollo's famous logo, an icon resembling the Chinese character of "humans" set against a bright red disk, and its sentimental theme song, "when the sun rises, our love for you is eternal," helped turn the health drink into a household name. By 1992 Apollo had transformed itself from a township village enterprise with assets of five million yuan ($625,000) into a huge corporation with one billion ($125 million). The tremendous success of its corporate identity strategy set off an emulative fever among other enterprises. "Image design" *(xingxiang sheji)* became part of the corporate vocabulary and a trendy social discourse. China's consumer public gained a heightened awareness of the value of commercial signs, insignia, icons, design patents, and, of course, company logos.

The link between corporate logos and the visual medium had a creative impact on advertising and the social landscape. Almost overnight, the huge red-and-white billboards on Beijing's Avenue of Eternal Peace advertising socialist virtues were upstaged by the more colorful ones promoting commercial goods. I suggest that Apollo's imported means of establishing its corporate identity was a watershed event not only for a commercial culture takeoff but also for a visual culture renaissance in post-Mao China. I want to call attention to a conceptual habit of ours: whenever we study contemporary Chinese commercial images, we automatically turn to media and advertising, bypassing the corporate sector altogether. How can we comprehend the rise of popular references to "culture as capital" *(wenhua ziben)*—that is, the transformation of cultural-symbolic capital into economic capital—in post-1992 China without giving due recognition to the visual turn of the corporate sector? My first goal in this book is to provide the missing link between corporate interests and marketing credos and the study of advertising and branding in contemporary China.

The challenges of writing such a book are many. My initial hurdle was to gain access to the ad industry, a world usually shut off to academic researchers. My plan got even more complicated as I realized that the "field" consisted of more than the advertising sector, which stands at the intersection of the media and the corporate sectors. I thus look at these two adjacent sectors as well and chart the complex dynamics that arise among them—the second goal of my book.

My third goal is to cultivate a cross-fertilization between academia and the advertising sector, and to write from an in-between, fluid perspective. Prior to 2002, I surveyed the literature on brands and branding as taught in U.S. business schools and waded through pioneering theoretical work in the field of cultural studies that treats ads as if they are nothing more than single-authored "texts." I also had the luxury of seeing thousands of Asian print ads and television commercials. These rigorous exercises gave me a strong textbook-based approach to advertising. But I was left craving the field knowledge that only an advertising agency can provide. By mere fluke, I was given the opportunity to work at the transnational advertising agency Ogilvy & Mather in Beijing for two summers, in 2002 and 2004. I went to Ogilvy to gain hands-on experience in branding a product from start to finish. I also took advantage of my privileged position at the agency to hunt for issues that galvanize the professionals on the front lines. I lived a double life as an academic critic immersed in the crisis-ridden daily routine of an agency.

My fourth and perhaps most challenging goal is to move those in the discipline of cultural studies from a focus on the ad as an authorial "text," flattened out for content analysis, to a focus on the ad as a "product," an assembly line output whose dynamics can only be captured through onsite fieldwork. I make production-centered issues—the processes of branding, specifically—my priority rather than the interpretation of how culture is represented in advertisements. This methodological emphasis is crucial if we want to explore the possibilities of moving advertising research and, by extension, pop culture studies in general beyond the staple question of representation into the domain of cultural production.

A long intellectual tradition has prided itself on critiquing commercial culture as "debased" and condemning consumption as "mass deception." But how can one undertake a genuine appraisal of commercial culture if it is already assigned an overwhelmingly negative value before we even begin our study? Is it possible to be a cultural critic while making room for industry frames of reference? I hope to join those who, in search of methodological renewal, go beyond the 1960s paradigm of "producers (as deceivers)" versus "consumers (as victims)." The institutional and social structure of control that underlies and legitimizes commercial culture is beyond my scope here. But by focusing on the site of production (in this case, the advertising industry), I seek to turn fieldwork into a tool with which to debunk the conventional dichotomies drawn between the local and the global, consumers and producers, and resistance and domination.

The integration of industry perspectives into advertising research enables us to mitigate problems arising from the conventional textual approaches to advertisements in more than one way. Analyzing the content of ads is problematic in markets like China's, where ads are, as elsewhere, increasingly made for target audiences to which the academic interpreter does not belong. An academic critic's like or dislike of an ad may thus matter very little in the final analysis. Seen in this light, while advertising studies in the humanities have long been built on canonical work in cultural criticism and social theory, it is time we also experiment with methods that give voice to the producers of ads (who are savvy consumers as well). Let us not forget that the best planner in an ad agency is often the most avid and smartest shopper of all. Equally important, an agency provides multiple access to real-life consumers. Not only do agencies rely heavily on regular focus group meetings, but strategic planners themselves—a subdivision of expertise within full-service agencies—are also privy to consumer insights gleaned from a variety of product categories. The bigger the agency is, the larger the number of its accounts, the more diversified these categories are, and the greater the scale of consumer insights provided. Full-service agencies can also afford to commission companies for multi-tiered marketing research (which is essential for an uneven market like

China's), bringing more consumers from diverse localities into contact with the planners.

A production-centered methodology, then, delivers more than just the producers' standpoint. It provides an easy way to enter the consumers' world and their points of view. When coupled with cultural analysis, this approach has several advantages. It remedies the short-term perspective of the trade literature on advertising by providing an integrative approach that brings all three fields (media, advertising, and the corporate sector) into the cultural equation simultaneously. It also goes beyond treating advertising as a mere psychoanalytic shorthand for the "discourse of desire," a theoretical hallmark of the humanities literature on the subject.

In the United States, advertising research on China has been dominated by case studies, practical tips about branding, and anecdotal literature. Euphoric in spirit and mostly focused on campaigns in TV and print media, these books fall short of probing more deeply into popular culture trends, largely ignore the impact of the digital revolution on marketing strategies and advertising platforms, and make blanket assumptions about market segments that blur gender, age, socioeconomic, and geographical divides in China. The best discussions of these topics, which this book taps substantively, have been published in Chinese.

I have written *Brand New China* for industry, advertising, media, academic, and general readers interested in gaining an in-depth understanding of the rise of China from the vantage point of branding and marketing culture. A total immersion in the rich worlds of producers, marketers, and consumers will also open up new ground for those who want to bridge the gap between theorists and practitioners.

I began this study as a "pure" academic. But frankly, after pulling all-nighters as a strategic planner in an ad agency, I can no longer think like the straight scholar I once was. It is my hope that this book will speak to all those in the multifaceted worlds I explore.

BRAND NEW CHINA

Introduction:
Framing Chinese Advertising

Commercial advertising returned to the People's Republic of China in 1979. What was once a young, unstable sector has taken big strides since then, turning into an industry with total billings of $18 billion by 2005, up 12 percent from the previous year, making up 0.78 percent of China's gross domestic product (GDP), and accounting for an impressive 1.92 percent of the country's tertiary sector (Guang 2006, 38–39).[1] The sheer size and scale of the Middle Kingdom lie behind its growth miracle. As of 2005, there were 84,272 ad agencies and approximately 9,650 advertising media. The total number of personnel employed increased from 700,000 in 2001 to 940,415 in 2005 (ibid.).

Commercial advertising in China was nipped in the bud during Mao's era. And few would disagree that the rampant consumer culture in China today is a mockery of the Communist revolution. But a facile exaggeration of the "discontinuity" between Mao's China and reform China has a drawback: we risk losing sight of the intangible link between China's socialist persona and its capitalist face that lies behind many success stories in corporate China. Channel distribution strategies like leading beverage producer Wahaha's "spider warfare" (that is, "countryside surrounding the city") are at the very heart of marketing with Chinese characteristics. Corporate branding of star enterprises like Lenovo and Haier relies

1

heavily on the disciplining power of corporatized Mao-speak and the Chairman's famed ideology of the "permanent revolution." Those business models have flourished and prepared ambitious Chinese superbrands to go global, reminding us of the stubbornness of the Chinese socialist legacy. Those who overlook socialism's deep roots in contemporary China and underestimate its ideological flexibility will find its market hard to crack.

Brand New China brings us to a close encounter with that market: its idiosyncrasies as well as its parallels to what has taken place in affluent Western societies. With an analysis that includes topics like the bobo fever and the single-child generation in pursuit of "safe cool," this book takes a critical look at contemporary Chinese advertising and examines branded phenomena in China—from product brands to corporate brands—how they have been created and what kind of challenges they pose to international advertising and to cultural *and* business globalization. Opinions are sharply divided on what the "new China" is like now that it is a member of the WTO. Some predict the "demise of the authoritarian state"; others consider China's ascent to the world stage to be a global self-promotion that will hardly put a dent in the state's capacity to control (Keane and Donald 2002, 208). With few exceptions, such as Zhao Yuezhi's longer view of China's integration into global capitalism (Y. Zhao 2003), critical literature on the WTO challenge is prone to reinforce a mentality dating from the Cold War in its treatment of the globalizing China either as the Communist "other" or as a foe involuntarily losing its own identity to become one of "us."[2] Post-2001 China is neither. It is heavily influenced by the ideology of global partnership while struggling not to become a mirror image of the United States. "Country branding" is more challenging than ever, and the emerging brand "new China" eludes ideological preconceptions.

New China, however, should be taken metaphorically rather than literally. Although the Chinese have captured their new vision in the catchphrase "created in China" (Keane 2007), the country is still seen as a world factory rather than as an innovators' heaven. The China of yesterday did not disappear simply because Shanghai has grabbed the attention of the world's luxury marketers. The number of the "Chinese middle class" is greatly exaggerated, and "new China" remains a highly stratified society, with a total of 26.1 million households living in poverty, where annual per capita income was less than $77 in 2004 (National Bureau of Statistics 2004; Zhu Qingfang 2004, 87–88). The gaps in disposable income between the city and the countryside jumped from 2.51:1 in 1998 to 3.23:1 in 2003 (Lu Xueyi 2004, 176). During the same year, although peasants made up 70.8 percent of the national population, they consumed only 35.1 percent of national goods output, with the result that the consumption capacity of the rural population is falling behind urbanites by at least ten to fifteen years (ibid., 177). All these statistics indicate the harsh reality of a deeply divided China, which is indeed brand new on the one hand, but still stubbornly old in countless ways, not least in its struggle with poverty and other social ills that have plagued the country for centuries.

Although I track the rising importance of rural consumers for advertisers, the new China treated in this book is primarily the urban face of a country in its integration into the global economy. By urban, however, I do not mean only the first-tier cities of Beijing, Shanghai, and Guangzhou that most Western watchers focus on. Due recognition must be given to cities on the second tier (for example, Hangzhou, Nanjing, Shenyang, Tianjin, Wuhan, and other affluent provincial centers) and to the third-tier, sizable, and relatively affluent county towns *(zhongxin cheng)* like Changzhou and Wuxi.

"Brand new China" and "branded phenomena in China" constitute two topical axes of this book. The third axis—the construction of the "local"—is indispensable to both academic and corporate discussions about international advertising in the new century. The temptation for a cultural critic to discover resistance wherever she looks is great. This book does not, however, replicate the dualistic thinking of "resistant *locals*" versus "dominant *multinationals.*" It explores crossover visions driven by synergy-making, and asks how one bonds with the locals—a concern of multinational and domestic Chinese advertisers alike. This task is pressing not least because of the analytical bias in our current literature on branding and advertising: a great deal of attention has been lavished on the localization of multinational clients (MNCs) and transnational ad agencies (TNAAs) in emerging markets. But "localization" is not an exclusive concern of the MNCs and TNAAs. The locals have a vested interest in it as well. This point is driven home by, for example, Wahaha's attempt to camouflage Future Cola as a "Chinese cola" when it is actually Eurasian. Very few "local" brands are purebreds these days, and national ownership says little about how a brand is actually perceived by target consumers. In fact, the entry of multinational clients and transnational ad agencies into the Chinese market brings into full relief the dominance of hybrid brands and joint venture models. Those mixed prototypes keep pushing consumers to renegotiate the meaning of localness and localization. What will emerge after the old paradigm of the "local" versus the "global" breaks down completely remains to be seen.

From a theoretical perspective, the task of moving beyond such a binary, or dualistic, conceptualization depends a great deal on how seriously we take "marketing" as an analytical tool and fieldwork as a key to our understanding of how culture, be it commercial or pop, is produced. Moreover, a systemic focus on how branding is done in the advertising industry has much to offer to academic fields largely confined within semiological, textual (Barthes 1972; Williamson 1978; Wernick 1991, 1997; Goldman 1992; Kellner 1995; McFall 2004), historical (Marchand 1985; Richards 1990; Lears 1995), and ideological (Anderson 1984; Jhally 1990; Mattelart 1991; Leiss, Kline, et al. 1997) studies. *Brand New China* integrates marketing perspectives into the study of branding, lifestyle culture, and corporate culture, and in so doing it fills in a gap in contemporary popular cultural studies. This investigation is not just a single-country exercise on China, but a methodological exploration that pertains to advertising research in general and to my study of the widespread hypotheses regarding the advent of a "Chinese middle class" and the rise of a "global youth culture"—propositions set in the controversial terms of Western sensibility.

ADVERTISING MEDIUMS

Advertising, *guang gao* in modern Mandarin, "communicating to the public" or in the broadest sense of "making goods publicly known," developed as early as commodity exchange took shape in human society. In China, as elsewhere, the earliest medium of advertising was oral and even musical. *The Book of Odes* (1027–476 BCE) recorded an entry in the "Hymns to Zhou" that tells anecdotes of street peddlers playing bamboo flutes to sell candies. Other variations of musical ads such as tinkers' clappers, waste collectors' bells, and the copper gongs of traveling sundries men are still heard all over China. Human voice is another commercial medium that has hardly gone out of style. Those who grew up in 1950s and 1960s Taiwan recall the melodious voices of soft bean curd vendors resonating through the night and at dawn. Today tourists strolling down the bustling Snack Food Street in downtown Wangfujing in Beijing are still beckoned earnestly by young shop clerks hawking their culinary specialties.

When the market developed further, the written word overtook the oral medium as a means of publicity. Signboards inscribed in calligraphy began to spring up all over the country as early as the Song Dynasty (960–1279). Two of the most renowned store signs, penned in literati-style calligraphy for Tongren Tang herbal medicine and for Quanjude Peking duck, first greeted the consumer public during the Qing Dynasty (1644–1911). The poetic and the commercial coexisted effortlessly in numerous other ads written in rhymed couplets mounted on scrolls and hung up at taverns during the same period. But the first Chinese advertisement in the genuine modern sense, complete with copywriting and a logo, is said to be a print ad made by a needle shop of the Liu family in Jinan district during the Northern Song Dynasty (960–1127). The ad extolled the fine quality of Liu needles and used the visual of a white rabbit holding a medicine pounder as the store insignia.

More modern advertising in China came into being after the first Opium War, which began around 1840. Individual advertisers evolved into an organized guild, commanding a vast network of commercial information and persuasion conveyed through modern mass media such as newspapers and later radios. Modern print ads first appeared in the foreign-owned papers *Shanghai xinbao* (Shanghai New Post) around 1861 and *Shen bao* (Shen Post) around 1872, courting the educated elites. But to reach the masses, who had limited access to print media (and eventually radios) at the time, foreign advertisers had to resort to a different medium more familiar to folk sensibility. These were Chinese New Year poster ads *(nian hua)*, also known as calendar ads, which grocery stores in Chinatowns today still parcel out generously at the cash register as the lunar New Year approaches. They cover a wide variety of subjects, from scenic spots, celebrity portraits, historical figures, religious rituals, and Confucian legends of filial piety to still objects of flowers, fish, and animals. In most instances, the early modern poster ads bore little relationship to the product being sold, which was usually relegated to an obscure corner of the canvas. My favorite example is a poster ad portraying a traditionally dressed young woman breast-feeding her mother-in-law (a Confucian tale), advertising a flashlight. Commodities featured most prominently were cigarettes, both foreign and domestic brands.

Print ads rose simultaneously with calendar ads to appear in pop magazines and journals such as *Dongfang* (Orient) magazine and *Liangyou* (Good Companion) during the May Fourth period (1917–1921). Even Communist publications such as Li Dazhao and Chen Duxiu's *Weekly Review* (1918) and Mao Zedong's *Xiang River Review* (1919) openly solicited advertisers and used ads as a way to promote "China-made" goods, progressive journals, and anti-imperialist ideology. Lu Xun—modern China's most famous Left-League writer-intellectual—spoke of the virtue of advertising in a matter-of-fact fashion. In his commentary on an eighteenth-century satire (edited by Liu Bannong), he said, "To print a book means to sell it in large quantities; to emphasize sales volume naturally means one has to advertise it; to advertise simply means to tout its strengths" (Lu Xun, "Wei Bannong tiji 'He dian' hou zuo," 1926, 286).

Meanwhile, in the commercial hub of Shanghai, a booming industry of designer art developed in tandem with calendar art to meet the demands of commercial clients.[3] Also popular in Shanghai was display-window advertising in big department stores like Xinxin and Yong'an. Splashy neon-light ads filled downtown streets from the 1930s till the clampdown of the Communist ideologues. Radio and film advertising, as well as poster ads along railroad lines, flourished after World War II. Colleges also started experimenting with classes in advertising during the 1940s and sent students overseas to study the subject. Ad companies mushroomed in big and medium-sized cities. The trend did slow down with the founding of the People's Republic of China, but by 1958, China had its first television stations for commercial broadcasting. During the same period, advertising ventured into hitherto inconceivable mediums, including railroad trains in which poker card boxes, lunchboxes, chessboards, passenger magazines, and decorative hangings were all allowed to display commercial messages. Window advertising in restaurants was exceedingly popular, too. At the crowded hot-pot restaurant Donglaishun (in downtown Beijing), chefs performed meat-slicing techniques behind a glassed box facing the street, pushing "window shopping" to the next level of creativity (Chen Beiai 1997; Yu and Deng 2000; Zhao Shen 2001).

The Cultural Revolution (1966–1976) brought an abrupt end to the budding commercial advertising. It was not until January 1979 that the first domestic TV commercial of post-Mao China, for a tonic wine, was aired by Shanghai television. Later that year, the municipal government of Beijing moved the Democracy Wall, where democracy activists had been permitted to post news and ideas since the preceding November, from Xidan to Yuetan Park, turning the original venue blasphemously into an advertising wall. Outdoor billboards began to mushroom soon after. Post-Mao China's first ad magazine, *Chinese Advertising,* was founded in Shanghai in 1981, followed by the authoritative *International Advertising* four years later. The Association of Chinese Advertising was established in 1983. It mediated between advertising agencies and the official regulator of the sector (the State Administration of Industry and Commerce that governs the entry rules for transnational ad agencies, among other things). But the quantum leap in post-Mao advertising was initiated by a historic policy change: in 1993 Beijing gave free rein to news media to run their operations as business units *(qiye danwei)* rather than as public units *(shiye danwei)*. The sharp decline of state subsidies compelled state media to seek advertisers as new sources of revenue. Commercial broadcasting gained its *raison d'être*. In 1995 the Chinese Advertising Law came into effect, putting the finishing touches on the new order. Commercial culture and commercial speech have become so well integrated into China's popular culture and social landscape that it is no longer possible for serious scholars of China to dismiss advertising as mere clutter and material culture as an illegitimate subject of study.

This book focuses on the last decade of the twentieth century and the first decade of the twenty-first—a fascinating period of China's accelerated integration into the global market system. Standing at the intersection of three fields—popular culture studies, advertising, and media studies—this volume combines the vantage point of marketing concepts and practices with that of cultural analysis. Among the topics I examine are global brands and international advertising; the competition between Chinese domestic ad agencies and transnational ones; the construction of the "local"; bourgeois bohemians and luxury consumption; "neo-tribes" as a marketing discourse; the psychographic profile of the new modern girl; the single-child generation and cool culture; the rise of blue-collar segments and the TNAAs' long march into the hinterland; the new ideology of "synergy" in corporate China; organizational storytelling and the making of corporate culture; the future of Chinese nationalism as a sales pitch; the impact of media policies over advertising; and China's Central TV station and the rise of regional media; the emergent new creative culture and Internet marketing.

China's entry into the World Trade Organization in 2001 has unleashed an extensive debate over the impact of "globalization" on the Chinese advertising industry. American models of branding keep pouring in. Others debate the applicability of Al Ries and Jack Trout's classic *Positioning: The Battle for Your Mind* (2001 [1981]) to the Chinese market. Some wonder whether corporate branding, a unique Asian strength, is inferior to the American paradigm of product branding. *Brand New China* places these debates at the intersection of dialogues that are at once commercial, socioeconomic, and cultural.

THE GOLD, BLUE, AND OTHER COLLARS

Without advertising media, goods cannot be made known publicly, and similarly, without consumers, goods cannot be sold. A production-centered approach thus necessarily gives priority to the consumer point of view.[4] My observations about Chinese consumers take various shapes in different chapters. Chapter 2 dwells on women consumers, Chapter 3 on mass consumers for fast-moving consumer goods, Chapter 5 on bourgeois bohemians, and a portion of that chapter combined with Chapter 6 are focused on a segment of the single-child generation—the "neo-neo tribes." It is clear that Chinese consumers cannot be lumped together into a fuzzy Chinese "middle class."

A useful exercise is to go over popular assumptions made by Western marketers about "Chinese consumers" and juxtapose them with insights given by Chinese marketers on the mainland. Two diametrically opposite marketing orientations are immediately obvious—one courting China's gold-collar segment *(jinling),* or luxury goods consumers, and another looking downstream at blue-collar consumers *(lanling).* But first, we may ask what the Chinese gold-collar's capacity for luxury consumption is.

The answer, though indirect, is optimistic, according to Western celebrity CEOs from Giorgio Armani, Brioni, Gucci, LVHM, and elsewhere who attended the 2005 *Financial Times* Business of Luxury Summit held in Shanghai. They believe that when the market peaks around 2010 there will be 100 million Chinese tourists buying premium goods abroad to avoid a new luxury tax at home (Movius 2005). A precise definition of the income benchmark for the target segment was missing, however. Although in the West, luxury consumers break down roughly into Aspire, Acquire, and Repertoire (with the latter two segments forming a substantial customer base), clearly the majority of Chinese gold-collar consumers are confined to the first category.[5] They aspire to own a brand but lack the resources to do so (Furman 2005). Yet the absence of a financial profile for this Chinese target has yielded forecasts depicting a country that will run ahead of the United States in the luxury game in the foreseeable future.[6] Alluring statistics have been repeated again and again online and in the Chinese press,[7] painting a rosy picture that has accelerated the gold rush of global luxury brands to China: "Prada chief executive Patrizio Bertelli predicted that by 2010, the Chinese consumer will have $500 billion to spend on luxury goods. You see it happening now, with the popularity of Internet and cell phone use. China may even overtake the U.S. [as a luxury market] by 2020" (Movius 2005). Bertelli's prophecy chimed in with similar messages drawn from participants attending another business forum, Extravaganza Shanghai, held around the same time as the *Financial Times* Summit. Those comments have tempted many foreign entrepreneurs into thinking that luxury lifestyles not only are catching on among the Chinese *nouveau riche* but are likely to percolate downstream to the "upper-middle class."[8] All these auspicious predictions point us to the cradle of Chinese gold-collar wannabees—the Yangtze River Delta—a geographical area covering the municipality of Shanghai and neighboring Jiangsu and Zhejiang provinces, where residents are said to have attained a GDP above $4,000 as of 2005, compared with China's national per capita GDP of $1,490 (Xinhua News 2005a,b). Prada and BMW may see them as a future gold belt. But compare these comments taken from an article on the Delta, published in a July 2005 issue of *International Advertising*, penned by two Chinese market analysts:

Why have people [living in the Yangtze River Delta] felt that their money is no longer worth a penny any more?

Home ownership expenses keeps shooting up . . . Last year, the salary raise for individual residents of Zhejiang Province was an average 10.4 percent, yet the private housing market went up as high as 21.7 percent. In 2004, housing took up 22.6 percent of a household's total expenditure. The increase over spending on food, clothing, medical service, cultural consumption and entertainment was reduced to a slim 9.5 percent. (Cai and Zhu 2005, 56)

A white-collar resident, Mr. Chen, said in an interview quoted in the same article, "We were paid a white collar's salary, but live the lives of the blue-collar. We invested everything into our house . . . We can no longer afford traveling, nor buying clothes that cost 400 or 500 RMB [$50–$63]. We won't turn on the air conditioner even in the hot steamy summer . . ." (ibid.).

The situation has worsened since education was deregularized by the government. Parents who can afford better schools for their children—the more affluent class and Bertelli's future targets—are stepping outside the system of free compulsory education and upping their investment in private schooling for their little "emperors and empresses." Higher tuition bills call for a more stringent budgetary discipline that cuts further into lavish spending.

If residents in the Yangtze River Delta feel strapped for cash, the well-to-do in other top-tier cities have fared worse. In 2007, the household per capita disposable income in the first quarter was reportedly $756 in Beijing, $871 in Shanghai, and $525 in Tianjin municipality ("Shanghai Leads the Nation" 2007)—figures too low to justify the widespread optimism shared by the Shanghai summit participants. What could have led those execs to imagine 100 million potential luxury consumers? The answer may lie in the tendency of transnational marketers to conflate Chinese white-collar workers with those who are genuinely at the gold-collar level. The former make up roughly 8 percent of the population—approximately 100 million consumers. Given that only a tiny fraction of households among them are earning more than $43,600 per annum—the benchmark for the Chinese "premier-league consumer" (a projection made in 2006 by planners at Ogilvy in Beijing)—Bertelli's vision of the quantum leap China's luxury industry will make in the future may well be a fantasy. In estimating how many consumers are truly gold collar today, Edward Bell, director of planning at Ogilvy Beijing, commented, "In the final analysis, I personally think that the real premium leaguers are pretty much only those dodgy businessmen (who bought state assets from government friends during the fire-sale days of the late 80's and earlier 90's) and the top tier of JV [joint venture companies'] employees. Between Beijing and Shanghai, there's about 1 million plus of these [people]" (Bell 2006).

If the critical mass of the gold-collar Chinese has yet to come into being and the white collars are pinching pennies, it is no wonder that China's blue-collar families—a critical mass larger than the white collar—have come into the limelight.[9] Heavyweight multinational clients like Coca-Cola and Procter & Gamble are diversifying from top to lower tiers by bifurcating themselves into premium and plebeian brands (Chapter 3). Indeed, a hot topic since 2004 or so has been to discover the "marketing opportunities" in the blue-collar market *(lanling shangji)*.

Spread among diverse age groups from eighteen to sixty-nine, 80 percent of Chinese blue-collar workers earn a monthly income of 1,000 yuan ($120) per individual. Seventy percent of households reach an income of 3,000 yuan ($365) per month. Their brand preferences lean toward domestic labels—Haier (in white goods), Da Bao (in cosmetics), Li Ning (in clothing), "Seven Wolves" and "Red Eagle" (in cigarettes).[10] They are primarily made up of well-trained personnel in traditional industrial sectors, skilled technicians in transportation, distribution, and construction sectors, women textile workers, behind-the-counter salesmen and company marketers, taxi-cab drivers, chefs in decent-looking restaurants, and even peasants engaged in modern farming technology (Yang Huishu and Huang Gang 2004; "Jiedu" 2004; Wang and Qiu 2004). They are considered a cut above those deemed "gray collar" (lower-level technicians and service personnel) and close in their pattern of brand adoption to that of the lower end of the white-collar stratum. The psychological profile of this segment sounds a tad boring: confident, optimistic, responsible, well-grounded mentally and emotionally. Less romantic than the white-collar workers, they pursue a lifestyle that squarely matches their income bracket. Thus emulative spending is not the norm. In fact blue-collar couples identify with very few brands, because paradoxically, although many brands are *made* for this segment, they are branded in white-collar language and images that alienate their real targets. To complicate matters, blue-collar Chinese do not form a homogeneous body.

They may be differentiated into three subsegments—"deep blue," which is the mainstay of the group, "ordinary blue" (the closest to gray-collar workers in taste), and "sharp blue" (the youngest among the segment, the best educated, and the most progressive, whose consumption pattern is close to that of the tail-end of the white collar). It is quite possible that blue-collar workers may join Chinese niche market consumers in forming the Chinese counterpart of the Long Tail, if the mobile phone, an affordable medium for the blue-collar segments, can be turned into a content-and-goods delivery tool, a low-priced distribution channel for all. The "Long Tail" is Chris Anderson's term that refers to the millions of small American niche markets with lower demand that collectively may, through cost-efficient digital channels, match or exceed the success of a few best-sellers (Anderson 2006). He argues that in contrast to traditional retail economics, which dictates that stores only stock "hits," a new business model initiated by Amazon.com and Google and enabled by digital search engines will create real market winners, because the actions of those in the huge number of smaller markets (the Long Tail)—their impulse to buy, sell, and distribute—will eventually outdo the big returns from mega hits.

Statistics about the exact size of the blue-collar segment in China are unavailable, but its members are spread all over the country, penetrating the metropolises, provincial centers, district cities, county towns, and villages—adding up to a population at least five times larger than the "middle class" concentrated in China's coastal regions. At first sight, these workers hardly seem in the same league as Anderson's Long Tail. Indeed, the analogy between the American and Chinese cases will only work if 3G phones stimulate the development of mobile data delivery services and m-commerce technology in tandem. Simultaneously, handset makers and operators like China Mobile will need to synchronize their efforts to provide chic phone features and bargain prepay services for MMS (multimedia messaging system) and audio and visual streaming. When Chinese

3G phones will evolve into cheap, mass-market handsets is any-body's guess. But when that happens, the Chinese tail, sure enough, will turn into an aggregate of hundreds of millions of blue-collar markets that luxury economics has written off. As the CEO of Horizon Research attests, it is a segment to be ignored at one's peril: "At the present moment, brands in China have all jumped on the bandwagon of gold-collar and white-collar brands . . . [But] China's white collars do not [even] add up to 20 percent of its total population . . . I mean that in China, the competitive advantage of white-collar and gold-collar brands is [actually] very weak. And yet [manufacturers and marketers] don't give a damn [about] the blue-collar market. Well, they may end up being neither here nor there and fall into a collar-less pit!" ("Fang Lingdian" 2004).[11]

Tending to both ends of the curve—the gold collar and the blue collar in the Chinese context—is a necessity for businesses seeking a strong foothold in China. Multinationals like Motorola and Nokia are recovering lost ground from Bird and TCL by rolling out low-end cellphones at 466 yuan ($58) for rural users ("Shichang" 2005). Gaining volume in the low-end market has indeed become a vital strategy for multinational clients whose profits previously came exclusively from premium consumers (Zang and Cheng 2005). This emerging competitive landscape wreaked havoc on the market shares of domestic peers. Statistics from 2005, for instance, indicate that the domestic share of the handset market dropped from 50 to 34 percent.[12] The entrance of MNCs to these poorer but more numerous markets will also put China's rural masses at the center stage of branding and marketing.

MAINSTREAM CONSUMERS: "FACE" CONSUMPTION, SAFETY APPEAL, AND THE NATIONALIST PITCH

Blue-collar consumers have also brought us a step closer to the concept of the Chinese mainstream consumer. Venturing into this discussion seems to go against the grain of positioning theories that emphasize "segmentation." Although I am in complete agreement with marketing gospel regarding the differentiation of markets (Chapter 2 is devoted entirely to "positioning" and Chapter 5 offers an exclusive look at niche markets and premium brand positions), at least one overall statement about China's mass consumers is possible. The current Chinese theoretical emphasis on market fragmentation and the rise of niches *(suipianhua)* is exaggerated ("Zhongguo guanggao ye" 2007), because in developing countries consumption is not all about lifestyle aspirations. Spending boils down to the size of one's pocket, especially for pragmatically minded Chinese mass consumers. In recent years, widening gaps between the ideal brand and the purchased brand are indicative of the declining power of image branding driven solely by aspirations. One set of statistics shows that "brand visibility," as a determining factor for buying a color television, has declined in Beijing from 59.6 percent in the first half of the 1990s to 33.9 percent in 2003 (Huang and Yang 2005, 27). A number one premium brand may not always wind up being the best-selling brand, especially in electronic appliance and computer categories.

Seeking one's "aspirations" is thus not an abiding concern for Chinese mass consumers. There are other rules of thumb for marketers to observe. Lu Taihong, a marketing professor and consultant in Guangdong, has edited a volume entitled *Chinese Consumer Behavior,* in which he enumerates the "archetypal characteristics" underlying this population's behaviors. Some are too familiar to elaborate: emphasis on saving for the future, ultra-sensitivity to price, prescribed spending on children's education, and so on. But two traits on his list call for a closer examination: the separation of the purchaser and the user through a gifting culture and through "face" consumption (Lu Taihong 2005).

The traits of gifting and "face consumption" *(mianzi xiaofei)* are key to our understanding of consumer behavior, especially during festival periods. Take the Autumn Moon festival, for example, in which, as a popular saying goes, "those who buy premium moon cakes won't eat them, and those who eat them don't purchase them" *(mai de ren bu chi, chi de ren bu mai)*. If you are mystified by this paradox, you have not fully grasped Chinese gifting culture. The majority of those who have bought pricey moon cakes are giving them to friends or seniors who are wealthier and higher in status than they. The moon cakes they eat themselves are the cheaper and most ordinary kinds. That is where the crux of "face" consumption lies. It is built on a gifting protocol developed for thousands of years side by side with the Confucian culture of hierarchy and the social networking system. This phenomenon of the separation of the user and the purchaser persists from one era to the next. The Cultural Revolution did not succeed in eroding the fundamentals of the Chinese "four olds" culture.[13]

Given that there is no real off-season for gifting in Chinese society, a lucrative marketing opportunity exists for those who know how to take advantage of it. Brain Gold *(Naobaijin)*, a health tonic brand, became China's number one gift brand, because it was advertised and then remembered as such. Linking products with the gift idea proved to be similarly effective for other product categories, such as cosmetics and health foods in general, all of which, if marketed correctly, can compete favorably with conventional gift products like cigarettes and spirits. Brain Gold's simple low-brow marketing strategy is a winner in that regard. A target for constant ridicule by elite admen, Brain Gold nonetheless created one of the most memorable tag lines China has seen, which even children can recite by heart: "I've got enough gifts this holiday, but never enough Brain Gold" *(jinnian guojie bu shouli, shouli zhi shou Naobaijin)*.

Moreover, Chinese face consumption complicates transnational marketers' theories about status consumption in China. These outsiders often overplay the Chinese fixation with "ownership and display" ("Luxury" 2005), which sounds more like a reference to behaviors characterizing the *nouveau riche,* a tiny segment in China that wears its wealth on its sleeve. For the majority of Chinese mainstream consumers, as the Brain Gold example indicates, one-upsmanship often means giving rather than owning a brand. What is displayed when gifts are given is usually not flaunted status but a more modest goal of everyday life in China: the maintenance of human ties *(renqing)* and the *guanxi* network in which reciprocity and multi-tiered gifting are crucial.

In addition to this centuries-old "face" ideology, another characteristic of mainstream consumption has also been underrated by transnational marketers—the appeal of safety. Given the overflow of counterfeit goods, Chinese consumers, especially mothers as primary purchasers, prioritize the brand appeal of "safety" over that of nutritional content for food and health products (Tang Ruitao 2005). The soap Safeguard fares amazingly well in China because it is marketed as a powerful germ-killer rather than as a skin lubricant. This basic preference for safe products cuts across all fast-moving consumer goods, prompting J.W. Thompson's CEO for its greater China office to conclude that "the fundamental essence of Chinese culture is not 'desire,' but the need for safety" (ibid., 118). Concerns for "food safety" reached a climax at home in 2005 when numerous cases of food contamination involving big-name retailers (for example, Kentucky Fried Chicken, Nestlé, and Bright Dairy) made headlines in quick succession (Liu and Zhang 2006, 69). In 2007, domestic food safety concerns felt the glare of the international spotlight, as a notorious case of tainted pet food ingredients exported from China to the United States led to the recall of more than 60 million cans of cat and dog food (Manning and MacLeod 2007). In the aftermath of that scandal, China's former czar of its Food and Drug Administration was sentenced to death (Beck 2007), a political example the government set up to appease Chinese consumers, whose trust in food safety standards had dropped to rock bottom. It is "safety" rather than "desire" that speaks to consumers across regions and social strata in China.

Chinese nationalism is one more trait that may affect the mainstream consumer. In times of affluence, nationalism is a weak card not often played by domestic manufacturers. Long gone are the days of consumer nationalism depicted in Karl Gerth's *China Made*. (Chapter 3 looks at the history of this subject at greater length.) But another round of nationalist consumer fever is possible, now that the 2008 Beijing Olympics are around the corner and China's space race with the United States is heating up. A well-known 2003 Ogilvy marketing survey, "Patriot's Paradox," examines the perceptions of Chinese youth regarding national and international brands. It finds the usage of international brands among the strongest patriots "nearly as high as [among] those with lesser feelings of nationalism" (Ogilvy & Mather 2003). The Ogilvy survey was conducted in the Pearl River Delta, a locale presumably less under the sway of Chinese nationalism than the rest of the country because of its proximity to Hong Kong, where Western influence dominates. Another geographically less partial report is more nuanced: "The Chinese university students in our study are young and open-minded and would not hesitate to buy any brand, Chinese or foreign, that has a high perceived value. But, nationalist appeals have a strong influence on older people and politically conservative consumers. Sometimes demographics alone can make a difference" (Ouyang et al. 2002–03). For instance, Beijingers rise well above their counterparts in Shanghai and Guangzhou in their preference for national goods. More interestingly, the Ouyang et al. survey underlines the importance of generational segmentation. A useful analytical model on that subject is provided by Lu Taihong:

- Generation X: Born between 1977 and 1989, they make up 23 percent of Chinese consumers;
- Chinese baby boomers: Born between 1961 and 1976, they make up 44 percent of consumers;
- Cultural Revolution Generation: Born between 1945 and

1960, they make up 33 percent of consumers. (Lu Taihong 2005, 206)

What is missing from this generational chart is Generation Y— those born after 1989 but before 2000 (ages eight to nineteen as of 2008), who make up approximately 14.5 percent of China's total population.[14] This generation's consumption capacity is not yet significant enough to appear on Lu Taihong's list.

Across the board, the perceived performance gap between national and international brands is expected to decrease over time. Brand choice for the boomers and the Revolutionary generation can vary; sometimes they may prefer national brands to foreign brands if all things are equal and sometimes they may not. Baby boomers, perhaps affected by the intense patriotic education they received as children, carry no obvious prejudices against national goods if they are well made, even though foreign labels score higher on their brand radar. The partiality for national goods among the Revolutionary generation is obvious, especially for those living in north China—the seedbed of anti-imperialism. For transnational marketers, the real battle between domestic and foreign brands will be waged at the doorstep of Chinese baby boomers.

The necessity of targeting high-end, mainstream, and blue-collar consumers simultaneously makes it amply clear that China is no easy market for multinational clients and ad agencies. Corporate China's drive to better its goods and services continues to pose challenges to MNCs just as they are trumping domestic producers by squeezing low-end markets. What makes the playing field even more fascinating is that transnational ad agencies are not as monogamous as their Chinese peers. Although it is still rare for a Chinese advertising agency to woo a multinational client, it is the goal of *every* transnational agency to court Chinese advertisers. As Charles Simpson at Saatchi & Saatchi in Beijing says, he is optimistic about winning over domestic clients who are now paying closer attention to branding (Hu Jing 2005, 116). As the proportion of domestic accounts in transnational ad agencies climbs steadily, we might wonder if, urged by foreign marketers, more and more Chinese corporations will be buying into Western theories of branding.

BRANDING

"Is Lenovo a brand? No. Is Haier a brand? No. They are brand names that aspire to be brands. But they [the Chinese] have to understand that branding is about the relationship with people both intellectually and emotionally. They have to have a consistent proposition they put in front of people" (Paterson 2004). Shelly Lazarus, who made this statement and who is chairman of Ogilvy & Mather Worldwide, found herself quickly pounced on after her comments were released in the Chinese press. She had to retract her remark ("I never said [that] Lenovo and Haier are not brands") and her Beijing colleague T. B. Song (the head of Ogilvy in Greater China) had to come to her rescue by explaining what "she really meant"—she was criticizing Haier overseas not Haier at home, and "the Lenovo [that was eyeing] a global market was not the Beijing-based Legend" (*International Advertising* Editorial Board 2005, 14, 12). Not to worry, he said, Chinese brands like Haier and Lenovo-Legend have already built a solid emotional bond with Chinese consumers at home.

Was this a tempest in a teapot? Not quite. Lazarus's comment triggered a period of self-reflection among concerned Chinese ad professionals, who asked whether China has real brands. But 2004 was a different era from the 1930s, when a condescending comment from a Westerner would have ignited outbursts revealing a deep inferiority complex. The discussions in the wake of the Lazarus incident were low-keyed and contemplative, marking a further erosion of Chinese nationalism in the advertising sector. Still, some professionals wondered whether corporate brands like Haier and

Lenovo were really nothing more than famous trademarks. They asked, further, whether corporate China had fallen victim to vicious pricing competition. If Asia's trading culture was inferior to U.S. marketing culture, should marketing and positioning be driving sales rather than the other way around? Another question was whether counterfeiting was threatening the development of brands in China, and in the end radical marketers asked if "positioning" was the ultimate answer to all their concerns.[15]

Chapters 2 and 4 address some of these issues. In the context of Lazarus's remarks, no consensus was ever reached. Suffice it to say that Chinese marketers fussed less about her comments than did Chinese advertising professionals. The latter are more enamored with American marketing theories of positioning and thus were more vulnerable to her criticism.[16] The former—marketing personnel at the helm of the ground operations of corporate China—are armed with success stories that fly in the face of Lazarus's classical approach to branding. Empirical evidence is helpful when it comes to a country as heterogeneous as China. If it is made up of more than 170 markets[17]—each with a population of approximately a million—it goes without saying that flexibility is required for success. A culture that takes a strong pride in the principle of "each according to its geo-culture" (J. Wang 2005b, 10–11) is naturally inclined to question the validity of overarching theories, especially theories coming from Western developed countries. This reaction should by no means be interpreted as a symptom of Sinocentrism. Different geographical and material constraints engender different problems that call for different solutions and experiments. Moreover, sporadic contestations of foreign ideas and foreign models have never prevented the Chinese from being intellectually curious about "universal truths," whether they are high cultural theories[18] or marketing models. Although constantly debating the usefulness of insights culled from Madison Avenue, Chinese marketers are often the most fervent translators and promoters of American theories of branding.

What is a "brand"? A frequently cited epithet goes: a product is made in a factory; a brand is bought by a consumer. In the American context, the word "brand" meant "to burn" a mark on livestock. Trade buyers used branding as a means of distinguishing cattle sold from different ranches. A rancher whose stock earned him a good reputation would find his brand much sought after, and the link between brand and discrimination was thus established. Commercial brands appeared in great numbers in the late nineteenth and early twentieth centuries, when trademark legislation was institutionalized to protect brand owners (Blackett 2004, 14). Many of today's best-known U.S. brands—Kodak, American Express, Listerine, Coca-Cola, Heinz baked beans, and Quaker Oats—date from that period. But for mass consumers of those early periods, a brand was not much different from a trademark. Back then, the upper class and the mass audience shared basically similar social instincts and emotions, and therefore advertisers "often saw little need to differentiate copy appeals" (Marchand 1985, 66). Advertising, rather than branding, was the major task of early-twentieth-century ad agencies. It was not until much later, in the mid-1960s, that the emerging class-mass distinction began to call for marketing strategies that differentiated rather than blurred. Getting consumers engaged meant selling them an emotional hook. Advertising entered what Ries and Trout call the "image era," leaving behind the bland "product era" (Ries and Trout 2001, 23–24) with its straightforward focus on product features and customer benefits. Icons and images soon took center stage, enabling consumers to acquire an emotional attachment to objects as nonsensical as an eye patch (the Hathaway Man) or a wrist tattoo (the Marlboro Man). Later the same magic appeared in a giant swoosh mark and small alligators sewn on shirts.

Standing behind the new era of brand symbolism was a visionary of the advertising industry—David Ogilvy.[19] Ogilvy conceives of a brand as a complex symbol, an "intangible sum of a product's attributes, its name, packaging, and price, its history, reputation, and the way it is advertised" (D. Ogilvy 1955). His most famous advertising campaign, "The Hathaway Man," ushered in a new advertising method aptly described by James Twitchell as a mental maneuver: "While you cannot change what the product *is,* you can change what it *means*" (Twitchell 2000, 136). David Ogilvy therefore chose to brand the man under the shirt, not the shirt itself. His sales pitch was a simple-looking black eye patch worn by a male model. A dose of mystique, danger, and romanticism was successfully associated with the Hathaway shirt. Rather than citing this ad as the beginning of the deception of mass consumers by advertisers, admen would rather see it as a moment of invention as significant as Newton's law of gravity.

From then on, the physical attributes of a product became less relevant to copywriting. The change in direction from selling the product to peddling a brand image paved the way for the emergence of new marketing concepts like "brand identity" and "segmentation" (not every segment is attracted to an eye patch). But by the 1970s, the cycle of mass production accelerated and the U.S. market overflowed with copycat goods in the same product category as the originals, befuddling consumers. Even image branding fell short of helping them make purchase decisions. The situation was more perilous for smaller emerging brands; major brand leaders had already gained a firm position in every product category, leaving hardly any breathing room for those who came after them. The number-two brands like Pepsi (next to Coca-Cola) and Avis (next to Hertz) had to find a way to carve out their own niche in a cut-throat market.

"Cherchez le creneau. Look for the hole," responded Al Ries and Jack Trout, authors of *Positioning,* the marketing bible that debuted in the mid-1970s (Ries and Trout 2001, 54). It is fine to be number 2 or even number 380 in the view of these authors, if the brand knows how to sell its positioning. The strategy is laid out as follows: create a position in your prospect's mind by taking into account your competitors' positioning and then zero in on the "hole." Classic positioning examples are: "Avis is only No. 2 in rent-a-cars, so why go with us? We try harder"; and "Come alive! You're in the Pepsi Generation." The latter campaign made advertising history by using lifestyle and attitude as an identity marker for the first time. Chinese case studies on positioning are provided in Chapter 2.

In the United States, by the late 1970s creativity was no longer seen as the most important factor driving a successful advertising campaign. Marketing began its subtle transition from verbal and visual imagism to strategic planning and "brand management." Creative departments in agencies began to feel the pressure of working *for*, not with, brand managers. By the mid-1980s, the traditional term "'brand image' was increasingly displaced by its solid financial equivalent, 'brand equity'" (Feldwick 1999, 70; 2002, 36). Simultaneously, marketing science institutes began to churn out commercial research that measured, tracked, and sought to show how to optimize brand equity. Although upon inspection, the core of "brand equity" still bore a close resemblance to David Ogilvy's concept of "brand image" (Aaker and Joachimsthaler 2000, 17), public relations and sponsorship appeared to have gained a much stronger influence than ever before.

Highly susceptible to new Western paradigms, the Chinese translated *Brand Portfolio Strategy* by David Aaker—the guru of brand equity theory—soon after the book was published in the United States in 2004. Today, David Ogilvy's best-sellers in translation lie side by side with Aaker's in Chinese bookstores, which reminds us of the curious coexistence, in every Chinese field and sector, of modern and postmodern Western theories that simultaneously poured into China right after the end of Mao's era. The once closed-door China had been abstinent in every regard. With the exception of Chairman Mao himself, brands did not exist in China from 1949 till 1978, nor did the notion of mass consumerism. Between 1978 and 1990, at the dawning of the reform era, the market was dominated exclusively by state-owned trademarks (known in Chinese as *paizi*). It was not until the late 1990s that terms like "*pinpai*" ("brand") and *pinpai zhanlue* ("brand strategies") came into currency and gave the old expression *mingpai* ("name brands") a new twist that resonates closely with the Western notion of branding.[20]

Historically, however, corporate China's initial encounter with Western-style "branding" occurred two decades ago, when the entire commercial sector took a dramatic turn to image design. It was not David Ogilvy who inspired the Chinese. In 1988, the Guangdong-based health-drink company Apollo imported, via Japan, an IBM-initiated management tool known as the Corporate Identity System (CIS).[21] CIS is made up of three subsystems: the MI (mind identity), BI (behavior identity), and VI (visual identity), referring, respectively, to a company's philosophy of management, concrete development and organizational strategies, and a company's visual identity. As we saw in the Preface, Apollo adopted the CIS strategy, particularly the VI, and saw its earnings balloon overnight. By the mid-1990s, books on CIS filled Chinese bookstores, showcasing the visual identities of lucrative businesses. Successful VI campaigns launched by Apollo and a dozen other corporations made the Chinese public all the more aware of the importance of corporate logos, mascots, and image culture in general. "Invisible assets" *(wuxing zichan)*—the core of "brand equity"—captured social imagination like no other word. That was the closest encounter the Chinese had ever had with Western-style branding before the advertising sector blossomed and evolved naturally into the next phase (that is, seeking Western paradigms on advertising and marketing).[22] Now full-service ad agencies (both domestic and transnational) in first- and second-tier cities in China seem to be following in the footsteps of pioneering American brand theorists and managers. "Marketing mix" rather than "advertising" has come to dominate agencyspeak. But while the Chinese will no doubt keep close track of the theoretical evolution of American marketing, whether they will continue to endorse trends that leapfrog China's technological infrastructure remains to be seen. A case in point is "relationship branding," with its emphasis on one-on-one dialogue through broadband. How fast will digital individualism trickle down from Generations X and Y to the rest of the Chinese population, whose primary medium is television and cell phone, not the Internet?[23] Is China's long-tail economy a mere fantasy?

INTERNET ADVERTISING AND USER-GENERATED CONTENT

Just as the Chinese "middle class" is not going to double in a decade or two, digital individualism is not going to take root anytime soon. And yet if Generations X and Y (those born between 1978 and 2000)—of whom many are addicted Netizens—make up 9.5 to 10.7 percent of the Chinese population, digital media and its impact on consumption cannot be entirely dismissed. This book places television at the center but treats digital media as well.

Television is a major advertising medium for the Chinese, because the national TV audience is 1.17 billion—a 98.2 percent penetration rate. The average viewer spends three hours daily watching the tube. In contrast, only 7.2 percent of the Chinese population were online in 2005, compared with 60.6 percent of Americans (Dobson 2005). Internet advertising made up 1 percent of national ad revenue in China in 2003, compared with 23.64 percent in television and 22.53 percent in newspapers (Zhang Haichao 2004, 21–22). The percentage rose slightly to 1.5 percent in 2004 (Jiang Wei 2005, 19). The slow growth of Net advertising notwithstanding, multinationals like GM, Coca-Cola, Motorola, and P&G are taking the lead in developing branded entertainment online.[24] The Internet is considered the fastest-growing advertising medium for Generation Y in China.

The 1.5 percent share of national ad revenue quoted above for Internet advertising looks less paltry if we compare it with the 3–4 percent share in Europe (2005) and the 5.5 percent share in the United States (2006) (Zhao Shuguang and Zhang Zhi'an 2004, 147).[25] A recent report published in *Business Week* bumps the Chinese percentage up to 2.3 percent (D. Roberts 2006). But the profit margin is so slim that one wonders how big Internet portals like sina.com and sohu.com survive. The answer lies in their multichain business model that relies heavily on games and short message service (SMS, or text messaging), rather than on advertising as a major income base.[26] Around 2003, roughly 64 percent of sina.com's revenue came from online games and mobile games as well as SMS content provision for carriers like China Mobile. Sohu.com fared the same.[27] In comparison, 99 percent of Google's income is advertising related.[28] But observers predicted that the Chinese balance would quickly change, and by 2006, Sohu was already earning about two thirds of its revenues from advertising (D. Roberts 2006).

For international youth brands, the Net is undoubtedly where the action is. In April 2005, Coca-Cola and Pepsi initiated a new formula of partnering with digital entertainment software giants worldwide. Two convergence commercials based on game narratives made a splash in the world of gamers and bloggers. Coke tied in with "World of Warcraft" *(moshou shijie)* (WoW) and Pepsi with "Magic Land" *(menghuan guodu)*.[29] In the weeks leading up to the launch and afterward, a co-branding campaign by McCann Erickson Shanghai hosted a two-day carnival, where twenty thousand consumers strolled through Darnassus, Stormwind Castle, and Thunderbluff—real-life replicas of WoW-themed zones. Ten thousand cyber cafés were adorned with Coke and WoW icons (Madden 2005a); a Chinese site for iCoke-branded World of Warcraft was simultaneously unveiled, accompanied by a commercial featuring pop sensation S.H.E. vanquishing an ugly ogre in a fantasy battle. In the commercial, S.H.E.'s magnificent three (Ella, Selena, and Hebe) confront a misogynist music exec who bids them to dress revealingly to sell more records. Enraged, the girls take a sip of Coke and morph into three Night Elves. Fully clad in medieval fantasy costumes, they combat their insolent boss, now an Orc character in the WoW universe. After a few magical stunts, the trio diminishes him to a half-naked clownish figure. The role-playing fantasy ends in a signature Coke tag line: "For satisfaction, look to yourself" *(Yao shuang you ziji)*. Pepsi responded swiftly to the challenge. It too announced joint marketing with an online game, "Magic Land." Pepsi's televised commercial, the "Birdman" chapter in the Blue Storm series, is a melodramatic adventure about trapped blue birdmen and heroic rescue missions.[30]

It is hard to tell which campaign, Coke/WoW or Pepsi/M-Land, got the upper hand in wooing 40 million Chinese gamers. One thing is certain, however. Convergence alone cannot lure Generation Y. If audience participation is not brought into the picture, producer-driven branded entertainment like the S.H.E. and Birdman spots may look like passive content of little interest to highly interactive end-users. In China, large-scale audience participation points to mobile media rather than to digital media. The *Super Girl* phenomenon is a case in point. A Chinese spin-off of the U.S. television show *American Idol* complete with SMS voting, *Super Girl* brought to its sponsor, Mengniu Dairy, $185 million in sales of a new yogurt drink (Madden 2005b). During the final contest in the 2005 season, a spot on Hunan Satellite TV, the reality show's host, cost $14,000 *per second,* topping the rate for prime-time television drama commercials aired on CCTV (China Central TV) (Yang Haijun 2005, 30). This success suggests that the Internet marketers' best bet is to create content tie-ins with TV and mobile media while maximizing the scale of interactivity.

Paid search platforms are another question. MSN's global launch of adCenter may be a sign that Internet advertising is coming back strong. Search marketing is evolving into a mainstream medium for advertisers in Japan and Korea, and the same is expected to happen in China. By 2007, the cost-per-click-thru was the most accepted system for search advertising there. But an additional caution was voiced by the China Internet Network Information Centre: search engines without a strong brand may go under, given that 34 percent of Chinese Web surfers use only one search engine, and 41 percent use no more than two (Wertime 2005). The current sentiments of online marketers in China are, to say the least, extremely mixed. Perhaps Chris Reitermann, managing director of Ogilvy One Beijing, best articulates the ambiguity of interactive marketing. "Key factors that will drive Chinese adspend online include, crucially, no history of direct marketing—meaning that marketers in China are likely to take to [the] Web's virtual infrastructure instead much quicker than their counterparts did in the U.S./Europe" (Savage 2005a). On the other hand, he cautions us against "over-selling the Web's cutting-edge capabilities" and the blog's potential as an advertising medium. India's example has reportedly been a sobering one for China: despite the quick growth of its online and wireless community, India has made slow progress in interactive marketing.

Perhaps "how fast interactive marketing is making headway" is not the real question. We might better ask what type of interactive content is best for an advertiser's online presence. Increasingly, the most exhilarating niche content appearing in China's cyberspace has been created not by advertisers and marketers but by the young users themselves. "The democratization of technology means that imaginations among Asian youth have ballooned." I quote from a research report of Ogilvy Beijing. Creativity is held in the hands of individual users, who produce media spectacles that have real sales value. The best example is the hilarious spoof of a 2006 film, *The Promise (Wuji)*, by famed director Chen Kaige (best known in the West for his *Farewell My Concubine*). Lampooning can be harmless, except in this case, amateur Hu Ge's "A Murder Brought on by a Steamed Bun" *(yige mantou de xue'an),* which drew comparisons to Monty Python in its satiric flair, was made up entirely of images lifted frame by frame from the parent film.[31] Hu Ge distributed the resulting underground video—nicknamed "Mantou" (the Chinese word for "steamed buns")—to his circle of friends, who promptly posted it on a video-sharing Web site. Within a month, it became a must-see for Netizens, triggering threats of legal action from Chen Kaige and rounds of social and legal debate over the boundaries of intellectual property rights. Such controversies are unprecedented in China. Of immediate relevance to advertising is the fact that "Mantou" turned out to be an effective marketing tool for Chen's film. Many "Mantou" fans, myself included, purchased Chen's original film after watching the spoof so as to better appreciate the latter—an excellent case of reverse advertising.

Another example of user-generated content generating sales is the much-publicized video by the "Back Dormitory Boys." Huang Yixin and Wei Wei, two college students at Guangzhou Art Institute, lip-synched their favorite songs by the Backstreet Boys and then uploaded the clips to Google Video.[32] They earned instantaneous fame and signed up endorsement deals with Motorola and Pepsi. The public's response to Motorola's online campaign was especially overwhelming. The two boys did their usual tricks with "As Long as You Love Me" on the Net. A simultaneous launch of a lip-synching and song remixing competition garnered 14 million page views. Visitors swarmed to the Motorola site and cast 1.3 million votes to pick the winner of the contest (Roberts 2006). The promotion generated not only headlines but soaring sales for Motorola's new phones.

The long line of amateur stars discovered online will follow in the footsteps of the Back Dormitory Boys and queue up as future brand ambassadors one by one. Meanwhile, social-network media are expanding the conceptual boundaries of branded content and offering convergence possibilities with blogs and podcasts. ChinaCircle (*Zhongguo yuan*)—a counterpart of MySpace—boasts of its ability to integrate product placement into Web 2.0 homepages. Seamless integration of ads into a ChinaCircle's user frame and other homepage decorative items has already brought multinational clients like Coca-Cola on board.[33] This latest development in social-network advertising may have a long way to go in China. The point to make is that pre-made and producer-driven content is no longer a draw for Netizens. User-generated content is the dark horse in the race by advertisers for creative ideas. Internet advertising will conceivably make headway as urban China's single-child generation (the likes of the Back Dormitory Boys and Hu Ge's online fans), 67–85 million of them, partake in the creation of a digitally based mainstream culture.[34] But for the rest of the nation—the other 1.2 billion in the audience—television remains king, and that is where major battles between corporate sponsors are fought. Television is the ideal medium in which to plant and build a brand in China.

WHAT LIES AHEAD: THE PLAN OF THIS BOOK

Brand New China examines a wide range of subjects related to three intertwined sectors—advertising, media, and the corporate sector. Brands covered span across food and beverages, distilled alcohol, white goods, cell phones, computers, Internet portals, automobiles, women's hygiene, real estate, and corporate brands as well as the country brand of China. My choice of brands and categories is primarily guided by their relevance to critical inquiries rather than by what they are in their own terms.

Chapter 1 anchors the analysis at the site of production—the advertising agency—and examines the trend of localization from the agency perspective. I investigate how "local content" is constructed and sample a mix of advertising campaigns commissioned by transnational, joint venture, and Chinese local clients respectively.

Chapter 2 opens with the theory of "positioning," along with examples, and highlights the fluidity and unpredictability of the process of branding. My emphasis is on the production of brand positions with reference to two campaigns for feminine care products. The demographic focus is naturally the new modern girl—the golden segment for the fast-moving consumer goods market. Applying the tool of Ogilvy's 360 Degree Brand Stewardship to the two case studies, I portray brand communications as a holistic project that produces meaning built on an equal partnership between the agency, the client, and consumers. The last portion of the chapter is written for those who wish to explore the new politics of culture beyond the consumer/producer and local/global dichotomies. To them I offer my speculations on the fusion of marketing research and cultural analysis and its impact on the scholarship of popular culture.

Chapter 3 examines corporate China's new drive toward crossover thinking and synergy making. I track the story and controversy of the Wahaha-Danone merger and assess the performance of global brands in generating synergy in China. Wahaha's "branded house" architecture is studied as a "synergy-driven model" in comparison with the "house of brands" approach characteristic of the Procter & Gamble strategy. To further explore the meaning of synergy beyond the register of joint venture brands and brand extension, I end with a discussion of nation branding (that is, branding "new China"), which calls for the convergence of multiple initiatives launched simultaneously by transnational ad agencies, the Chinese state, and domestic superbrands traveling West.

Chapter 4 continues the theme of reciprocal flows but shifts attention to the corporate culture of two superbrands, Haier (white goods) and Lenovo (computers). Central to my exploration is the debate over the conceptual divide between corporate branding and product branding. I devote an entire chapter to corporate branding in part to demonstrate the lessons we can learn by exploring corporate culture from the vantage point of organizational storytelling.

This brings us not only to the rich anecdotal literature of Haier and the cartoon series bearing its name but to the two online debates that erupted around Lenovo triggered by Chinese bloggers.

Chapter 5 treats an understudied subject: the reciprocal relationship between lifestyle cultures and marketing through an examination of bobo fever in urban China. How did an imaginary class of "bourgeois bohemians" emerge in a country where the bourgeois base is statistically small and where the bohemian equation is nonexistent? To shed light on the "pop culture turned marketing fad" syndrome, I introduce the concept of the "neo-tribes" and map the pathways that link style cultures to consumer segmentation.

Chapter 6 tracks the relationship between music and youth culture in China in the context of transnational cell phone branding. Through a case study of Motorola, I discuss the fledgling mobile data industry in China and other factors that accounted for the uphill battle of transnational cell phone makers to sell mobile music in China. The urban single-child generation features large in this study. Several assumptions held dear by transnational marketers are put to the test. The conceptual distinction between music "tribal cultures" and music "subcultures" is emphasized. I also elucidate how such a differentiation offers clues about mainstream cool culture in China while helping marketers arrive at a clearer definition of the target segment for wireless music.

Chapter 7 is devoted to media buying and media planning—the placement of advertisements after they are made. I examine the tortuous process of the commodification of state-owned Chinese media. The vicious circle of the opening, retrenchment, and readjusted partial opening of the programming content industry is characteristically Chinese and socialist in nature. The complex structural dependency among the media, advertising, and corporate business sectors is laid bare in the dual contexts of CCTV's annual advertising auctions and China's landmark media policies. TV drama as an advertising medium is given special attention, and the future of product placement is discussed.

The Conclusion brings us to the eve of the Olympics in Beijing and to the new developments in Internet marketing and grassroots digital culture that are paving the way for a major shift in the creative content and form of Chinese advertising. The Olympic spectacle of a "new China" is more tantalizing than ever. I close with a reflection on the theoretical and methodological ground opened up in this book.

CHAPTER 1

Local Content

The very idea of global advertising runs counter to the marketing concept: it takes insufficient notice of the requirements, needs, attitudes, mind-sets, traditions, and expectations of the target group in the individual country.

Roderick White (2000)

In the late 80s and 90s we saw a huge swing towards international advertising as brands became preoccupied with globalization. In the new century we are seeing a significant move away from that . . . towards [a] market specific approach.

Mary Teresa Rainey (2001)

Both Mary Teresa Rainey of Young & Rubicam, a transnational ad agency, and Roderick White, at London-based Conquest Consultancy, describe TNAAs' retreat from globalism as a fait accompli. The job of a successful transnational advertising company, in their view, is to stay on top of the cultural values specific to the target market.

36

THE REVERSE TREND OF LOCALIZATION

These two epigraphs sum up the general trend of industry opinion regarding global marketing and advertising. By 2005, the anti-globalization perspective sounded far more acceptable than in the late 1990s, when Marieke de Mooij first broached her thesis about "national cultural value systems" (de Mooij 1998, 2003).[1] In an intriguing turn of events, her controversial idea that markets remain stubbornly national finally won the day. As the appeal and practice of standardized advertising across multiple markets steadily declined, companies jumped on a new bandwagon: "localization." John Philip Jones describes the almost feverish changes: "The proportion of 'substantially localized' campaigns increased from 20 percent to 35 percent. The proportion of partly standardized and partly localized campaigns rose from 10 percent to 55 percent. The proportion of 'fully standardized' campaigns fell from 70 percent to the remarkable low of 10 percent" (Jones 2000, 5). These statistics testify to the new tactics of transnational ad agencies, whose raison d'être used to be confined to the hypothesis of convergence. Multinational corporations have tripped up more than once by banking on the appeal of sameness. A recent example, Nike's snazzy "Chamber of Fear" commercial, bit the dust in the Middle Kingdom because of its sacrilegious treatment of the dragon—a totem animal—and its "disrespectful" portrayal of Chinese kung-fu masters ("China Bans" 2004).[2] The battlefield is strewn with failed global ad campaigns (see Chapter 2 for more examples). The reverse trend of localization has stolen the scene. In the twenty-first century, "going local" is the ticket to success for multinational brands.

The issue of "localization" needs to be examined from the perspective of advertising agencies and sample pitches that are sensitive to the locale, made by domestic, JV (joint venture), and transnational advertisers to authenticate their brands in China. Their experience sheds light on current academic discussions of "cultural globalization." Only ultranationalist advertising professionals and theorists who have never spent a day in an agency would seriously pit "globalization" against "localization" by positioning them as contesting discourses.

Meanwhile, the savvy practitioners out there in the field are much too busy camouflaging their brands (sometimes as "domestic" and sometimes as "imported") to care about making a fixed choice on one side or the other. Does it matter if they brand a product "local" or "global"? Whenever I raised such a question, the response of admen and -women—whether Brits, Aussies, Americans, Chinese, Japanese, or Bulgarians—was a uniform "Why bother?" with an added chuckle. This typical view is well represented in the words of Ilya Vedrashko, a former account manager at Young & Rubicam in Bulgaria and a new media strategist at Boston-based Hill & Holliday:

> I think that the key to understanding the global-local paradox lies in the mantra that branding is what happens *inside consumers' heads.* Corporate ownership or place of manufacturing do not matter unless they are clearly and purposefully manifested. Consider Guinness, a brand owned by Britain's Diageo Group. But for most consumers, Guinness is seen as one of the strongest Irish symbols, as strong as St. Patrick's. It has been sold in Russia for quite some time too and taken as a popular high-tier imported brand. Now, on July 1, 2005, Diageo entered a partnership with Dutch brewer Heineken and will begin brewing Guinness in St. Petersburg. But will it remain an "imported premium Irish beer" in the mind of Russian consumers for long? Its brand "identity" is a mixed bag. Is it British, or Irish, or Russian? (Vedrashko 2005)[3]

The identity of a brand is a projection made by the consumer, and it is nothing more than the result of a successful pitch. In the words of Eric Rosenkranz, the president of the ad agency Grey Asia Pacific, "the advertising agency doesn't own the brand . . . The person who really creates the brand is the consumer" (Rosenkranz 2001, 35). If a brand is perceived by the target segment as "local," it *is* local even though it is owned by a multinational. Chapter 2 on Kotex and Chapter 3 on synergy offer many Chinese examples illustrating the same logic. Comfort & Beauty, a feminine napkin, has always been seen by users as a local "Chinese" brand even since its acquisition by Kimberly-Clark; Wahaha works hard not to reveal the Eurasian origin of Future Cola by marketing it as the "*Chinese* cola." To frame the "local" as contesting the "global" is beside the point precisely because those two scales are not mutually exclusive. The actual practice of both domestic and multinational advertisers overturns such rigid dichotomies. Consider another quote from Bruce Oltchick, former executive vice president of advertising sales at Star TV:

> "What makes a brand local today?" A great question . . . The answer is: "the consumers' perception of the brand." The best example is a U.S. example: Most U.S. consumers would claim that Haagen Dazs is a foreign brand. It's not. It's American. What makes a brand "local" is how intimately it's perceived by consumers and how relevant it is to them. In reality, it's irrelevant who owns the brand or who manufactures the brand, or who markets the brand, etc. (Oltchick 2004)

Perhaps the best-known example of brand-identity crossovers is McDonald's. James Watson and contributors to *Golden Arches East* argue that many East Asians have ceased to consider McDonald's "foreign," because it is now seamlessly integrated into local lives. Cultural globalization, Watson argues, should not be seen as straightforward "Westernization" (Watson 1997). More and more pop cultural studies grounded in nuanced ethnographies make similar observations: that an ideologically pitched dichotomy such as the global versus the local can be a false one that "hides more than it reveals" (Condry 2006, 2).

Once we throw the local–global dichotomy out the window, we need to replace that framework with new inquiries. But we need to look beyond the merry-go-round of "cultural authenticity," a perspective that revolves around the local–global axis and that structures the current debate on international advertising. Instead, I find it more useful to start with the site of production itself—advertising agencies—and explore a set of production-centered topics, among them, the international agency model of the Association of Accredited Advertising Agencies (4As), the presence of international agencies in China and their skirmishes with domestic companies, and the flap over the challenges posed by an alternative discourse known as 4C (Chinese/Consumer/Consensus/Communication).

At the heart of this chapter is the production of the "local" by domestic ad boutiques (agencies with specific creativity profiles) and by TNAAs. "Chinese" content has been construed in various ways. As we sample a few advertising campaigns that have captured "localized creativity"—campaigns rolled out by transnational corporations, joint ventures, and local clients—we will find that each campaign takes a different approach to "local" aesthetics and to the notion of creativity itself. Mapping the agency landscape also reveals what kind of comparative advantages or disadvantages a local agency has over TNAAs. No less important, "localization" may acquire new meaning if we shift our analytical locus from the international–domestic axis to the tiered internal markets of China itself.

THE WTO COUNTDOWN

To gain easy entry into the ad agency environment in China, we will start with China's historic agreement with the World Trade Organization in December 2001. By the end of 2005, for the first time since 1978, foreign ad agencies under sole ownership were allowed to operate in China. Anxieties about an "imperialist takeover" triggered furious domestic debates about the impact the WTO would have on the Chinese advertising industry. Opinions culled from trade magazines revealed familiar polemics that have been recycled throughout modern Chinese history, in which resistant nationalists have fought against advocates of total Westernization—in this case, both reacting to paranoia about the WTO:

- Globalization is the ruling paradigm. Chinese ad professionals should embrace it heartily.
- Chinese culture is beautiful. We have to insist on cultural protection and preservation by emphasizing "national attributes" *(minzuxing)* and resist the infiltration of foreign elements into the sector.
- Globalization is a [cultural] imaginary serving cultural imperialism. The return-to-origin approach will not help. China cannot escape the ultimate destiny of total subjugation to capitalist imperialism of the developed West. (Xu Chun 2003, 91)

Such reactions, ranging from boundless optimism to ultra-pessimism, pictured a domestic advertising industry under siege in the face of the WTO challenge, whether timidly acquiescing to the West or caught in a fierce fight to preserve its "Chinese identity." But as Chapter 3 demonstrates, polarized sentiments of nationalism and wholesale Westernization were by no means the predominant reactions expressed in 2003. A more powerful discourse on "synergy" emerged around the same time, showcasing corporate China's growing appreciation for the fluid crossings between the local and the global, and with it, a budding faith in the cross-fertilization of Chinese norms and international standards. There are many choices for the Chinese other than subjugation or resistance, given the closing gap between local and transnational knowledge of branding, marketing, and corporate management. The versatility of domestic Chinese agencies should not be underestimated.

Defense Strategies

The number of advertising agencies in China was an astounding 84,272 in 2005, a 10.6 percent increase from the previous year (Guang 2006, 38). Although the sector appears extremely crowded, breathing space is provided by the notoriously short span of Chinese advertisers' commitment to the agency they have signed with. Unlike the United States and Japan, where an agency's contracts last an average of 10.5 years in the former and 5.6 years in the latter, Chinese corporations are prone to roam from one agency to the next. A 2003 tally by Huang Shengmin reports that 41.3 percent of them dissolved their agency partnership in less than two years, while 34.9 percent maintained a three- to four-year relationship. But very few made it through their seventh or eighth anniversary with an agency—a slim 4.8 percent (Huang Shengmin 2003, 178). The revolving door syndrome has been indicative of several anomalous practices prevalent in the sector. First, medium- and small-sized domestic ad agencies are master hijackers of clients from other agencies. And it takes very little to nourish small minnows in an ocean. Second, they court clients with rock-bottom prices. Third, vicious competition led to the infamous practice of charging clients no commission fee *(ling daili)*, scaling back further the shrinking profit margin of all agencies (Zhao Nannan 2002).[4] Cheap services are a dime a dozen, and Chinese domestic advertisers enjoy tremendous leverage over transnational agencies in cutting a deal. The advertising market in China is one chaotic playing field where improvisation rules. The small player is versatile and, sometimes, the fittest.

One may argue that, over time, demands for branding expertise will wean advertisers from makeshift boutiques and propel them to seek international 4A companies. Yet the needs of Chinese corporations for professionalized brand communications take time to nurture. Faster triggers for a complete shake-up of the advertising sector were China's WTO agreements. Starting in March 2004, foreign agencies could hold majority stakes in a joint venture up to 70 percent (Qu 2004). By the end of 2005, they could enter China with sole ownership status. The tidal wave that resulted has been expected to affect big domestic agencies in tier-one cities more adversely than agencies in tier-two, tier-three, and lower-tiered cities, because the latter are seen as ideal joint venture partners who possess the special knowledge regarding a locality eagerly sought by transnational agencies reaching out to the uncharted inland markets of China.[5] The joint venture model drives a cooperative rather than a confrontational relationship between local agencies and transnational agencies in second- and third-tier cities. The real front line in this imaginary combat is drawn between TNAAs and the domestic heavyweights in first-tier cities and special municipalities.

On the eve of the maturation of the WTO agreements, many proposals were made by Chinese critics to redefine the terms of engagement in the upcoming duels within the advertising industry. The key winning factors were said to have changed from "creativity" and "talent discovery" to capital and scale (Guo Jin 2005, 15).[6] Since a creative business is a business first and foremost, the argument went, perhaps the domestic biggies should start thinking about "consolidation" *(zhehe)* in preparation for the "foreign onslaught."

Industry integration as a defensive strategy has ample precedents. The Chinese model of "conglomeration by administrative order," however, defies the Western understanding of mergers. Through state-orchestrated conglomeration, the industrial and media sectors were broken into clusters of strongholds to better oppose the expected massive "alien infiltration" (J. Wang 2003, 249–250). Nobody can play the WTO card more skillfully than the socialist state. The China Cable Network Company, majority owned by SARFT (the State Administration of Radio, Film and Television), was established in 2001 to absorb local cable operators all over the country to eventually run one third of the cable TV market (China Online 2001). Large-scale consolidation in the audiovisual media sector of the early twenty-first century was, in fact, a replay of the reorganization of the press in the 1990s (Y. Zhao 2000). Other examples of scale economies abound. In December 2001, a number of state-owned broadcasting companies were merged to form the China Broadcasting, Film, and Television Company. This new conglomerate took over the "management of the central platform through which foreign TV companies transmit satellite signals to China" (China Online 2001). Chapter 7 will return to this topic and examine state-orchestrated mergers in the context of Chinese media policy reform. Right now, the urgent question on the table is whether the scaled-up integrative moves that have already taken place in print and audiovisual media also occur in the relatively autonomous advertising sector.

Surprisingly, as of early 2007 Beijing's attitude has been one of noninterference. An official spokesman from the SAIC (State Administration of Industry and Commerce) stressed the importance of the survival of the fittest (Qu 2004). Some critics in the advertising sector, on the contrary, recommended voluntary consolidation of top domestic agencies so as to preempt merger initiatives coming from transnational agencies (Guo Jin 2005, 16). In this we see a fascinating example of the Chinese reflex for "centralization"—with or without the state's push. Underlying such a proposal for "consolidation" was a defense mechanism triggered by the countdown to December 2005, when the floodgates that had hitherto kept medium and small international agencies out would be flung open.

Optimism Prevails

Not everybody had his finger on the panic button. Some critics rebutted the foreign monopoly thesis and recommended a wait-and-see attitude. These observers typically believed that China's advertising market was big enough for contending parties to coexist. Moreover, they felt, domestic giants could work productively with transnational titans to cultivate a self-regulated, more normative advertising market for China. Those and other similar "synergistic" predictions were borne out in part by the new confidence of Chinese admen in the steady growth of their country's GDP. Many saw an increasingly competitive corporate China as a cure-all for the domestic advertising industry. To the extent that transnational ad agencies' boom in China was dependent on their transnational accounts—so the argument went—so would domestic agencies be able to count on thriving domestic clients for a stable supply of revenue flow.

Meanwhile the negative press about Ogilvy's and Saatchi & Saatchi's wrong-headed choice of visual cues added more fuel to industry criticism of Chinese clients' infatuation with the 4A "myth." Many 4A agencies were seen as following the trite formula of skin-deep linguistic sinicization (Fu 2004, 53).[7] The morale of domestic agencies was further boosted by an increasing number of multinational clients seeking local agencies for a new facelift (for example, Danone's contract with Black Horse Ad Company) and cases of transnational agencies losing local clients to domestic new arrivals (as in the exit of Weiquan and Six Spirits from Bates to a new Chinese boutique) (Onicek 2003, 38).[8] All those instances demonstrate that "synergy" may not be a far-fetched abstraction after all. Despite some gloomy forecasts, plenty of optimism about the continued flourishing of domestic agencies even after China's accession to the WTO could be found.

The Odds

The early years of the new millennium were a time of crisis but also a time of blurring boundaries and new opportunities. Amid the cries of "the wolves are coming," symbiotic relationships of TNAAs with domestic agencies, which fostered mutual learning as well as benign competition, were said to characterize the "mainstream melody" in the new century (Wu Xiaobo 2003, 12). Ambitious Chinese admen began to believe that together with the branding resources provided by the TNAAs, they could localize global knowledge to perfection. This commitment to a reciprocal engagement in an "advertising commons" should nonetheless not be taken at face value. Reciprocity does not always translate into equality. Too often the 4A spokesmen are overly eager to conflate those two concepts. An adman for the transnational agency Leo Burnett says, for instance, that in his view, "there is no longer a distinction between international 4A companies and domestic companies. To develop [in a foreign market], an agency needs to localize itself 100 percent. So I thought whether we are talking about Leo Burnett, Ogilvy, or Dentsu, those agencies have deemed themselves 'local'" (quoted in Onicek 2003, 40).

This synergy talk may bring to mind our earlier discussion about the increasing blur between an "imported" brand and a "local" one in the mind of a consumer. But the identity of an agency can by no means be assessed by using the same crossover logic. Although it is easy for a transnational to declare its new-found "localized" identity, the reverse is hardly true for local agencies. It is one thing to postulate synergy, but another matter to ignore the disadvantages domestic Chinese players have suffered. Not all agencies are equal.

TNAAs have obvious advantages in talent recruitment (the lure of higher salaries), resource mobilization, and accumulated expertise in product branding.[9] A quick look at a 2003 survey of the Big Ten in China tells us more than half of the story (Guoji guanggao and IAI International Ad Research 2004, 12–15). The huge gaps in billings by foreign agencies versus Chinese agencies (marked by asterisks) are significant:

Saatchi & Saatchi	$338 million
McCann-Erickson	327 million
Leo Burnett (Shanghai)	325 million
Dentsu (Beijing)	291 million
Future Advertising Co.*	147 million
Guangdong Ad Co.*	135 million
Shanghai Ad Co.*	116.5 million
Shanghai Lowe	83.75 million
Dayu Beijing Co.*	48 million

When we move to another chart (Lu Changsheng 2004, 119–120) comparing the annual growth percentage of one against the other, the unevenness of competition is equally revealing:

	2001–2003 growth rate
Saatchi & Saatchi	93 percent
McCann-Erickson	95 percent
Beijing Dentsu	111 percent
Ogilvy (Shanghai)	49 percent
Guangdong Ad Co.*	50 percent
Shanghai Ad Co.*	48 percent
Beijing Ad Co.*	5 percent
Shanghai Arts Co.*	22 percent

On average, the total billing of domestic Big Tens in 2003 amounted only to 53.8 percent of the total income turnover of the transnational Big Ten (ibid., 120).

To be fair, one conspicuous advantage enjoyed by domestic agencies is their autonomy and, consequently, a faster line of communications conducive to efficient decision making. The TNAAs, on the other hand, are bogged down by the cumbersome long chain of command that originates from their headquarters (usually located in New York or London) and moves down to the continental (the Asia Pacific), then to the Greater China region (Hong Kong, Taiwan, and the PRC), and finally to country offices (for example in

Beijing, Shanghai, or Guangzhou). Sometimes even the smallest decision has to travel office by office all the way up to an agency's global headquarters. When regional executives are reluctant to assume responsibility for a decision, the ball is kicked from one court to the next, wearing out the patience of Chinese clients who are not used (and probably never will be) to such rigid business protocols. In short, domestic agencies can make the best of their autonomy to ensure a fast execution of their clients' campaigns, and no less important, to react at lightning speed to the capricious policy changes made by the government (Chapter 7 discusses the effect of changing policies on the advertising sector).

But international companies hold a trump card in their hand: the "4A" epithet. The acronym stands for the Association of Accredited Advertising Agencies and privileges American advertising practices. Many Chinese have even mistaken "4A" to mean the "American Association of Advertising Agencies." The assumption is not far-fetched, given that branding manuals based on American standards sell like hotcakes in Chinese bookstores. The manuals lay down in fine detail the division of labor between subdisciplines[10]—a model that big domestic companies are now copying verbatim. By 2007, generally speaking, the classic American paradigm of branding, which emphasizes the importance of segmentation, was gaining ground in China.

Two cases—the Libo Beer campaign by Bates, and the Harbin Coke Windmills commercial by DMB&B—provide useful examples of the ways in which 4A agencies operate on the ground in China. The creative sensibility underlying both campaigns was often referred to by industry critics as "seamless localization." The Libo television commercial, in particular, could easily pass for an "authentic" Chinese ad. Each campaign makes a different pitch to sell the "locale," but both demonstrate how TNAAs in China can progress from shallow nativism to a more sophisticated rendering of "local content." A sure sign of this development is the way in which the slogan "think globally/act locally" has increasingly been upstaged by "think locally/act locally" as the twenty-first century has begun. Although many agencies like Bates and Leo Burnett were slow to downplay the mention of "global standards" in their company literature, the wind has definitely shifted not only toward locally produced campaigns but toward deep "local content." Before 2000, few foreign companies were successful in delivering a creative campaign genuinely in tune with the cultural logic and "idiosyncrasies embedded in the mother tongue of Chinese" (Feng 2005, 108), but the best among them have now steered away from token sinicization.[11] This adjustment is an inevitable result of the increase in local Chinese clients that are now represented by 4A companies. Lowe boasted a portfolio with 40 percent local clients; J.W. Thompson, 30 percent; and Ogilvy Shanghai, 50 percent (Nie and Ma 2003, 23, 14). Alliances between local advertisers and 4A agencies seem more and more tangible as well.

But even by 2005 or so, the majority of Chinese manufacturers still habitually sought services from local ad boutiques—the most notable among them being Ye Maozhong, Pingcheng Company, and Blue Flames. Often, local clients might be curious enough to approach a 4A company but would get cold feet halfway through and back off from the agency's recommended strategies. Memorable television commercials for domestic brands bearing 4A hallmarks were still in short supply in the early years of the new millennium. In comparison, joint venture brand owners were more adventurous partners with 4A agencies.

"Libo Beer Is Why I Like Shanghai So Much!"

The ad campaign for Libo Beer, a JV brand seeking market rejuvenation, was launched by the TNAA Bates in Shanghai in 2001. At first glance, the popular campaign did not seem to rely on any gimmicks. Both the print ads and the television commercial highlight the brand's association with local consumers' shared memories about Shanghai as a place close to the heart. A simple narrative format was used, and the resulting commercial was a smashing success, reaching not only its target audience—young white-collar salarymen in Shanghai—but also local mass audiences. The campaign turned a new page in Chinese branding and advertising, because Bates captured the essence of the brand identity of Libo in a recurring positioning statement—"why do we like Shanghai so much?" The underlying strategic concept is simple: Libo, an old Shanghai beer, has been with "us" through thick and thin. The beer brand, the campaign says, witnessed all the growing pains of Shanghai throughout the reform era. This was a unique selling proposition that competitors like Budweiser and Tsingtao Beer were unable to claim. Invariably, each Libo advertisement highlights a memorable spot in the city that once carried a profound symbolic meaning for the Shanghainese. Each spot is expected to resonate with the locals and evoke memories that only the locals can savor. Told from the visual point of view of a little boy growing up in Shanghai, the commercial folds his personal memories into local, public memories. To make the synthesis work, each commercial showcases an unforgettable public space and public event in Shanghai of the 1980s: a sensational swim-wear exhibition featuring female models baring their arms and legs (the first in local history) and dancing in a department store; the swarming crowd at the Shanghai Stock Market Exchange on its opening day; the statue of Colonel Sanders standing cheerfully outside Shanghai's first Kentucky Fried Chicken; a local hair parlor where the now grown-up boy gets his first perm (a passing fad in Shanghai); an outdoor billboard carrying the once popular city propaganda of capitalist work ethics; and skyscrapers under construction at Hengxin Square.

The success of this formula tells us that locality sells. It also validates what Judith Farquhar says about the place reserved for "history," especially China's socialist past, in the mind of Chinese consumers today. The *Other* of the "global" is neither a local cultural essence nor a timeless national identity. Globalism's *Other* is a people with a shared past and a shared locale (Farquhar 2001, 125). Not just any locale that may provide a trendy translocal experience, but a hometown where lives are anchored and memories can accumulate. The Libo commercial says Shanghai is the best place to be. Both Shanghai residents and ad industry circles reveled in this message. It matters little if some academic critics contest that the cityscape unfolded in the commercial looks anonymously urban, "not specifically Shanghai."[12] What matters to the advertiser and the ad agency is the response of their target segment—the local Shanghainese who were supposed to recognize the locale in this commercial as none other than Shanghai itself. They obviously did.

THE "LOCAL" IS A CONSTRUCT

Fanfare about the Libo campaign quickly spilled over into variety talk shows in Shanghai, which rolled live interviews of old and young Shanghainese strolling down the streets reciting the tagline and singing the theme song. On the surface, the creative idea and execution of this campaign shows a strong adherence to local aesthetics: it moves away from image strategies based on abstract visual cues back to the traditional storytelling format most familiar to Chinese audiences. Pointed criticism of the commercial's irrelevance to migrants in Shanghai by some admen (Huang and Ye 2001, 72) only further validates the campaign's success in connecting to its target audience—local Shanghainese.

But the "localness" of this campaign cannot be taken at face value. First, the campaign is all about "emotional branding," a global marketing tactic at its best (Travis 2000; Gobé and Zyman 2001). Bates was reluctant to expose the 4A methodology underlying the Libo campaign. Had they made the knowledge public, they would not have received so much excellent press for "thinking Chinese" *(Zhongguo siwei)* (Nie and Ma 2003, 17).

Second, the Chinese ad industry was infatuated with Libo precisely because it was seen as a rare instance of market segmentation at the time. Up until the recent turn of the century, most Chinese and JV manufacturers advertised rather than branded their products, because it was too costly to buy the expertise in brand communications offered by 4A agencies. Libo's branded personality— "it is an old friend in our hometown"—lies at the heart of the campaign's success. Needless to say, it was an unorthodox practice at the time to sell a brand by building emotional associations with target consumers. The campaign was a masterpiece of segmentation, the norm for modern American advertising that I will treat in detail in the next chapter (Aaker and Joachimsthaler 2000, 31–93). Another intriguing detail is how unintelligible this commercial was to the rest of the country outside greater Shanghai. That is exactly where the true meaning of "local" lies—a shared history and a shared system of reference.

Last, we should ask whether the campaign, as legendary as it was, created a sales miracle for Libo. The answer is ambiguous. Prior to the campaign in 2000, Libo's market share in Shanghai was 16.5 percent, trailing far behind the number one beer, Santory (57.75 percent), and its national share was reportedly a slim 6.12 percent (Lin Sanzho 2004). After the launch of the Libo campaign in late 2001, the market share was said to have jumped by 20 percent the following year ("Difang xing pijiu" 2004). No follow-up statistics validated signs of sustained growth, although the Chinese marketing literature online and off indicates that Libo now leads Tsingdao—the national best-seller—in Shanghai at least. Verifying those statistics is difficult. But it is indisputable that Libo's market is now well rooted in greater Shanghai. It is also certain—something that advertising execs don't want to hear—that brand visibility does not automatically translate into towering sales figures.

Meanwhile the campaign has entered Bates's archive as a successful trophy of localization.

A success it was indeed, especially if we are told that Libo is strictly speaking not a "local" Shanghai beer but a JV brand posing as an authentic local brand.[13] This news brings us back to the futility of insisting on the clear distinction between what is "local" and what isn't. Even if the campaign may not have reaped consistently hot sales, it did accomplish one major feat—branding Libo as the only beer in Shanghai bearing genuinely local roots. This case illustrates that the "local" is almost always a construct.

The Coke Windmill Commercial

The same strategy of localization holds true with a totally transparent global brand like Coca-Cola. Made in Harbin, a famous Coke TV commercial is a sixty-second spot built on the visual motif of the windmill. It offers a *mis-en-scène* of North China, complete with a soundtrack of festive Chinese music. We witness small children wearing brightly colored Chinese cotton jackets, running around in a rich sea of Chinese red—red sails at a small harbor and red windmills blowing in the north wind in a remote rural village where peasants, old and young, are cheerfully greeting what seems to be the new year's fresh snow. Of course, a Coke bottle colored in the subtle shade of Chinese red emerges in the final shot to solve, light-heartedly, the mild suspense created by the seemingly purposeless assemblage of random shots and images.

An executive at the Atlanta Coca-Cola headquarters testified to the enormous success of this "localized" commercial, which was also very well received in other parts of Asia, in Europe, and in America ("Asia Television Commercials" 1999). The Harbin Coke commercial will go down in the corporate history of Coca-Cola as a well-executed example of its new company motto—"think locally." What interests me is multinationals' claims on the "localness" of campaigns that feature local scenery and local people engaged in ethnic festivities, when, in fact, both the campaigns' communication strategy and creative execution bear unmistakable imprints of the branding formula characteristic of 4A agencies.

In the case of the Harbin commercial, its visual language is clearly Western—tilt camera angles coupled with compositions dominated by strong visual cues. One should also note the total absence of a narrative cushion (to which Chinese TV viewers are most accustomed) for those loosely strung images. No stories were embedded in the commercial. To top that, the brand personality underlying the visuals is unfailingly the same old Coca-Cola that we have known from the days of the Hilltop commercial and "Mean Joe Green" up to the more recent polar bear series—a happy, warm, rosy-cheeked, communally conscious, reverent, festive, and fuzzy personality.[14] This commercial drives home a pedagogical lesson for those celebrating the emerging "local" sensibilities of McDonald's, Coke, and other transnational corporations. Precisely because there is a burgeoning Western market for "difference" (that is, the exotic sells), accentuating local content has more to do with these corporations' new marketing strategy than their promotion of local cultural specificities. Not surprisingly, the total disappearance of the word "global" in the new Coke company mantra—"Our business is local, close to home" and "think locally and act locally"—has strengthened the company's portfolio and pushed its sales up to $15 billion per year. Can we take the signifier of the "local" at face value? The answer is no.

4A versus 4C

Both the Libo and Coke commercials illustrate how "content localization" is much more complex than meets the eye. At the same time, the industry perspective—the blunting of friction between the "local" and the "global"—might take the edge off the politics of culture. If there is no point in distinguishing local from global, and if the "local" is a construct emptied of the politics of resistance and is nothing more than a marketing ploy, perhaps politics has no real bearing on advertising?

Those supporting the thesis of "advertising imperialism" in the classic *Madison Avenue in Asia* (1984) would counter that not only is this sector not politics-free, but the penetration of the TNAAs into a "sovereign nation" can be seen as a contemporary variation of colonialism. The thrust of those and similar critiques can be summed up in the words of a Filipino critic: "That advertising has become a very influential force in [a developing] society all the more underscores the need to de-Westernize it" (Anderson 1984, 61–62). Chinese nationalists would endorse this recommendation whole-heartedly. In 2001, an aggressive discourse of resistance—known as, and centered on, the 4C concepts (Chinese/Consumer/Consensus/Communication)—broke out to challenge the dominant 4A model.

Although a 4A affiliation represents a standard of professional ethics and therefore a sufficient level of public trust, the 4A has no administrative or executive power. Companies that come under the 4A banner make a pledge to protect consumers from deceptive advertisements and shield competitors from unfair practices via self-regulations. The first Chinese 4A was founded in Guangzhou in 1996; Shanghai followed suit in 2001; a Beijing-based 4A association did not come into being till 2005. Chinese 4As insist (at least in theory) that they aspire to transcend the self-interests of individual companies and that their sole aim is to promote fair competition and raise service and management standards. Regardless of such altruistic rhetoric, the 4As, especially the Guangzhou branch, are perceived as private clubs with membership restricted to only the transnational ad agencies.

Probably because most domestic agencies are unable to gain a 4A affiliation due to strict entrance criteria, iconoclasts within the local advertising community began to develop a contentious discourse challenging the international 4A norm.[15] The xenophobic sentiment toward the 4As was probably also fanned by Chinese admen's anxieties about China's accession to the WTO. A 4C campaign unfolded in 2001 in the popular trade magazine *Modern Advertising (Xiandai guanggao)* to defy the 4A formula. An account of 4C is included here despite its quick passing, because it was symptomatic of a persistent anti-Western undercurrent in China's advertising sector (and indeed in many other sectors). Time and again, this inflammatory sentiment is reactivated by international crises that set off the Chinese sensitivity to the issue of national sovereignty. Ultra-nationalist discourses explode in response to the unequal power relationship China is seen to suffer. The accession to the WTO no doubt intensified the crisis mentality of those radical elements in the sector lying in wait for another opportune moment to oppose Western norms.

The 4C was no simple business discourse about numbers or alliterative labels. It was a manifesto complete with modernist and postmodernist social theories evoking Max Weber, Giddens, Habermas, Keynes, Lyotard, and Foucault. Put briefly, the 4C concepts were theoretically embedded in an oppositional and thus a dichotomous framework: Chinese versus American, consumer versus advertiser, consensus versus hegemony, communications versus broadcasting. Many 4C manifestos have been set forth since September 2001. The piece that caught my attention starts with an emotional appeal to local ad agencies—"look straight into the eyes of the Chinese consumer" (Yang Wen 2001, 16). Domestic agencies are advised to bear in mind three sets of psychological characteristics said to be uniquely Chinese, each of which is pitted against what is allegedly seen as "Western." They are family-centered subjectivity versus individual-centered subjectivity; practical rationality versus absolute rationality; and the continuum of the Self and the Other in sharp contrast to the Western epistemology of the subject-object dichotomy. This model privileges, as the second C indicates, a consumer-based pattern of knowledge in defiance of the 4A regime, in which the advertiser is seen as the magnet. According to the author, the 4C shift of conceptual anchor from "advertiser to consumer" introduces a significant break in the notion of communication. The 4C condemns the unilateral broadcasting model in which the advertiser speaks *to* the consumer. It promotes, instead, a dialogical, consensual mode of communication. What follows is a predictable critique—à la Foucault—of the discourse of hegemony seen as inherent in the broadcast model.

Seen from the vantage point of the ad industry, the 4C discourse is riddled with questionable premises. Could an adman afford to critique consumerism, the raison d'être of advertising? Second, the modern Western concept of branding and marketing is totally anchored in consumer insights, which means that the 4C proposal for a paradigmatic shift from the manufacturer to the consumer took place long ago. Third, few successful advertisers and ad agencies in urban China today resort to the outdated notion of a "homogeneous" Chinese consumer market. Regional differences are well acknowledged in the marketing lingo of tiered cities, a topic I discuss further in Chapter 5. The marketing appeal of tier-two cities (for example, Chengdu, Wuhan, Shenyang, and Chongqing) has now outweighed that of tier-one cities (Beijing, Shanghai, and Guangzhou)—which are seen as already oversaturated. Even third- and fourth-tier cities have begun to command attention from multinationals. The market culture characterizing each tier is markedly different. And to push the argument of segmentation further, within each city cluster, consumers are broken down further into subsegments. The uneven development of local and regional markets has made marketing in China both a challenge and a headache. A "brand-seeker" prototype in Beijing may only count as a "brand-adopter" in Shanghai, because usually Beijingers are less trendy than the Shanghainese. And we have not even addressed the thorny issue of how to match consumer segments with the increasingly differentiated media audiences in China (for details see Chapter 7). The 4C vision of a "Chinese" mass market characterized by a single psychological formula is anachronistic, and a sure recipe for marketing failure. The practical value of the 4C is thin.

The quick demise of the 4C, however, does not mean the end of anti-4A and anti-TNAA sentiment. Chinese admen and -women will always harbor complex feelings on the issue of localization *(bentu qingjie)*. I continue to come across statements like the following—"Only by rebelling against the mainstream can we find our own way . . . the so-called international mainstream is but an illusory master narrative that we ourselves created. Hardly any [savvy] creatives in the world will recognize that mainstream as a *real fact*" (Guangzhou Editing Department 2004, 12). This quote sounds all the more intriguing because it was taken from an interview with Zhang Xiaoping—the main organizer of the Guangzhou 4A affiliates. The irony seems clear: there is little qualitative difference between 4C advocates and Chinese 4A architects in their distaste for global norms. It seems that many native talents working in 4A companies are rebels in disguise. Consider these words from another 4A adman:

> Those foreign bosses [in 4A companies] are bragging about their lead in localization. They are actually clueless about local thinking, they just started to speak Mandarin Chinese.
>
> If you are strong in local thinking in an international agency, you will be very miserable. You will find few people with whom you can communicate and interact.
>
> You are asking me who controls the future of the discursive power of the 4As in China? Well, Western foreigners, Hong Kongese, and Taiwanese admen and women represent the "ruling party," and us native talents, the "opposition party." (Fu 2004, 51, 54)

These three quotes are telling; they validate my own observation that regardless of how high local admen have climbed on the executive ladder of a 4A company, the smarter they are, the more likely they will be entertaining thoughts of opening their own agency and being a *bentu* professional some day.

THE BENTU IDEOLOGY: LOW-BROW LOCALISM WITH CHINESE CHARACTERISTICS

Bentu is the Chinese word for "local," and *bentu hua*, "localization." Appropriately, after discussing how the TNAAs construct the "local," we are now turning to local aesthetics subscribed to by *bentu* agencies. Their efforts often boil down to an earthy, noisy, and straightforward aesthetic of mass appeal. If you are a connoisseur of hip Western commercials, or if you are an American bourgeois bohemian with a one-downsmanship sensibility (see Chapter 5), you will find a typical Chinese commercial pitched by a domestic company nothing short of aesthetically revolting. My own viewing experiences of those *bentu* ads occasionally yield pleasant surprises. A CCTV commercial selling Naobaijin (a popular Chinese brand of health tonic that I discussed in the Introduction) impressed me with its unabashed display of the spectacle that translates into the sensational, hustle-bustle crowd effect.

I often had to rein in my appreciation for Naobaijin commercials when in the presence of 4A admen and -women, who detest low-brow localism.[16] But TNAA professionals need to heed the golden rule of advertising—that the aesthetics don't matter so long as the ad is a good pitch to the targeted consumers. This principle is particularly relevant for multinationals eyeing the Chinese inland markets. As the new decade of the twenty-first century wore on, international 4As made a stronger effort to emulate homespun Chinese aesthetics. Ogilvy, for instance, resorted to traditional paper-cut art to advertise China Mobile during the Lunar New Year festival.

畅享移动新年话

我越心动世界情

全球通 GoTone
A世界·心响往
中国移动通信 CHINA MOBILE
Beijing 2008
北京2008年奥运会合作伙伴暨北京奥组委合作伙伴

辞旧岁，一年一度的手机更新换代又开始了。享受生活了，这个新年，全球通准备了精彩贺岁好礼，让我们低低畅享移动新生活！

【新鲜畅享】手机短信登录动梦网(wap.monternet.com)或发送"05"至"18632"、"MO"彩讯上网，带来更多手机信息，多彩的节日图铃下载，有着的在线游戏逗逗乐，洋尽的手机资讯浏览，尽享节日精彩；手机拨打12590700，语音尊享特有手机节日点播音。

【环球畅享】出国过节无论您到哪里，只要开通全球通国际漫游业务，都能随时随时候邮上网，收发短信，彩信，分享节日气氛。

【倾情畅享】18岁大方待先看，新年音乐乐为我开。

【倾享畅享】积分兑换包括定制手机在内的多种精彩礼品，让新年更添新气象。

* 活动详情请查询10658090或请咨询当地各移动营业厅公告，中国移动通信有权对此次活动作解释权。

Ornately donned folk pantheons familiar to the masses (for instance, red-faced Lord Guan and the plump Longevity Star) are
made even more jovial with cell phones placed in their hands! (Lao
Han 2005).[17] A busy, multicolor visual of this sort adds to the melodramatic affect dear to ordinary Chinese sensibilities.

A less straightforward but equally earnest mass-line approach
was adopted by Nike. The sports giant had a traumatic year in
2004 because it had to apologize to the Chinese for its "Chamber of
Fear" global campaign that featured a kung-fu master fallen on
all fours. J.W. Thompson in Shanghai reversed Nike's fortunes
in China with an indelible series of five-second commercials celebrating the Nike spirit in creative flourishes true to the spirit of vernacular Chinese localism. The spots focused briefly on ordinary
Beijingers showing off their athletic reflexes or consciousness at
various uncanny moments during the day, such as in the commercial "Pop Corn," in which the sound of a street vendor's pop corn
popping prompts a young man who is tying his shoes to dart
forward like an Olympic runner. The campaign (with the tagline
"Sporty Encounters Made Anytime and Anywhere") restored
Nike's image and won it a trophy at the eleventh Chinese Ad Festival (Xiao Tong 2005). What greeted us in these campaigns was
not something new but an intensification of a localizing trend that
Coca-Cola and Marlboro had mastered so well in China. Both multinational companies are pros at manufacturing Chinese sensibility.
Coke made several renowned commercials exploiting the Chinese
sentimentality with regard to soccer games (see Chapter 3).
Marlboro's disadvantage (cigarettes ads are not allowed on Chinese
television) was handsomely offset by its thematic "Celebrate the
Lunar New Year" television commercials that are thoroughly "Chi-

---

Opposite page: Lord Guan, with a cell phone in hand, in a print ad for
China Mobile celebrating the Lunar New Year. China Mobile and Ogilvy
Beijing.

nese" (Meng Xiangsheng 2002, 291). In place of Marlboro Country and the rugged cowboy are China's wild West and its darkskinned rustic drummers immersed in an action-intense harvest ritual. Marlboro's signature machismo (Twitchell 2000) is given a very local treatment indeed.

In this competition for nativist appeal, domestic agencies have an edge, according to Ye Maozhong and Wu Xiaobo, two of China's strongest spokesmen for localism with Chinese characteristics. Ye's career as an adman started in 1993. By the late 1990s, he was already widely quoted in trade magazines as the dark horse of advertising. Wu Xiaobo, a CEO at Pingcheng Ad Company, was the brains lurking behind campaigns of famed local brands like Ningbo Bird, a cellphone brand ("2003 Zhongguo guanggao ye" 2004, 19).

Ye Maozhong, in particular, has a charismatic presence, because his nationalist pride is well blended into pragmatism and a passion for advertising so intense that his company became a magnet that drew an endless supply of famous local clients. Ye's motto is an unswerving "cater to consumers but never guide them" (ibid.). He gave bundles of marketing tips in his single-authored volume *Chuangyi jiushi quanli* (Creativity Is Power), among them, "we make ads to please the masses," "one should not have a blind faith in the 4A agencies," "agencies make a mistake by preferring 30 seconds to 15 seconds," "you should try to mention a brand's name at least three times in a 30-second spot and twice in a 15-second one," "real creativity is grounded in thorough marketing research," "a good ad meets two goals: first, it drives the consumer to buy the product; second, it makes the consumer like the brand." The mascot of his company is the wolf. According to Ye, "wolves are excellent team players. They are also ferocious and powerful" (Ye Maozhong 2003, 360–410).

Chinese consumers, especially the middle and lower-middle classes in tier-one, -two, and -three cities and further below, much welcome Ye Maozhong's advertisements. Northern consumers appreciate his Beijing-specific sensitivity more than southerners. The lower the tier goes, the more appealing his brand of creativity is. I was particularly impressed with a campaign for a tonic drink for businessmen in which Ye made a clever, nuanced pitch to reference the sexual prowess of male targets. The trick hinges on a simple, smart pun on the Chinese word *gan,* which means "dried up," "liver," and "bottoms up" all at once. A male exec is seen being wined and dined at company parties while his wife is pacing to and fro at home, worrying about his alcohol intake hurting his liver and making him "dried up." Audiences watching the Ocean King Tonic series chuckle at the innuendo and memorize the brand name instantly—which means half the task is already accomplished.

"Localism with Chinese characteristics," at its core, takes place in a close linguistic encounter between consumers and taglines. In China, sophisticated verbal play often builds brand equity faster than a well-executed visual image. I am, of course, referring to mass market consumers, not niche segments. It is this deep appreciation for the double entendre and an acute sensitivity to wordplay that lie behind the mass appeal of Ye Maozhong's advertisements. Audio aesthetics please Chinese people (literate and illiterate alike) in a way that that clever images cannot match. Consider the taglines Ye created for Yili ice cream cones—"tai kuazhang le ba!?" and "Yili sige quan, chile jiu zhidao." Rendered into English, they sound like a mouthful—"isn't it too exaggerating?" and "count the four rings inside Yili ice cream when you are eating it." The Chinese original has a telegraphic terseness in perfect accord with the tonal beat and thus possesses a pleasant singsong quality that kids—Yili's target consumers—especially enjoy. Ye's 2002 account for Mengniu Dairy (Yili's major competitor) pushed the verbal trick to a new level of innovation. Naming the product *Suibian* (instant metamorphosis) ice cream, he weaves the motif of "transformation" into a sequence of frames showing kids biting into the ice cream and turning instantaneously into a Batman, a Spiderman, and a Harry Potter in quick succession. The eight- to sixteen-year-olds love the commercial. And the brand name *Suibian bingqilin* is tonally so rhythmic that reciting it feels like practicing a tongue twister. Other memorable cases of audio-localism include Wahaha's jingle "hele wahaha chi fan jiu shi xiang" (drink Wahaha, you will eat more), and Beck's "ting ziji de he beike" (listen to yourself, drink Beck's).

Punning taglines aside, there is something more to Ye Maozhong's work that distinguishes him from other well-known local talents. The brand of localism he sells is tinged with a unique urbane flavor that came from his clever sampling of Western cultural highlights. Not only does he make reference to Batman, Spiderman, and Harry Potter—icons of American pop—but he uses the opening movement of Beethoven's Symphony No. 5 to good melodramatic effect in the Ocean King tonic series. But if you call his creative instinct "cosmopolitan," he will likely take offense. To him, the three syllables of ye-mao-zhong stand for a *bentu* brand in itself that sells "Chinese localism."

Ye Maozhong is just another example that validates the truism well known to advertising professionals: what makes a brand "local" has everything to do with the emotional identification of the consumer with that brand. Intimacy can be built through a variety of means—through identification with a local icon like Ye (that is, the "strongman" phenomenon), through product adaptation (Kentucky Fried Chicken) and localized creative content (Nike's "Pop Corn"), or through positioning adaptation (Marlboro in Hong Kong) and distribution channel strength (Wahaha and Bird), and even via elaborate public relations maneuvers (Coca-Cola).[18] To complicate matters, localization means different things to different agency players. For Ye Maozhong, it translates into a specific creative approach (dramatizing verbal and audio puns) that speaks to mass consumers. For Blue Flames (a successful boutique with bill-

Frames from a TV ad for Mengniu Dairy *Suibian* Transformer ice cream show a small customer turning into Batman. Mengniu Dairy and Ye Maozhong Advertising Company.

ings exceeding 300 million yuan), "localization" is equivalent to national and cultural purity.[19] For transnational 4As, the spectrum of localization is a much more extended one: from capturing the essence of sportiness in quotidian activities (Nike), to celebrating the Spring Festival in a small northern village (Coke), to brainstorming for a Chinese tagline (Buick).[20] Finally, foreign agencies that abide by the following rules of the game (a selective list) may also be successful in localization:

1. Emphasize team playing and communal and family values even if your target segment is teenagers;
2. Use extreme caution whenever you try to make an appeal to humor or sex;
3. Pick warm, sincere public relations activities that are modest in tone;
4. Instill modern sensibility into familiar Chinese idioms, allusions, stories, or fables;
5. Use storytelling and other more indirect creative methods to appeal to the southerners, but feed Beijingers more serious and information-oriented ads. ("Zai Zhongguo" 2005)

In the end, the definition of what counts as a local advertisement or a local brand is up for grabs. Only consumers have the final say.

A final word of caution for multinationals rushing into rural China, who will be challenged by the need for localization in ways different from what this chapter has covered. The strong roots of localism in the hinterland make product adaptation a definite priority over marketing and advertising. Many categories we take for granted in urban China may face a difficult entry in rural towns. The fast-food category is one such example. "Targeting underserved areas where there is little competition may enable western firms to establish market dominance" (Eckert, Haron, et al. 2004, 172)—I quote Kellogg marketers of Bugles who envision themselves making a sweeping claim on the snack food market in

China's vast underdeveloped regions. Yet that vision betrays a lack of understanding of rural Chinese consumers. When it comes to matters of the palate, "locality" is more than a construct. Foreign logos and suave brand strategies cannot anticipate quick rewards in the hinterland, where single-child families do not dominate. Fast food like hamburgers or snack foods like chips will not find an easy footing. If one day rural folks do take a fancy to Western fast food, I'd bet that Kentucky Fried Chicken will fare better than McDonald's, because not only do Chinese people love chicken more than beef but the Chinese dishes on the KFC menu will be a definite draw for country people.

Next time in one of my sojourns in Beijing when I find no seats in overcrowded Chinese fast-food venues (the Yonghe Soybean Taiwanese franchise comes to mind), I will be happy to go to a KFC for a bowl of mushroom chicken porridge and taste their fried chicken wings marinated in salt and pepper and star anise powder. I may even try their "Old Peking Style Chicken Roll" with scallions and sweet bean sauce tucked inside. Although that will be a far cry from authentic, meticulously sliced Peking duck wrapped in steaming hot paper-thin Chinese pancakes, I will prefer this KFC dish to a hamburger at McDonald's. If there is anything left that stubbornly resists the blurring of boundaries that this chapter harps on, it is our culinary sensibilities that remain loyally local, especially for those Chinese living in tier-two and tier-three cities, provincial and county towns, and villages of all sizes. I join world gourmet eaters to pay tribute to those cooks who have preserved centuries-old recipes and resisted the trendy fusion styles, and who continue to cater to local and regional taste buds. "Am I lovin' it?" is a famous tagline of a McDonald's campaign turned into a query.[21] The hamburger king had better speed up its product adaptation before inland Chinese consumers think twice about how to answer that question.[22]

CHAPTER 2

Positioning the
New Modern Girl

"Listen to yourself, drink *Beck's!*" (Beck's Beer)

"*'Fifth Season'* is *in!*" (JianLibao)

"Even a child like me yelps too, at the first gulp, Qoo!" (Coca-Cola)

"A comfortable feeling just like any other day." (Comfort & Beauty)

"Positioning," the basic tenet of contemporary American advertising, is the practice of segmentation in a cluttered marketplace. As a primary tool of communication, it helps a brand become what it is, as opposed to something it's not. The brand positioning of a product can be as imaginative as the Qoo profile in the epigraph above, or as literal as Haier's "sincerely forever" or Volvo's "safety." To segment means "to limit." Thus a shampoo brand targeting "people with hair" is a marketing joke, risking total irrelevance in today's highly differentiated market. Not all consumers are equal (Stockdale 1999). The concept of "narrow cast" is in and "broadcast" out. The fruit beverage Qoo in China, for instance, is tailored for children aged five to eight; Comfort & Beauty, a feminine-care brand, targets females who seek reassurance; Beck's beer beckons freedom seekers; and the Fifth Season, a new leisure drink series launched by Guangdong-based JianLibao, targets fad-seeking youths. Even the youth market is becoming highly segmented in China these days.

Positioning and its journey through China can be illustrated by examining several case studies; looking at the way in which a typical 4A ad agency identifies and creates a "position" for a brand also shows how branding works. Branding road maps developed by transnational ad agencies tend to resemble one another, because they follow similar paths blazed by master theoreticians such as David Aaker, Al Ries, Jack Trout, and Ogilvy's own—David Ogilvy—who retains his legendary stature as a brand visionary to this day. I will rely heavily on Ogilvy's 360 Degree Brand Stewardship as a basic tool in my explorations; this approach stands out as a highly efficient instrument, easy to learn and implement. I familiarized myself with it during my fieldwork at Ogilvy.

The most important rule for branding is articulated by Al Ries and Jack Trout: "Positioning is not what you do to the product. Positioning is what you do to the mind of the prospect" (Ries and Trout 2001, 2). This view, cited frequently in agency manuals and theoretical literature on branding, is well aligned with the shift in American advertising from a product-centered trajectory to a consumer-oriented marketing perspective. Beck's commercials in China provide a good example of ways to create a "position" in the prospective buyer's mind.

BECK'S BEER

Beck's "position," simply put, is "freedom of choice." Those familiar with the social ethos of post-1989 China can well imagine the
popularity of an advertising campaign rooted in the notion of
"choice." Debuting in the mid-1990s in Beijing, only half a decade
after the Tiananmen Square crackdown, this smart Beck's campaign
fed disillusioned urban youth the ideology of individualism. The allure of such a message couldn't have been better timed: June 4,
1989, crushed the utopian yearning of students for (fuzzily defined)
political reforms; the early 1990s that followed are remembered as
an age without heroes and heroism and an epoch of profiteering for
all (J. Wang 1996). Pop culture crowded the market, streets came
alive with store logos and goods, and advertising began to take on
the full-fledged influence we associate with the West. A budding
sense of individualism accompanied the rampant commercialism.
Imagine the fanfare created by the Beck's campaign: although the
Chinese people were not permitted to deviate from the norm of col-
lectivity, they were free at last to consume commodities they chose
for themselves. Beck's will be remembered as one of the earliest
Chinese ad campaigns to pioneer the concept of "positioning."

One Beck's commercial opens with a field of blooming sun-
flowers facing the sun. (Note the allusion to Mao as the "sun.")
Suddenly, one sunflower turns to the west, where a bottle of Beck's
beer stands and beckons to it. At that instant, a male voice chimes
in: "Listen to yourself, drink Beck's" *(ting ziji de, he Beike)*. In another variation of the same concept, a family of crabs is moving
sideways and in a single tight row. One crab suddenly spots a bottle
of Beck's beer in the sand. Without turning its body around, the
lone crab breaks ranks and starts walking forward toward the bottle. The same tagline is played at that moment.[1]

Needless to say, those two commercials stood out dramatically
from the dominant socialist advertising of the early 1980s that con-

veyed nothing more than information about the price and availability of a commodity. The heavy emphasis on the use-value of goods was often cited by outsiders at the time as a manifestation of the "material backwardness" of socialist China. The Beck's campaign was one of the early precursors of image advertising that emerged in the mid-1990s. Increasingly, Chinese commercials delivered the same messages that Westerners are bombarded with—that consumption is not about replacing worn-out material goods themselves but about the choice of a particular style of life. With Deng Xiaoping's blessing, status consumption and market ideology do not always contradict party ideology in China.[2] They make strange bedfellows, for better or for worse.

Marketers in China, in fact, are good at tweaking the superficial contradictions between the "free market" and the "communist state" into a unique selling point. Such a twist was exactly what made the Beck's campaign tick. What turned Beck's beer into a cultural event was more than the wayward mood of an "independent" crab or a "free-spirited" sunflower. Underlying the subliminal images of "a sunflower turning West" and "a crab stepping out of line" was a subtle ideological critique of what socialism stood for. The message was a seditious one, and calculatedly so.

But Beck's was hardly going preachy. The company had a single-minded goal like all other corporate clients—finding a position that resonated well with prospective consumers or, more specifically, a position that was already lurking in their mind. Savvy brand architects do not aim at creating something new. They tap into what is already there in the prospect's mind and recharge the connection. Branding is more about resonance than inculcation. What Beck's delivered was nothing more than the younger generation's desire to go against the grain in an era bound by political taboos. Instead of staking out a new cultural position, the beer simply unearthed what was on the minds of the unruly youth at that particular historical juncture.

FIFTH SEASON

As "differentiation" became the golden rule for Chinese advertising in the twenty-first century, brand positioning like Beck's (which sells an attitude) no longer raised eyebrows. Copycats filled the market. Fifth Season is a new subbrand launched by the JianLibao Group, one of south China's largest sports drink companies. JianLibao's heyday had come and gone in the early 1990s, when its carbonated drinks, known as China's Magic Water, were best-sellers on a par with Coke and Pepsi. But the state-owned company soon staggered under the weight of bad management and fierce competition. In 2002, a new president was brought on board to re-build JianLibao. To turn the company around, he made two deci-sive moves: he changed the flagship product of JianLibao from sports drinks to leisure drinks; and he steered away from a single-brand strategy to create a subbrand called "Fifth Season," planning to phase out its association with JianLibao gradually. Both tactics worked. Sales of the subbrand reached $62 million in early 2003 (Liu Botao 2003). Although JianLibao's fortunes rose and fell in subsequent years (the company was bought out by Taiwan's Uni-President Food Company in 2005), Fifth Season remained the cor-poration's banner brand (JianLibao 2006).

The subbrand's success had everything to do with its position-ing strategy. Targeting fifteen- to twenty-five-year-olds, Fifth Season gave birth to a chic, tantalizing urban metaphor of a "mood sea-son," an alternative mental space outside and beyond the four sea-sons (Xiao Zhiying 2002, 55). The brand plays successfully on the concept of *linglei,* the Chinese term for the "(alternative) other," now a powerful marketing concept for lifestyle categories in China as we shall see in Chapter 6. Fifth Season's brand identity is narcis-sistic, rebellious, dreamy, and faddish. Its tagline was "Fifth Season is *in!*" And its brand position: "Enjoy a relaxing life, express your-self at will." This may sound dangerously close to the positioning of other premium leisure drinks. China's urban beverage drinkers have a tough time deciding which brand truly speaks their mind. But the pitch of Fifth Season accomplished one important mission—disassociating JianLibao from the image of tonics and shifting its personality away from "sports" to an expression of *au courant* personal choice.

Is Fifth Season cool? Those who saw the drink's advertisements reacted in different ways. My favorite is a television commercial that parodies its Taiwanese competitor Master Kang. We see a Ren Xianqi look-alike (Ren is the celebrity spokesman for the rival brand) cruise past a mom-and-pop shop on a bike. He eyes the beverage drinks on display in the store. The shop owner throws him a Fifth Season. In a similar stunt act to impress the bystanders as he did in his Master Kang commercials, the look-alike Ren, still sitting on a moving bike, tries to catch the bottle in one fell swoop but misses it and falls flat. The voice-over says: "Don't play cool, if you are not made of cool material!" The comparative mode is set in motion but rendered tastefully and won the heart of the fun-loving late teens and twentysomethings, Fifth Season's major target.

EVERYTHING YOU WANT TO KNOW ABOUT QOO

We have only a short distance to travel from drinks that look cool to a drink named Qoo, one of Coca-Cola's hottest offerings in East Asia as of 2005. As most Asian Qoo fans know, the Qoo character originated in Japan. The country of origin of Qoo is significant in our discussion of brand positioning, because "segmentation" is not the norm in Japanese marketing. Marketers there place a greater emphasis on corporate branding instead. The highly successful Qoo is therefore an even more interesting case of brand positioning.

A low-sodium beverage, Qoo takes on subtly different personalities in different regions. It was launched in the fruit juice category in Japan and China, but advertised in Taiwan as a sports drink (with fortified Vitamin B6, Oligo, and amino acids) said to be good for children's muscle growth, digestion, and neuro systems.

In Japan, the little blue mascot was a male character even though the original brand was designed to appeal to both children and their mothers. Drawing on consumer feedback, Coca-Cola Japan Company (CCJC) discovered that low-percentage fruit juice drinks are very popular with married Japanese women who have children aged three to ten. Those young mothers, research indicates, feel nostalgic for their own childhood and dote on Japanese cartoon *anime* characters. Their children, in contrast, are less drawn by cute and sweet characters and relate more to more sophisticated, precocious characters such as "Chibi Maruko-chan," a cute nine-year-old girl with a great imagination, and "Shin-chan," a kindergartener whose antics are the subject of the series "Crayon Shin-chan" (Yoshito Usui 2002). The challenge for CCJC marketers and creatives was to find a happy compromise between the two market segments of mothers and children, and they searched for a concept that would capture this in-between quality. The winner was "qoo"—a sound uttered by an adult after drinking the first gulp of beer in great satisfaction. Out of the sound emerged an animated cartoon character that looks precocious, not at all childish despite its childlike face. A theme song was created for the character: "Even a child like me yelps too, at the first gulp, Qoo!" The song was set to blues music to enhance the character's mellow aura. An entire profile was devised, including information that the Qoo character was "a little bit taller than a table," had been born in the woods, hated bullies, only said "qoo," "weighed as much as three pineapples," loved to dance, and was seven to ten years old. From product design to brand personality and on to communications planning, Qoo exemplifies one of the best integrated communications strategies ever devised in Japan.

In 2001, Qoo beverage went abroad. It soon became the third-largest subbrand of Coca-Cola in Asia. But the challenge of retain-

Coca-Cola Japan's Qoo beverage. Photo: Yuichi Washida.

ing its Japanese character had just begun. The biggest challenge lay in building consistency from the diverse segmentation strategies adopted by Qoo's respective foster homes. When introduced into Singapore, Qoo the character was mutated into a gender-neutral creature, half feminine and half masculine. In Germany, the precocious side of the Qoo character was let go, because the German team insisted that as a children's brand, the characteristics of Qoo should be confined to "childishness alone." In China, although the drink was given a name whose meaning stays very close to the original spirit of Qoo—*kuer,* "children of cool" (a pure linguistic coincidence)—the brand has also undergone a similar process of infantilization as in Germany. Chinese Qoo drinks are heavily advertised as calcium- and vitamin-rich to appeal to parents' anxieties about children's calcium intake. As Qoo mania spread over the rest of the world, maintaining its original brand concept became more and more difficult, since there is no such thing as a stable global children's segment.

My discussion of Beck's, Qoo, and Fifth Season should make it clear that advertising is not a sledgehammer pounding down on consumers. It is primarily about segmentation, or occupying a position in the mind of target segments. Beck's (in China) and Qoo (in Japan) testify to the validity of rule number one in the positioning bible—the easiest way to blast into your prospect's mind is to get there first (Ries and Trout 2001, 19–21). But there are also positioning strategies to cope with the problem of being number two. The most popular strategy is to try to be the *first* to occupy the second position (Pepsi Cola after Coca-Cola) or to try to reposition your competitor and burst its bubble in the way that Fifth Season did to Master Kang, and Tylenol to aspirin.

At times, however, repositioning a strong competitor may prove difficult, especially in the category of fast-moving consumer goods (FMCGs), where megabrands like Procter & Gamble and Unilever dominate. To compound the problem of jousting with global players whose pockets are deep, countries like China and Japan discourage openly comparative advertising. Under such circumstances, repositioning one's own brand may be a more viable alternative to attempts to repositioning a competitor's. Here our fourth epigraph above becomes relevant. "A comfortable feeling just like any other day" is a tagline for Comfort & Beauty (C&B), a joint venture feminine-care brand owned by Kimberly-Clark (KC). My discussion of C&B serves a number of purposes: it provides a perfect example of a repositioning campaign; because of my own familiarity with the campaign, I can use C&B as an entry point to examine Ogilvy's tool, 360 Degree Brand Stewardship; the Kotex and C&B brand merger (KC&B)—part of the original repositioning scheme—has rich implications for the debate over global campaigns and international advertising; and, by extension, through the KC&B case study, we can reevaluate the usefulness of old paradigms that pit "local culture" against "global culture" and shed light on the question of "agency." And it must be said that the global Kotex Red Dot campaign has entertainment as well as pedagogical value.

COMFORT & BEAUTY: THE NEW MODERN GIRL

Feminine-care products like Comfort & Beauty share a market segment that overlaps with the one for cosmetics, shampoo, and fashion, namely, women from their late teens to their late forties. This general segment is said to be the most powerful in China today, with the percentage of women employed in professional and technical jobs reaching 38.1 percent of the total workforce in urban China, translating into more than 42 million women with income (Kang 2005). But potential Chinese female consumers far exceed that number. Marketers have long been aware that married women, whether they are working women or not, hold the purse strings of Chinese households. And yet it was not until early in the twenty-first century that they started trumpeting the observation that young Chinese women are carving out more autonomous gender roles and are more ready than ever to spend for pleasure. Any useful discussion of C&B, and indeed of any products catering to the second sex, needs to begin with the changing self-perceptions, defined in marketing terms, of young women in tier-one and tier-two cities. I say "young" women because in China today, the twentysomethings are corporate clients' dream segment for product categories centered on self-expression. Capturing the aspirations of these trend-seekers has emerged as a top priority for marketers in China.

> I am center of the world, I am the focal point. (Prystay 2002, A11)

> Career is the way to prove my capability but 'strong woman' loses the essence of being a woman. (Ogilvy & Mather Asia Pacific 1999)

> Family and child are my duty, but not my whole life. (ibid.)

> There are various roles I have to perform . . . Most of the time, I am seeking for applause from the audience. (ibid.)

Marketers seeking consistency can detect a pattern from these statements: young women in contemporary China cast themselves in the image of smart, attractive, and resourceful women who need their own space and time; they also long to reward themselves. Gone is the era of self-sacrifice their mothers and grandmothers lived through. Advertisers attempting to court the new modern girl have to salute *her* achievements and fuel *her* fantasies. A similar perspective was echoed by Linda Kovarik, a strategic planner at Leo Burnett: "We are seeing a rise in materialism and ego. [Chinese] women are expressing themselves in a way their mothers couldn't. Brands need to offer them room to be vain . . . As marketers, we can definitely explore more archetypes: woman as hero, woman as lover, woman as creator, explorer" (Prystay 2002, A11).

Have transnational marketers overrated the new modern girl's yearning for independence? The recent blogs of Sister Lotus and Rowdy Swallow offer a few clues. Wildly controversial, these women have been seen as transgressors and held responsible for an outbreak of "tramp culture" *(jian wenhua)* (Li Guoqing 2005).

> Behold my sexy, bewitching appearance and my incorruptible temperament! Wherever I go, I attract the relentless gaze of the crowd and become the focal point of their attention. (Sister Lotus 2005)

I don't need to obey you [men]; I won't flatter you, adore you, or pay attention to you. I am amusing myself and fretting by myself. I complain to myself, live and shall die alone . . . (Rowdy Swallow 2005)

These quotes, especially the second one, touched a chord that mere sensationalism cannot explain. Reading them makes one wonder if the offense of "vulgarity" is the real issue. Sister Lotus's saucy photos showing her licking flowers and thrusting out her C-cup chest may fool us into thinking that online smut is ravaging China. But there's no denying that she's got an attitude, and reportedly declared with audacity—"I will not be censored"—against a government ban (Cody 2005). The equally infamous Rowdy Swallow, who posted nude images of herself online, filled her blogs with cyberfeminist manifestos and passionate defenses of prostitutes as human beings who should have full rights. Swallow and Lotus share a determined defiance against public censure. Using digital media as a means of viral communication, they join ranks with Mu Zimei, whose notorious sex diary and lovemaking audiotape started a blogging fever in China in 2003.[3] One important entry of Mu's online diary was ignored in most tabloid portals: "I faithfully record how I live. I don't care about other people's interference or sabotage. I don't give a damn if the mere mention of my name scares men to death" (Wang Bin 2005). Fans and nonfans alike wonder if these women's desire for the public gaze can be neatly pared down to narcissism. Are they lurid exhibitionists or liberated women, tramps or iconoclasts? We may not succeed in pigeonholing them, but one thing is certain: although the trio was not consciously aware that the personal is political, the digital media, which Lawrence Lessig calls technologies of self-expression (Lessig 2004), are fanning a cyberfeminism in China that defies the quick dismissal of puritan censors.[4] Few may follow in the trio's footsteps, but their fan clubs have multiplied with cheers coming from both sexes. Regardless of whether the majority of Chinese women have the nerve to become daredevils, feeling feminine and wanting to be expressive and carefree (though not duty free) are aspirations that resonate with young females in China today. C&B's repositioning campaign catered to this segment.

Modern Comfort for Modern Women: C&B

"Once we begin to look at 'comfort' seriously it becomes a very complex idea" (Taylor 2003, 95). The depth of this insight did not escape the Kotex C&B team. In the summer of 2002, Kimberly-Clark (hereafter KC)—the manufacturer of Kotex—was in the midst of relaunching C&B, a local Chinese brand it had acquired. The relaunch was originally conceptualized as a way to associate Kotex with C&B. The ad agency's account team and strategic planners turned to consumer insights for a refreshing angle to rejuvenate the brand's position of "comfort." As a product benefit, "comfort" spans several emotive categories that range from domestic to physical and emotional comfort, and involves attributes that stretch from pleasure and leisure to privacy and intimacy, including a sense of liberation that results from one's total immersion in nature. Women in Wuhan, for instance, define the core attributes of "comfort" differently from their counterparts in Shanghai and Guangzhou. To compound the difficulty, transforming C&B into a co-brand with Kotex entailed moving it from the low end of the market to an upstream position. Placing the brand between "value" (low-end) and "premium" meant reaching several market segments at the same time—the medium and high-end value market as well as the low-end and medium premium market. Each segment's threshold for "comfort" is quite different, not to mention locale-specific differences.

C&B has raised the first generation of sanitary-pad users in China. Since its acquisition by Kimberly-Clark in 1994, it has been labeled a mom's brand. Several repositioning campaigns were made prior to 2002, but they did not succeed in shedding its old-fashioned image. In 2002, KC worked with Ogilvy to make two radical moves—leveraging the global signature of Kotex to revive C&B and courting younger women users in urban China. Ogilvy's assignment was to project the market strength of the co-driver brand and develop a new concept to capture the twentysomethings. The old C&B position, "a comfortable feeling just like any other day," came under close scrutiny. The campaign planners also revisited Kotex's global positioning in preparation for the co-brand launch. On the eve of the 2002 campaign, KC's double jeopardy was obvious: while C&B was a popular brand in the low-end market, Kotex lagged far behind Whisper and Sofy in the premium market. Merging those two value-polarized brands, each with its own weaknesses, would be no easy task for marketers.

The winning concept, after months of research and negotiations between KC and Ogilvy, was "Free myself, do whatever I want [on those days]." The new pitch was a dramatic departure from the earlier position of "feeling comfortable," because it targeted "freedom seekers" rather than C&B's conservative "comfort seekers." The "Free Myself" ad campaign was aired in four cities in the fall of 2002. Market shares and brand awareness went up. But the campaign posed several intriguing questions for researchers like myself. First, contrary to KC's original plan, it did not introduce the co-brand "Kotex" nor did it highlight the revamped position of "freedom seeking." Instead, the repositioning campaign was focused on a new product feature, a blue strip on the pad, nicknamed "Instant Blue Absorber" *(shun xi lan)*. The co-driver brand "Kotex" all but disappeared on the new packaging. The five letters appeared in tiny script, visible only if you looked for them carefully. In a campaign involving two brands, one low-end and "local" and another premium and international, we might anticipate that "Kotex" would take the driver's seat to resuscitate C&B. But it didn't. Kotex's presence was diminished, and it evolved from a po-

The "Blue Strip" *(shun xi lan)* is just visible on the pad under the center bottle. Kimberly-Clark.

tentially dominant co-brand to a shadow endorser of C&B. To make it even more intriguing, in the final execution, the Free Myself television commercial did not fully dramatize the radical concept of "do whatever I want." This is a case where the communications goal set for the brand was revised continually, and the end result surprised even those closely involved in the relaunch.

360 DEGREE BRAND STEWARDSHIP

The KC&B case can be analyzed in many ways. The most instructive way is to reconstruct it in the context of Ogilvy's 360 Degree Brand Stewardship. To begin by reading the advertisements as "texts" with meanings to be assigned by the researcher is not useful, since I do not belong to the target segment of young women and thus am in no way privileged in analyzing the ads. However skilled I am in structural linguistics and social theories, I am not entitled to monopolize the interpretation of an ad produced for targets drastically different from me in age, mindset, cultural practices, professional bias, consumption habits, and emotive structure and experiences. Advertising research is much more than "reading an ad" from our own vantage point. An ad is a product first and a text second. Meaning production in advertising can only be grasped if we turn from a holistic, semiotic approach to production-centered trajectories. Here I want to extend an observation made by Sahlins (1976), Appadurai (1986), and McFall (2002) a step further. Not only does the meaning of material objects derive from their use and the context of that use, it finds its way into a brand through the elaborate teamwork of branding, which involves consumers working in tandem with marketers and advertisers.

Once this critical reorientation is set in motion, we may ponder how a strategic concept like "Free Myself" got written and at which stage of the branding process it was written. The role of consumers is of crucial interest, both for the specific feedback they provided and how it was integrated into each step of putting the campaign together—concept writing as well as creative execution. Such questions also hold the key to solving the enigma of why KC's co-brand strategy was tossed out halfway through the execution of the repositioning campaign.

"Where Is the Brand Now?"— Scanning Comfort & Beauty

"Where is the brand now?" is the first question confronting marketers when they reposition a brand. In our current context, how did C&B fare in the mind of target consumers in the summer of 2002? The ten-year-old local brand scored high on "channel" (how well the brand reaches consumers in the trade environment) and "goodwill" (thanks to an excellent distribution and retail network and a strong rapport with middle-aged women) but was found lacking in "visual," "image," "customer," and "product"—brand equity categories used by Ogilvy to scan the health of an existing brand.[5]

We are entering the territory of 360 Degree Brand Stewardship, a proprietary tool of Ogilvy & Mather built on communications strategies involving a multidisciplinary approach to advertising. The classical departments in a full-service agency are account services, planning, the creative department, public relations, and accounting. In the old days, each department sat apart, with account planners and creatives driving the action and taking charge of brand strategies. The lead department used to be advertising, and the primary mediums were television, newspapers, billboards, and magazines. A message input or a unique proposition was usually the end-point of the advertising. In comparison, 360 Degree branding stresses thinking about a brand in its totality and the coming together of all the disciplines of the agency to work from the very start as a brand team. The key words are "strategic planning" rather than "account planning," "brand team" rather than "account team." This macroscopic model throws open the definition of "advertising medium" to embrace anything that moves (or not) as a potent medium carrying a brand message (Blair, Armstrong, and Murphy 2003, 7). The end goal is a holistic communications plan that aims to achieve total brand exposure. Partial communications solutions such as print ads, television commercials, or Internet banners are passé. Originating with Ogilvy in Asia, the 360 Degree paradigm is rich with culturally specific media options unique to the Asia Pacific region: bicycles in China, i-mode in Japan, wells in India, elephants in Thailand, and puppet shows in Indonesia, just to cite a few examples. Today the "total branding" approach characterizes the general shift of transnational advertising agencies from traditional advertising toward a communication-centered marketing approach. Ogilvy's 360 Degree paradigm is exemplary not least because it has grown into a famous brand in itself.[6]

As the initial step in its 360 Degree analysis, the agency scanned the C&B brand and identified a set of problems that plagued the aging brand. It was perceived as insufficient in the categories of "image, visual, customer, and product." The customer base of C&B, as we already know, was confined to older women; its image was seen as gentle and caring but not inspirational; its visual impact was weak and its package design dull (the "product" category will be discussed later on). The scan results played a crucial role in defining the brand challenge for C&B: make the idea underlying the relaunched brand more radical to renegade C&B users. The scan also helped set the objective for a repositioned C&B: capture the unique personality and aspirations of the new C&B girl. Once the challenge and the objective for a campaign are determined, the team moves on to the next stage—concept writing—which eventually yields the sterling pitch for the campaign in the making.

Brand Audits

At this critical juncture, the production of meaning in advertising follows a path entirely different from that in literature or other elite forms of writing. Concepts do not sprout from the mind of planners and marketers. They are culled from brand audits, which take the shape of focus group discussions.[7] In a market as diverse as China's, nearly two dozen audits are done with focus groups spread throughout cities in different tiers. Participants include the users of the target brand and competitor brands as well as nonusers. I watched a few videotapes of focus group discussions held in Beijing and was present in a mock audit unrelated to the campaign in question. The "play" element is crucial to those audits. A range of verbal and nonverbal approaches build pathways into the mind and emotions of the participants, among them, personalizing the brand, making collages, role playing, and sentence completion (Lannon 1999, 47–48).[8] My favorite audit tools are personification and collages. The interviewees are asked what sort of a person a brand might be if it were alive, and the result is a fascinating array of celebrity personalities ranging from business tycoons and politicians to pop singers and television and movie stars. An equally productive brand-personality probe is to switch categories. Ask if a cellphone were a car, what kind of a car would it be? Pushing focus groups to think visually through collages is yet another way to tap into the rich repository of the consumers' unconscious. To do so, the marketer brings to the focus group a collection of images clipped from magazines or downloaded from the Internet. Depending upon the cues given by the marketer-interviewer, each participant will pick and choose images from the collection that may bear inspirational clues about the target brand. No choices by an interviewee are ever useless or superfluous. An individual participant's sensibility and her emotional association with the brand are what a marketer hopes to capture during these brand audits, which generally last three hours per session.

The success or failure of a campaign is half-determined by how well the brand audits are executed. Productive sessions enable marketers to assemble the brand profile and to find valuable pointers toward new concepts for a campaign. C&B's audits, for instance, yielded a brand portrait with the following characteristics: middle-aged, over forty, a yesterday person, and an introvert who paid little attention to her appearance.[9] Younger consumers in the focus groups wanted C&B to evolve into a less ladylike brand and acquire a personality like a friend's. How to rebrand it in that direction depended upon how C&B's target consumers perceived "comfort" in their own terms. Therefore the most important question raised during the audits was phrased as: what is a "comfortable feeling" for you?

The insights derived from those audits—twenty-one of them altogether—broke down the notion of "comfort" into five types. Respondents in second-tier cities were prone to associate "comfort" with simple pleasures in daily lives ("sitting in front of a window watching raindrops and listening to music," "watching Korean TV drama in bed," "sitting in air-conditioned rooms chatting with friends"). Middle-aged respondents prized inner tranquility as a comfort benefit. But many women in their late teens and early twenties described comfort in terms of immersion in the beauty and energy of nature ("feeling the ocean and bathing under the sun," "walking in the woods"). Most agreed that life "shouldn't be too exhausting" and believed feeling content to be a crucial component in a comfortable life. An equally large number of focus group participants expressed a desire to feel worry-free and carefree ("want to fly," "let my inspirations run free").

In follow-up concept testing discussions, target consumers continued to cue in the agency and the client. When asked if any of the concepts listed above captured their aspirations during their periods, participants voted down "inner tranquility" "simple pleasures," and "feeling content" because they were considered "not exciting enough." They were seeking more "inspirational elements" to insert into their daily comfort zone. Armed with those concept evaluations, the agency then designed a communication package that sold back to the target segment the same set of preferred messages.

Concept 1, 2, 3, Testing, Testing

Among the five types of comfort mentioned above, the "worry free/carefree" notion was chosen to be fine-tuned for further concept testing with focus groups, out of which emerged the winner concept "Free myself, do whatever I want." It was during this stage that additional nuanced feedback was given by interviewees. Although "free myself" stood out as the best-received concept by all age groups, target consumers were also wary of promoting the user image of an aggressive career woman toiling day and night at work, a lifestyle seen as irrelevant to them. Thus Ogilvy's effort to push a radicalized image of a freedom seeker was not endorsed by KC. Would the new C&B girl be an aggressive type, "striding fast on the street, waking her best friend up in the middle of the night because she wants to chat, losing her temper because she feels like it, plugging her ears when her mother is preaching"? This description was written and recommended by an Ogilvy planner, but it was rejected.[10]

A young Chinese woman is typically less radical than the average ultra-independent, carefree young American woman. If we divide the feminine-care market into three major segments—duty seekers (the old C&B), freedom seekers (Sofy and Whispers), and reassurance seekers (Kotex)—young Chinese women are situated closer to "reassurance seekers" than to "freedom seekers." In October 2002, the female protagonists who greeted the audience in the "Free Myself" commercials turned out to be two ordinary girls—modern-looking but without a distinct zeitgeist. One young girl was reassuring her companion, chattily, that the new C&B's blue-strip feature would provide them the best protection during those inconvenient days. "Freedom seeking" gave way to "reassurance seeking"—the global positioning of Kotex. It was a compromise creative execution and a contradictory one, too: the combination of downplaying the Kotex brand name while promoting its brand position seemed at cross-purposes.

KOTEX AND THE RED DOT CAMPAIGN

The fact that Kotex served as the backseat driver of the C&B campaign lets us examine how local and global brands interact. The case demonstrates once again the crucial role consumers play in tipping the balance of the local-global scale.

From the very beginning, Kotex C&B was supposed to be relaunched as a joint-venture brand, with the assumption that Kotex would bring in brand equity to resuscitate the ugly little duckling C&B. Indeed KC's original mission was to fold C&B into its new Kotex parent and market Kotex-C&B as a single brand. But during concept testing in Chengdu, Wuhan, Beijing, and Nanjing, it was found that Kotex's English name could not be used to endorse C&B. Most focus group interviewees failed to associate Kotex with its existing Chinese name, *gaojiesi*. The two brands were also considered too far apart in user profiles and brand images to merge with each other. Kotex's global personality is summed up in following terms: a twenty- to thirty-year-old white-collar woman, very capable at work, clean and graceful, contemporary in her look, a bit cold and unapproachable. It is a profile only marginally relevant to young females in China. Consumer feedback led to two subsequent decisions by KC—miniaturizing the word "Kotex" on the new package and revoking the original co-branding plan. In subsequent above-the-line advertising, Kotex was not even mentioned, creating the impression that C&B was the primary driver. The downplaying of the Kotex logo was understandable, but C&B remained driven by the Kotex brand position ("reassurance seeking"), a highly contradictory strategy at first glance.

The Blue Strip: Shun Xi Lan

"Reassurance," as we have seen, is a product benefit (that is, leakage protection) highlighted in the 2002 "Free Myself" campaign. A new product feature—the blue strip (nicknamed *shun xi lan,* or "instant blue absorber")—enabled the two chatty girls to "reassure" each other that C&B offered them the best protection. Instead of the carefree mood of the new C&B girl, the "Free Myself" commercial highlights a product upgrade by turning the blue strip into a unique selling point. It was an unexpected move. In contemporary advertising, where mood dominates positioning strategies, differentiation achieved through product features goes against the grain. Kimberly-Clark banked on the odds that by deviating from the cliché strategy of "image and mood differentiation" (used by Whisper and other peer brands), KC&B could cut through the clutter of "freedom seeker" brands. The strategy worked. The "blue strip" gave C&B an edge in the packed market. It quickly evolved into a new subbrand name in its own right and made *shun xi lan* a cutting-edge offering from KC China (Hu Jin 2005). Most intriguingly, *shun xi lan* was launched as a subbrand of C&B to target younger segments while staying totally dissociated from Kotex. This plan is a stellar example of a triple-pronged branding approach, with C&B and Blue Strip tucked into the "local" brand portfolio and Kotex a stand-alone foreign offering. The "blue strip" also has a visual equity not to be underestimated. The poetic Chinese translation not only pared the functional association down to the minimum but successfully teased out an optical and metaphoric richness absent in the original English. Turning a function back into an image is an unconventional marketing tactic and was a coup for Kimberly-Clark.

The "Free Myself" campaign thus was not centered on a freedom-seeking concept or plot. It was driven by a communications strategy consistent with the global positioning of Kotex: the blue strip reassures the user that she is well protected. KC's strategic position was twofold: keeping C&B's name intact while debuting a modernized subbrand whose position was aligned with Kotex. Better still, *shun xi lan* sounds "local," syllable by syllable. That association may have helped the subbrand retain some mom and auntie users, while its contemporary look appealed to younger targets. Few consumers would discover that *shun xi lan* and *gaojiesi* were made by the same multinational company.

Red Dot or Not: That Is the Question

The example of the "blue strip" drives home a lesson crucial to our understanding of Western advertising theory and practice: consistency is the key. An MNC rarely changes the positioning of its global offerings—it may change the creative executions, but not the position; streamline, but not mutate. Brand positions stay constant (unless they are relaunched), but we may ask whether creative styles travel intact, and how global advertising campaigns fare outside the postindustrial, developed world. At issue are the creative executions of a global brand in a specific locale.

Kotex's Red Dot campaign of 2000 is relevant here. To streamline the image of Kotex, the campaign used a red dot as a symbol for menstruation. All Red Dot advertisements, whether they developed in the United States or in other locales such as China, share a minimalist style, modern and aesthetically vibrant, a creative approach that resonates well with young women in Europe and North America. But when Red Dot spots were imported into the Asia Pacific markets, they fared poorly. Asia's problem with the Red Dot, simply put, resides in the fact that images do not translate well from culture to culture. The campaign was pulled out of Vietnam by a senior Communist Party member who thought the Red Dot was too suggestive for Vietnamese viewers. In China, younger consumers are more or less oblivious to the visual symbolism of the Red Dot; older women dislike the image because of its strong association with blood. All over Asia, especially in north Asia, the advertising campaign did not increase sales as planned. In Korea, consumer resistance to the Red Dot gave birth to a White Dot campaign, which drew on Korean women's fondness for cleanness, purity, and freshness—qualities associated with the color white rather than with cardinal red.[11] Because of Korea's success with the White Dot and regionally specific feedback on the Red Dot, KC revoked its pan-Asian strategy by splitting the Asian Pacific KC headquarters in two—north Asia and south Asia—with Korea KC now leading the north Asian branch offices (China included). In the early years of the new millennium, it was Korea KC who assisted the China KC branch office in developing alternative, non–Red Dot (NRD) campaigns.

The different aesthetic choices between the mainstream Red Dot and the NRD spots are especially striking if we juxtapose one ad from each category and compare the focus group's reactions to each ad. We will start with "Fish," a spot developed in Beijing but with an underlying creative idea based entirely on the "red dot" concept. The basic plotline of "Fish" is made up of three sequences: fish are together → one fish is trapped by a net → the stray fish swims back to the group again. The corresponding human story behind "Fish" also progresses in three stages: a young girl is having a good time with her friends → her period comes and she feels distraught and unsocial → Kotex enables her to feel secure and sociable again. The audience studies undertaken to test the ads raise questions about whether target consumers decoded the spot in the way marketers intended. Ideally, we want to capture or recapture what was going on in the minds of both the sender and the receiver to determine what meaning each visualized. And finally, what does the particular process of encoding and decoding an advertiser's message tell us about the complex relationship between consumers and producers?

Although those questions (the last one especially) are still debated in cultural and media studies and will probably remain unresolved, sophisticated industry research provides us with methodological tools by which the audience's voice can be heard. The four tables I include below are culled from charts in a marketing research

TABLE 1 Encoding "Fish"

Images shown to focus group	Intended message
A group of black fish swimming	Together with friends
↓	↓
One fish turns red	Period comes
↓	↓
A net appears	Barriers during period
↓	↓
It is trapped by the net	It is trapped by the barriers—isolated
↓	↓
Product window (3 layers with wider middle layer)	Excellent absorbency/Safe-fit feature of middle layer
↓	↓
The red fish escapes the net	Gets out of isolation
↓	↓
Rejoins the group	Back to friends—to normality
↓	↓
The fish are giggling	An emotional pay-off

report commissioned by Kimberly-Clark. There are two tables for each commercial under study, one describing the visual encoding and the audience interpretation that the marketers hoped for, sequence by sequence, and the other showing what the focus group actually thought it saw and how it decoded the images. We will begin with "Fish" (see Table 1). The left column lists the visual cues for each of the micro-units of the plot contained in the right column.

Table 2 records the target group reception and breaks it down into what the members thought they saw (in the left column) and how they interpreted those visual cues (right column). Items crossed-out on the left are cues that were not picked up.

A comparison of Tables 1 and 2 indicates that although the fo-

TABLE 2 Decoding "Fish"

Actual perception	Actual interpretation
A group of black fish swimming	Together with friends
↓	↓
~~One fish turns red~~ (not perceived)	Period comes (determined by guesswork)
↓	↓
~~A net appears~~ (not perceived)	~~Barriers during period~~ (not perceived)
↓	↓
~~It is trapped by the net~~ (not perceived)	It is separated from others (guesswork)
↓	↓
Kotex appears	General pad benefits
↓	↓
The red fish escapes the net	~~(not understood)~~
↓	↓
Rejoins the group	Back to friends
↓	↓
The fish are giggling	To be free

cus groups grasped the triple-layered plotline, most of them missed the color change of the black dot to red. The symbolism of the net also went unnoticed: "Seems that all fishes are red from beginning to the end" and "I see only red fishes" were typical reactions. Likewise, the symbolic meaning of the red dot escaped them completely: "I only see the red fishes, there is no red dot," or "it seems there is a red dot, but I don't know why it is there." However, all the interviewees of Chinese origin (Taiwanese focus groups included) were quick to recall the phrase "like fish in water" *(ru yu de shui)*—a famous proverb—underscoring the lesson that image decoding has more to do with cultural than visual competency. Many participants found "Fish" monotonous in color and deprived of a "human touch." The distaste for abstract image cues was apparent. What was intended to be crisp and clean came across as lacking in visual appeal to the target segment.

From "Fish," we turn to a non–Red Dot spot, "Surprise," which was presented to focus groups on hand-drawn story boards. The human motif was played up and its color scheme purposely complicated. Not a trace of red-dot-like symbolism was visible, but we must ask whether this creative idea was better endorsed by the focus cells. In Table 3 I render what was intended and in Table 4, what was received.

Both mainland Chinese and Taiwanese interviewees failed to grasp why the girl was sneaking around in public places. "Fear of leakage" and her desire to be left alone were not picked up. Although the notion of parental supervision was too obvious to be missed, none caught the voice-over "[the young girl] is confidently facing her suitors," a cue crucial to our decoding the subsequent scenes involving the two boyfriends. KC China eventually shelved the NRD campaign because consumer responses at the testing stage were not overwhelmingly positive. The television commercial for "Surprise" was never made, which shows the speed with which the corporate client responded to consumer insights. Consumers play a leading role as the brand production chain progresses, not only determining the concepts behind each campaign but also having an important effect on creative ideas and eventually on the decision whether or not to make an ad. Target consumers are omnipresent throughout the entire process of branding—from positioning, concept writing, all the way to creative execution—a point often missed by those unfamiliar with how advertising works on the ground.

The next two sections focus on more academic issues concerning the use of fieldwork in cultural studies, the oversimplified construct of producer versus consumer, and the inadequacy of the global versus local analytical model. More business-oriented readers may

TABLE 3 Encoding "Surprise"

Images shown to focus group	Intended message
In the shopping center	Public place no. 1
↓	↓
Girl is hiding/escaping/looking around	Wants to be alone
↓	↓
Rushes to the elevator/quickly closes the door	Wants to be alone
↓	↓
A lot of people around	Public place no. 2
↓	↓
Sneaking to the car in the parking lot	Public place no. 3
↓	↓
In the car, bag on the back seat	Introducing the product
↓	↓
Product window (3 layers with wider middle layer)	Excellent absorbency/safe-fit feature of middle layer
↓	↓
Reaching home	Finally she can be alone
↓	↓
Mom and two young men	More confident about facing people, even two boyfriends
↓	↓
Girl laughs	Her old happy self again

wish to skim this material or turn directly to Chapter 3. I should quickly note here, however, that it is futile for us to debate which of the two terms—local or global—is more privileged in corporate world decision making today. The best way to exit from the false dichotomy is to turn our attention elsewhere—back to the consumers and to the question of cultural production.

TABLE 4 Decoding "Surprise"

Actual perception	Actual interpretation
In the shopping center	(Scene too busy to understand)
↓	↓
Girl is hiding/escaping/looking around	Wants to avoid being discovered
↓	↓
Rushes to the elevator/quickly closes the door	Wants to avoid being discovered
↓	↓
A lot of people around	(Scene too cluttered to understand)
↓	↓
~~Sneaking to the car in parking lot~~	(Not understood—too cluttered)
↓	↓
~~In the car, bag on the back seat~~	(Not understood—too cluttered)
↓	↓
~~Product window~~	About the pad (no leaks)
↓	↓
Reaching home	Just reaching home
↓	↓
Mom and two young men	She can have more admirers
↓	↓
Girl laughs	Being happy because of more boyfriends

ON FIELDWORK AND THE
PRODUCER/CONSUMER DICHOTOMY

Our knowledge about consumer proactiveness is useful to the on-going academic debate on the encoding and decoding of media messages by the consumer-audience and its power relationship with the producer. In other words, consumers are active meaning-making agents rather than passive recipients of producers' messages. But as we saw, Kotex's target segment didn't decode the commercials in the ways intended by marketers/producers. At first glance, it may appear that this observation compels us to endorse the mainstream academic reception theory that audiences are autonomous and media texts are completely open for interpretation. The problem with such a view lies in the slippage of an "active" audience into an "autonomous" audience. I agree with James Curran that the issue of media power/domination should not be written off too quickly (Curran 1990). But it would be equally problematic to support the reverse argument, denying members of the audience any claim or capacity for being agents on their own terms. Those who do deny the idea of audience participation in making meaning contend that audiences don't have the power to set the agenda within which the text is construed, even though they have plenty of leeway in interpreting a text (in this context, a television commercial) and in creating meaning playfully all the time. The agenda setter—the culture producer—is seen as a puppet master who manipulates intentionally—a critical insight that makes sense until we examine advertising as a specific cultural industry.

The case study of C&B and Kotex throws into question the premise of "conscious orchestration," because it demonstrates that neither corporate advertisers nor consumers can stake an exclusive claim on making (and controlling) the meaning of material culture today. The complex process of branding constitutes layer after layer of negotiations between all three parties (the target consumers, the corporate advertiser, and the ad agency), which makes any attribution of power to just one party highly reductionistic.

Furthermore, not enough awareness is paid to the fact that the "consumer-producer relationship" plays itself out differently from one cultural industry to the next. How publishers, authors, and readers relate to one another in the book industry is bound to be different from the ways in which big music labels, indie labels, musical artists, and their fans relate in the pop music industry. Besides, within the advertising industry itself, the consumer-advertiser relationship looks different from one product category to another. Target consumers in self-expressive product categories (such as fashion, cell phones, footwear, and fast-moving consumer goods) are more powerful drivers in determining concepts for advertising campaigns than their counterparts in medicine, electrical appliances, and real estate. In all these categories, the consumers participating in marketing focus groups are usually primary users of the product, and to split hairs over which users are "active" and which are "passive" hardly affects the conceptual stability of the "consumer-producer" relationship.

But if we turn to video games, automobiles, and software and information products, where lead users are increasingly encouraged to modify and develop product concepts (and thus unwittingly destabilize the cozy dichotomy of "producer versus consumer"), it becomes obvious that consumer research requires ethnographies on different kinds of user participation produced at different moments of a product's life.[12] Just as I argued earlier that research on branding should necessarily be focused on the production of advertising campaigns, "user-centered innovation" (Von Hippel 2006) compels researchers to examine the changing corporate process of renovation, which can only be effectively captured through on-site fieldwork in companies specific to a given product category.

Critical theory on the subject has been slow to recognize that no two cultural industries are alike and that furthermore, the consumer-producer relationship changes from industry to industry and from one product category to the next. Eager pursuit of an overarching ideological framework—either empowering or dismissing the consumer—has led most academic researchers to devalue or shun fieldwork in the culture industry. Yet without focusing on a particular industry and "getting one's hands dirty" in the field, it is difficult to go beyond the either-or mode of critical thinking and pose new questions. Problems become defined in dichotomous terms, begging polarized answers.

I should add that blogging and role-playing games like Second Life, a 3-D virtual world entirely imagined, created, and owned by its residents, provide an even bigger playroom for consumers who are shaping corporate agendas in directions formerly unimaginable. New media have rapidly eroded the boundary between a producer and a consumer, giving rise to new conceptual categories like the "prosumer."[13] Although there is always hype about flashy trends, the explanatory power of binary logic is decreasing day by day.

Even within the context of traditional media, focus groups and target segments pull the strings, from brand audits to concept writing and from concept testing all the way to creative execution. Advertisers and ad agencies cede this decision-making power to consumers out of sheer necessity. Today's market, especially for those in the developed world, is oversaturated and splintered into innumerable niche markets where individual consumers can make or break a brand. Their likes and dislikes are bending advertisers' preferences. Skeptics may insist that in developing countries like China, consumers are nothing more than blank canvases. That might have been the case in the 1980s and 1990s, but today smart media are nourishing fickle Chinese urban consumers who are not unlike their counterparts in Western markets. The notion of "brand loyalty" is on a short leash in China, where 80 percent of female respondents claimed to have switched brands at least once or twice in 2004 ("Chinese Women Score Lowest Brand Loyalty" 2005, 10). Transnational ad agencies have brought to China contemporary advertising tools that enfranchise consumers to a degree unknown to scholars still entrenched in the paradigms that grew out of the early periods of consumerism.

Fieldwork does not by any means hold an exclusive claim to methodological effectiveness. But just as describing the melodies flowing out of an instrument requires knowledge of how it is played, writing about advertising without practicing it is unsatisfactory. Fieldwork also provides analytical options other than a choice between romanticizing the audience/consumer and theorizing the total domination of media institutions. David Morley notes that the ethnographic turn in cultural studies is a healthy, inevitable trend despite the need to be mindful of its limits (Morley 1997). Some ask whether fieldwork in research on cultural industries (and, in my case, immersive participant research) risks compromising scholars' critical calling. But as George Yudice argues, the contemporary system of corporate control is premised less on commodification—the Adornian critique—and more and more on the monopoly of intellectual property rights (Yudice 2003).

To be more specific, the new momentum for critical studies of pop culture lies not in the social theorists' critiques of "commercialism" but in consumers' struggles over digital rights management (DRM). This pivotal issue arises from the convergence of viral marketing, new media, and grass-roots creative communities online, as we shall see in the Conclusion. Those who pay close attention to new marketing trends (buzz marketing and blog marketing) will recognize that user-generated content dominates virtual space, which is pushing the digital (copy) right(s) movement to the forefront of the debate on "corporate power." Fieldwork alone cannot enable us to perceive the interrelatedness of these new and diverse fields of activity. But access to industry vantage points helps researchers quicken the pace of conceptual discoveries. Indeed, the terms of a new consumer activism have already been redrawn by the digital generation: Naomi Klein's clarion call of "no logo" (Klein 1999) sounds less and less relevant in an age of open content movements like the Creative Commons. The burning question in the new century is not whether one should wear a brand or not (we are all consuming brands regardless of our ideological stripes),[14] but rather how individuals can fly in the face of corporate control of intellectual property by creating brands of their own. On the next horizon of cultural production, the consumer *is* the producer and vice versa. The new fight is all about the freedom to distribute one's own creative work on one's own terms and about the utopianism of building digital commons to make human knowledge available for all, free of charge.

TRANSNATIONAL ADVERTISING AND THE LOCAL-GLOBAL QUESTION

"Consumer versus producer" is only one set of supposedly binary terms that the Chinese case studies show to be more complicated than was once thought. Let us return to another, already mentioned: "local versus global." The Red Dot controversy has pedagogical lessons to deliver here as well. We have seen that the conception of the "local versus global" divide—C&B versus Kotex—does not work. It is pointless to ask whether Kotex or C&B was the primary driver in the 2002 campaign, or to sort out whether *shun xi lan* (the Blue Strip) is a "local" or a "foreign" brand. What matters is the target consumers' perception. Chinese consumers saw both C&B and the Blue Strip as local brands even though both are owned and manufactured by Kimberly-Clark. Hence most users will never guess that Kotex underwrites the brand position of the new C&B. This lack of awareness does not, however, mean that they have been duped, unless their purchasing decision relies totally on the "national identity" of a brand, which in itself has become a questionable category given the complex crossover brand traffic these days. Moreover, one can never overestimate the importance of pricing strategy and product quality to consumers in general, not to mention savvy, capricious Chinese consumers. We can see, in the growing complexities of brand identities in the age of globalization and consumers' perception of them, that a brand is a cultural construct. Both C&B and *shun xi lan* are hybrid brands. Determining whether they are local or global is to fall back into the trap of either/or thinking. Rather than being local or global, cultural production today is hybrid by default.

A critical mass of theoretical literature in multiple disciplines critiques this superficial dichotomy between "globalization" and "localization." Jan Servaes and Rico Lie are critical of the prevailing view in communication studies that global media dominates. We are reminded that "co-production" inevitably blurs the distinction between those two dialectically opposed registers (Servaes and Lie 2001; Servaes 2003).[15] Stuart Hall's eloquent probing into the "aesthetics of the crossover" flings open the door between the two terms. He exposes the extreme resilience of postmodern globalization as it works in and through local specificities and uses the metaphor of the diaspora to show that the locals, too, want to speak across the boundary of the place of origin (Hall 1991). Michael Hardt and Antonio Negri recognize the political valence behind the concept of a localist opposition to globalization but prefer an internationalist strategy over a "localist" strategy, given that the production of locality is also an effect of globalization and that locality's resistant underpinnings are thus built on false grounds (Hardt and Negri 2000). Dan Schiller hesitates to pit cultural imperialism, a threat brought on by globalization, against a putative "national cultural identity" because, as he says, contemporary human engagements have come to be identified "as a continuing interaction rather than a summary end point" (Schiller 1996, 95–96). Critical geographers strike similar notes by resorting to the conceptual language of "scales" in arguing that power relations in a society can vary considerably depending on "who controls what at which scale," which implies that neither the local nor the global has theoretical or empirical priority in shaping reality (Swyngedouw 1997, 140–141). Cultural anthropology is perhaps the discipline most invested in process-based methodology (that is, ethnography) and the most insistent in subverting the local-global dichotomy (Allison 2006; Condry 2006; Manalansan 2003). Occasionally cultural studies critics can transcend the Hegelian dialectic (to which Hall and Hardt are bound) and allow a locale to drive the research agenda and thus succeed in usefully complicating the relationship of diametrically opposed geocultural divides. A good example is George Yudice's *The Expediency of Culture,* which includes a chapter on Miami as a cultural-economic corridor between Latin America and the United States. His emphasis on reading "culture" in terms of an international division of labor lays out the processes of a new "international networking and partnering" in the production of culture that cuts across the developed and developing world (Yudice 2003, 192–213). Indeed, scholars of international cultures have an edge over others in complicating the terms of the debate. Precisely because they have access to the ground operations of a locale and are thus more sensitive to nuances unknown to those writing from the transcendental trajectory of a global theorist, they are more resistant to reducing the "local" to a simple discursive foil for the "global" and nothing else. Like Latin American studies, the China field also produces scholars engaged in destabilizing the older concept of "local" and "locality" while keeping a vigilant guard against a hyperglobalist perspective. Tim Oakes, Louisa Schein, Yuezhi Zhao, Carolyn Cartier, and the authors in *Locating China* all bring focused attention to the transfers of meaning between different scales embedded in a locale—that is, the local, the regional, the national, and the global, as well as the urban and the rural (Cartier 2001; Y. Zhao 2003; J. Wang 2005a; Oakes and Schein 2006).

With few exceptions, however, the existing literature in the debate over global-local dialectics is preoccupied with theorizing about the process of hybridization rather than allowing the process on the ground to unravel and speak for itself. More often than not, researchers resort to the analytical strategy of "glocalization" as a way out. Yet to pare the complex processes of cultural production down to a neat neologism avoids the real issue, not to mention the problem that the descriptor "glocal" flattens out scalar differentials that vary from one nodal point to the next on the production chain. By lumping together the concepts of "cultural content" and "cultural production," the descriptor eventually doesn't tell us much about either. More dangerously, once de-hyphenated, "glocal" creates an illusion that we have escaped the maze of the local/global dichotomy, when, in fact, as long as we steer away from the process of cultural production, we run the risk of retracing our steps and returning to where we started—a metaphorical debate about "culture" understood in ideologically polarizing terms. To extricate ourselves requires the shift of analytical focus away from "content" to "production," so that different analytical questions can emerge. Investigating what actually happened in an advertising campaign and the ways in which interventions by focus groups took shape has allowed us to understand why the marketers' original directions and agendas change. Production-centered questions enable us to disentangle, step by step, the elaborate process of the enculturation of C&B as a brand.

We have seen how, at each stage of the branding process, whether it is account planning, communications planning, creative execution, or public relations, local and global strategies play themselves out to different degrees by different players. The "positioning" of C&B, for example, is split into product positioning (the blue strip) and concept positioning (comfort). "Comfort" further breaks down to "daily comfort" types, "self-expressive" types, "nature lovers," and so on, a conceptual mosaic far too irregular to correspond squarely to the local/global scheme. Another question concerns the place of public relations (PR), a modern Western discipline. I once asked Scott Kronick, the PR manager of Ogilvy Beijing, how he viewed the issue of global cultural hegemony. He responded: "Our [Ogilvy's] office and business culture is very local, and proudly so."

But this is not to deny that his staff follows the Western PR model whenever they are commissioned to develop PR strategies for corporate clients in China. There is no contradiction here. Rather, to pursue a Western PR model from a local cultural base reveals the locals' desire to acquire knowledge and skills they don't have. Indeed, local Chinese agencies are busy learning how to brand and qualify themselves as 4A companies, and transnational agencies like Ogilvy & Mather and Saatchi & Saatchi want to adapt local ways and look local. Pragmatism, not ideology, is the driving force here.

As long as there are markets, there are people; wherever there are people, values differ and communications strategies have to adapt. Thus there are no (successful) global communications strategies, even though there are global products and global brands. The Red Dot campaign called into question the very notion of "global communications strategy." The campaign made clear that a standardized visual stimulus fails to communicate the same message to target consumers around the world. Thus it is not true that advertising concepts based on strong image cues are able to cross borders more easily than campaigns based on copy (de Mooij 1998, 31). Just imagine how an average Western woman would respond to the "white dot."

Localizing communications strategies is the name of the game for savvy multinationals today. I cited a few such examples in Chapter 1. The Harbin Coca-Cola commercial is an excellent case in point. Even joint venture advertisers like Libo Beer have resorted to the strategy of localization ("Libo Beer is why I like Shanghai"). In these examples, locality itself is turned into a commodity and loses its valence as an ideological marker. The emphases on local identity and local culture are nothing more than marketing strategies prevalent in the era of globalization. Nor do I see the trope of the "local" as a ruling metaphor for resistance. The old paradigm of "domination versus resistance" has only limited explanatory value for a world grown too complicated to be neatly polarized.

This chapter has demonstrated the way in which advertisers and ad agencies get wrapped around the consumer's finger. Her wish is my command: I have highlighted the consumer's vantage point while showcasing the marketing tools developed by Ogilvy to breed brand loyalty in China. In the next chapter, I shift my focus to corporate clients and examine how domestic companies and MNCs in contemporary China use the other elements in the marketing mix (such as distribution and retail channels, price, and goodwill strategies) to their advantage. We are moving into a terrain where business-centered marketing is given a primary focus. The issue of national sovereignty returns and it promises more, not less, drama.

CHAPTER 3

The Synergy Buzz
and JV Brands

China's TCL Group acquired GoVideo recently. But in the U.S. market, TCL will continue to use the brand name of GoVideo to sell color TVs and DVD decks.

Guoji guanggao (International Advertising), September 2003

The a priori for localization *(bentu hua)* is globalization. Without globalization, localization cannot emerge.

Wu Xiaobo, manager, domestic Chinese ad agency (2003)

At the foot of the Badaling Great Wall, a new theme park of Chinese brands will be built. A thousand well-known Chinese brands will be exhibited in an area that spans 100,000 square meters.

Guoji guanggao (International Advertising), September 2003

In the first eighteen months after China's accession to the World Trade Organization, the sentiments of Chinese corporate and advertising sectors changed in visible ways. Emerging confidence in the competitiveness of Chinese brands could be seen, while forward-looking entrepreneurs grew to appreciate globalization in its role as a facilitator of a positive cross-fertilization of global canons with local norms. The new buzz word was, and is, "synergy." The simple, ideological view declared in the short-lived 4C manifestos pitting the "Chinese" against the foreign global competitor—a sure sign of cultural defeatism—has receded.

This chapter's three epigraphs, all taken from China's trade magazine *International Advertising,* exemplify the changing terms of the Chinese debate on "localization versus globalization." TCL, China's leading television and mobile-phone manufacturer, took over GoVideo but made the practical decision to retain its local, American brand name, a strategy to which MNCs often resort after their entry into an indigenous market ("Shichang da cankao" 2003). TCL is playing the same game as a multinational, plotting smartly to expand its global presence.

Wu Xiaobo—author of the second epigraph—may sound like an old-fashioned dialectician. But this young manager of a domestic Chinese ad agency is no dogmatic Hegelian Marxist. Wu's assessment of the increasingly self-conscious dialogical relations between "localization" and "globalization" points to a new perspective in China's advertising sector that sees the TNAAs and domestic Chinese agencies as interacting with each other in synergy *(hudong hezuo),* constituting what he calls a new order of localization, something remarkably different from Chinese practices of the 1980s and 1990s.[1] This synergistic ideology will continue to define the mainstream vision of Chinese advertising industry for decades to come.

Meanwhile, the old ethos has died hard. The third epigraph signals the return of the imperium complex—Chinese cultural nationalism replayed in better times via a theme park of name brands at the Great Wall ("Shichang da cankao" 2003). The Chinese hang-up with "Chineseness" is rooted in the nation's historical memory of 1840 (the Opium War), a humiliating national past that extended well into the 1930s and 1940s when China was in the throes of semi-colonialism, and ceded territories to invading foreign powers. The consumer nationalism known in earlier periods, however, should not be conflated with a contemporary Chinese publicity campaign to promote the building of a "great wall of brands"*(pinpai changcheng)*. The point is not whether Chinese consumers and entrepreneurs are nationalistic but what kinds of historical conditions have enabled different phases of consumer nationalism to emerge. In this case, a proposal for such a theme park would have been ludicrous in the late 1990s, since corporate China had few Chinese brands to showcase. But by 2003, the spectacle of an entertainment park complete with streets dedicated to entrepreneurs like Zhang Ruimin (the founder and CEO of Haier) delivered a somewhat different historical lesson. It reflected a national sensibility no longer caught in an edgy defense of endangered sovereignty as it once had been.

Controversial as this theme park may sound, its historical significance needs to be assessed on different grounds: the ruling metaphor here is not a combative "anti-imperialism" but the celebration of "abundance." If built, the park would do more than merely showcase national icons; it was also supposed to house a permanent exhibition on branding. It could conceivably be constructed as a project that documents branding and marketing theories/practices popular in both the modern West and contemporary China, in short, a project that cannot be neatly contained within the old ideological frame of Chinese nationalism. Even when that frame is present, it exists in a new context.

News about the construction of the theme park has been scarce since 2003, even though more and more Chinese brands have made names for themselves. In the fall of 2003, the ten best franchise brands were announced in Beijing, among them, Quanjude Peking Duck and Malan Handmade Noodles—domestic brands sharing the spotlight with Unilever and Kentucky Fried Chicken ("Shichang da cankao" 2003, 137). The gap between local and transnational knowledge of branding, marketing, and management is getting smaller and smaller. Industrious Chinese advertising professionals have been quick to pick up the lessons taught by multinationals, and they envision that "in fifty years we will get to the destination which took capitalist countries hundreds of years to reach" (Huang Zongkai 2003, 13). That's no exaggeration. Not only has the strength of Chinese brands grown, but Chinese firms are undergoing a creative transformation in both directions simultaneously: localizing global knowledge and practices with a heightened sense of cultural subjectivity, on the one hand, and gaining a deeper appreciation of the mutually constitutive relations between the local and the global, on the other (Simons 2003). In this mellower phase of localization, crossover traffic is merging from both directions—multinationals are enthusiastically localizing while Chinese companies are courting transnational capital in the name of a more accommodating nationalism. Both parties recognize the symbolic value of the "local" and play it to their own advantage.

I focus in this chapter on the joint venture of Wahaha and Danone (the French food and drink multinational)—the early successful partnership and a snapshot of the two companies' ferocious spat in spring 2007. The synergy logic is further extended to my discussion of Procter & Gamble and Coca-Cola. In all four cases, I pay particular attention to the ways in which each corporation leverages the bipolar flows of synergy to strengthen its business in China. Although synergy making between Chinese advertising agencies and the TNAAs has been going strong and is widely celebrated, there is no denying that the Chinese JV model in other business sectors was put under close scrutiny in the aftermath of the Danone/Wahaha dispute. "To JV or Not to JV" picked up a new satirical beat in Western law and business blogs. As of mid-2007, industry observers and the public were still busy sorting out the charges and countercharges hurled by both parties at each other and trying to decide, if possible, which partner was less guilty in the brawl.

The French conglomerate accused Wahaha of violating their original contract for setting up mirror operations that bottled and sold the same drinks as the JV company. To get even, Danone sent an ultimatum: either Zong Qinghou (founder of Wahaha and CEO of the joint ventures) had to close up all the operations in which Danone was not currently invested, or accept its bid for a 51 percent stake in those units, a move described by Zong as a low-price forced buyout, which would make the French company the owner of the Wahaha brand. Zong rejected both demands with indignation and retorted that Danone was no monogamous partner either. He proclaimed the French had done even greater damage to the partnership by investing tens of millions of yuan in numerous other competing diary and beverage makers in China (Lu Yuliang 2007; Zong 2007).[2] On the list were Shanghai-based Bright Dairy, Huiyuan Juice, Robust bottled water, and Mengniu Dairy. The verbal duel soon escalated to a new level when the Wahaha CEO unleashed a media campaign to court public sympathy. Alleging that Danone's "hostile" acquisition plan was creating a monopoly control of the Chinese beverage market, Zong made a plea for governmental intervention to protect endangered Chinese national brands. A lawsuit was in the works. It appeared there would be no winners if they failed to settle their differences.[3]

Danone taught Wahaha a hard trademark lesson. The row also made it clear to the Chinese that a win-win solution in business-to-business partnerships is easier said than done. Many now ask whether there is other ways of talking about generating global synergy for the locals beyond simply equating it with cash-register partnerships and joint ventures. I will turn to this question in the last section of this chapter, arguing that an equal investment in the synergy exercise can be made by TNAAs in China and, above all, by the socialist government itself. The larger issue is branding the nation. It requires a different kind of synergy that drives the partnership of all who have a stake in marketing the "new China."

UPSTREAM, DOWNSTREAM, AND CROSSOVERS

For multinational companies in China, the synergistic phase of localization in the twenty-first century means rolling out a new marketing strategy: landing their brands in the hinterland. The concept of the "local Chinese market" extends beyond oversaturated hub cities to tier-three, tier-four, and other lower-tiered county towns and villages. The aggressive push inland by big-league manufacturers of cell phones and fast-moving consumer goods has made headline news. One should not, of course, imagine that all Chinese peasants can automatically be turned into market segments. Chinese rural targets are made up of tiers based on disposable income, and the viability of rural segments is category specific—soap, shampoo, and cell phones are more relevant to rural consumers than computers and red wine, for instance.[4] Predictably, this new marketing trend of privileging rural consumers has also brought about a significant change in China's media environment: it has enhanced the status of local media outlets, enabling CCTN (China *County* Television Network) to present itself as a competitor of the dominant China Central TV in courting advertising revenue. By the same token, crossbreeding travels in a different direction: while transnational brands are trickling downward, domestic brands are moving upstream. Rejoice Shampoo's entry into second- and third-tier markets ($1.20 a bottle) and Motorola's debut of its "township cell phones" (as low as $40) are complemented by the parallel movement of domestic giants Bird and Lenovo, who bid for premium cell-phone users in first-tier cities ($230 for a new model).

In this new order of synergy, mixed breeding is as popular as crossbreeding. Domestic Chinese conglomerates with ambitious expansion plans can no longer afford to stay purely "local" for long.

Many JV brands have come into being since the mid-1990s. The decisions by Wahaha and Robust (the second-largest Chinese bottled water producer) to dance with Danone may be seen by ultra-nationalists as a "sell-out" to "foreign imperialists," but corporate mergers are simply how big business gets done in the era of globalization. To expand market share and to answer Beijing's policy call for *zuoda zuoqiang* (scale economies) and *pinpai guojihua* (internationalizing Chinese brands), one after another, local magnates have opted to take up multinationals' offers for joint ventures. The catch is that many foreign partners have moved to control a majority of company shares a few years later (as Danone did with Robust), prompting the Chinese press and industry critics to ask once more whether Chinese "national brands" are an endangered species. This question sounded even more urgent after 2005, when China was obliged to deepen its WTO commitments, and, naturally, during the Danone-Wahaha public wrangle.

The response of advertising professionals to the question is mixed. For some, who owns or markets the brand is irrelevant, since a brand's identity rests with consumer perceptions. International brands can be marketed as if they are "local." For instance, American consumers perceive Häagen-Dazs as a foreign brand even though it is completely American. By the same token, as we saw in Chapter 2, Comfort & Beauty (a sister brand of Kotex) will always be seen by Chinese women as a "pure" local brand, because its multinational owner, Kimberly-Clark, purposely camouflaged it as such. Conversely, while multinationals excel at disguising their offerings as "local," domestic brands also practice cross-dressing to perfection: Wahaha's Future Cola, Libo Beer, and even Tsing Tao Beer are all masked as "Chinese" when in fact they are JV brands.

The public's lack of information about the national origin of brands does not mean that all customers are dupes. In the eyes of the cosmopolitan, younger generation, it is futile to pin down the "national" identity of a brand when crossover traffic and crossover identities are increasingly the norm. The era of globalization is rightfully characterized by the growing dominance of hybrids over purebreds, mixed assets rather than pure assets.

The consensus among seasoned marketers is: the more sophisticated a market is, the less likely it is that consumers will be obsessed with the purity of a brand's national identity. But the facts of the China market may defy this analysis, as new twists on the old frames of ideology and nationalism keep emerging. The haunting question—"what makes a JV brand 'Chinese'?"—is one of pressing importance to both business elites and the general public in China. Given China's history, it is no surprise that the revelation of the JV status of a high-profile national brand like Wahaha early in the new millennium reactivated the siege mentality and triggered a heated debate in the press.

JOINT VENTURE BRANDS AND
THE QUESTION OF "CHINESENESS"

Wahaha emerged from that crisis unscathed as a "Chinese" brand, which makes us wonder why the Chinese public, as nationalistic as they were, continued hailing Wahaha as the jewel of "national" brands even after its well-publicized merger with the French Danone Group. I argue that the definition of and consensus about "Chineseness" have changed with the emergence of new social dialogues, or discourses, trumpeting the logic of synergy.

Throughout the 1980s and 1990s, the Chinese perception of a "local," "national" product was determined primarily by who owned the majority share the Chinese company—a prescribed minimum of 51 percent. This "majority-stake" formula was itself quite a departure from earlier criteria prevalent during the national goods movement of the 1920s and 1930s, when the purity of assets—100 percent of shares—was a non-negotiable requirement for products labeled "Chinese" (Gerth 2003, 196). Standards have eroded since the late 1990s as asset hybridization has become the norm (J. Wang 2004, 15–17).

Take one of Wahaha-Danone's joint ventures, Future Cola, for example. The subbrand is marketed as a "local" Chinese cola even though Danone owns 51 percent of the trademark. Because CEO Zong Qinghou kept the mixed-breed origins of Future under wraps, rumors about a reputed "51 percent stake held by Danone" ran wild in early 2002, triggering a widespread panic about the "dwarf syndrome" of Chinese national brands (Yan and Fang 2002; Yang Youzhong 2002). The Chinese public pressed the question of whether Wahaha had lost its majority share to Danone. We now know that the rumor was true, as Zong Qinghou himself confessed, belatedly, in 2007. But back in 2002, he insisted that Danone's total share in the Wahaha/Danone joint ventures did not exceed 32 percent (Yan and Fang 2002, 10). Both his critics and his sympathizers now wonder if Mr. Zong deceived the Chinese public knowingly five years ago or whether he was truly ignorant of "how capital and mergers work" then, as he now says.[5] I have always suspected that Zong was silent about Danone's 51 percent share of Future Cola for fear of compromising the positioning of Future as an "authentic" Chinese brand.[6]

The year 2002 was an exceedingly tricky year for Chinese businessmen engaged in joint ventures. China's accession to the WTO provoked rounds of agitated public debate about the cons of the new open-door policy. It was a pressure-cooker situation for a Chinese entrepreneur who had, knowingly or unknowingly, licensed a renowned national brand to a joint venture in return for foreign investment. This may not appear to be an abnormal business practice by international standards, except that Zong Qinghou understood the Chinese complex about the purity of national brands and he wanted to be a winner in both worlds. To ensure that Wahaha would remain "Chinese" in the eyes of domestic consumers, Zong Qinghou invented new definitions for what constituted "national content" (of Chinese goods) by coining a new catchphrase—"joining assets without joining brand names" *(he zi bu he pinpai)*. A new set of standards for "national brands" was born, principles known as the "Three Insists" *(sange jianchi)*. For Wahaha this meant joining assets without joining brand names, insisting on the autonomy of Wahaha's management, and no layoffs of Wahaha employees after the merger (Chen and Zhou 2002).

What Zong didn't reveal then, but became crystal clear during his 2007 showdown with Danone, was that "not joining or sharing brand names"—the first Insist—was only partially true. Not only had Zong signed a contract in 1996 licensing the Wahaha brand to the joint ventures (Wahaha and Danone co-owned thirty-nine of them), but he agreed to a fifty-year licensing term. In yet another dramatic turn of events, he also confessed that the original of that contract was never submitted for approval from China's Trademark Office (Lu Yuliang 2007), implying that it is, therefore, not legally binding. *Bu hepai*—"not joining brand names"—in a double twisted manner is thus neither true nor false.

A model national entrepreneur back in 2002, Zong won the hearts of many admirers for holding on tenaciously (and "successfully") to these three conditions, which became a viable paradigm replicated by the Robust Group in its deal with Danone half a decade later. Predictably, the doctrine of the Three Insists successfully shifted the mood of the Chinese press and reinstated Wahaha's image as a national brand. This incident illustrates clearly the constructed nature of "Chineseness." The "local" or the "national" attributes of a brand are nothing more than discursive categories reinvented throughout history as the Chinese tackle changing challenges to issues of autonomy. In comparison with the era of the national goods movement in the 1920s and 1930s, today the facile equation between foreign presence and foreign domination has grown weaker and the earlier Chinese compulsion to define material goods only in terms of national assets has subsided to a significant extent.

This decrease doesn't mean that the current climate will not be challenged by delicate cases like the Danone-Wahaha conflict or similar cases in the future. Five years ago, however, a high-profiled fight with an MNC would have deified Zong and hushed his critics. In mid-2007 the sentiment was mixed. The best, and the most surprising, rebuttal of Zong's viewpoint came from a governmental spokesman, who refuted the idea of "pure" national brands and saw eye to eye with transnational marketers by stating that the concept of national origin itself is misleading (Wang Zhidong 2007). Many others considered the Wahaha founder a culprit and held him responsible for disgracing China in the international court of opinion. The information laid out in this chapter is equally illuminating—Zong Qinghou was as dishonest to his own compatriots about the Three Insists theory as he was about the brand licensing contract he sealed with Danone. Although very few applauded Danone's aggressive way of handling the crisis, Zong is facing legions of domestic critics who fault him for mixing economics with nationalism (Fang Jun 2007). Even those who have compassion for him agree that he is no Chinese Merchant of Venice.

Although it is hard to predict the fallout of this incident on purchasing behavior, should Danone proceed with a lawsuit,[7] China's backpedaling to the early days of consumer nationalism is out of the question, especially on the eve of the Beijing Olympics. Besides, Chinese consumers themselves have contributed to the weakening of the connection between consumerism and nationalism. Quality and price matter as much to them as the national origins or ownership of a brand. "Nationality" still counts, but only one out of the four traditional categories that characterized "national content" in the twentieth century has survived the passage of time (Gerth 2003, 18). "Management" remains a viable category to help determine what makes a brand "Chinese" today, but the other three categories—capital, raw materials, and labor—have all ceded their place to "brand name" as the category evoking the strongest association with the name of the nation. We have seen how fast the ground can shift once again in light of the Wahaha-Danone struggle. Even the purity of national brands matters less than it used to.

THE WAHAHA MODEL: A BRANDED HOUSE

Wahaha's resilience as a national brand underlines the mythic stature of the Wahaha model, frequently cited by Chinese marketers as a cardinal example countering the American paradigm of positioning. To appreciate that model fully, we will look at the famous channel distribution strategies of the beverage magnate as well as the overall architecture of its brand. This is probably an appropriate historical moment to review Wahaha's past as its future is held in abeyance. Many factors have played into its miracle sales, which reached $1.24 billion in 2005 (Miller 2006), among them a radical strategy to extend its brand with numerous subbrands, smart media strategies that ensure that their television commercials reach rural households in the hinterland, and the company's cordial relationship with the Chinese state. Danone's transnational capital further consolidated Wahaha's hold on the domestic Chinese market as it steadily expands westward. Zong Qinghou's success rests on his strategy of building a network of middle distribution channels so seamlessly spun across the country that they are compared to spider webs.

Spider Warfare (Zhizhu Zhanyi)

"Spider warfare" is a metaphor for market infiltration that privileges middle distribution channels over retailers through the building of a *lianxiao ti*, a complex "body of a tiered system of distributors" (Wu Jing 2002, 22–24). Zong picked only one wholesale distributor in each market region. The designated first-channel distributors were then held responsible for setting up a dense network of secondary channels, followed by networks of third-tier distributors and end retail shops formed in the same fashion. The overall network is tightly knit, with each tier parceling out Wahaha products only to those on the next tier and no further. The network also allows Wahaha to focus its management skills and resources on the very tip of the pyramid, limiting first-tier distributors to the cream of the crop—only 1,000 of them across the entire country.

Wahaha's hugely successful spider web strategy is much celebrated by corporate China. Rooted in the military tactic of "villages surrounding the city" or "flanked attack" *(ceyi jingong),* the strategy pushed Future Cola deep into Jiangxi, Xinjiang, and Heilongjiang—China's interior provinces—and reaped an impressive national market share of 10 percent in the category of carbonated drinks by the early days of the new century. Wahaha's plan owed a great deal to the heritage of Chairman Mao's guerrilla warfare. In much the same way that Mao's Red Army avoided a face-off with Chiang Kai-shek's urban forces, so did spider warfare allow Wahaha to dodge a frontal encounter with Coke and Pepsi. The web-spinning strategy also enabled the Hangzhou-based enterprise to cultivate rural consumers' awareness of the cola category, bringing benefits to all cola makers, including its competitors (Guo et al. 2002, 93–94). Future Cola is, of course, only a small victory among many for Zong Qinghou. Wahaha's capture of the market lies mainly in the staple categories of milk drinks, fruit drinks, and bottled water. Zong has attributed the company's leading position to his emphasis on "channels" first and "branding" second. Or, more precisely, he made an unprecedented move by turning a distribution strategy—spider warfare—into a brand itself.

Wahaha's savvy understanding of the rural market can also be found in its media-buying strategies. The Jiangxi Miracle is a good example. In 1998, when the Future drink line was first launched, Wahaha's Jiangxi branch manager purchased media spots worth 7 million yuan from Jiangxi Satellite TV, a station ranked low in its national penetration rate compared with other provincial television stations. The payoff was swift: sales of Future drinks reached 200 million yuan in 2001. The daring decision to buy so many spots from the satellite TV company was based on the often neglected fact that most villagers and townspeople in the mountainous province could only receive two channels—CCTV and Jiangxi Satellite TV (Ji Xin 2003, 93–95). Rural China, of course, was not the only target of Wahaha's advertising campaigns. Zong Qinghou's "blanket impact" strategy exposed Wahaha's brand to every available locale and medium, advertising it from the countryside to towns and metropolises on radio and CCTV, in newspapers and magazines, and on the Internet.[8]

Branding Future Cola

I mentioned earlier that Wahaha's branding is weak. The company has an advertising portfolio dominated by bland aesthetics and the clichéd marketing formula of celebrity appeal.[9] Future Cola, in particular, demonstrates Wahaha's lack of strategic consciousness with regard to developing flexible brand architecture. From the very start, this JV brand was positioned against Coke and was branded as a "national" cola ("our own cola"). The pitch of Chinese nationalism distanced Future immediately from Wahaha's two core values—"feeling healthy and young." For an extended period, jokes about Future Cola's "dismal future" provided comic relief in trade magazines. One witty jingle poked fun at the cola's Chinese name ("Unusual Cola," *Feichang kele*) in a tongue twister: "Unusual Cola, unusually absurd; Unusual Cola, its end is coming" *(Feichang kele, feichang kexiao; Feichang kele, feisi buke)*. Proving the pessimists wrong, Future Cola sold very well in rural markets. Thanks to Zong Qinghou's spider warfare tactics and the cola's affordable price and nationalist appeal, it was and still is the most visible cola brand in rural China. But the "Chinese cola" strategy went stale by 2000. Two years after Future Cola's launch, sensing that the pitch of nationalism couldn't carry the subbrand much further, Wahaha rebranded Future by bringing it back to the core value of the master brand—"feeling young."

But that's not the end of the story. Occasionally, irrelevant catchphrases have flitted across the television screen and made one wonder if the identity crisis of Future Cola had been resolved. I once caught a glimpse of a television commercial in which a bride and groom seized a bottle of Future during their wedding ceremony while we heard a voice-over saying: "Future Cola, an unusual choice" *(feichang kele, feichang xuanze)*. Not only was there little connection between the tagline and the product, but Future's brand character was virtually nonexistent in the spot. The Future drinks (which come in apple, orange, and lemon flavors) have no coherent and clear identity other than their CSD (carbonated soft drink) content. My confusion deepened as I came across another Wahaha category—carbonated fruit juices—a product line different from cola drinks but whose brand identity overlaps with the Future line, since both are associated with fruit flavors.

Wahaha as a Branded House

The case of Future Cola raises many questions for brand theorists: Would it have served Wahaha better if Zong Qinghou and his brand managers had developed Future into a stable co-brand with a meaningful co-driver role? In other words, should they have turned Future into a stand-alone subbrand with its own brand personality that could add an attribute or a beneficial association to the mother brand, much as Blue Strip did for Comfort & Beauty, and Sprite for Coke? We need to ask what kind of "brand architecture" Wahaha has built and whether this structure is sustainable as China's soft-drink market differentiates further. The speed with which Wahaha expands its brand boundaries begs the question of how much further Wahaha can extend its product line without overstretching itself and cutting into its brand equity.

Wahaha's portfolio is cluttered. It currently has eight major beverage lines that range from bottled water, milk drinks, fruit juices, tea drinks, sports drinks, CSD drinks, and nutri-express drinks to tonics for children. Each series of products further extends into diverse subseries. The extreme case is the milk drink category, which subdivides into fifteen subbrands. Like GM and Mitsubishi, Wahaha pursues a branded-house strategy. This strategy allows the master brand to serve as an umbrella under which new offerings accumulate (Aaker and Joachimsthaler 2000, 118–127). It is a simple formula to extend a brand. When successfully implemented, it can enhance brand clarity and synergy; when it fails, it creates a jumble of unconnected products, as in the Future series.

Unchecked brand extensions are looked upon suspiciously by American brand theorists like David Aaker, Al Ries, and Jack Trout. Successful extensions of subbrands in Western markets under a single master brand like Virgin are rare exceptions. Western subbrand strategies more often result in stand-alone brands whose connection to the manufacturer and to the mother brand is purposely not made known to the general public, resulting in what may be called a "house of brands" architecture. To avoid a potentially negative impact on brand associations, many of these stand-alone subbrands also stay unconnected to each other, as is true for Banana Republic and Gap, Jaguar and Ford, Tide and Bold, and Anthropologie and Urban Outfitter.

In contrast, Wahaha is a branded house like Virgin, where the master brand serves as the dominant driver with a large number of subbrands tugged along under its banner like mere descriptors rather than co-drivers of the overall brand. The mindless proliferation of subbrands with lackluster personalities can pose real dangers for a manufacturer with branded-house architecture. Thus

Wahaha's plan of rebranding Future Cola—the flagship of the Future line—seemed to signal an overdue advance in branding. A repositioned Future Cola (or Future Lemon) might grow into a genuine subbrand that could impart energy and character to a mother brand on the verge of becoming a five-hundred-pound gorilla.

But Future Cola's struggle with that co-branding opportunity only lasted for a short while. It was eventually folded back into the staple Wahaha brand identity, "feeling young," and thus lost the flexibility needed to create an identity of its own. Meanwhile, new developments in the beverage market continued to hold off Wahaha's prospects of radically changing its brand architecture. In 2001, a month after Coca-Cola debuted green tea drinks, the Chinese company announced that it, too, would enter the tea market with a new line of Future Tea drinks ("Coca-Cola Moves" 2001). For classical branding theorists, Wahaha's adherence to the extension strategy seems baffling. But interestingly many superbrands in China (for example, Haier, Lenovo, and the herbal medicine Tongren Tang) also subscribe to the same branded-house approach. Such a strong Chinese preference for brand extensions runs counter to mainstream American branding theory.

This predilection has critics at home, too. Corporate China's reservations about Wahaha's brand strategy are old news, too anecdotal to merit serious consideration. The initial critiques of Wahaha's brand extensions were partly driven by the nationalist critics' frustration with the Danone "takeover" and apprehension about a massive "invasion" of multinationals in the wake of China's accession to the WTO. As time went on, more seasoned interpretations began to appear to challenge standard, conventional criticisms of Wahaha's branded-house strategy. Ong Xiangdong, the manager of a communications and marketing company in Shanghai, has presented such a refreshing perspective in his *Bentu pinpai zhanlue* (Local Brand Strategies). Instead of viewing line-extension as a "trap" (Ries and Trout 2001, 124), Ong gave Wahaha's brand strategy a thumbs-up.

Ong's book highlights the inevitable discrepancies between (Western) theory and (local) practice and in so doing, lays bare the impact that a market's specific characteristics will have on the business and branding strategies of its native manufacturers. For Ong, Western preferences for the house of brands strategy (as in P&G, for example) make perfect sense in the West. In mature markets such as the United States, laws regulating corporate monopoly and commodity production/distribution are well in place, the environment for capital investment is healthy, and swift capital accumulation allows corporations of all sizes to come into being and compete with one another. As a result brands are crowded together in search of the same clientele, yielding a highly differentiated market in which producers have to split hairs to achieve unique product branding.

The Chinese market, in contrast, has its own idiosyncrasies. Ong argues that Wahaha need not emulate P&G's strategy of nurturing stand-alone subbrands, with each commanding a distinct brand personality (for example, Pantene, Head & Shoulders, Crest, Tide, and Whisper). Different rules of the game are generated by a market condition characterized by many as "irregular": counterfeit goods are everywhere; transparency in market mechanisms is lacking; reliable information about commodities is so scarce that consumers distrust small, unknown brands. On top of all these irregularities, product and food safety laws and drug regulations are largely unenforced. An insufficient legal infrastructure has also left manufacturers unprotected, so small companies can neither survive easily nor win the trust of insecure consumers. To compound the problems, slow asset accumulation in China prevents small corporations from becoming viable, so that only a handful of state-funded monopoly enterprises dominate. The principle of scale economies ordained by the government has also encouraged Chinese companies to scale up through horizontal extensions of their brands.

In the final analysis, the priority that Chinese consumers place on safe consumption lies at the heart of their sustained loyalty to colossal, highly visible corporate brands. The importance of safety appeal can be seen indirectly in the escalating bids by so many corporations, regardless of their budgets, for five-second spots on CCTV throughout the 1990s. The bidding craze, as argued in Chapter 7, should not be attributed to the "irrational" media-buying behaviors of corporate China. Instead, such bidding is symptomatic of small- and medium-sized domestic corporations' efforts to turn into big players overnight by becoming what are called king-bidders, a goal that is itself a response to consumers' perception that "size" matters. The equation between "size" and "safety" cannot be overestimated in the Chinese market. In such a climate, corporate branding necessarily outweighs product branding. From Ong's perspective, Wahaha's aggressive extensions built corporate brand equity at lightning speed, which is seen as an eminently reasonable solution specific to the Chinese market environment. By the same token, Ong attributes the failure of Whirlpool's early venture in China to its adoption of a co-driver brand strategy (Whirlpool-Daffodil and Whirlpool-Snowflakes) (Ong 2002, 9). Whirlpool would have fared better, Ong maintains, had it stuck to the practice of a single dominant driver (that is, Whirlpool), dropping hyphenated local brand affiliates altogether.

In this view, Wahaha's branded house is seen as a winning strategy because its massive brand extensions leverage the master brand across multiple product markets that are not yet dominated by big brands—another circumstance drastically different from the Western market, where no categories are left unclaimed. Speedy horizontal extensions have enabled Wahaha to establish its brand visibility very quickly in multiple product lines, allowing it, for example, to capture the bottled water market even though the company's initial staple product was milk drinks. This same strategic logic also makes Ong endorse Wahaha's entry into the nonbeverage categories of rice porridge and children's apparel (ibid., 219), moves that had provoked criticism from Chinese brand watchers.

Brand strategies are, therefore, always place-specific. It is futile to discuss the advantage of one type of brand architecture over another without returning such discussions to the context of specific market conditions and specific market cultures. For Ong, practice needs to be privileged over theory. Since there is no universal human condition to speak of, brand strategies practiced in different locales are necessarily diverse. Marketing teaches us two important lessons: no two markets are identical, nor is national culture a homogeneous entity.

Ong does not reach a definite conclusion regarding which strategy, branded house or the house of brands, will eventually prevail as the Chinese market grows more mature and splinters into niche segments.[10] He strongly hints, though, that model-sensitive and synergy-conscious Chinese entrepreneurs will continue to scrutinize Western brand theories without feeling overly anxious about "total Westernization," a scenario imagined by Chinese anti-WTO advocates.

THE DANONE EQUATION

Wahaha's partnership with Danone began in 1996, much earlier than China's entry into the WTO in 2001. The merger helped Wahaha take on new subsidiaries and brought them world-class advanced production lines from Germany, the United States, Italy, Japan, and Canada. The cash flow also helped Wahaha to expand westward (to the cities of Tianshui and Guilin), and come out on top in the bidding battle for China's scarce water resources. In June 2001, the joint venture made industry headlines by setting up a subsidiary at Mount Tai in Shandong Province, a highly strategic move for their three-year-old bottled mineral water business. The mountain, a UNESCO World Heritage site, is celebrated for the supreme quality of its mineral water. Similar expansion plans are in the making all over China, thanks to the merger with Danone.

By the early 2000s, the synergy between the two partners had just started to have an impact on China's beverage industry. Danone is as savvy a player as Wahaha is. With a foot in the latter's door, it began a series of acquisition offensives in China. In 2000, the French conglomerate purchased Robust, and a few months later, it scooped up 50 percent of the shares of Shanghai Meilinzhengguanghe Water Ltd., China's biggest bottled water company. Danone's acquisitions dealt a heavy blow to its global competitor Nestlé (Lin Lingdong 2000). All of a sudden, the French giant was a force to be reckoned with. Forecasts predicted that Danone would hold 20 percent of China's water market in ten years. In 2001 it also made a parallel entry into the dairy market with the purchase of a 5 percent equity stake in the Shanghai Bright Dairy (Liu Lijun 2001).

Predictably, Danone's strategic move into the bottled water and dairy sectors set off a wave of anxiety in the Chinese press. But this time, the nationalist rhetoric was offset by seasoned industry analyses that played up the theme of "equal partnership." Disclosed details of those deals were focused on the gains for the China side and the give-and-take logic of "synergy." In the official statements released by Meilinzhengguanghe right after the acquisition, nationalist sentiments ran high.

> I made two requests to Danone. First, Meilinzhengguanghe must become China's largest bottled water company . . . Second, our joint venture should create a new brand [equivalent to] Evian in France that is fully Chinese. (Zhang Li, vice general manager of Meilin, 2000, in Lin Lingdong 2000, 7)

But a more representative view on the dawning of a new era of cooperation was well articulated by Robust's president and a Danone spokesman—both driving home the theme of synergy in an up-beat tone.

Many people think internationalization means exclusively going abroad. They forget that internationalization is a two way street. In-ternationalization doesn't exist if we only go abroad without allow-ing foreign companies to enter the China market. Let's take this co-operation with Danone for example. This cooperation aims at improving Chinese enterprises and China's economy with foreign funds, instead of giving our market to foreign companies. (Robust president He Boquan, 2000, ibid., 10)

It could be misunderstood if we use the word acquisition. We want to cooperate with good local partners but not to integrate them. On the contrary, we will support and develop the existing local brands and cooperatively create a healthy water market. (Danone spokes-man, in Liu Lijun 2001, 3)

The irony of these three statements is obvious with changed circum-stances. Neither Zhang Li, then the vice general manager of Meilin, nor He Boquan, then the president of Robust, foresaw that they would soon lose their companies—brand name and management rights—to the astute French investor. Danone's friendly declaration that "we want to cooperate with good local partners but not to in-tegrate them" could have been repeated verbatim at their press con-ferences in 2007 for good comic relief.[11]

Back in the early 2000s, major presses were filled with reports on the increasingly pragmatic Chinese orientation toward foreign part-nerships, an attitude expressed most eloquently by He Boquan. His emphasis on a "two-way street" echoed the same commitment to bilateral growth pledged by Danone to nurture Chinese brands, a utopian vision now crippled by what transpired in 2007. Sadly so, especially because the Chinese people would rather focus on 2008 than rewind history back to 1840.

An article entitled "The Death of National Brands" best captured that sense of tension embedded in the ambivalent Chinese attitude toward joint venture brands. The two authors of the article deplored Robust's loss of its management autonomy to Danone soon after the latter raised its ownership share in the JV to 92 percent. Following the resignation of the entire Chinese management team, Robust's He Boquan was quoted lamenting, "This was my first lesson on China's accession to the WTO" (Yan and Fang 2002, 62). Citing numerous cases of Chinese brand failures attributed to mergers with multinationals, the two authors fell right back into the ideological rut of Chinese nationalism. But the staggering list of the "four ways of dying for a Chinese brand" was prefaced by a cautionary note of their own: "In the era of global economy and internationalization, discussions of the rise and fall of Chinese brands from the narrow angle of nationalism may sound prejudiced and short-sighted" (ibid.).

Their words were a self-correction and a self-critique quite typical of the general Chinese sentiment in the first years of the new millennium, and, I dare predict, representative of the spirit of the country in the wake of the Danone-Wahaha debacle. Asset acquisition has become an indispensable means for Chinese companies to expand businesses at home and to develop brands that can go global. Synergy-seeking at the cost of economic sovereignty appears inevitable, even if it sounds illegitimate to ultranationalists. Moreover, one should remember that a brand's identity is always up for grabs. In all probability, Robust, known in China as *Lebanshi,* may still be seen, and drunk, as a local "Chinese" brand.[12]

COCA-COLA AND PROCTER & GAMBLE

A discussion of synergy is insufficient without a look at two major transnational conglomerates whose presence in China is much more visible than that of Danone. We have examined the impact of transnational mergers on domestic Chinese brands. But the new era of crossover synergy has also influenced the marketing strategies of the two prominent global brands in China—Coca-Cola and Procter & Gamble.

Future Cola's hold on rural China has been strong since its launch in 1998. Good channel distribution is one factor, but another crucial determinant of its popularity rests on price—Future Cola is six cents cheaper than Coke and Pepsi.[13] To compete, Coca-Cola launched cheaper colas in returnable bottles, cutting the price of a can down to twelve cents. The new concept was "Coke costs the same as water" (Chang and Wonacott 2003, 4), a strategy indicating that the multinationals have come a long way in China. Only a few years ago, localization was focused primarily on product content and creative executions of ad campaigns. For example, Kentucky Fried Chicken serves egg drop soup in China; the menu of the McDonald's in Hong Kong features curry chicken rice and roasted chicken rice in mushroom sauce. Unilever's shampoos add black sesame and ginseng variants. P&G's hair care lines are fortified with a strong antidandruff formula to cater to Chinese consumers. Less well known is Leo Burnett's Hong Kong Marlboro man, a neat-looking family man who hops into a private jet heading for his ranch, flanked by a bevy of assistants and friends (Ong 2002, 99–100). Product and brand localization has become both a necessity and a cliché, it seems.

Coke's twelve-cent solution, like Danone's courtship of Wahaha, Robust, and Shanghai Meilin, represented a new direction in localization efforts by multinationals. They have learned how to think like the locals and to strategize in a Chinese way. We saw how Danone piggybacked on the success of domestic Chinese brands and how it developed an acquisitions formula that acknowledged the Chinese demand for brand independence for a short while, before it pulled the rug out from under their local partners. Coke's solution to the Future Cola challenge was also intriguing precisely because it, too, went beyond skin-deep localization. As a seasoned global player, Coke owes its pervasive presence in China to a comprehensive localization plan ranging from raw material purchases, personnel training, and folk culture research to localized ad campaigns and public relations sponsorships. Most celebrated is Coke's commitment to Project Hope, which had built fifty Hope elementary schools and a hundred Coke Hope libraries in rural China by 1999. With such well-received corporate branding in constant motion, Coke and its subbrands Sprite, Fenda, and latecomer Smart (known as Xingmu in China and branded as a "local" offering) have built remarkable market strength and brand visibility in China's CSD drink categories (Meng 2002, 280). The twelve-cent strategy is a master stroke from its increasingly localized think tank. Coke knew it could not beat Wahaha's channel strategy and took the pricing route instead.

P&G too moved its brand downstream under the pressure of competition. In 2001, local Chinese skin-care brands Dabao and Little Nurse edged themselves to the front of the line; Shulei and Xiashilian (a Unilever offering) broke the monopoly hold of Pantene and Head & Shoulders; Qiqiang seized considerable market share in detergents. P&G reacted to this series of crises by changing its price tags. In 2003, it announced a plan to further shed its blue blood and reach out to the masses in India, China, and Thailand ("P&G tries to reach out to the masses" 2003). Brand watchers in China have argued that the new strategy could backfire if it ends up alienating the gold-collar segment—young and middle-aged urban Chinese women known for their superiority complex vis-à-vis the rurals (Jin Ke 2003). Observers also claim that lower prices offer no guarantee of attracting rural consumers if distribution problems are not addressed by P&G.[14]

These critics put too much emphasis on whether P&G and Coke's discount strategies were endangering their premium brand positions in China. By 2005, three of P&G's brands—Rejoice, Head & Shoulders, and Pantene—succeeded in claiming the largest China market shares in the shampoo category, dismissing any worries about the negative impact of the MNC's pricing tactics, which were, after all, a favorite tactic adopted by local companies (Yuan Fang and Wu Qi 2005, 12–13). P&G's profit margin was expected to rise further after signing a memorandum of understanding with China's Commerce Ministry to join the "Ten-Thousand-Village Market Project," an ambitious plan aimed at setting up 250,000 rural chain stores by the end of 2007 ("China's Commerce Ministry" 2007).

Coca-Cola fared equally well—its sales volume in China surged 22 percent in 2005 to 900 million cases (Patton 2006). But the comparative advantage of Coke in China, I should say, rests on another strength it enjoys. The world's biggest soft drink maker has integrated its brand name successfully into the fabric of everyday life in China through high-profiled PR campaigns (Siewert 2002). In addition to Project Hope, Coke was the official beverage and major sponsor of the Chinese national soccer team when it sought to qualify for the World Cup finals in January 2001. Loyal Chinese fans watching the 2001 game fondly remember the "Team China" commercial, which features a Chinese boy presenting a Coke bottle filled with Chinese soil to the players and wishing them a "homegrown advantage" in the game. The moment was a highly emotional one that consecrated the bond between the soft drink multinational and the Chinese audience craving a world soccer championship. If we were to run a brand popularity contest to measure the goodwill generated by multinationals in China, Coca-Cola would undoubtedly rank at the very top. One cannot say the same about P&G, but its corporate image is too strong to be adversely affected by its rustication campaign. On the basis of my cell phone study (discussed in Chapter 6), I observed that regardless of product categories, transnational companies are moving toward multitiered pricing while building distribution strength in rural townships. The margins of comparative advantage held by domestic Chinese companies are getting slimmer and slimmer by the day.

These new market trends have much to tell us about doing business in the era of globalization. The strong and powerful excel in aggressive, noiseless localization and make no pretense about it and need no local partners (Coke and P&G). Perhaps the current hype about "synergy" is nothing more than an acquisitions card played by second-tier multinationals (Danone) and a window of opportunity opened up for local corporations dreaming big about the future (Wahaha). Precisely because it takes time for a domestic company to grow big enough to cut merger deals on equal terms with heavyweight multinationals, the current synergy buzz may for now be more utopian than real.

But perhaps the Chinese need not cling to the traditional concept of a business partnership as far as synergy is concerned. There may be other means of adding cachet to Chinese brands beyond participating in joint ventures. Is it possible to envision other partners in synergy for Chinese corporations than the MNCs—a different sort of partner who might place a higher value on marketing the "new China" as a brand?

BRAND CHINA? SAATCHI & SAATCHI'S VISION AND THE BEIJING CONSENSUS

One set of partners who have a bigger stake in marketing the "new China" than the multinationals are the transnational advertising agencies. The TNAAs are better positioned than MNCs like Coke or Danone to help Chinese enterprises build their names. To begin with, this job is part of what agencies are paid to do. Second, less conflict of interest exists between the client and the ad agency than between, say, a Chinese beverage maker and its French counterpart. Better still, more and more TNAAs are invested in country branding, which treats image problems associated with the place where a product is perceived to be manufactured. "If a 'brand' is defined as an experience, then some of the world's most powerful and recognizable brands should be countries," says René Mack of Weber Shandwick Worldwide, an agency involved in creating the Country Brand Index (Shandwick 2005), a yearly index of countries' positions as brands. Indeed, consumers—tourists, residents and retirees, investors, and media journalists—make "place decisions" all the time (Kotler, Haider, and Rein 2002). *Anime* and high-quality electronics are associated in our minds with Japan, automobiles with Germany, fashion with France, software and spirituality with India. The fortunes of a national brand can rise and fall; Brand America's problems in the post–Iraq War era are just one example (Anholt and Hildreth 2005).

"Made in China" is a hard sell to many international "place buyers." In fact, China's image has continued to take a beating in the decades since the U.S.-led Cold War media campaigns targeting "Red China." News about censorship linked to Google in China, the stringent firewall deployment online, and China's violations of intellectual property rights coupled with its record of human rights abuses rightfully bring it negative press, but the reporting is not sufficiently balanced by a similar number of equally newsworthy stories about its achievements gained in domains other than those of economic prowess.[15] Lenovo's odds of garnering goodwill among Americans are not great when the U.S. Congress harps on the "security risks" of buying computers from the company (Blustein 2006). Taking on the task of refurbishing a tarnished name is no easy task. Thus one should give credit to Saatchi & Saatchi for initiating the idea of repositioning China as a country brand.

In 2001 Saatchi & Saatchi Guangzhou brought back China's first prize from a prestigious international ad festival—a silver lion from Cannes for an ad promoting P&G's Head & Shoulders. The news was touted in China as the beginning of the international recognition of "creativity with Chinese characteristics." But Saatchi & Saatchi had loftier ambitions than just producing award-winning Chinese ads for global clients. As far back as 1998, Kevin Roberts,

S&S's CEO, had wanted to make "made in China" a premium global brand. In his address to the American Chamber of Commerce in Shanghai, Roberts fleshed out this vision in great detail. He reiterated the same goal in 2002, at the tenth anniversary celebration of Saatchi & Saatchi's entry to China, when he renewed his pledge to help domestic Chinese brands go global (Nie 2002). No one disagrees that China is the "perpetual market of tomorrow" and the world's largest selling and buying country, but as a brand, the country's name is a negative factor for many and anathema for some.

Saatchi & Saatchi's vision of "Brand China" resonated with many Chinese entrepreneurs. Such an endeavor does not only involve the capital investment made by multinationals to nurture domestic brands. In order for "Brand China" to become a reality, synergy must also exist across all sectors of the economy. What is needed is a long-term "coordinated and consistent delivery of messages about Chinese products [not only] by many brands in many product categories" (K. Roberts 1998, 5) but also by an army of transnational advertising agencies all working toward the same goal.

Roberts cites the Sony story to nonbelievers. If "made in Japan" succeeded in shedding its earlier "cheap and chunky" brand image, "made in China" can one day emerge as chic. Following the same logic of naming the core values that now drive the Sony brand (that is, compactness and quality in minute detail), Roberts cooks up a recipe for "Brand China" (ibid., 7):

wisdom	energy
mystery	vitality
spirituality	high intelligence
harmony	high craft
invention	industriousness

The stereotyping revealed in this list may scandalize China specialists and cultural theorists. But branding is all about boiling down perceptions to their essentials. Nobody is more self-conscious than the brand stewards themselves about the artificiality of brand construction. A brand is no different from any discursive construct. Precisely because the attention of consumers is a rare commodity, efforts at branding intensify the desire to abridge and elide. To rise above the information clutter, a brand's DNA is crystallized into a few pithy campaign concepts. One can poke fun at Roberts's list, but it seems beside the point to do so. Numerous counterexamples, of course, can be found to rebuff the attributes on his list. "Harmony"? This Taoist value was never really prevalent in China even in imperial times. A "mysterious" and "spiritual" East?— Orientalist thinking long debunked in academia. "Invention"? We are back to the Chinese obsession with the Four Great Inventions and the "Empire of Heaven" complex. What about the features on the right? I suspect that Roberts consciously grouped the ten attributes into two columns: on the left are cultural traits of an "old China" cast in an image of the "Orient" that caters to the imagination of a less sophisticated Western consumer public; and on the right, a cluster of contemporary virtues which, in Roberts's mind, justifies the rise of China as the most exciting emerging market in the world.

Despite the reservations one may have about stereotyping, some marketing truths are evident in Roberts's project of rebranding China. In addition, the target consumers for Brand China are neither cultural critics nor China specialists but the average Joes and Janes among global consumers, whose images of China are more likely nurtured by the old television show *Kung Fu* or the more recent movie *Seven Years in Tibet* than by PBS China documentaries or Edward Said's *Orientalism*. Roberts's list is by no means far fetched by marketing standards.

Attention should nonetheless be turned away from stereotyping to a more relevant issue, namely, the kind of soft power[16] Roberts wants Western consumers to associate with China:

The pragmatic Chinese mix of spirituality and esoteric philosophy with material life is perfect for the emerging global consumers. Chinese ideas such as Tai Chi, Chinese healing, and the Tao are increasingly popular in the West. Feng Shui is another brilliant idea which has hit the architectural mainstream in the West. There are numerous products with a unique Chinese angle which could be included under the Brand China banner such as textiles, ceramics, herbal remedies, medicines, teas and beverages, and even furniture. (ibid., 8)

Unfortunately, this softer, spiritual, and earthy "Brand China" is not a mental map powerful enough to help the Chinese turn their country brand around. "Made in China" will need a genuine makeover on a much larger scale than the Sony story or a list of imagined "Chinese" attributes. Only then will a breakthrough of China as a country brand be possible.

The solution is certainly not that China should be split into "ten regional brands," as Gilmore and Dumont propose (Gilmore and Dumont 2003, 28). The marketing of a place or locale involves multiple stakeholders, which means that China's biggest stakeholder, the government, needs to be brought on board to treat the country's image problems. Colombia is the major exporter of coffee to the United States today, thanks to a successful marketing campaign by the National Federation of Coffee Growers of that country; Britain was marketed by Tony Blair in 1998 as the cradle for "creative industries," and today it has become the world's most credible exporter of cool design culture. A country branding campaign orchestrated by a government is nothing unique. In the case of China, however, we run into a classic dilemma: "Relying on government leaders to devise a country's branding campaign is particularly risky if politicians have image problems of their own," a comment about Ghana which is equally applicable to China (Opoku 2005).

Against all odds, though, the Chinese government started the process of rebranding China in 2002, and its vision was cogently argued in Joshua Cooper Ramos's controversial "Beijing Consensus" (2004). Ramos made a daring proposition: that the "Beijing Consensus" will replace the Washington Consensus, neoliberal development economics enshrined in the Washington-based international financial institutions, as the dominant model of global development for third world countries. Without going into details about Ramos's thesis, suffice it to say that both the conservative and the liberal ideologues in the West (from academia to media outlets) were deeply offended by the alleged succession in paradigms to come. Chinese intellectuals at home weren't slow, either, in picking on Ramos for overstating Beijing policy as "consensual" when in fact internal debates about a "Chinese development model" are far from being settled.

The document, nonetheless, is a fascinating window into the new identity of China, whose rise on the global scene was marketed by its own government as a "peaceful emergence" (*heping jueqi,* literally, rising precipitously in a peaceful way). The concept was charming but short-lived and later morphed into the more neutral-sounding "peaceful development."[17] A brainchild of the veteran Party theoretician Zheng Bijian, the political discourse of "peaceful rise" was intended to serve two purposes: rebutting the twin theories of the "China threat" and the "China collapse" set forth by pundits in Washington, D.C., and describing to the whole world the new-century role China sought as a cooperative and responsible international player.

"The Beijing Consensus" was based on Ramos's conversations with Chinese policymakers and written as an exegesis of Zheng's initial ideas. Two primary visions laid out in the Ramos white paper are directly relevant to country branding: the vision of a new China intent on balancing the gaps in living standards between the rich and the poor; and the vision of a country relying on innovation-led growth to overcome the knowledge divide between itself and postindustrial societies (as opposed to building technology from the bottom up and sequentially). Although this sounds like a China hype based on a "virtual China: the promise of what the People's Republic could become, rather than what it already is" (Leonard 2005), country branding, like product branding, is all about aspirations and not about reality. Seasoned marketers would have to agree that a green, equitable, and responsible China driven by innovation and reined in by peaceful diplomacy is a better marketing concept than Roberts's simple, depoliticized version of a new China. It is not a modest proposal by any means, but if the Chinese government is genuinely sincere about a complete image makeover, it will need to take its own prescription in large doses.

Meanwhile, in undermining the Western dualistic mode of thinking about China, Ramos's paper is a long overdue antidote to the perspective of mainstream Western media. He has useful lessons to impart to those wishing to get into Chinese heads.[18] One does not have to agree with him completely, but his streetwise take on China deserves attention. Ramos argues, for example, that China "does not believe in uniform solutions for every situation . . . It is pragmatic and ideological at the same time, [with] little distinction between theory and practice." To illustrate such flexible practices, he cites Deng Xiaoping's famous saying—"groping for stone to cross the river"—indicating, in perfect agreement with current Chinese leaders, that this strategy has led the country onto the "best path" for modernization (Ramos 2004, 4). He expresses admiration for Chinese intellectuals and policymakers because the level and intensity of their open-ended thinking about Chinese society is, according to him, missing outside the PRC, where foreign China watchers and scholars are usually driven by an "antiquated dualism of 'engage/contain'" (ibid., 10), a style of political maneuvering typical of a Cold War mentality.

To explain the priorities of the Chinese agenda, Ramos gives us another popular saying of Deng's, "whether it is a black or white cat doesn't matter as long as it catches the mice," meaning that practice (catching the mice) is more important than ideology, be it socialist or capitalist (white or black), when it comes to ways of reforming China. Giving a new twist to Deng's metaphor, Ramos describes the mantra of the new regime as, "the color of the cat *does* matter. The goal now is to find a cat that is green, a cat that is transparent" (ibid., 23). A greener environment and transparency in governance is no mere rhetoric from the socialist government, Ramos says. It is revealing of China's desire to keep up with the modern Western norm. The Chinese, he also tells us, have little interest in copying the rest of the world but want "to control, localize and administer their own global future." This independent mindset has led them to oppose "the kind of mail-order prescriptions of the Washington Consensus and distanced them from the whole history of first-world economic advice" as they diligently pursue their own path (ibid., 32–33). Ramos's empathy with and respect for the localization of ideas and ways of life are what make him a different policy analyst from those in the developed world. Here is a Western interpreter who values difference as much as similarities and even more important, he tries to dig deeper into the appeal of localization to the locals.

The "Beijing Consensus" is many things at once—a policy advisory, a semi-official discourse, and, less consciously, a brand statement for a new China still in the making.[19] My juxtaposition of Ramos's white paper and the Saatchi & Saatchi initiative is meant to lay bare the strength and weaknesses of each exercise. Roberts sees China as a plastic cultural object devoid of politics, while Ramos sees China as a clear subject, self-conscious of its own political vision. But "The Beijing Consensus" has thus far had a small audience and a short shelf life, in part because it is not completely certain whom Ramos saw as his target audience. Was he speaking to scholars, policymakers, the general public, or people of specific nationalities? His target consumer turned out to be an audience of many faces, too elusive to capture. To compound the audience problem, a country brand that has no widespread buy-in from its own population is not grown organically and, when presented to the world, may be treated as nothing more than state propaganda. Herein lies a crucial difference between nation branding and product branding: a consumer brand knows exactly whose buy-ins it seeks and gives the target segment a central role in the process of branding—a process much harder for country branding to achieve.

Saatchi & Saatchi's "Brand China," on the contrary, is an excellent case of precise targeting. The segment Roberts privileged is Generation Y—the children of baby-boomers, born between 1982 and 2000 (Howe, Strauss, et al. 2000)—the "most receptive Western audience yet for Brand China" (K. Roberts 1998, 8). Members of Generation Y are more open-minded than an average global consumer, because "locality" for them is often nothing more than a marketing label. There is thus a built-in paradox in Roberts's Brand China project: it markets China as a "national" brand, but to sell it, "Brand China" must appeal to the new global aesthetics of Generation Y on whom no one race, country, or culture can put an exclusive claim. In that generation we find the so-called hub influentials, an urban population whose formula for success and whose tastes for cell phones, music, handbags, wine, and cuisine bear closer resemblance to their counterparts in other global metropolises than to their sisters and brothers residing in their home towns and home countries (Stalnaker 2002). Roberts is betting on the appeal of high-value Chinese goods to customers of hub culture styles around the world.

That would surely be a brand spectacle. But to succeed in destigmatizing the name of China and turning it into a hot ticket on the international marketplace, more than a single agency's participation and effort will be required. For "China" to make a triple leap of this kind, advertising agencies working in multiple sectors will need to cooperate with domestic corporate clients. The result would be synergy on a grand scale, and for this a top-down (that is, government-driven) orchestration is out of the question. For such synergies to emerge and eventually converge, major stakeholders for a "brand new China" will need to implement their respective visions simultaneously—Ramos's China rising peacefully as a responsible global citizen and a compassionate reform-minded government at home; Roberts's China transforming its old charms and creativities into new hub-era fantasies; joint venture partners in China honoring the rules of the game while understanding the Chinese need for brand autonomy; and China's prized entrepreneurs making huge strides in internationalizing their home-made brands.

CHAPTER 4

Storytelling and
Corporate Branding

Reciprocal flows, by definition, do not flow only in one direction. Not only is traffic initiated from the West, but increasingly Chinese superbrands are traveling the opposite way. The Chinese excitement about the westbound voyage is real. But brands strong enough to migrate overseas must first be superbrands at home. Thus a new kind of "brand nationalism" has taken hold and triggered questions like "Why don't *we* have *our own* Samsung or Sony?" After the PC maker Lenovo's acquisition of IBM's ThinkPad and the bid of Haier, a domestic appliance giant, for Maytag, national hopes for the global reach of Chinese brands grew almost feverish.

Looking at the Big Two provokes questions about what their corporate culture is like and how well they will adapt to the Western market environment. Further, I explore whether changing business strategies in corporate China and corporate America are reconfiguring the old dichotomy that pits the Asian preference for corporate branding against the priority Americans place on product branding. We can also learn more about Haier and Lenovo's culture if we examine it from the vantage point of organizational storytelling. This last topic incorporates an examination of the media's role in corporate storytelling. For example, Haier's corporate ideology is dramatized by a cartoon series, and the controversy that erupted around Lenovo was triggered by bloggers. The implications of the old and new media for corporate branding, and of organizational narratives for institutional discipline, will shed light on our understanding of Chinese corporate culture.

Until now, Chinese corporate culture has grown out of a larger marketing environment in which the importance of brand management gives way to corporate management, brand culture to corporate culture, and brand identity to corporate identity. But whether such a manufacturer-driven business environment can produce globally competitive brands is a significant concern.

"I NEVER SAID THAT HAIER AND LENOVO ARE NOT BRANDS"

As we saw in the Introduction, late in 2004 Shelly Lazarus, the chairman and CEO of Ogilvy & Mather Worldwide had to defend herself for saying that Lenovo and Haier were actually not brands at all and that "so far China has no brands in any real sense" (Tang Yong 2005). Here I wish to tease out Lazarus' veiled criticism of China's brand environment in her subsequent interview with the *People's Daily*, from which the above heading was taken. Speaking in a seemingly conciliatory mood, she explained why megabrands are not necessarily strong brands and why a stellar international brand isn't the same as a superbrand at home. In plain language, homegrown stars may still not be savvy enough to go primetime in the international market. Lazarus complained that the Chinese business habit of squandering big money on advertisements yielded only "short-term returns but [would] not generate longer term growth [of the brand]." She asked whether Lenovo and Haier, whose corporate tactics had worked miracles in the domestic market, had developed a sustainable long-term brand building strategy that would help them nurture an emotional bond with local customers *abroad*. To that thorny question her answer was no. It is thus unclear whether these Chinese brands will be able to win over global consumers en masse. A further, though less obvious, issue is that in their gigantic growth, the brands may collapse under the weight of their own mythologies.

Shelly Lazarus brought the Chinese dream of making their brands Olympian down to earth. Thus far, the Big Two have been preoccupied with the making and branding of corporate culture at the expense of brand culture. This activity has not been the oversight that Lazarus implied, but a choice in keeping with the branded-house strategy favored by East Asian corporate giants, who extend product lines under the umbrella of a master brand. In Japan, for instance, huge trading companies like Mitsubishi, Sony, and Suntory can walk with impunity into neighboring product territories and create strong leverage for their offerings across product lines. Their brand resources have primarily been used to build their company names. Haier, Lenovo, and Wahaha have followed suit.

In contrast, there are few corollaries in the Western market, where stand-alone brand architecture dominates, for such enormous brand stretch (Owen 1993). Over time, the subbrand strategy, or the "House of Brands" approach, has nourished a Western marketing culture that gives priority to product branding over corporate branding. In addition to frowning on practices like those of Haier and Lenovo, Western marketing literature in general has taken a critical stance toward the trade-dominant Asian business culture, seeing it as deeply marred by an emphasis on short-term gains and tactics. It is said to be a profit-conscious trading culture whose "sales/margin oriented logic" breeds a marketing environment that privileges selling and distribution rather than branding and marketing (Blair, Armstrong, and Murphy 2003, 208, 211). This same "mercenary tradition" has reputedly paved the way for the Asian emphasis on corporate brand equity over product brand equity. To remedy such a "disadvantageous" business practice, Chinese corporate managers and advertising professionals have been advised to replicate the Western marketing paradigm.

This ongoing debate about the pros and cons of the Asian and Western trading paradigms will not subside anytime soon, especially given that the new century is dubbed the "Asian" century. Meanwhile, digital media are changing the terms of this debate faster than the CEOs are. The convergence of business thinking is already creating fascinating mirror images impossible to imagine even half a decade ago: the West is reassessing the value of corporate branding while an entrepreneurial China finds itself actively engaged in learning about the tricks of brand management. This point of analytical equilibrium is predictable, given the strength of synergy thinking that has sprung from both sides of the Pacific.

All these inquiries are linked. We may ask whether the advantages and blind spots of the Chinese corporate-centric paradigm can generate incentives for product innovation as efficiently as the Western brand-centric model. We also need to explore how paradigm crossovers from both directions are made possible and what role the Internet plays in creating new business strategies. My starting point is storytelling, which draws us into the heart of the corporate culture of Haier and Lenovo.

CORPORATE CULTURE AND ORGANIZATIONAL STORYTELLING: THE HAIER WAY

"We will use a diverse array of entertainment assets to break into people's hearts and minds . . . We're moving to ideas that elicit emotion and create connections . . . [ideas] whether [in] movies or music or television . . . are no longer just intellectual property, they're emotional capital" (Jenkins 2004). These remarks were made by Steven J. Heyer of Coca-Cola in a keynote speech delivered at the Madison & Vine Conference in 2003. He was referring to a catchy business trend: the fundamental human desire for entertainment has turned stories into a golden means of communication and led corporate America to rediscover the marketing value of storytelling

(Stark 2003). This is nothing new for Asians. The Chinese and the Indians have inherited centuries-old traditions of oral storytelling that have found their way into these cultures' characteristically drama-rich television commercials. We all know that "a good story sells." A related and yet understudied topic is the ways in which corporate branding can be built on organizational tales.

The Chinese culture has a long tradition of tale-writing and oral storytelling. Much to everyone's surprise, the horrid chapter of the Cultural Revolution brought that ancient art to a new height. During the ten years of turmoil and cultural liquidation, no modern entertainment genres survived except the eight model revolutionary plays and operas. The entire nation, especially the "sent-down youths" exiled to the countryside, were left to their own pleasure-seeking devices. Storytelling was a popular pastime for all. It is no accident that today's CEO celebrities like Zhang Ruimin (Haier) and Liu Chuanzhi (Legend-Lenovo), erstwhile sent-down youths during the Revolution, are eloquent storytellers who have relied on the power of narrative to give their corporations a distinct and often dramatic personality.

Corporate storytelling is central to the mythmaking of Haier and Legend (Lenovo's Chinese name). For Haier, for example, famous tales such as the "The Sledgehammer," "The Third Eye," and "Little Prince" are as integral to the Haier legend as Zhang's management philosophy. The tradition of oral storytelling coupled with a residual Maoist penchant for slogan literature have created a rich repertoire of anecdotes that define the Haier Way. Haier's organizational stories enact the archetype of the epic, complete with the rise of the hero from anonymity, conflicts and crises, struggles against the odds encountered, and the ultimate triumph over adversity.

The adventure began in 1984, when Zhang Ruimin took over a sinking ship, the Qingdao General Refrigerator Factory, an old company whose name was associated with substandard refrigerators. He oversaw eight hundred employees who had no incentive to improve productivity. The socialist system of the "iron rice bowl"—guaranteed life-long employment—emerged as the first antagonist, a larger-than-life one, in the saga of Haier's quest for success. One can imagine the difficulties facing the modern manager by just glancing at the Thirteen Articles, a set of new regulations Zhang Ruimin established for the factory workers, among them, "thou shall not knit during work," "thou shall not steal from public properties," and "thou shall not pee on the workshop floor." From there Zhang built, step by step, eighteen design centers, ten industrial parks, 58,800 sales agents, and 11,976 after-sales service centers in 160 countries (Yi and Ye 2003, 4). Today Haier has diversified its production line into white, black, and brown household appliances incorporating 15,100 models of appliances in categories as wide ranging as refrigerators, freezers, wine coolers, air conditioners, washing machines, cell phones, water heaters, microwave ovens, irons, TVs, DVD players, and even computers (Haier 2007b). In 1996 Haier established its first overseas base at Jakarta, and in following years, in the Philippines, Malaysia, the Middle East, the United States, Yugoslavia, and Western Europe. To see how Zhang Ruimin got that far in a matter of two decades, a few select organizational stories will provide some clues.

The Sledgehammer

A year after Zhang Ruimin took over the Qingdao Factory, seventy-six refrigerators were found to be defective. A refrigerator at that time cost $100. An average worker's monthly pay was only $5. Seventy-six refrigerators added up to three months' salary for five hundred workers. If Zhang had followed past practices, he would have parceled out those deficient goods to prized employees or used them as soft bribes for officials. But he ordered them smashed with a sledgehammer in front of four hundred teary workers. The whole incident was videotaped. Zhang and Chief Engineer Yang

Mianmian fined themselves three months' salary (Sun Jian 2002b, 46–50). The message was clear: defective products are junk; substandard employees producing substandard products will be punished. "Zero defects" *(ling quexian)* has been firmly in place as a key performance concept since then (ibid., 48), and quality control is now one of the most remarkable strengths of Haier. "Haier" means "higher" in its English slogan. Going higher and higher each time is a new tagline, a metaphorical blueprint for globalization.

The "Third Eye" Is Watching

A significant portion of Haier's assets originally came from the coffers of Qingdao City, as we shall see below. Yet even with the blessing of the local state, Haier's venture was not risk free. There are three realities in China, according to Zhang, each requiring monitoring by a watchful eye. Under a planned economy, an enterprise only needs one eye to look out for governmental decrees; in a normalized market economy, two eyes are required, with one focused on internal company affairs, and another on the market. But the Chinese transition from a planned to a commodity economy took a complex, zigzag course. A sensitive third eye is thus called for to capture China's unpredictable policy shifts, which vacillate between socialist and capitalist economic thinking (Chi Shuangming 2004, 165–166). Haier's "third eye" is adept at spotting opportunities triggered by Beijing's fickle policy directives.

The major shift occurred in 1992, when Deng Xiaoping went south and gave a series of reform talks to boost the market economy. One of his famous sayings on that trip instructed the people to "make bold experiments, do not take gingerly steps like a woman with bound feet" (ibid., 166). Special economic zones were set up. Enterprises were encouraged to think outside the box. This open policy prompted Zhang and his Haier comrades to make an ambitious plan to build a modern industrial park. With governmental approval for a loan of 1.6 billion yuan, Zhang purchased 800 *mu* (approximately 5,000 acres) of land in the eastern part of Qingdao as the future site for the park. But the loan was suddenly frozen as a result of central credit tightening. Zhang Ruimin bailed Haier out by going public on the Shanghai Stock Exchange. It was a narrow escape: Haier raised 369 million yuan with its initial public offering, or IPO (ibid., 166). The industrial park was built as planned. When all three eyes were well coordinated, miracles could happen. Right before the company went public, Zhang changed the brand name of his joint venture from "Liebherr Haier" to "Haier"—and a national brand was born.

Big Yam and Little Prince: Tales of Innovation

After Haier pushed its products into China's interior, rural consumers living in the southwest sent innumerable complaints about the "poor quality of the water pipes" in the washing machines. An investigative team was sent to settle the grievances but found that the pipes were blocked by yam skins, because peasants had used the machines to wash yams. Instead of instructing the masses to stick to clothes washing, Zhang Ruimin made a strategic move and designed a new machine with enlarged pipes, better drainage, and dual washing functions. The new product was rightfully named Big Yam, and has become one of the best-selling washing machines in rural China (Su and Chen 2003, 120). The entertaining tale of Big Yam has been woven into the company literature and given a rich pedagogical value on a par with that of the Sledgehammer and Little Prince.

The birth of Little Prince was no less dramatic. Since the mid-1990s the pace of work has picked up in the cities, and time has become a precious commodity. Urbanites can no longer afford the old habit of doing grocery shopping daily. A new weekly shopping routine has developed, which in turn requires a bigger freezer capacity.

But frugal households were reluctant to part with their old refrigerators even though the freezer space was now too small for food storage. Haier seized the opportunity to discover another new market. Out came Little Prince, a low-budget small freezer that does not require much floor space in overcrowded Chinese apartments. It provides the extra freezer space most families crave. A perfect win-win solution with Chinese characteristics.

Little Prince and Big Yam are hardly stand-alone subbrands. Both offerings are branded with Haier's name and remain function-driven products without unique brand personalities. The corporate-centric paradigm of Haier—the conflation of product identities with company identities and the unchecked horizontal and vertical extensions—has generated incentives for product innovation as strongly as the Western brand-centric paradigm. A built-in system of innovation is rooted in Haier's desire to satisfy consumers, which holds the key to the company's quick ascendance in the Chinese market. Few appliance makers can beat Haier's lightning speed in product innovation. Today the company portfolio includes 13,000 models of appliances. Concomitantly, the spectrum of prices for a single product category has kept extending: you can find Haier air conditioners for as low as $225 apiece and as high as $1,463 (Haier 2007a). Typically, customers are given two different models to choose from at every $6 increment.

Some skeptics attribute Haier's success to budget pricing more than to its strength in product innovation, neglecting the scaling of prices Haier is known for. Such views are made even more problematic because since the late 1990s, domestic superbrands have entered the high-end market with premium prices catering to affluent urban customers, while multinationals are becoming competitive in their pricing in rural markets, a crossover phenomenon I analyzed in Chapter 3. In any case, Haier's example is a powerful rebuttal to the widely held view that the corporate-centric paradigm is lacking in both work efficiency and a drive to innovate—advantages credited to the brand-centric paradigm alone.

The Wolf Theory and Other Tactics

Theoretically, Zhang Ruimin would be the last person to choose between these two paradigms, because his vision for globalization is highly accommodating. The corporate-centric approach may have suited a mass market like China's, but Haier must gain expertise in niche marketing and branding to make its mark abroad. Both Chinese and American analysts have paid attention to his corporate tactics for global expansion. Among these globalization tactics is the CEO's famous "three one-thirds" vision, which takes a three-pronged approach to overseas expansion: one third of Haier's products are made and sold domestically, another third are made domestically but sold overseas, and the last third will be both manufactured and sold overseas (Sun Jian 2002a, 87–88). Zhang's "wolf theory" is formulated in similarly tactical terms. There is no better way of outsmarting "wolves" (a metaphor for rival foreign companies), he says, than becoming one yourself and breaking into the other wolves' home turf.[1] His answer to the WTO challenge can be summed up as "dancing with the wolves, sharing the market with international brands" (Wang and Kang 2002, 47).

Has Haier International been a success? Zhang Ruimin has been quoted saying, "We have succeeded in completing only one and a half steps toward globalization, but not all three steps required for the task," meaning that the Haier brand has traveled out of China and entered halfway into overseas markets but has stopped short of morphing itself into a well-known global brand (Liu Yinghua 2005). Zhang admits with some regret that Chinese corporations have lost the historical opportunities they had to become name brands abroad by sheer means of massive capital accumulation.

Money alone can't do the trick. He has come to recognize that "the only way to become a global brand is through innovation and the speed to innovate" (ibid.). This last statement makes one wonder whether the CEO has transcended his founding vision, that is, an engineer's obsession with product innovation. He needs to be flexible enough to switch gears from a manufacturer-driven mentality to a consumer-oriented one, from corporate centrism to brand empire-building. Reaching out to Western consumers is crucial.

Haier has strong advocates. Donald Sull, the author of *Made in China: What Western Managers Can Learn from Trailblazing Chinese Entrepreneurs*, has endorsed its "consumer pull" strategies and named it the most valuable Chinese brand ("Haier Goals" 2005).[2] But critics are quick to cite Zhang Ruimin's hasty moves, especially his quick expansion overseas. Size doesn't automatically translate into quality, they argue. Nor can huge coffers alone make a global brand today. Buying name recognition as Haier did at every step of the way is not the same as building a brand strategically. The company's diversification scheme at home and abroad is seen as "driven by opportunism and desperation, not [by] good strategy" ("Haier's Purpose" 2004).

The most stringent critique has come from sociologist Jiang Ruxiang, who sees a systemic problem ingrained in the mentality of Chinese CEOs. In his view, corporate leaders like Zhang Ruimin and Lenovo's Liu Chuanzhi are heavily influenced by traditional tactical thinking, which is microscopic in nature, propelled by (and confined to) the strategist's sense of serving the prince. This "servant mentality" engenders a hierarchy ruled by man not by charter, a system paling in comparison to a contractually based modern Western corporate setting that separates the CEO from the company (Jiang Ruxiang 2003). The conceptual difference, put metaphorically, is that between Machiavelli and Thomas Hobbes. In this view, Zhang Ruimin is no Jack Welch, his hero. Chinese corporate strongmen treat their companies as a personal patrimony, a possession in line with the medieval concept of *dominium*. Zhang, like his other Chinese counterparts, rules by princely charisma. The conflation of a leader's personal convictions and the company core values runs parallel to another striking characteristic of corporate China, namely, the lack of a genuinely independent commercial culture free from the push and pull of state power.

Sun Tzu, Chairman Mao, and Organizational Discipline

Jiang Ruxiang's critique of Chinese strategic thinking is relevant here. There is a logical connection between the organizational stories we have just reviewed and strategic thinking with Chinese characteristics, among them, a leadership cult, a war room mentality, and a monarchical management style. Although a strong man has stood behind every world-class corporation (Jack Welch, Bill Gates, Steve Jobs, and so on), middle-aged Chinese CEOs came from a five-thousand-year-old lineage of military strategists, many of whom, like Sun Tzu, were more disciplinarians than visionaries. Monarchs who cared deeply about values, like Mao Zedong, often overlooked the limitations of their founding vision and surrendered themselves to leadership cults and turned deaf to criticisms. The deification of the "Zhang Ruimin spirit" at Haier seems to point to a similarly dangerous path: the lack of the flexibility of a founder to evolve beyond his earlier strategic vision. Both Sun Tzu and Mao, I should note, are role models for Zhang and Liu.

"The consummate leader cultivates the moral law, and strictly adheres to method and discipline; thus it is in his power to control success" (Sun Tzu 2003, 17, 20). Sun Tzu's classic on the art of war (dating from the fifth century BCE), as we know, is not only a familiar handbook for Western business strategists but a bible for Chinese entrepreneurs. The concept of "attack by stratagem," seamless organizational discipline, and the proverbial equation of the business world with the battlefield *(shangchang ru zhanchang)* are what drive Zhang Ruimin's wolf theory and Wahaha CEO Zong Qinghou's spider warfare. Liu Chuanzhi of Lenovo has also been known to see himself as a generalissimo, scouting terrain, crafting plans, and running Lenovo like a "boot camp" (Ge 2003b, 15). One of Zhang Ruimin's three most favorite books is said to be *The Art of War.*[3]

Even more important than Sun Tzu was Mao Zedong's influence on Zhang Ruimin's generation of corporate leaders. A devout Communist Party member, Zhang is less an ideologue than a utopian thinker whose idealism, a hallmark of the Cultural Revolution, survived the catastrophe intact. Many analysts point out correctly that the Haier Group is ultimately government controlled ("Haier Goals" 2005), echoing Jiang Ruxiang's lament over the inseparability of the state and corporate China *(zheng qi bufen).* But shorthand statements like this tell us little about Zhang's complicated, positive relationship with the CCP.

What the sledgehammer smashed in 1985 was not only the seventy-six refrigerators, but the state socialist work ethic itself. The story of Haier, however, didn't follow a typical capitalist storyline. Zhang Ruimin is far too utopian a communist and much too wise a strategist to brand socialism an antagonist. Legally, Haier is a "collective enterprise" whose assets are "owned" by all employees. Yet it is not listed in full on the stock market. "Collective ownership" in the reform period is in essence a euphemism for the "diversification of state capital" rather than an equation to "privatization" understood in Western terms. Such an investment body consists of a mixture of stakeholders whose origins and identities are difficult to define. This modern version of mixed ownership is promoted fervently by the Party state precisely because it seeks to re-contain, rather than exclude, state capital.

The municipality of Qingdao has played a major role in transforming Haier into a conglomerate through a series of administrative fiats. In 1984 the city rounded up several dilapidated state-owned electric plants, set up the Qingdao Refrigerator Factory, and appointed Zhang as the new helmsman. In 1992, it facilitated the birth of the Haier Group by orchestrating another merger between the refrigerator factory and the Qingdao Air-Conditioning Plant. It was reported that Haier's middle-level managerial personnel are all Communist Party members ("Haier Rises" 2001). All this serves to illustrate what the commissioned Chinese and Western authors of Haier's history felt reluctant to highlight, namely, that the paragon of China's "private" entrepreneurs Zhang Ruimin has cultivated and maintained strong ties with the Communist Party. The blurred boundary between the "private" and the "public" is, in fact, a norm in post-Mao China. It is somewhat revealing that American media have said little about Zhang's ideological loyalty to the Party. The shyness of Western journalism may have to do with liberal media's apprehension that a more nuanced evaluation of "the Haier Way" might compromise our mythmaking about emergent Chinese "private" enterprises. After all, American neoliberalism cannot imagine any other relationship than an oppositional one between the communist state and the "free market." Conceivably, the pleasure derived from an imagined victory of capitalism in communist China would have been much tempered if Zhang's ideological statements—"I am not only an enterprising leader, more importantly, I'm a Communist Party member"—had been trumpeted in mainstream U.S. media ("Haier Rises" 2001).

If Zhang's statement, which appeared in the *People's Daily*, does not seem entirely credible, *The Haier Way* documented an interview with Zhang Ruimin in which he was quizzed on his choice of December 26, Mao Zedong's date of birth, as the official birthday for the Qingdao Refrigerator Factory. Zhang appeared evasive. The authors pursued their line of logic:

"But you respected Mao. For instance, you copied the 'school principle' in Mao style on the central wall of the Haier University. You constantly emphasize the importance of being practical and realistic, which are frequently quoted Mao doctrines. Also, you traveled all the way to the hometown of Jiao Yulu, who was a role-model Mao had set up for the whole nation to learn from. And, like Mao, you want to do something big." (Yi and Ye 2003, 173)

"You want to do something big" is right on target. Zhang's expansive vision for Haier and his voluntarist convictions are signature traits of Maoist revolutionaries. His style of pushing Haier's engineers to outdo themselves is also reminiscent of the Chairman's famous theory of the "permanent revolution."[4] In the specific context of product development, he says, "All innovations are fleeting and relative . . . From the day when a new product comes out, you have to negate it and move on to invent a newer and better product. You will have to be on your tiptoes as if treading on thin ice all the time" (Ge 2003a, 33–34). True to that spirit, Haier churned out twelve successive generations of Little Prodigy, the world's smallest washing machine.[5]

When the thought revolution of Mao's style wedded Sun Tzu's stalwart discipline, it is not an exaggeration to say that an imperial subject was born. The Haier Man and the Lenovo Man—company employees—are all terra cotta soldiers in a hierarchically structured collective, who owe absolute loyalty to the supreme commander, the CEO. Devotion needs to be maintained and discipline administered. An inner logic connecting organizational stories to the Chinese mode of strategic thinking is evident. On the surface, the Sledgehammer episode acts as a symbolic landmark in Haier culture. Little Prince and Big Yam were woven into the living folklore of the company because they embodied the value of innovation. But there is more to organizational storytelling than the inculcation of corporate values.

Storytelling and Corporate Culture

Progressive organizational studies do not treat corporate tales as innocuous artifacts or as simple metaphors of core values (Martin

1990). Important events—such as the controversial firing of Lenovo's chief engineer (an episode I will treat later)—do not automatically generate stories that are broadcast to employees and recorded in company brochures. Stories that survive the ups and downs of an organization's history are most likely didactic, and if regularly reinforced, they program discipline and social control. Once crystallized, the Sledgehammer, Little Prince, and similar stories became part of Haier's disciplinary apparatus. Popular organizational stories, in that sense, represent the ideological "unconscious" that employees unknowingly internalize. Cute Little Prodigies are excellent propaganda tools to drive home the ideology of the "permanent revolution," and the symbolic Sledgehammer hangs above the head of those toiling on the workshop floors. Surveillance is unnecessary if self-discipline does the policing job. If we ask who in the end controls these stories, we see that here Sun Tzu meets Mao: the supreme leader himself. The postmodern, deconstructionist take by scholars of contemporary organization studies—"once told, the story becomes contestable"—is probably much more relevant for General Electric than for big Chinese corporations like Haier (Gabriel 2000, 117).

Nor are all methods of discipline translatable into stories and metaphors. At Haier, corporatized MaoSpeak—neologisms and slogans—compete with stories like the Sledgehammer in driving efficiency and productivity. Zhang's famed OEC management model is one example. "O" stands for "overall," "E" for "everyone," "everything," "everyday," and "C" for "control and clear." Put together, the acronym means a daily discipline that requires every employee to accomplish the work target for each day, with a 1 percent increase over what was done the previous day (Yang Keming 2003). "Be practical and realistic," a famous Mao quote, is said to be a guiding principle behind Zhang's management philosophy (Yi and Ye 2003, 85). Other catchphrases in Haier's "Little Red Book" include "React in speed and move promptly" (*xunsu fanying mashang xingdong*), "Follow difficult markets first and easier ones later, and export our brand name to the world" *(xiannan houyi, chukou chuangpai),* "Let a luminous East light up the West" *(dongfang liangle zai liang xifang)* (Liu, Zhao, and Zhang 2001).

The continuity between Mao's China and corporate China is most strikingly revealed in corporatized MaoSpeak. Language is a construct built on deep ideological origins. The Maoist lingua franca at Haier is symptomatic of strategic thinking that carries cultural and ideological baggage. But those insisting on deciphering the saying "Let a luminous East light up the West" within the simple frame of Maoism or Chinese nationalism miss a qualitative change in the trans-oceanic flows of the new century. As business globalization deepens, there will only be "strong" or "weak" brands rather than "national" or "transnational" brands (Blair, Armstrong, and Murphy 2003, 207). The notion of a "luminous East" may refer to the sped-up reality of the reverse brand traffic from Asia flowing westward. It is difficult to tell whether this would result in a kinder globalization than the one steered by New York– and London-based multinationals.

We can be certain, though, that as more and more Asian brands invest, or even succeed, in localizing themselves in the developed world, the real debate will drift away from the now dominant thesis that a brand's identity is nation bound. Old ideological associations between the "local," the "margin," and the "national origin" are breaking down, just as the stubborn identification between "globalization" and "Westernization" will. Despite the critics' reservations, an example like Haier, with its westbound ambitions, is truly instructive and even refreshing. Whether a successful transplant across the Pacific will take place soon, the Haier Way is ultimately a story about the next phase of globalization: an increasing volume of brand traffic flowing from the developing world to the modern West.

LEGEND-LENOVO: CONTESTED HISTORY
AND STORYTELLING ON THE INTERNET

No other corporation in China has capitalized on the new momentum of globalization faster than Lenovo, the country's leading vendor of personal computers (PCs). In 2005, the company made global headlines with its acquisition of IBM's personal computing business. The merger was said to create the world's third-biggest PC maker, with annual sales totaling $12 billion. Originally known as the Legend *(Lianxiang)* Group, the company had been established in Beijing by eleven scientists from the Chinese Academy of the Social Sciences (CASS), a government think tank, in 1984. They started off as a small distributor for Hewlett-Packard and AST Research (a PC manufacturer), gradually gaining technological and managerial expertise from the latter.

In 1999 Legend outshone its competitors by inventing the first-generation user-friendly Internet-enabled Chinese computer. The Pentium-based Conet PC came bundled with a modem and brought "one-touch-to-the-net" services to home users, putting an end to the cumbersome registration processes of logging-on that had been required. In 2003 Legend changed its name to Legend-Lenovo and soon became the Lenovo Group Limited. They produce not only PCs but also handheld devices, mobile handsets, motherboards, IT consulting services, and other wireless solutions. According to an interim fiscal year report, approximately 1,446,600 Legend PCs were sold during the first half of FY2001/02, representing a yearly incremental growth of 17.8 percent (Liu Chuanzhi 2001).

In 2004 the Group's net profits jumped 16.2 percent from the year before ("Lenovo Posts" 2004). Although there have been widespread speculations about the dip in its stock—down 26 percent during the first quarter of 2006 (Cantrell 2006), Lenovo weathered the Big Blues and gained in fast-growing PC markets.

According to a report on the full year 2006/07, its worldwide PC shipments grew more than 17 percent during the fourth fiscal quarter, "well ahead of the industry average of approximately 11 percent" (Lenovo 2007). It's no small achievement that the brand of choice for China's average PC user is Lenovo rather than Dell, IBM, or Toshiba.

Many of my comments on Zhang Ruimin are applicable to Lenovo's founding father and former chairman of the group—Liu Chuanzhi. Lenovo's steady ascent to prominence has had everything to do with Liu, a hybrid of Sun Tzu and Mao not unlike Haier's CEO. Like Haier, the company is partially state-owned but privately run. The Group owns 61 percent of its holdings, of which 65 percent belong to the think tank CASS, and 35 percent to Liu and twenty-seven other original Legend employees (Paul 2002).[6] The government accounts for more than 18 percent of Legend's PC sales.

Lenovo, like Haier, is replete with the lore and myths extolling the founders' vision. The CEO is a supreme strategic planner true to Sun Tzu's ideals and spirit. In terms of both the scale and the consistency of creativity, corporate tales spun by Lenovo pale in comparison to Haier's. But Liu Chuanzhi is fond of fables, perhaps because they work so well as teaching tools.

In 1988, Hong Kong Legend was established to distribute foreign-brand computer products for Beijing Legend. Lenovo was a startup company at that time. It had a solid technological and financial base at home, but little knowledge about the international computer market. Liu Chuanzhi compared his company to a big, strong blind man. In contrast, Legend's Hong Kong JV partner-to-be, a small company jump-started by graduates from London University, lacked the technical know-how it needed, even though it had built strength in international trading. CEO Liu compared it to what he called a "crippled clairvoyant." Working together, went the fable, the "blind man" and the "cripple" doubled their comparative advantages (Ge 2003b, 5). In 1994 Hong Kong Legend was listed on the Stock Exchange of Hong Kong. By 2000 the joint venture became one of the constituent stocks of the Hang Seng Index, laying down a solid foundation for scale economies and pushing Legend a step closer to becoming an international information technology (IT) company.

"Puffy buns versus real buns" is a fable about agenda-setting for corporate founders, who appear in the account as two bun peddlers. The first peddler is an old woman at a train station. Her agenda is to cheat people whenever she can. Treating all customers as people she will only serve once, she puts little stuffing in her buns but makes them all look puffed up and deceivingly big. Naturally, her business fails to grow. The second bun peddler has a completely different agenda. Planning eventually to build a franchise from the base of his small street stall, he works to perfect each bun to please his customers. His good reputation eventually helps him achieve his dream. Legend aimed at becoming the second peddler: it crawls along at a steady pace, but set its revenue target at $10 billion by 2005, a goal easily met (Lenovo 2006), and planned to enter the Fortune 500 list about the same time, a wish fulfilled as of 2005 (ibid., 12).

These two fables illustrate Lenovo's organizational storytelling culture and give away the zeitgeist of a corporation built on a rigorous and sometimes humorless discipline. CEO Liu has been seen as a smoother and more sophisticated strategist than Zhang Ruimin. He has often acted like a corporate twin of Mao and led his followers like the supreme commander of the Red Army. Like the Chairman, he has had a penchant for aphorisms and has been known for golden one-liners such as "a small company handles business, a big company handles people *(zuoren)*."[7] Mottoes extolling the leader's wisdom are given precedence over product tales in Lenovo's company literature. All this sounds familiar: the leadership cult and slogan fever constitute an integral part of the double heritage of Maoism and traditional Chinese military culture. Unlike Haier, however, Lenovo's company history has not been so neatly contained within the carefully managed narratives scripted by Liu's cult followers. What makes Lenovo such an unusual case for organizational story-telling is the challenge Chinese bloggers have posed to its official history. "Once told, the story becomes contestable"—an unlikely scenario for Haier—does ring true for Lenovo.

What Bloggers Can Do

The "blogging revolution" has pushed viral communication to new heights. Technorati, a global weblog organizer that helps people search for and organize blogs, tracked 51.3 million blogs world-wide in 2006, with about 1.2 million posts daily.[8] In the United States alone, an estimated forty thousand new blogs were created every day in 2005 (Baker and Green 2005).[9] In contrast, in August 2002 China's top weblog site—BlogChina (bokee.com)—was established with only 200 bloggers. But by 2004 the site was experiencing an explosive upsurge of more than 100,000 visits per day, thanks to a kiss-and-tell online diary penned by a twenty-five-year-old sex columnist known by the alias "Muzimei."[10] Even by July of the previous year, Muzimei had already become the most searched-for name on Chinese Internet portals, "surpassing one occasional runner-up, Mao Zedong" (Yardley 2003). Soon the story traveled across the ocean, and China's new Web craze was summarized by a single label: "bedroom blogging."

The hype could not have been further from the truth, however. There are at least two million blogs in China (Duncan 2005), and most have nothing to do with backstreet trysts and sex scandals. They cover subjects ranging from politics to social networking to pop music. Blogging as citizen media has a bright future even in a nation patrolled by legions of Internet policemen and -women. Chinese chat room culture, if the case of Lenovo provides any clues, is extremely contentious.

On January 16, 2004, blogger Wang Yukun, a former researcher at the State Council of the PRC, the highest executive organ of state power, published on BlogChina a long post entitled "The Eternal Trauma in the History of Corporate China, A Comparative Analysis of Commercial Humanism—Sony vs. Lenovo." Relentlessly critical of Lenovo's vision, Wang revisited the story of the conflict between Liu Chuanzhi and Ni Guangnan (chief engineer and Liu's erstwhile right-hand man) and the latter's ignominious dismissal in 1999. He framed the struggle in terms of a tragic confrontation between knowledge capital (Ni) and mercenary opportunism (Liu). Ni's exit, Wang said, deprived Lenovo of the historical opportunity to invent the first "China chip" (Wang Yukun 2004, 37). Wang denounced Liu Chuanzhi's triple model of *"mao gong ji"*—developing "trade, manufacturing, and technology" in that sequential order—and trumpeted Ni's vision that reverses the priorities: "technology first, manufacturing and trade later" *(ji gong mao)* (ibid.).

Wang Yukun's blog arrived at a time when Lenovo's stock had dipped and the company's diversification strategy into the Internet and software applications had run into a brick wall. To make matters worse, the company's innovative plan to develop core computer technologies had also stalled. Those who had counted on Lenovo's leadership in forming homegrown standards in the high-tech field were bitterly disappointed. It seemed that China was fated to pay "patent rent" to multinationals for decades to come, and that the shift from "made in China" to "made by China" was still far away. Looking back into Legend's history, critics saw the firing of Ni Guangnan as a serious setback for Lenovo's research program and its ability to deliver Chinese high-tech patents and technical standards.

Wang Yukun's harsh criticism touched a chord in the bloggers' community. An extensive online debate about Lenovo's organizational culture unfolded in early 2004. Many bloggers echoed Wang's pessimism, but an equal number of them defended Liu Chuanzhi. Despite such diverse opinions, both the pro-Liu and anti-Liu factions agreed on one fundamental point: that their critical examination of Lenovo converged in a deep reflection on the Chinese dream of strengthening the nation through science and technology. A typical view was articulated by a blogger named "bluethinker":

> What we are really concerned about is not Liu Chuanzhi and his problems per se . . . but our dream about techno-nationalism. It was a dream born from the Opium War and the May Fourth Movement especially; a dream spun by the Hundred Days' Reform, by Sun Yat-sen's vision for saving the nation through the development of business and industry, and by those 'Four Modernizations' talks [of Deng Xiaoping]; it was a dream come alive with the slogan that "science and technology are the primary force of production" and the [call for] a national campaign of Informationalization . . . Time and again, we dreamed the same dream of rejuvenating the nation through science and technology . . . Why has Lenovo become our target? Because in Lenovo we entrusted so many of our precious dreams. (Bluethinker 2004)

One such dream has been the invention of "China chips"—a word pronounced in Chinese exactly like "Chinese heart"—further fanning the passion of techno-nationalists. Ultimately there was poetic justice for the pro-Ni camp: after exiting from Legend, the former chief engineer worked with Beijing Zhongxin Microsystems Co. Ltd., under whose auspices the first China chip, nicknamed "Ark No. 1," was unveiled in April 2001 (Liu Juanjuan 2006). So perhaps Liu Chuanzhi *was* shortsighted as Wang Yukun alleges. Yet online criticisms during this round made only a small dent on the public perception of the CEO. Lenovo's reputation did not suffer until the outburst of the second online polemic, ignited by a "Lenovo Man"—an employee.

In March of the same year, Lenovo's ISP (Internet Service Provider) and ICP (Internet Content Provider) strategies were aborted. A massive layoff forced out 5 percent of the company's Beijing-based employees in three hours (Ling 2005, 386). Watching his traumatized coworkers packing up one by one on short notice, an agitated employee, Mao Shijie, wrote an eyewitness account of the heart-wrenching incident and posted it on "Prickly Plums" *(Laermei)*, a company BBS (electronic bulletin board) set up in the new century as an open forum on which employees were encouraged to post critiques of the company in the same spirit of the Hundred Flowers campaign launched fifty years earlier by the Chinese Communist Party.

Mao Shijie's diary was quickly copied by colleagues and friends and circulated beyond the company over the Internet. Worse, it was given a catchy title: "Our Company Is Not Home: An Eyewitness Account of Lenovo's Lay-off." In the diary, Mao mourned for the failed integration of Lenovo's IT strategies, faulted its early expansionist vision, and asked who should be held responsible for such a strategic fiasco. "Whose fault was this? Our leaders'! All of our strategies, including FM365, were heading in the right direction and generated big revenues, but who made it fail? . . . We ordinary workers were shouldering the burden of the mistakes committed by our leaders . . . Don't you ever look upon our company as a home . . . We all made contributions to it, but it didn't return our affections like our parents" (Mao 2004). Mao Shijie's accusations were a slap in the face of a company that prided itself on making its workplace environment a closely knit family culture. Within five hours after the diary was posted, 104 had responded (Wang Yukun 2004, 390). Many echoed the same disillusionment shared by Wang Yukun about Lenovo: "China's IT banner is in the hands of Intel, not Lenovo's. How incredibly sad this is! It is the sadness of Legend, the sadness of Legend Men, and the sadness of China's IT industry" (Wuming 2004, 329). The vision spelled out in 2001 by Yang Yuanqing (the new chairman)—that Legend-Lenovo would be transforming into a cutting-edge high-tech and IT service company—now suffered a serious blow in the public eye. By July 2004

Legend had closed its IT service division and repositioned itself as a computer and cell phone manufacturer, to the dismay of many sino-techno-nationalists.

FM365.com: A Billboard Story

Mao Shijie's diary mentioned FM365—an Internet portal started by Legend at the peak of its ill-fated diversification campaign. The rise and fall of that portal is of interest for two reasons. It created one of the most celebrated billboard advertisements in China and showcased one of Legend-Lenovo's earliest attempts to go international. FM365.com was set up in June 2001 as a broadband service joint venture, in partnership with AOL Time Warner. Each company pledged $100 million for building the portal in the years to come. The grand scheme would enable every purchaser of a Legend PC to "get access to the latest AOL software and many of the services available to the online giant's U.S. subscribers" (Einhorn and Webb 2001). The deal, analysts predicted, was "likely to accelerate a shakeout of China's main portals" (Shameen 2001) and would enable FM365 to trump China's Big Three portals—Sohu, Sina, and Netease. But the partnership with AOL came to a quiet, untimely end in January 2004, almost coinciding with the incident described below.

The real drama and the sequence of events behind the demise of FM365 were expunged from Lenovo's official chronicle. But unofficial reportage peppered the Internet. On December 1, 2003, Internet surfers logging onto 365.com found a classified web portal, FM265, instead. Had 365 been highjacked or sold? Speculations ran wild online until it was confirmed that a Hong Kong–based domain-name registrar, "265.com," had purchased 365 for $120,000. Staff from Legend were initially ignorant of the transaction and insisted that 365 had not shifted ownership. The disavowal made Legend the laughingstock of the Net. The two portals remained overlapped for a month while Legend scrambled to manage the chaos. This was the first signal to the public that the IT company was running into roadblocks with its much touted expansion into the Internet business. The PC maker would soon revert to its earlier focus on building its specialty sector rather than dallying with "multiple-sector businesses" *(duoyuan hua)*, one of which had been the ill-fated FM365 ("FM365 huigui Lianxiang" 2004).

The demise of 365.com kept chat room traffic busy for months. Detractors now faulted Legend for building a portal at a time when the Internet bubble had burst. The debut of 365.com, however, had been a highly positive event not only for the public but for the entire Chinese advertising industry. To examine that event, we must backpedal to April 2000, to the climactic billboard campaign that unveiled FM365. Nicholas Tse, Hong Kong's heartthrob and a pop singer turned actor, was signed on as the celebrity endorser for the new portal. But from the start, the campaign was wrapped up in riddles. On April 12, 2000, jumbo billboards appeared in the streets of Shanghai, Beijing, and Guangzhou featuring Tse posing an enigmatic question: "Who will be my heartthrob on April 18?" Neither the product's identity nor the advertiser's was given away. The only thing printed on the billboard was Tse's signature (Meng 2002, 34). Serialized five-second spots ran simultaneously on the major TV stations of the three cities. As April 18 drew nearer, the mysterious ad triggered escalating curiosity. At first, it was speculated that a surprise concert might be held by Tse on that day. Fans started making phone calls inquiring about the shadow concert, overloading the telephone lines of big performance stadiums. In Guangzhou, twenty billboards were missing, all allegedly stolen by Tse's fans. Internet traffic was congested as bloggers swarmed into chat rooms trying to solve the puzzle. On the evening of April 17, large crowds gathered at the billboard sites waiting anxiously for the unveiling of the riddle-solving board. A wait of six days had been calculated to bring the public's mood to a boiling point.

The climactic moment arrived on the 18th with a big surprise: the mystery female—whom the public expected to be Nicholas Tse's secret paramour—turned out to be FM365.com, and the masked advertiser, Legend. The board showed Nicholas Tse opening up his arms to embrace the new Internet portal, with a tagline reading "Genuine feelings are interactive—FM365.com!" The carefully orchestrated media event was an ingenious stroke, except for two glitches. The Internet press conference thrown by Legend on April 18—another surprise for the public—to create a second climax to the multimedia launch of 365.com turned into a fiasco. The webcast had to be aborted minutes after Liu Chuanzhi and his chief commanders went live online to connect with journalists and end-users. The responding traffic was so heavy that the server crashed, and the "virtual press conference" ended in dropped connections and content blackout (Ling 2005, 338).

The second glitch was no less embarrassing, although it could in no way have been prevented. A month before this media event reached its climax, buzz agents began sending rumors that Nicholas Tse and Faye Wong (another celebrity singer and the female lead in Wong Kaiwai's *Chongqing Express*) had fallen in love. A parallel rumor ran that the couple was paid by a Beijing conglomerate to have a rendezvous in the capital and to star in a hundred-million-dollar advertising campaign. Legend's first enigmatic billboard begged for a tease, but Pepsi stole a good portion of the momentum. On April 18, the day of reckoning, Pepsi ran a full-page color print advertisement in *Beijing Youth Daily* featuring Faye Wong with the taunting line, "Who makes your heart throb? Pepsi!" Legend's theatrical debut of FM365 was almost nipped in the bud and Pepsi reaped half of the harvest. This billboard campaign was China's first case of suspense marketing. It was likely inspired by an infamous 1981 billboard campaign in Paris that came with three sequential posters. The first one showed a young woman in a bikini, saying, "On September 2, I will take off the top." A new poster appeared on that day featuring the topless model. This time around she made another promise, "On September 4, I will take off the *bottom.*" With the same intense curiosity of the Parisians, Chinese audiences were waiting to uncover the mystery on April 18, utterly spellbound and totally entertained.[11]

For at least a short while, Legend kept the public enthralled about FM365 with other newsworthy media stories revolving around it. Various new content platforms were set up, among them, a public education program on e-commerce, an official Chinese Web page for the smash-hit movie "Crouching Tiger Hidden Dragon," an Olympics page, an online stock market channel, an Online College of Go game, news-sharing programs with the *Beijing Daily* and *Beijing Evening News* (Meng 2002, 37–38). The list ran on and on. All these endeavors, including Legend's tie-in with AOL, went into the garbage in 2004. Although FM365 was now leased to a broadband multimedia venture, Sun 365, Lenovo's share in the joint venture (a reported 15 percent) was so low that it looked almost as if Sun Media had been granted the right to use the portal brand for free ("Sun New Media" 2005).

The year 2004 was one to remember for the Lenovo Man and Woman. The severing of ties with AOL in January took place almost simultaneously with FM365's exit and the posting of Wang Yukun's biting blogs. The infamous layoff in mid-March and employee Mao Shijie's diary exposure were a PR disaster for the company. It appeared that Lenovo's struggle with its public image at home was doomed. Then came a sudden series of surprises: on March 26, Lenovo held a press conference announcing its successful bid to the Olympic Committee to serve as a TOP (The Olympic Partner Program) sponsor. The PC maker was signed on to provide desktop and notebook computers, servers, and technical support, among other things, for the 2006 Olympic Winter Games in Torino and the 2008 Olympic Games in Beijing. The following year saw an even bigger publicity coup for Lenovo—its acquisition of IBM's

PC arm. To explain this stunning rebound, a different spin on the turbulent year of 2004 now surfaced: it was said that Chairman Yang Yuanqing had purposely employed a double-edged strategy, namely, retrenchment at home and expansion overseas (Ling 2005, 394–398).

I have now come full circle with my argument—by 2005, Lenovo had crossed the Pacific and gone global. Together with Haier—the other paragon of corporate branding—it needs to get deeply engaged in the American style of marketing and product branding. To humanize itself in Western markets that have never heard of Lenovo, a heavier investment in the "software" of communications—storytelling—seems indispensable. This is an Achilles' heel for the PC maker: with the exception of the billboard campaign for FM365, Lenovo has taken a backseat approach to communication strategies that bond with customers at the emotional level. A powerful corporation like Lenovo will always possess tremendous resources to hire corporate writers to pen sanitized anecdotes and cleanse its official history of unsanctified hearsay.[12] But that's not the same as creating communications that build entertainment value and emotional capital into the brand. More important, digital media now allow smart consumers to find the chinks in the armor and revolutionize the ways in which official organizational storytelling can be *undone*. Lenovo has a lot of catching up to do in the area of brand communications.

"The Haier Brothers": Branded Entertainment

Lenovo's weakness is Haier's strength. In Zhang Ruimin one finds a savvier player in his use of media to dramatize corporate ideology. Not only has Zhang known how to take full advantage of the media to promote his corporation's identity, he has gone far ahead of his competitors by dabbling in serialized "long-form" content and entertainment media.

It is only appropriate that a corporation that places such high value on linking business to culture has produced China's longest-running cartoon TV series, "The Haier Brothers." It debuted in the early 1990s on CCTV and lasted for eight years. Cartoon marketing was reportedly an influence that came from Japan (Lin Zimin 2003). During the 1990s, Japanese cartoon figures like Dolaamon, a robot cat from the future, made animation characters into idols all over Asia, kicking off a new marketing trend. Marketers searching for a new border-crossing visual language constantly looked to cartoon idols as product endorsers. Animated figures are more trendy and charming than real-life celebrities and they are affordable, with no strings attached. Unconstrained by the laws of gravity, they zoom in and out of the imaginative space with absolute flexibility. Cartoons are an ideal medium for a corporation that thrives on adventure metaphors. The Haier brothers in the series—a dark-haired boy and his light-haired counterpart in their Speedos—symbolize friendship between Haier and its German investor, Liebherr. The print corporate logo also showcases the two kids cuddling together, one eating an ice cream cone (alluding to Haier's core business of making refrigerators) and the other giving a thumbs-up sign. Together the cute duo plays out Zhang Ruimin's bold vision of globalization in animation format. An indigenous cartoon culture was in demand in China; Haier saw the opportunity and added another chapter to its legendary corporate culture.

The cartoon series is a fable for universal love and the power of positive thinking. As symbols of intelligence, bravery, and compassion, the two boys demonstrate the utopia of "East meets West and the Rest." Genuine multiculturalism requires a lot of long-distance traveling. Appropriately, the brothers and their traveling companions have a wanderlust just like the company they serve as a logo for. Their fervent quests for knowledge send them out to the sea, through the sky, and into outer space. Starting from the Pacific, they travel to the North Pole, fly over the Mediterranean, drift

The Haier Brothers. The Haier Group.

through the Persian Gulf, follow the Silk Road, and move on and on tirelessly. Together they travel across five continents, four oceans, and fifty-six countries, survive 238 ordeals, and cover roughly 120,000 miles ("Haier xiongdi" 2001). From Egypt to the South Pole, hardship and calamities are conquered through nonviolent means. What is remarkable about the Haier brothers is their phenomenal capacity for altruism, a quality inherent in the moral character of Haier that Zhang Ruimin captured in his metaphor of "Haier as ocean." "Haier is like an ocean . . . What is most spectacular about the ocean is its altruistic giving year after year in silence. Its selflessness is in full exposure . . . Let us burst open all the barriers standing in our way and roll forward like the waves" (Zhang Ruimin 2003, 36).

An animated promethean vision like this coming from an appliance maker is impressive enough, not to mention that the Haier Brothers cartoons were one of the earliest specimens of the long-form content in advertising. The series goes back to 1993, a decade ahead of postmodern advertising's emphasis on branded entertainment in drama format. In the West, branded content is known as the antithesis of the thirty-second commercial and is often associated with product placement, as in Coke's sponsorship of *American Idol*. "The Haier Brothers," however, departs from the conventions of contemporary branded entertainment. Not only were celebrity stars and directors not hired (just think of Madonna and Ang Lee in the BMW short films), but no Haier products were placed in the cartoon.[13] The two cute brothers are Haier's ambassadors for globalization. Together they deliver an expansive, friendly, and, above all, utopian view of the world. Some might question whether the series is worth Haier's investment of 15 percent of its advertising budget.[14] It humanized the appliance brand and generated tremendous goodwill even among nonusers. Can we put a price tag on the tale-telling appeal of a brand? It is worth a king's ransom.

Back in 2001 there was much fanfare over Haier's contract with

American TV marketers to bring the cartoon series to the United States (Deng 2001). The deal may have fallen through, since no up-to-date information seems to be available. American children may find the series too tame and its animation too static. But such a reaction may not be a real loss for Haier. The last thing Zhang Ruimin should do in the United States is to replicate his old strategy of emphasizing the corporate brand and corporate image—what the cartoon was made for—at the expense of product branding. We are back to the debate raised at the beginning of this chapter: is the Asian preference for corporate name branding responsible for the dearth of global Asian brands? Should profit-driven Asian companies shift gears and invest more in product branding as Shelly Lazarus had suggested?

"Corporate branding"—building equity in a corporation's name and identity—is crucial to doing business in China, where consumers' emphasis on safe consumption draws them to colossal, highly visible corporate brands, as Chapter 3 showed. Not surprisingly, China's Big Two subscribe to a marketing approach that prioritizes corporate management over brand management and corporate ideology over product image branding. Foreign manufacturers entering the China market will need to follow suit to win the trust of Chinese consumers.

Meanwhile, judging from the inroads Haier and Lenovo have already made overseas, we see that globalization flows in both directions. Chinese superbrands have started localizing themselves in Europe and America in much the same way that McDonald's and Procter & Gamble have indigenized themselves in developing countries. As the momentum of strategic localization picks up, "hegemony" may no longer be equated with U.S.-based multinationals alone. The Haier Way may mutate as it develops different localized Haier cultures around the globe. In fact, Haier is facing the same problem that McDonald's encountered in China ten years ago: how to localize in the target market. It is difficult to tell how fast these enterprises that once cashed in on the value of collectivism at home will adapt to cultural climates oriented toward competition, capitalist style. Will Zhang Ruimin and Liu Chuanzhi's penchant for collectivism (à la Sun Tzu) get in the way of their appreciation of the jungle law practiced in "The Apprentice"?

It is still too early for us to answer the question. But we can be certain that the simple equation between product branding and the "Western paradigm" may not hold much longer. Westbound Chinese corporations like Haier and Lenovo have no other choice but to master the art of product branding to survive in overseas markets. But the changing scenario may not tilt the balance and lead to the waning of the corporate-centric paradigm characteristic of Asia in general. I argue that the Internet is paving the way for a renewed interest among American entrepreneurs in corporate or master brand marketing. A convergence of business thinking is taking place. "Which paradigm will prevail?" is a question that is less and less relevant to the spirit of the synergetic twenty-first century.

Many U.S. brands, as we have seen, do not carry the name of their companies. These companies have a diverse brand portfolio of subbrands that cater to multiple consumer segments simultaneously. This is especially true for fragrance and clothing name brands, which need different subbrands to reach different retail channels. L'Oréal has spun out Lancôme for upscale retailers and department stores, Maybelline for drug/discount stores, and Redken for beauty salons. Each subbrand may also dominate a particular niche segment and a different functional category, as in the case of Toyota's Camry and Lexus, or P&G's multiple offerings such as Pert Plus, Pantene, and Head & Shoulders. The multiple retail channel and multiple category approach necessitate the "house of (sub)brands" architecture that contains independent stand-alone brands. Prior to the arrival of the Internet, consumers had little knowledge of the connections between a company and its various subbrands. If problems arose with one subbrand, a company could easily phase it out with no adverse consequence to the equity of the master brand and the other subbrands.

But digital media have changed the power equation between consumers and manufacturers. They provide smart, curious consumers a powerful tool to unveil a manufacturer's identity and render its brand portfolio transparent. Once consumers begin to associate subbrands with each other, one brand's problem will affect the reputation of another. When that happens, companies run the risk of losing some of their corporate brand equity. We begin to see more and more examples like that of Ford, which has returned to corporate image campaigns to refurbish its ailing name. The Ford ads aired in October 2005—two TV spots titled "Innovation" and "Compass"—featured chairman and CEO Bill Ford in a showroom with engineers talking about product innovation and safety. The commercials also bundle the Ford name with the company's Volvo brand, which has a known strength in safety standards. Developed by two agencies owned by the world communications giant WPP, Penn Schoen & Berland and Ogilvy & Mather-Detroit, the ads marked Ford Motor's first major corporate advertising since 2001 (Thomas 2005).[15] Corporate branding is coming back to the States.

Not everybody considers it a winning strategy. "What doesn't work for Ford are ads that sell the brand without the real product. That's old-fashioned advertising that has less and less credibility," says one analyst (Nussbaum 2005). But that perspective misses the point. The newer ads raised awareness of the corporate brand by confronting "the problem that Ford has, which is being pretty stodgy as a company" (Howard 2006). As an additional benefit from the campaign, attaching Volvo's safety appeal to the brand image of Ford allows the company to leverage the brand equity of a stellar subbrand. "This is an interesting strategy, since the company is essentially hedging itself by trying to build value in Ford; in the future, they can use the Ford name to help any of their other brands. If they are successful in turning around the brand, Ford can then go out and use its name to help their struggling subbrands such as Lincoln and Mercury" (Khalfan 2006). I quote Jameel Khalfan, a former student of mine at the Sloan School of MIT, because he first brought to my attention the compelling argument that corporate branding has a future in the United States. Like many other students, Jameel lives on the new media and carries the conviction that the Internet is changing corporate practices noiselessly.

Before long, "the houses of brands" will no longer be able to protect their anonymity. They will soon have to concentrate on strengthening corporate brand equity to minimize the impact of consumers' new desktop research habits. Coca-Cola, I am told, ran an ad featuring its multiple offerings, such as Powerade sports drinks, Dasani bottled water, and Minute Maid orange juice. P&G has also taken steps to associate its flagship brands with one another in order to boost brand awareness both in the United States and, not unexpectedly, in China. What do all these examples tell us about the old dichotomy between product branding and corporate branding, and our habit of attributing the former to a characteristically "Western practice" and the latter to "Asian and Chinese" idiosyncrasy? Single-minded either/or thinking will continue to be challenged by Generation Y consumers like Jameel and his media-savvy pals. In the brave new world of convergence, paradigms travel both ways. Shelly Lazarus's advice for Chinese entrepreneurs is only partially valid.

CHAPTER 5

Bourgeois Bohemians in China?

If the American economist Thorstein Veblen lived in urban China today, he would be impressed. Nowhere else would he find such a large population so eager to practice his theory of "pecuniary emulation" (Veblen 1994), what writer Timothy Sexton has called a kind of "keeping up with the Joneses." The phenomenon begins with those sitting at the top of the social pyramid, whose consumption standards become emulated by those in lower tiers of society.[1] You are what you consume. That is, consumption is built on a tiered logic: for those situated lower on the hierarchy, there is no faster way of acquiring social prestige than copying the lifestyle of those higher up. Louis Vuitton, Prada, BMW, and Fendi, for example, all regard China as the center of turbo-growth, because their near-term investment will pay off "in secondary cities like Dalian, Shenyang, and Chengdu, where second-tier status as a city translates into *first-tier* desires by the residents" (Stalnaker 2002, 175). In August 2002, when I finished my internship at Ogilvy, "third-tier" cities (southern county towns) had already entered the marketing lingo, suggesting that average residents in affluent county townships would soon be catching up with second-tier desires. A game of musical chairs was set in motion, with lower tiers busy making an urban imaginary that is always and already a tier higher. All this, I propose, is the social logic of consumption Veblen elucidates so well in *The Theory of the Leisure Class*.

Market segmentation fuels the engine of emulative spending. In Chapters 1 and 2, I examine the material processes of advertising and marketing *in situ* by focusing on the elaborate "assembly line" of commercial branding and the tiered construction of meaning in specific advertising campaigns. Now we turn to the upstream market and its niche segments to explore the mutually constitutive relationship between marketing and style cultures. We will see how marketing research serves to bridge the two subjects of study, popular culture and consumer culture, a link often ignored in academic scholarship.

Through a discussion of bobos ("bourgeois bohemians") and the phenomenon of other "neo-tribes" in China, I will examine the logic of Chinese market segmentation. Bobos can also be seen both as a pop cultural and as a marketing phenomenon, and their existence points to the need to give marketing a place in transnational pop culture studies. I look at the contemporary mutation of the anthropological concept "tribe" into a new marketing term, *zu* or *zuqun* ("neo-tribe"), and the challenges this new term poses to the old notion of "subculture." An underlying theme of this chapter is that delimiting and naming the target segment for a product is what makes emulation possible. The consumer identifies with a given sociocultural segment, or "tribe." And as we shall see, the "tribal" logic of consumerism found at the higher end of the consumption ladder is an imaginary space crisscrossed with various funny terms that have evolved from the concept of the "neo-tribes." An investigation of Chinese bobos and *xin xinrenlei* (the neo-neo-tribe) introduces the real and the imaginary benchmarks for membership in each tribe.

Indeed, if consumption is conceived as an upward spiral movement that progresses tier by tier, the upper echelons hardly sit idle on top of the social ladder, waiting for those below them to catch up. An upscale marketer's job is largely confined to splitting those who are further up in the social hierarchy into tinier and tinier market segments. These niche segments set high-end consumers apart not only from the masses but also from one another.

At first glance, the myriad "tribal" discourses now circulating in urban China seem nothing more than novel marketing strategies targeted at the newly affluent. But the question of whether marketers can create wants, as the 1960s mass culture critique would have us believe, has no easy answer. Cultural producers today do not have the faith of their early 1900s counterparts in their power to control the minds of consumers (Ohmann 1996). As a society grows more affluent, successful marketing increasingly depends on unearthing consumers' own preferences and desires and then selling them back to target segments, as we saw in Chapter 2. Tribal logic, for example, would have no purchase if it had not tapped into the existing anxieties of the socially privileged. They are anxious not to be caught by the mass consumers who are busy emulating them. Thus those further up the social ladder—neo-tribes like the bobos—play the game of differentiation as fervently as those down below. In consumerism, differentiation and emulation are two sides of the same coin. China is no exception.

BOBO FEVER

"These are highly educated folk who have one foot in the bohemian world of creativity and another foot in the bourgeois realm of ambition and worldly success. The members of the new information age elite are bourgeois bohemians. Or, to take the first two letters of each word, they are Bobos" (Brooks 2000, 10–11). David Brooks's *Bobos in Paradise: The New Upper Class and How They Got There* is a comic work of sociology on the rise and cultural impact of America's new elite in the age of the knowledge economy. The facetious celebration of weddings of the 1960s counterculture and the 1980s overachievement craze triggered bobo fetishism in China. In September 2002, the Chinese translation of the book arrived in major cities and became an instant best-seller. *Xiaozi,* "petty bourgeoisie," a term trendy only a year before, became passé overnight. "Everybody else is already a bobo, what are we waiting for?!"—blasted a popular declaration. As 2002 drew to an end, the bobo became a Chinese poster child without a hint of irony.

A Chinese word, *bobo,* was coined to sound almost exactly like the English word. But many others resort to an indigenized version of the original—*bubo*—a combination of the first syllable of the two Chinese words, *buerqiaoya* (bourgeois) and *boximiya* (bohemia). The term advanced to the number three spot on the list of top ten Internet words in China in 2002, trailing "keep pace with the times," and the "Three Represents" (Mooney 2003).[2]

A small café near Southeast University in Nanjing named itself Bobo Café, a perfect example of a second-tier city teeming with first-tier desires. There was at least one Web site, *Xici hutong* (www.xici.net), that at one time posted a Bobo page and provided advice on how bobos were supposed to act, where to find them, and how to become one. After answering some multiple choice questions (for example, "Are you satisfied with your life?" and "What do you think of Italian fashion?"), Web surfers could assess their bobo potential ("Zhongguo Bubo zu" 2002). In the capital, businessman Zhang Luzi opened the DIY@bobo Bar to provide a home for this new social group. There was also a short-lived Bobos Club in Beijing that sponsored lectures on *fengshui* and other topics related to "spirituality." The list goes on and on. A bobo marketing craze appeared in first-, second-, and third-tier cities, and an entertaining debate unfolded in the press and on the Internet.

Advertising copy cashed in on bobo fever:

ALCATEL OT715 "Have you ever heard of 'Bobos'? . . . a social group in search of freedom, challenges, and spiritual fulfillment. They are keen on creating the genuine meaning of life for themselves. A bobo demands the best from life. They are seeking products of exquisite taste and quality, but more important, products that display character and the essence of a free spirit. Bobos have been looking everywhere for an ideal cell phone. Not until now have they found the new Alcatel OT715 . . . It combines the 1970s retro style of elegance and the cool attitude of the twenty-first century" ("Bubo zu de xin chonger" 2002).

LEGEND SOLEI NOTEBOOK E100 "A well-cultivated person will not stoop to compete to be number one among average Joes and Janes. A bobo is well cultivated. His notebook displays a style of simplicity. Bobos love country folks, a weathered fisherman, a craftsman in the remote countryside, or a short and plump artist who dances simple folk dances and sings simple folk songs. To bobos, these simple-minded country people look serene and peaceful. Although they are poor, they live a rich life . . . Corresponding to the fundamental spirit of the bobos is the simple but smart looking E100. It is clothed in simple dark blue, but its keyboard and LCD screen shine in fashionable silver. A contradictory color scheme like this matched with a daring design delivers a jazzy sense of romance for bobos" ("Yidong Bobo zu" 2003).

GREAT WALL "PROSPERITY NO. 2," SHENZHEN Prosperity No. 2 was a new "theme" apartment complex built by one of Shenzhen's oldest real estate corporations, the Great Wall. A major promotion was launched in spring 2003 targeting neo-tribes as diverse as the Visual Tribe, the petty bourgeoisie, the bobos, and the IFs (International Freemen/women).[3] In lieu of a plain real estate brochure, Great Wall printed a cultural manifesto in a "white paper" that introduced various apartment blueprints, custom-designed for each tribe. Interwoven into some thirty different architectural layouts were semi-literary attempts like the following:

If life has so much fun, why do I care for anything else?
Life is like a rendezvous for a matinee. Whether it is tragic or
    comic, it is worth waiting for.
If a space is too small, one will give it an opinion discount;

If it is too big, it's hardly ideal.
Only a space that displays wisdom will hit the perfect 10.
  ("Changcheng dichan" 2003)

Target consumers are supposed to grasp the synergy between "culture" and "architecture" and come to appreciate the "culture" (whatever that means) that underlies the deep infrastructure behind Prosperity No. 2.

BOBO INTERNATIONAL, CHANGSHA, HUNAN PROVINCE "In Bobo International, you get a perfect view of the mountains and hear the sound of the Xiang River gently stroking the banks. If you want to snack, turn on the electric burners. In a few minutes, you will be enjoying a drink with your beloved under the moonlight—over a few simple appetizers" ("Bobo guoji" 2003).

From category to category, from copy to copy, the word "bobo" and the accompanying descriptions deliver a single message: premium value. If you spot what looks like tongue-in-cheek humor in this advertising copy, be assured that irony has no place in marketing plans in China. Chinese boboism has retained none of Brooks's satirical edge. What reads like a parody to nontarget segments (say, cultural theorists) actually touches a deep chord in China's fad enthusiasts, who are searching for a lifestyle breakthrough. Many such bobo campaigns, including the next one we will look at, have gone way over the top.

THE GUANGZHOU PROJECT: SEARCHING ONLINE FOR BOBO PROSPECTS The corporation in question, let us call it S Real Estate, is located in Guangzhou. It singled out bobos as its target clients. To pare down advertising expenditures, the company relied on the Internet for promotions and devised an elaborate communications plan. To identify the target segment and attract its consumers' attention, several online activities were launched simultaneously: a search for bobos in Guangzhou; a contest for the ten coolest bobos in Guangzhou; a Web editorial called "Bobos and Their Poetic Lives"; an online serialized story penned by a fictional bobo living in the S apartment complex—"Love Soars on the Wings of Poetry: The Confessions of a Bobo"; a Flash animation site advertising the "happy lifestyle of bobos" and the brand essence of the S apartments (happy life = freedom + wealth + mindfulness).

The maximum impact of this communications plan can be gauged from the questionnaires for the online bobo search:

1. Do you look for something cool about a refrigerator rather than its cooling function when you shop for one?
2. Are you one of those who often wear hiking boots and ski glasses or some unconventional gear to work?
3. Would you be willing to give up your job at the drop of a hat and go to a far-off place for a month?
4. Do you feel that being single for the rest of your life is no big deal?
5. You are an atheist. But if one day you fall in love, will you feel that it's God's will?
6. Is it unbearable if your living space does not give you a poetic sense of life?
7. Is it torture to live in a place that looks just like any other place without a personality? (Lin Jingxin 2003)

These ten queries are accompanied by follow-up instructions. If you answer "yes" to *any* of the questions above, contact the S Corporation immediately. You are a prospective bobo qualified for incentive awards comprising a surprise gift and a complimentary day trip to the S apartment complex. And mind you, if you are interested in running for the ten coolest bobos championship in Guangzhou (activity No. 2), all you have to do is to enter a prose-writing contest by submitting the most "poetic" and "personality building" experience you have ever had. A selection panel will pass the verdict. The ten winners will be given the title of *Bubo jueshi*, Sir Bobo!

THE DEBATE: BURSTING THE BUBOS' BUBBLE

Not every one, of course, bought in to the trend or fell for the overblown marketing ploys. After the initial fanfare waned a little, Beijing's authoritative lifestyle magazine, *Life Weekly*, was quick to point out that there were very few bobos in China. But others, like Ye Ying, the editor of "Lifestyle" at the *Economic Observer*, were reluctant to underestimate the appeal of the bobo lifestyle to urban youth (Ye Ying 2003). It was most likely, she predicted, that the fever would linger and, I would add, especially in places where one finds a critical mass of the nouveau riche. This observation may not be far off the mark, particularly in the changing social climate of the post–Jiang Zeming era. The original bobo spirit—an affluent class opposed to soulless materialism—had touched a raw nerve in China's rising social elite.

The social value of affluence in a socialist country is never stable. In 2003 and 2004, being labeled "rich" brought mixed blessings. Closer social scrutiny was only one small inconvenience the rich had to endure. More onerous was the societal guilt trip that took away the pleasure of being an upstart. A new generation of Party leaders was touting the politically correct slogan "social justice" *(shehui gongzheng)*, restraining, at least in theory, the ethos of mindless materialism. Media attention was lavished on the "*san nong* problems (peasants [*nongmin*], villages [*nongcun*], and agriculture [*nongye*])."[4] President Hu Jintao moved "poverty alleviation" and "social conscience" to the top of the national agenda. Premier Wen Jiabao made headlines in the early months of 2004 with a personal campaign to help rural migrants collect overdue wages. One result was a backlash against the new rich and their unconscionable behavior. Paul Mooney's report in *Newsweek* quotes a Beijing writer saying, "People look down on the nouveau riche, and that's why [the] Chinese are keen to add the bohemian title" (Mooney 2003). Numerous instances emphasizing the social costs of materialism gone berserk can be cited. In 2003 a second-degree murder trial involving a rich woman running over a peasant in her BMW stirred up media furor. In 2004 the murder of four dorm mates at Yunnan University by a poor peasant student, Ma Jiajue, triggered another round of social criticism. This time, the materialistic society at large was blamed for its indifference to a tortured student trapped in extreme poverty and driven to insanity. Although "wealth" will never become a stigma for the rich in the same way that "poverty" is for the poor, the Chinese court of public opinion has declared the rich "guilty," signaling a profound shift in the collective emotional identification away from the nouveau riche toward both the old and the new poor. The bobo phenomenon thus provided China's new elite with an opportunity to reconcile materialism with spirituality, and elite status with egalitarian ideals.

The fever, interestingly, struck a chord with social critics as well. It rejuvenated a perennial question: just how large is China's "bourgeoisie"?[5] China has never had any bohemians, but should the bourgeois side of the equation be taken for granted? *Life Weekly* posed these questions, and its answer was "perhaps China does not have real bobos, because the Chinese 'middle class' has not been fully formed" (Miao, Lu, et al. 2002). The editors went on in a satirical vein, saying that *bu* (bourgeois) was what the Chinese were really after, and identification as *bo* (bohemian) was a dispensable sham. The advertising of S Real Estate validates such a view. Perhaps the bobo concept traveled so well in China precisely because it pinpointed the double lack of both bohemians and bourgeoisie. Rule No. 1 in the Great Book of Consumption: naming a lack is the fastest way to guarantee its quick rise in demand.

IN SEARCH OF THE "MIDDLE CLASS"

The bourgeois question predictably elevated discussion of bobos to a level that only serious sociological researchers could participate in. But the transition of a lifestyle topic into a sociological one did not occur. Nor was the challenge posed by *Life Weekly* answered by cultural critics. By spring 2004, not many follow-up discussions on the controversy had reached the public arena. One reason could be that the public's attention was diverted from the question of the "middle class" to the new benchmark for prosperity, namely, *xiaokang* (the "small well-being," a cut below the "middle class").[6] Although south China has a bigger stake in promoting the discourse of the "middle class," the north and the rest of the country have been drawn to *xiaokang* as a policy concept that is deemed more relevant for its less affluent population.

The middle-class question, however, demands attention not least because it too often gets lost in the ideological shuffle. As shown above, Chinese boboism resided precisely in the promoters' belief in the separability of class from taste and was, in the end, a thriving social imaginary that did not correspond to the bobos as a real social class. In contrast, David Brooks's American boboism is unmistakably a caste phenomenon and fundamentally a class formation. Is the term "Chinese bobo" a misnomer? Statistics regarding the Chinese middle class provided much fuel to those critics who debunked the bobo phenomenon. They held that the future of Chinese boboism hinged on whether there was a bourgeois base to begin with. Seen in that perspective, the bourgeois equation is essential for boboism to take root in China and is worthy of critical attention.

A research report by Li Chunlin appeared in *The 2004 Analysis and Forecast on China's Social Development,* providing statistics on the Chinese middle class (Li Chunlin 2004). Four criteria are outlined in modern sociology to assess whether one belongs to the middle class: professional status; income; patterns of lifestyle consumption; and subjective cognition. The data for the Chinese study were collected by a research team at the Chinese Academy of the Social Sciences engaged in a project called "Structural Changes of Contemporary Chinese Society." Between November and December 2001, the team collected data from people between sixteen and seventy years old living in twelve provinces, special municipalities, and seventy-three districts and counties. At the end of the research period, they had obtained 6,193 valid samples.

First, 15.90 percent of those surveyed were categorized as middle class by profession *(zhiye zhongchan)*. Five professions—Party and political officials, the business managerial class, private entrepreneurs, technical skilled labor, and office workers—were labeled "white collar" professions.

Second, 24.6 percent were deemed middle class by income. There was no standard mean for all the regions surveyed. Income gaps between different places were huge, with the monthly income of townspeople exceeding the villagers' by 2.5 times; the average income in areas of developed regions exceeding that of underdeveloped regions by 2.5 times; and the income of townspeople living in developed areas exceeding the peasants living in underdeveloped villages by 5.4 times. If the *national* income index were used as the standard for social classification, there would be some odd results: those living in the metropolis whose economic condition was inferior might be categorized as "higher income earners," and those who were relatively wealthy in underdeveloped regions might be termed "low income earners." It is therefore necessary to recalculate the "mean" on a regional rather than on a national basis. The surveyed areas were divided into six regions: comparatively well developed towns, cities, and districts; developing cities, towns, and districts; underdeveloped cities, towns, and districts; well-developed villages and rural areas; developing villages and rural areas; and underdeveloped rural areas. The research team derived the average individual monthly income region by region. Those whose income rose above the mean in each region were counted as the "middle class"; those below the mean were not.

Third, 35 percent of those surveyed were middle class by standards of consumption and lifestyle. Like the income index, a universal standard for the "middle-class lifestyle" was hard to define, let alone to achieve, in a country as culturally diverse as China. Li Chunlin and her research team argued that with some exceptions seen among middle-aged and young people in metropolises, "so-called middle-class culture has not appeared in China." Since a specific standard of "cultural" consumption was absent, the researchers developed an elaborate point system for measuring each household's capacity for consuming medium-range and luxury goods. "Middle-class lifestyle goods" were divided into four categories: necessity electric appliances (such as a color television, refrigerator, and washing machine); medium-level consumer goods (such as a telephone, mobile phone, CD player, microwave, and an air conditioner); luxury goods (such as a computer, camcorder, piano, and motorcycle); and ownership of an automobile. Each of the items listed in the first two categories was worth 1 point; in the third category 4 points; while households that owned a car received 12 points. The "consumer middle class" *(xiaofei zhongchan)* resulted from the calibration and comparison of the total scores earned by each household. The 35 percent figure, however, failed to acknowledge the wide gaps in consumption patterns between urban and rural China (50.2 percent and 25.1 percent, respectively) and between generations (young people between the ages of twenty-one and thirty scored 41.8 percent and the older generations, 24.1 percent).

The last category, "subjective cognition," yielded the largest percentage. As many as 46.8 percent of those surveyed considered themselves to be members of the "middle class." Gender difference was minimal in this category. Schooling mattered little. Of those who had not gone beyond primary school, 40.8 percent identified themselves with the middle class, compared with 72.9 percent of college graduates. Approximately 31.1 percent of those who had never gone to school at all considered themselves "middle class" as well.

These are fairly reliable statistics. However, if the four criteria are combined to arrive at a comprehensive index for the middle class, then the proportion of people in the Chinese bourgeoisie drops to 4.1–6.0 percent. Even in big cities, the percentage is as low as 8.7–12 percent. That is, the percentage of Chinese who are white-collar workers, whose income falls into the medium range, whose consumption level reaches the median, and who at the same time identify themselves as middle class is only a little above ground level.

Official statistics, leaked in January 2005 from the National Bureau of Statistics, used different criteria from those of the CASS team in 2001, and the findings for the "middle class" stirred up some controversy. The bureau set the annual household income for a middle-class family of three members at a minimum of 60,000 yuan (approximately $7,300) (Yu Jinjin 2005). By that criterion, there were only 5.04 percent middle-class families in urban China as of 2005, nearly five times lower than the 24.6 percent figure for "middle class by income" published in the CASS 2001 report. Although the bureau projected that by 2020 the figure could jump to 45 percent, the huge discrepancies between the CASS figure and the bureau's became an immediate topic of contention. Optimists like Lu Xueyi, the former head of the Institute of Sociology at the CASS, argued for a more relaxed criterion (Zhang Liming 2005). For Lu, the key benchmark for the Chinese bourgeoisie was not income but profession. He observed, as an example, that "a white-collar worker making a monthly income of 3,000 yuan is middle class, but *not* a taxi cab driver making 5,000 yuan" (ibid.).

The gloomy picture from the bureau also spurred some interesting castle-in-the-sky exercises. A survey conducted by Yahoo

China, which involved as many as 110,000 Netizens, drew a jovial composite portrait for the most affluent among the Chinese middle class—about a third of the class. What was their lifestyle like? They drove Peugeot 307s or Audi A42.4s, earned a monthly income of $1,200, lived in fancy high-rises like "Toronto Forest," used Sony notebooks at work, enjoyed the restaurants in five-star hotels, and vacationed in Paris and East Africa (Yahoo 2005). Yahoo's optimistic findings, however, actually pertained only to the "gold collar" residents of China, not the white collar.

CLASS OR TASTE: A LEAP OF FAITH

Instead of asking "Where are the Chinese bobos?" we may now ponder, "Where are the Chinese bourgeoisie?" China has a long way to go before a real caste with an economic power equal to that of the American yuppies-turned-hippies (obsessed with one-downsmanship) will emerge. Yet meanwhile, the bobos as an urban imaginary and marketing in the name of the bobo seems to have paid off. This phenomenon is a Chinese paradox. Nothing seems to stop the Chinese from indulging themselves in a social imaginary that fans their dream of being part of the global, "cosmopolitan" culture.

Bobo fever was indicative of a symptom that I will call "a leap of faith in separating taste from 'class'" (as in *jieji*, "[social] class"). Chinese cultural brokers sold boboism in China as a lifestyle fad rather than as a product of a class culture. Did it really matter if China did not have bobos so long as upscale consumers wore the bobo lifestyle on their sleeves? Marketers couldn't care less. But it is fascinating that China's social commentators were oblivious to the real meat in *Bobos in Paradise*—the historical rise of the bobo in America as a class of its own. Although David Brooks argues that the bobos' meritocratic culture thrives on blurring class distinctions and that Marx's theory of "class conflict" is invalid, a close reading of his book provides a detailed sociological profile of a new American upper-middle, establishment class, which, in his words, defines the "parameters of respectable opinion and taste" (Brooks 2000, 41–46).

Chinese bobo fever can be seen as a social conversation, or discourse, that decoupled the bobo "class" from bobo "taste." Journalists able to make that mental leap contributed a variety of articles on "lifestyle choices" by Chinese women who yearned for the social status that foreign upscale brands can bring. They might save for months, for example, to buy a whole set of Chanel cosmetics even though they would never be able to afford a Chanel evening dress (Ye Ying 2003). "A person's taste in life and her 'style' determines her social status. And taste can only be expressed through one's daily lifestyle," said Shi Tao in his preface to the Chinese edition of Paul Fussell's book *Class* (Shi 1998a,b; Fussell 1992).[7] Perhaps taste has become the fastest shortcut to higher social class and social status. Pierre Bourdieu said that "taste" is a class-determined construct (Bourdieu 1984), but Shi Tao and like-minded Chinese bobo promoters have declared the opposite—one doesn't have to be an aristocrat to act aristocratic—bypassing the sarcasm underscoring the writings of Fussell and Brooks altogether.[8]

The popularity of *Bobos in Paradise* and other similar books about lifestyle choices points to a cultural symptom prevalent in twenty-first-century China. Urban China has been overcrowded with social trends that usually emerge in the West in post-affluent societies where luxury is less about owning and displaying one's wealth and more about simply being and enjoying. Less becomes more. But when will Chinese niche consumers be able to appreciate "one-downsmanship" when they have not had enough practice with "one-upsmanship"[9]—"face" consumption *(mianzi xiaofei)?* Questions like taste, the "freedom" of lifestyle choices, and one-downsmanship have come to plague a country where only 4.1 to 6 percent were deemed middle class in 2004. Before wealth accumulates and trickles down to the masses, anxieties of abundance have already hit taste fanatics and the would-be bobos. Gaps between the post-affluent urban imaginary and social reality have continued to widen as the duels between cool hunters and social critics linger on. The spectacle may be fascinating for Western trend spotters, but for the majority of Chinese for whom social classes conflict rather than blur, the urban imaginary closing in on them seems to be spinning out of control. But when is China *not* overheated about the catch-up game? Meanwhile, bobo fever turned out to be a passing trend, overtaken by other, flashier neo-tribes.

BOBOS AS A MARKET SEGMENT

In many regards, urban China is an endless fashion race trying to beat escalating turnovers. The protagonists come and go. But the marketers stay. Bobo fever was not only a popular cultural phenomenon but a marketing phenomenon, and some of the shrewdest observations about the fever were made by marketers. In April 2003, a group of eighteen of them gathered at Beijing's Postmodern Tower for a brainstorming session sponsored by *Successful Marketing,* a trade magazine. Their agenda: What kind of "marketing opportunities" *(shangji)* will bobo fever offer to Chinese marketers?

There can be no better venue for a marketing symposium on the bobos than the Postmodern Tower in Beijing. Located about a quarter-mile from the real estate hot ticket SOHO Tower, *Houxiandai-cheng* (literally, "post-modern-city") is built on the new urban mythology about a "backstreet" lifestyle.[10] Everything that people already own or have made a pledge to is relegated to what is called their "front street" lifestyle—out of date, homogeneous, constrained, and insulated. "Backstreets" promise not so much pleasure as anti-mainstream living at odds with banal middle-class taste. The Postmodern Tower's target segment is, appropriately, the bobos. Inside the Tower, everything is pared down to Rule No. 4 in the Bobo Code of Financial Correctness: "You can never have too much texture" (Brooks 2000, 92). Craggy brick walls without decorations, bare unfinished wooden floors pieced together with irregularly shaped planks—the Tower exudes the bobo's spirit of calculated casualness.

The Bobo Symposium

Several questions were put on the table at the bobo symposium. How many bobos really are there in China? Can a minority group like that support a product line? The crowd was divided. But regardless of the issue of the number of bobos, the marketers were in strong agreement about the necessity of cashing in on the trend. You don't have to believe in the leap of faith to take advantage of it. The following is a sample of comments from symposium participants:

"The bobos are all pursuing distinct personalities. They have purchasing power."

"Bobos have dreams. So they are easy targets. They can be easily moved by 'concepts' and 'storytelling.'"

"Sell them the bobo spirit."

"Chinese society will witness an increasingly large affluent class. Although we will probably never be sure whether X or Y is a bobo, we will surely see them display some bobo characteristics such as a preoccupation with creativity and spiritual values."

"Our marketing opportunities will rest on whether we can provide products with added values that transcend materialism. For instance, sell ambience and service at entertainment venues such as bars and restaurants."

"You can detect a new social tendency now. Business behavior must be wedded to cultural concepts. Only when competition takes place at a certain cultural height and at a spiritual level can you make your products stand out."

"Bobos value personal experiences. They like to be adventurers. But they are not iconoclasts. Nor are they opposed to being trendy. Their main value coincides with the core values of society. That's the fundamental reason why they are so successful . . . We should not associate boboism with a fad or with an act of rebellion. We should not look upon them as mere upstarts either. They don't ever rebel." ("Bubo zu shangji" 2003)

DINKs and Other Neo-Tribes

The last quotation is especially revealing in its no-nonsense assessment of the bobo unconscious, in China at least. But understanding who the bobos are is one thing, and motivating them to spend is another. They need a reason to buy. Marketers at the symposium argued that the answer to the million-dollar questions of what bobo desires are like and how they can be captured was simple. Give them "ID [identifying]" labels. Sell them distinct personalities. The symposium named such a desire the burning need of Generations X and Y to broadcast to the world, "Who I am!" (Liu, Wang, et al. 2003).

The bobos were not the only group that craved self-validation. Barely had one tribe entered the spotlight than a series of others emerged to upstage it, all coming at stunningly short intervals. Other consumer societies have neo-tribes as well. But the frenzy in China tops them all, leading to headlines like "The IFs Have Come. Don't You Ever Mention Bobos Anymore!" Meanwhile the International Freemen are fighting for the limelight with another tribe dubbed the DINKs—Double Income No Kids.[11] The tiny stage is getting very crowded.

Stratification of the population into smaller and smaller customer segments has indeed come into vogue since the new century began. Chinese marketers claim that they are merely following the social desire for such differentiation. And in the case of bobo fever, they could hardly catch up. Some symposium attendees were honest about the necessity of meticulous segmentation. Marketing follows the 20/80 principle: 80 percent of a society's purchasing power is concentrated in the top 20 percent of consumer elites. Ironically, high income earners have grown increasingly indifferent to consumption. Old demographic indexes like "age" and "income" are not strong identity markers for niche markets anymore. Premium consumers need catchy cultural identities to distinguish themselves from their fellow elites. Thus the marketing craze for fastidious positioning churns out one tribal label after another.

MICHEL MAFFESOLI AND THE TRIBAL PARADIGM

The Chinese may have gone to an extreme, but the fever for "neo-tribes" was a "foreign" phenomenon transported from Taiwan, Hong Kong, and Japan. Perhaps what is happening in China is only a hyperbolic version of consumer society in general. The connection between consumerism and the theory and reality of neo-tribes is our next topic.

French sociologist Michel Maffesoli has said that contemporary consumers live in "the time of the tribes," which has witnessed an explosion of style cultures. Tribes are organized around brand names and role-playing fantasies. Old categories such as core identity, subjectivity, autonomy, and even subculture have fallen short in accounting for new forms of "sociality." Maffesoli distinguishes the "social," defined in terms of the "rational association of individuals having a precise identity," from "sociality," the highly unstable space where a multiplicity of contingent tribal circles intersect and make meaning based on the whatever is happening at the time.

Maffesoli is both fascinated and repulsed by the chameleon instinct of the performing self that drives today's consumer culture. Sometimes he complains about the "conformism" of youth culture and reveals a nostalgia for the old concept of the "individual," which he sees as stable and unique: "What we are witnessing is the loss of the idea of the individual in favor of a much *less distinct* mass." "The dramatic authenticity of the social is answered by the tragic superficiality of sociality," says Maffesoli (1996, 76), betraying thinking that could be categorized as "conventional." But despite a small handful of slippages, Maffesoli maintains consistently, true to the Weberian spirit, that "identity is never, from the sociological point of view, anything but a simply floating and relative condition" (ibid., 65). He describes the cultural moment of neo-tribalism as a multitude of changing and fluid networks "confirmed on a daily basis" (ibid., 97).

There is a flip side to this phenomenon, as Maffesoli implies: the guarantee of group solidarity of the neo-tribes becomes dependent on, and as fragile as, their occasional gatherings (and dispersals). He thus raises new questions about solidarity: what happens to human fellowship in the new age of media convergence? In particular, how is "solidarity" registered, felt, and articulated differently when interactions occur in different media simultaneously? For all the Alices who wander into the wonderland of ever-increasing URL links while listening to their iPods and playing mobile games, finding their way "home" is the least fun option of all. The journey continues. Maffesoli's *The Time of the Tribes* teases out the technological aspects of the tribal paradigm that, as we shall see, lie at the heart of the emerging tribe of the day, *xin xinrenlei* (the neo-neo-tribe).

But Maffesoli provides only a theoretical skeleton, rather than real-life examples. Here we will examine the social mosaic of neo-tribes in motion. The instantaneous rise of the bobos and other tribes in China is highly instructive for broader inquiries into the tribal question at large.

A "Post-Subcultural" Era?

A discussion of Maffesoli would be incomplete without a mention of the impact that his theories have had on earlier paradigms of sociality, especially Dick Hebdige's concept of "subculture," which sees radical members of the British working-class youth culture (skinheads and beatniks, punk rockers and dancers) as challengers of aesthetic and social conventions not directly, but obliquely, through style.[12] One could say indeed that the tribal paradigm can only make sense if it is set off *against* the earlier paradigm of subculture. Hebdige's punk groups "posed the clearest threat to law and order" (Hebdige 1979, 110) by pledging group solidarity and total commitment to subversive activities against the sacred. Maffesoli's neo-tribes, in contrast, do not take part in the resistance to the power structure of the day. His specimens—today's teens— are trend seekers without showing an interest in declaring guerrilla warfare on the status quo. We may ask whether the theory of "subculture," which is predicated on a simple dichotomy between a monolithic mainstream culture and politically conscious resistant subcultures, is still valid in our knowledge-based information society where the old boundaries between "culture" and "economy," "activism" and "consumerism" can no longer be as clearly drawn as in Hebdige's time.[13]

Perhaps the most concentrated effort to reconceptualize Hebdige's old paradigm can be seen in the Vienna symposium "Post-Subcultural Studies" held in May 2001. A new field was said to be born, with a large contingent of European researchers of youth culture who share an overriding interest in examining dance and music style cultures. Most participants in the symposium agreed on the demise of the "subcultural heroism" of the 1970s and 1980s (Weinzierl and Muggleton 2003, 6–9). But the allure of alternative models such as Maffesoli's must be balanced by a caveat—he theorizes "politics" away too readily. If the "optimum strategy" of the neo-tribes is "to tap into a number of lifestyles, adopting whichever one best fits the situation to hand," their irreverent energy appears to be utterly purposeless (Clarke, Doel et al. 2003, 137). How to push the increasingly instantaneous tribal formations toward a redefined "activism" constitutes one of the central missions underlying the new critical literature that touts the arrival of the "post-subcultural" era.

The paradigmatic shift from subculture to neo-tribe can be seen in urban China as well. Anyone familiar with the clubbing and music scene in the Chinese metropolises is struck by the frantic tribalization of new taste cultures. Gone are the days of Cui Jian, the father of Chinese rock whose song "Nothing to My Name" became an anthem for Tiananmen student protestors. So is Chinese subculture with *angst*. Singers Jay Chou, Faye Wong, and Pu Shu, each a spokesperson for at least one major commodity product, are now the hottest pop icons. Rebellious postures are chic, but they have little to do with iconoclasm. China's young generations are courting a "safe cool," a partygoing esprit unattended by the kind of soul-searching sought by the proponents of the new European post-subcultural movement bent on repoliticizing youth cultures with a carnivalesque twist.

But one should not, of course, analyze what is emerging in China by taking a European model as a starting point. The temptation to make such a comparison is, however, difficult to resist precisely because cool marketing and global branding have given new impetus to the formation of the target segment called "global youth"—international urban youth in their late teens to early twenties. It is a transnational marketer's ultimate dream: enabled by digital technology and international marketing, a global youth culture seems to be converging from the Atlantic to the Pacific and Indian oceans. Yet an easy equation between the West and the rest as maintained by earnest advocates of cultural globalization is misleading. "Cool" music and "alternative" youth in China hardly signal the same thing as their counterparts in Euro-America—a subject I treat in the next chapter. The concept of "convergence," however, has real value when applied to the East Asian equation. Just as satellite stations like Star TV have initiated a process of programming integration at the regional level (J. Chan 1997), so are East Asian youth cultures now converging in a new tribal sensation—*xin xinrenlei.*

XIN XINRENLEI: THE EAST ASIAN CONNECTION

Maffesoli's theory is borne out in East Asia, where market segmentation in tribal terms has taken on a life of its own. Maffesoli's *tribus* has splintered into tiny subdivisions, each half a generation apart, in places like China, Taiwan, Hong Kong, and Japan. Not surprisingly, neo-tribes in China, such as the bobos, DINKs, and IFs, are now considered rather conservative in their taste, because as the established social elites, they are not as cool as their successors, the neo-neo-tribe *(xin xinrenlei)*—Asia's hottest market segment. Members of this emerging tribe are in their late teens and early twenties and cross gender divisions. They have a symbiotic existence with high-tech communication gadgets. Their threshold for irreverence is immeasurable. And with less money than the bobos, they are no easy prey for mainstream consumerism.

Maffesoli should be given credit for mentioning that "the feeling of tribal belonging can be reinforced by technological developments" (Maffesoli 1996, 139). But when he penned his theory of neo-tribalism in 1988, he hardly foresaw that technology itself could create a tribe of its own, complete with characteristics that even sound alien to the "neo-tribes." In China, the neo-neo-tribe is the first generation who grew up in the Internet chat rooms. Their counterparts in Japan are participants in a vibrant cell-phone youth culture that has just begun to sweep urban China.

It is not a coincidence that the Chinese term *xin xinrenlei* is a transliteration of the Japanese term *shin shinjinrui,* introduced to the mainland via Hong Kong and Taiwan. In Taiwan, the term is used almost synonymously with "Generations X and Y." In Japan, it refers to the post–second-baby-boomers generation, who are now in their late teens and early twenties, according to Yuichi Washida, the director of Hakuhodo Foresight, a research arm of the parent company that develops methods of forecasting "future scenarios" for their clients (Washida 2003).[14] He pays specific attention to female *shin shinjinrui,* also nicknamed *kogals,* famous for their vivid makeup and fashionably blonde look. They have rather weak ties with their family members and tend to prefer friendships over family bonds. Many analysts say that this trend has grown as a result of advances in information technology (Washida 2004).[15] To push Washida's insights a step further, I consider *kogals* to be "hub influentials," discussed in Chapter 3, and the generic category of the "neo-neo-tribe," a hub-culture phenomenon spread all over Asia.

Chinese Xin Xinrenlei

Xin xinrenlei wear their hair in all kinds of colors. Their cool faces give an exaggerated cold blank stare. They are dressed in plastic and metal looking clothes . . . They just want to look different. They are trend pursuers. They are a superficial and restless tribe . . . There is another way of portraying them: if you look human, then you do not belong to the neo-neo-tribe yet. (Longyuan huquan, undated Internet post)

A magazine categorizes them into four subspecies: Net bugs, CD rats, barflies, and car wolves . . . But because the members of the neo-neo-tribe do not have much dough, there can only be a few 'car wolves' among them. (Longyuan huquan, undated Internet post)

Xin xinrenlei are inexplicable. So far we have not yet figured out their lingo, behavioral code, or life philosophy. The so-called neo-neo-tribe should not be seen as a mere signpost for a certain historical period. More important, it points to an uncertain ideology. In China, this tribe's ties with traditionalism are disappearing. Their thoughts and views on life are rapidly aligned with the international norm. Born in the late 1970s [author's note: they were actually born between 1989 and 2000], they are distanced from "tradition." Their knowledge about the past has been channeled indirectly through movies, novels, and TV drama. Their literary sensibility has been nurtured by Japanese manga. This is a generation that was fed by "fast food culture" while its members were growing up. Compared with the previous generation, they are much more independent, will-ful, and self-centered. Their way of absorbing things is DIY [Do It Yourself]. Indoctrination and preaching find no place in their lives. (Guoke 2003)

Having fun is the most important thing in life . . . Acting "cool" is the art and wisdom of a rebellion against a mediocre life. ("Xin xinrenlei de 'ku' shenghuo" 2003)

Pinning the neo-neo-tribe down to a consistent profile is dif-ficult. Many real-life *xin xinrenlei,* the ones I found at China News Online—Xiaolong (Little Dragon) and Nina—seemed much tamer than the imagined specimen (Yu Ruidong 2002). This is a genera-tion known to care about nothing but "fashion," "hair styles," "computer gadgets," and "relationships" (ibid.). But "fashion" here takes on a meaning that is different from what it means to the neo-tribes. It points to an attitude rather than to glittering material objects.

Otaku and Kogal

For a quick comparison, consider what the neo-neo-tribers' Japa-nese counterparts are like.

These two types, "otaku" and "kogal," do not mean male and fe-male, although their correlation with gender is high. The initial male consumers have particular characteristics . . . they usually find out about new information and [high-tech] products very soon. They also tend to focus on technical specifications and quality to satisfy deep and narrow personal desires . . . people called "otaku" are those who tend to be isolated from their friends and families. They love playing games and reading comics alone rather than enjoying sports or joining community activities . . . [Later,] the meaning of "otaku" was gradually expanded to include people who were generally thought of as techno-geeks or nerds . . . "Otaku" are usually impulsive buyers of electronic devices in the very early phase of the development of products, and also abandon them easily if they find the product unsatisfactory.

In contrast, most "kogal" (literally, "girlish female") are very active young girls, who love shopping, chatting, and being fashionable. They are surprisingly good inventors of new ways of using electronic devices. As opposed to "otaku," the "kogal" do not buy things impulsively. However, once they buy a product, they become frequent users. For instance, today, average "kogal" use their mobile phones 24 hours a day and seven days a week. Through this heavy use, they find a variety of curious ways of using mobile phones quite different from the regular ways that are explained in the instruction manuals. They are the people who started changing the ringer tones from boring beeps to various trendy popular songs by inputting music data by themselves several years ago, and changing screen savers on mobile phones from boring defaults to very cute pictures. They also turned the behavior of exchanging mobile e-mail into a basic part of their lives. They love taking pictures of themselves, so we can conceive that the original idea of today's camera-phone is based on their needs. (Washida 2005, 27)

Washida's account of the Japanese *shin shinjinrui* breaks down into largely gender-specific *otaku* and *kogal,* a marked contrast to the gender-neutral Chinese *xin xinrenlei.* And *kogal*'s social networking and shopping patterns hardly fit them squarely into the category of "rebellious youth." Indeed, we can debate whether *otaku* or the Chinese *xin xinrenlei*'s attitude is reminiscent of Hebdige's subculture paradigm or of Maffesoli's tribal logic. But the question of rebellion is a red herring. "Having fun" and "doing whatever I want to do" are the keys to unlocking the enigma of the neo-neo-tribe, regardless of which culture they come from. Another point of entry is technology. A classic visual image of a member of the Chinese neo-neo-tribe is a "lone figure bent over a computer like a big shrimp." But even that image is bound to change soon as wireless entertainment enables Chinese teens to do what Japanese kids, crazy for their cell phones, are best known for—sitting in crowded plazas with pals, swapping p2p music files on smart phones, and messaging furiously with each other while busily playing online fantasy games.

IN LIEU OF A CONCLUSION: THE SAMMY POINT OF VIEW, HONG KONG STYLE

The case of an advertising campaign in Hong Kong for San Miguel Light Beer, one of the leading brews of the beer division of the giant Philippines-based San Miguel Corporation, provides one more look at tribal cultures. The campaign is about "attitude," and its target, Hong Kong's neo-neo-tribe.

How to position a light beer that is a line extension of an aging flagship brand posed a challenge to the Ogilvy Hong Kong team. The breakthrough came when researchers started inserting San Miguel Light right into the social space of young drinkers. The research question was: what is going on in their fickle minds? (Ogilvy Guangzhou 2002). Through a five-pronged approach, a mosaic of stories and dialogues among and about those youngsters was assembled. Together they revealed a pattern of consistent "attitude":

"Their conversation is disorganized, there is no subject or theme, they live in a blue sky conversational world . . . as the conversation goes . . . , they start to shift to other things." (interview with a City University sociology lecturer)

"The most difficult problem is 'what to eat' . . . Simply thinking about what to eat will spend us a day." (overheard)

"Who will be calling me? Who will have nothing to do now? After calling him, I'll call someone else who has nothing to do." (overheard)[16]

This tribal group seeks instant gratification rather listlessly, but it is a deeply bonded crowd. Thinking that home is the "most boring place of all," they are "driven out into the metropolis of urban Hong Kong." They are crazy for visual and sensory stimuli, "anything that hints of mischief-making, that is visually fun . . . But everything is instantly disposable" (Blair, Armstrong, and Murphy 2003, 75–76). They move on quickly to the next "hit."

This profile is similar to that of neo-neo-tribe members in other Chinese metropolises. They are crazier and wilder than the Japanese *shin shinjinrui,* but they all share the same C-culture—cartoons, computers, comic books, and Nintendo games. They speak and consume the same visual language. Based on those field observations, the brand personality for San Miguel Light took shape quickly. He is a little guy who follows his own instincts, who does not give a damn about public opinion, a trickster guided by impulse rather than by rational thought. "Watch out, I have something wild inside me!" A new mascot was born: Sammy.

When I first encountered this naughty little devil in a series of print advertisements for San Miguel Light, I saw him as an obnoxious male prankster and a highly gendered invention. However, that cartoon figure, juvenile and delinquent, appeals to the target consumers regardless of their gender. He is the "ultimate spontaneous animal" that lurks in the hearts and minds of the Hong Kong neo-neo-tribe, an unstoppable phenomenon. He is everywhere. Private Sammy moments are posted in public. The Sammy "virus" was un-

Sammy acts up in an outdoor San Miguel Light ad. Ogilvy Beijing.

leashed openly on television, billboards, and print ads.[17] He popped up in shops, public lavatories, bars and restaurants, on the streets, at Metro stations, as tattoos and stickers, any medium you name, braving the public, "I dare, do you?" He pees whenever he can't hold it; he turns off the light switch when walking by a lady's room; he moons you and dares you to spank him; he farts purposely in a crowded elevator; he targets the urinal from a far distance; he shows love to a young girl by pushing her off a cliff. Scatological humor is his trademark. The taglines feature Sammy-style outbursts: "Come on, man!" "Hey man, that's fun." "Maybe we don't need to take things that seriously." He is in our face, asking, "Will you be Sammy enough when your chance comes?"

If you feel timid answering these challenges, you are simply not a member of the Hong Kong neo-neo-tribe, but you may still qualify for its other Chinese or its Japanese incarnations. We can find Sammy's Golden Rule—"my only rule is to bend the rules, disruptively but not destructively"—performed by his counterparts in China, Japan, and perhaps in other parts of Asia. In Sammy we see the rise of a hot East Asian youth cultural phenomenon.

I began this chapter with the bobos, an imaginary class, and end with the neo-neo-tribe, a real-life social segment. I have yet to spot a TV commercial that captures the dual traits of the Chinese bobos, namely that they have to practice both one-upsmanship and an imaginary one-downsmanship at the same time. Such real-life specimens are rare, to say the least. In contrast, the visual representation of *xin xinrenlei* has flooded the media precisely because it is a tribe rooted in reality. Real bobos may be scarce, and yet by 2006, minimalism began to gain momentum and the trend of calculated casualness—a trademark of one-downsmanship—could be seen in fashion, conveying the message that simple style itself is stylish. In-your-face luxury may slowly give way to understated aesthetics, as marketers at Ogilvy Beijing predicted. Regardless of which way Chinese taste culture is heading, the arrival and popularity of both bobos and neo-neo-tribes is a sure sign of the tribalization of the Chinese market. The theorem of the tribal discourse aside, we have examined two other important questions. Although no quick answers can be found, the taste versus class question and the theoretical possibility of an emerging global youth culture point to the heart of my critical concern: the importance of taking "marketing" into serious account in any study of regional and transnational popular cultural trends. As we have seen, marketers only need to take a tiny step to turn a popular discourse about a tribe into a new marketing phenomenon. And one can certainly argue the reverse. Indeed, it is difficult to tell which comes first—a real-life tribe or its incarnation as a market segment. Either way, when marketing meets culture, can a new pop culture movement be far away?

CHAPTER 6

Hello Moto:
Youth Culture and
Music Marketing

The "neo-neo-tribe" social segment comprises only part of the single-child generation, which numbered approximately 111.9 to 142 million as of 2005.[1] Each of those "little emperors and empresses," as they are called, is said to have a total of six parents (their grandparents on their mother's and father's sides plus their own parents), who spend an average of 50–70 percent of the household's income on them for their needs or desires, which range from education to designer brands (Lu Taihong 2005, 381). Utterly spoiled and with an overblown view of themselves, this epicurean generation worships high-end brands and enjoys using its debit cards. The mindset of this generation is best captured by a popular expression: "Every day is sunny and tomorrow will be even better" *(tiantian you yangguang, mingtian hui genghao)* (ibid.). As a group, they are the source of the unique phenomenon of "one-family two-tiered consumption"—with parents using lower-tier brands in order to save for their child, who purchases premium brands (Chen Subai 2005). This generation is also media savvy, well informed about cutting-edge global trends, and enamored of cool communication gadgets. The parents may possess only an old Bird, but their single child is holding a Motorola or Samsung while constantly thinking of upgrades. This chapter focuses on this mobile tribe—their likes, the boundaries of their imagination, and the product category that matters the most to them, cell phones.

CELL PHONE

A news release in December 2003, from metro China, speaks of Shanghai, Beijing, and Guangzhou as having all fallen under the spell of the *Cell Phone* phenomenon. But despite appearances, the penetration rate of mobile handsets in tier-one cities was not what this "phenomenon" referred to. The buzz had been created by *Shouji* (Cell Phone) (2003), a best-selling film directed by Feng Xiaogang, the champion of China's cool cinema, who has a knack for creative marketing.[2] The film reaped a box office of fifteen million yuan in the first three days after its premiere and became the year's most profitable Chinese film.[3] The behind-the-scenes trickster of this crowd-pleaser is a Motorola 388C. The tragicomedy begins when one day, its owner, an adulterous married man, leaves his Motorola cell phone unattended at home. Who picks up his ringing cell unwittingly and answers his girlfriend's call but his wife, who happens to have taken a day off from work. One steamy discovery follows another, all mediated by Motorola handsets. Various Motorola models, the abettors of the "crime of intimacy," are given center-stage treatment. Every betrayal teaches us a bit more about how to operate the tiny box. This smart product placement was a stroke of genius for a cell phone maker whose fortunes were said to be on the decline.[4] The hype about *Cell Phone* turned Motorola—the film's primary sponsor—into the most talked-about mobile phone brand in the country and helped Motorola evolve into a bona fide entertainment brand.

MOBILE MUSIC INITIATIVES

"Mobile music" is said to cut across cultural borders, luring cool global youth to become earnest buyers of music handsets. But it is unclear how well this formula was working for Chinese youth as the new millennium progressed. Whether the relationship between music, youth culture, and cool culture in metropolitan China is similar to that in other metropolises is an open question. Central to my inquiry is a field project on "Cool China" conducted at Ogilvy Beijing in the summer of 2004. Although my critical perspectives on Motorola's brand strategies are based on independent academic research unrelated to my Ogilvy fieldwork, part of the chapter will draw on a digital photo-narration project I designed at the ad agency. This qualitative research sought to discover consumer insights into the youth market in China. I was also keen to explore whether the digital photo-narrative could be a useful methodology for future research on youth culture across national borders.

Since the turn of the twenty-first century, Motorola has been preoccupied with redefining its niche in China's oversaturated mobile phone market. The handset maker was faced with a conflicting set of representations: as a brand name, Motorola was seen as both old and new, and its culture both hidebound and progressively modern. Chic advertising images associated with the "Moto" campaigns and smart product placement in feature films had raised the visibility of Motorola as an adventurous brand in China. But when it came to preferred brand choices, Nokia occupied the number one position across all age groups. Korea-based Samsung emerged as the leader of cool aspirations for the younger segment, narrowly trailing Motorola in a tight race for second place. Under these circumstances, Motorola needed a quick revival—or a revolution.

The company's answer was to try its global formula on China—launching a music marketing platform targeting youth. Motorola was certainly not alone in jumping onto the bandwagon of wireless music. Nokia was heading in the same direction by partnering up with Warner Music and Loudeye, a global leader in digital music platforms. But Motorola seemed further ahead in creating hip headlines with iconic products like Razr V3 and RokrE1 and in staying active with sponsorships of live media concerts (like the

Redfest in Singapore) and creative festivals involving international DJs (A. White 2005). The underlying premise for these initiatives was transnational marketers' well-known assumption that music is the fastest way into the mind and soul of today's youth. The title of a news release of July 26, 2004, came as no surprise: "Motorola and Apple Bring iTunes Music Player to Motorola's Next Generation Mobile Phones" (Motorola 2004a). The partnership enabled millions of music lovers to transfer their favorite songs from the iTunes Jukebox to Motorola's next-generation "always with you" mobile phones via a USB or Bluetooth connection.

The handset maker's efforts to create an interface with mobile music proceeded at lightning speed. Even prior to the Apple deal, a marketing package with MTV worth $75 million already signaled Motorola's plan to transform itself into an entertainment brand with strong musical offerings (Morrissey 2003). The year 2004 was an extraordinary one for the company: it launched the MotoMusic Web site, enabling subscribers to download music, including songs performed by cutting-edge, "emerging" artists in China (Motorola 2004b).[5] The July deal with Apple further consolidated the brand's association with "cool" music. Both the "emerging artists" platform and the iTune-enabled cell phones aimed to create a mobile music society thriving on cool culture. Music marketing also enabled Motorola to stretch its business model from the provision of voice, SMS, and MMS service to value-added management of music applications and music content.

In late 2006, more hot news broke out: Motorola was reaching out to China's youth market with a music-optimized Rokr model and a Web site—China's largest DRM (digital rights management) music download site—"with full track and ringtone downloads for up to 15,000 songs costing 25 cents each" (Madden 2006a). Optimism about the sales of music handsets continued to grow.[6] There was a hitch, however. Eighty-five percent of Chinese youth—the target for the new Rokr—don't pay for music downloads (Synovate

2006). They also spend only small amounts on music CDs, even though they are listening to more music than ever. Are these free riders willing to pay for downloads from RDM-armed Web sites? Why would we expect Chinese youngsters to abstain when American college kids routinely use Kazaa, LimeWire, BitTorrent, and other peer-to-peer file-sharing services to download unauthorized music? Students whom I surveyed at MIT often complained that "commercializing MP3's is a poorly executed process." Granted that there are sporadic industry efforts to spread legal downloads, but as Albert Park, a student in my 2007 Advertising class, points out, "they are all hampered by restrictions in terms of burning to CDs, playing on different computers, etc." (Park 2007). Furthermore, if Chinese mobile users purchase music phones simply to look cool holding them, and opt out of buying downloads from MotoMusic, will Motorola's model be sustainable?[7]

Industry experts had mixed opinions. But cultural critics should ask different questions. The phenomenon of music marketing has taken over the handset industry, but nothing substantial on the subject has been published either in academia or in the trade. Various assumptions have been made about the relationship between music and youth culture in China, yet little research has been conducted on the cultural drivers behind the musical preferences of the country's youth. Moreover, "consumer insights" from the youths themselves have been the weakest in the research chain. Whenever the term "youth" is mentioned, it is cast in the same frame as "global youth," and the pattern of Chinese youth's music consumption is taken to be comparable, if not now then in the near future, to that of young Europeans and Americans. Is Kenny Bloom's Mogo.com.cn, a digital video platform with music channels on hip-hop and alternative rock, going to revolutionize the music tastes of Chinese youth? Can one assume that the relationship between "youth" and "music" in China is evolving into the same as that in developed Western countries?

FROM MUSIC CULTURE TO YOUTH CULTURE

During my fieldwork at Ogilvy in 2004, I wondered whether the reigning Western model of youth music and subculture was a good starting point for China analysts and marketers. To be sure, music is the global language of the "New Generation," but cutting-edge youth in the West like to be perceived as anti-fashion and anti-brand, and they embrace music that smacks of radicalism. But the relationship of cool Chinese youth to music may resist being depicted in equal terms. We need to pursue the connection, if any, between cool Chinese music and punk or alternative rock. Another unknown is whether the arrival of third-generation (3G) mobile services (which will enhance roaming capabilities and multimedia data delivery) and greater bandwidth capacity will change the Chinese file-sharing habits. In the course of my contacts with Chinese youth online and offline, on the streets, and in the food courts and music stores in Beijing, the question of whether Chinese hip-hop and punk fans are equivalent to the radical elements seen on New York and London streets kept popping up.[8] I wondered whether "music" was the primary driver for Chinese youth culture, and whether my Cool China project could be reduced to a cool *music* project.

To answer these reservations, my research at Ogilvy resulted in a location-sensitive study in which "youth culture" was given priority over "music culture." Results of initial interviews with young people from a diverse range of age groups confirmed that, generally speaking, while market segmentation of tweens and youths in the West takes place primarily on the basis of their musical taste (Lindstrom and Seybold 2003, 20), no such equation exists in China. Not only do Chinese youths have extremely eclectic musical preferences, but they bond quickly with singers who have a knack for creating a "chop-suey" musical experience. Loyalty to a single pop singer rarely occurs for long, and Chinese youth do not adhere to a stable set of mixed genres. Musicians who have a shifting fusion of styles stand a better chance of appealing to this fickle clientele. This finding contradicts an additional assumption made by many transnational music marketers: that Asian youth, like their counterparts in developed worlds, are increasingly willing to follow a particular type of music (such as hip-hop).

Transnational youth marketers' logic that "brand preferences correlate with musical taste" (ibid., 21) is thus difficult to sustain in China. "Music" is a backseat driver, second to clothes fashions, in the total picture of cool culture consumption, and its influence on brand adoption, though no doubt important, should not be overrated. Furthermore, transnational marketers who believe that cool music means edgy content will be surprised to find that Chinese "cool youth" do not consume indie labels. The intimate relationship of cool culture and alternative music, which seems a marketing given in developed worlds, is a risky assumption in China. The urgent research question is less about cool music and more about the culture and characteristics of *linglei* ("other species") youth themselves, as we shall see.

MOTOROLA AND MOBILE DATA IN CHINA

Motorola serves as an excellent vehicle for my inquiry into both youth culture and cell phone branding, not least because the handset maker's mutation from a technological brand to a "cool" brand in China connects three stories simultaneously: the shifting brandscape of China's mobile phone market, music marketing, and the association of mobile music with cool culture.

China's cell phone market has come a long way since 1995. Back then, 85 percent of China's total market shares were divided among Motorola, Nokia, and Ericsson, and another 10 percent were distributed among Siemens, Samsung, Philips, and Panasonic. Local Chinese makers did not enter the fray till 1998, with only a slim share of 2 percent. By the end of 2002, however, that had risen to 30 percent, breaking the market domination of transnational handsets (Ji Xin 2002b, 56). The turning point came in 1999 with the entry of the "Three Musketeers," domestic heavyweights Ningbo Bird, TCL, and Xiaxin. Bird and TCL, in particular, commanded marketing strategies that put their transnational rivals on the defensive. TCL entered the competition from the premium end by developing cell phones enabled by WAP (Wireless Application Protocol);[9] Bird launched a distribution "channel" offensive by developing a seamless web of 50,000 handset shops and service centers spread among district towns, county towns, and in second- and third-tier cities, bypassing the metropolises where transnational handsets were dominant. Such a powerful channel strategy, which can best be captured in the Maoist slogan "the countryside surrounding the cities," is characteristically Chinese, one that Wahaha and other domestic superbrands like Lenovo and Haier have also employed with great success, as we have seen. National brands controlled 50 percent of the market until 2004, when competition again turned in favor of rival multinationals. Nokia and Motorola's cheap "township cell models" began to penetrate low-end markets ("Guochan" 2005). Meanwhile, domestic brands were moving upstream: Bird and Lenovo's premium cell phones cost as much as $157. Crossing over from the lower end to the premium is a difficult climb. Bird went into retrenchment in 2005 (Zang and Cheng 2005); domestic peer TCL also got badly squeezed.[10]

In such a competitive environment, Nokia, Motorola, and other competitors are all eager to spend on branding and advertising.[11] Also worth noting is the shift of corporate focus from technology to design and the rise of music marketing worldwide.[12] As "musical taste" emerged as an important demographic index in developed countries, music content and music applications were also pushed to the top of the agenda for transnational handset carriers. All of a sudden, mobile phone makers were devising business strategies that integrated "mobile entertainment" into portable devices. Entertainment and telecommunications industries began to invest heavily in revenue-sharing models that allowed cross-fertilization among all the major players on the value chain: content providers (such as Disney, Fox, Sony, Universal Music), carriers (AT&T, Verizon, China Mobile), handsets (Motorola, Nokia), and technology (Apple, Microsoft).

In China, the new partnership model lagged behind for a number of reasons, one of which was the weak chain in the mobile data industry and Chinese consumers' reluctance to pay for mobile content. True, mobile entertainment began to generate a buzz in metropolitan China: ringtones, image messages, Java games, MMS horoscopes, EMS pictures, and SMS jokes are all available on chic handsets. The major push for developing the mobile content sector was driven by the government, which was intent on shoving the cell phone market from voice communications to the data service market. Authorities anticipated that future revenues would shift away from simple access fees to billed services for infotainment and mobile transactions.

Reality, however, has lagged far behind. The statistics on cell phone usage in China deliver a cautionary tale: attracting Chinese users to buy MP3 phones is one thing, but persuading them to spend on mobile data is another. The penetration rate of multimedia messaging services (MMS), which enables a phone to handle images, video, audio, and rich text, was relatively low compared with that of SMS (short text messaging). The optimists would argue that revenue streams are rising. Pyramid Research, a growth strategy expert for communications, media, and technology companies, provides statistics that show a rosy picture in a number of areas (see Table 5).

The figures in Table 5 indicate the obvious: that thus far mobile data in China is still dominated by SMS and ringtone downloads and that the usage of MMS is climbing while music application us-

TABLE 5 Mobile Data in China, March 2007

Mobile data users	2003	2007
SMS	217,953,000	562,873,000
Ringtone applications	907,000	199,689,000
MMS	1,840,000	58,213,000
Email	920,000	24,337,000
Music applications	0	9,702,000

Source: Pyramid Research.

ages are trailing behind. While useful, these data provide nothing more than a set of numbers that tells us very little about the human equations that need to be factored in for us to derive any reliable projection of the growth trend in the future. What are the user habits and attitudes, preferences for content, and interest levels for mobile data services and applications in China? The Asia/Pacific Mobile Consumer Services Survey conducted in 2006 by IDC (a global market intelligence company specializing in information technology) provides a few clues; see Table 6 (Wong, 2007).

For data services and applications other than P2P text messaging, I will provide only a snapshot of the first three major inhibitors, since the other categories are statistically not very significant. As Table 7 shows, with the exception of the photo image pass-on service, the two major inhibitors for the use of more advanced features are "cost concerns" and "no need for service." The second runner-up in deterrents—the inability of the phone to support the function—can be interpreted either way in the Chinese context, that is, the user may, or may not, use the function even after he or she upgrades the mobile phone, given the income constraints on cultural consumption discussed in Chapter 5.

These figures belie international marketers' assumptions that a Chinese MMS culture is as ready made as a Chinese youth culture. Given the statistics, the so-called application revolution from

TABLE 6 Reasons for not using P2P data service, China (%)

N = 1,006 respondents who are cell phone users[a]

Survey question: What are the reasons for lack of usage or low usage of the following services?

Send a P2P (person-to-person) text message

Cost—expensive, unsure how much it costs, do not wish to pay	13.8
No need for service	62.1
Unaware of service	0.0
Mobile phone does not support the service/application	10.3
Do not know how to use	10.3
Not user friendly	10.3
Difficult to use	3.4

Source: Adapted from Alayne Wong, *Asia/Pacific Mobile Consumer Services Survey, 2006,* IDC, 2007. http://www.idc.com/.

a. Eighty percent of the Chinese respondents were selected from the major first-tier and second-tier cities of Beijing, Shanghai, Chengdu, Tianjin, Wuhan, and Hangzhou. Twenty percent were chosen from the third-tier cities of Guilin, Zhuhai, Yuxi, and Xianyang.

text-based dialogue to rich content, from mobile communications to mobile transactions, hasn't taken place yet. However, transnational marketers are still highly optimistic about the future: they predict that value-added services such as music and video downloads will skyrocket once they are launched, now scheduled for 2007.[13] I will turn to Europe as a benchmark for what China may become.

Europe's mobile operators plan to grow data revenue tenfold within five years. But in "Limits to Growth for New Mobile Services," industry analyst Michelle de Lussanet found this prediction much too optimistic. Her 2003 projections showed that two-thirds of European operators would begin to offer 3G streaming in 2004, and that the figure would rise to 91 percent in 2005. But only 16 percent of Europeans would use 3G even in 2008. She expected that only one in four consumers would have a 3G-capable handset in 2008, and only one in four of those—6 percent—would use stream-

TABLE 7 Reasons for not using other data services, China (%)

N = 1,006 respondents who are cell phone users[a]

Survey question: What are the reasons for lack of usage or low usage of the following services?

Use SMS/MMS services for contests/polls/raffles/voting (such as TV voting)

Cost	23.2%
No need of service	57.2
Mobile does not support the service	14.2

Download icons/screensavers/logos/ringtones

Cost	23.0
No need of service	50.0
Prefer usage via fixed-line Internet (PC)	13.8

Send photos taken with camera phone to another person

Cost	7.6
No need of service	33.5
Mobile does not support the service	43.4

Browse the mobile Internet (such as the operator's portal and others)

Cost	24.4
No need of service	29.9
Prefer usage via fixed-line Internet (PC)	26.5

Download MP3 music track files and short video clips

No need of service	30.9
Mobile does not support the service/application	39.7
Prefer usage via fixed-line Internet (PC)	12.5

Source: Adapted from Alayne Wong, *Asia/Pacific Mobile Consumer Services Survey, 2006,* IDC, 2007, pp. 20–25. http://www.idc.com/.

a. Eighty percent of the Chinese respondents were selected from the major first-tier and second-tier cities of Beijing, Shanghai, Chengdu, Tianjin, Wuhan, and Hangzhou. Twenty percent were chosen from the third-tier cities of Guilin, Zhuhai, Yuxi, and Xianyang.

ing services regularly (de Lussanet 2003). Two problems stand out among the major roadblocks for the spread of 3G-enabled services in Europe: the clashing of operators' mobile Internet suites with handset vendors' goals and the fact that consumers' disposable income is sharply limited. The latter deterrent is especially relevant to the Chinese: if the Europeans are reluctant to double their mobile phone bill, the Chinese will be far more resistant to paying for new content. The bottom line is "income threshold" and the budgeting habits of Chinese people, both of which will change little with the advent of 3G. Incentives have to be built into budget-saving prepay packages. Those who use streaming services regularly will most likely be the expatriate communities and gold-collar residents in metropolitan China. Third-generation mobile services, in other words, are an enormous luxury for the "middle class"—who make up less than 10 percent of the Chinese population. The profit margin may be smaller than expected for operators and handset vendors.

As of 2004, China's Monternet (Mobile Internet), a unified nationwide mobile data service platform, has a value chain of more than five hundred service and content providers (including Sina, Netease, Sohu, and 263.net). Subscribers can gain access to data as diverse as news, entertainment, finance, online gaming, and other multimedia content. The growth of the market is reportedly 15 percent a month (Ransdell 2002). The initial press hype notwithstanding, Monternet's wireless content and application provisions are primarily SMS based and news dominated. Sites specializing in stocks, sports, and entertainment news enjoy much heavier traffic than those providing MMS content. General statistics in 2004 revealed a slim slice of 20 million MMS users in comparison with 199 million SMS users.[14] Statistics from 2007 (see Table 7) spelled out three major obstacles for improving the frequency of the users' access to Monternet. Added to "cost" (24.4 percent) and "no need for service" (29.9 percent), the third factor standing in the way is "prefer usage via fixed-line Internet (PC), a high 26.5 percent. Handset makers dreaming big about selling out their stocks of smart phones in China face two major tasks. The first is to change the Chinese mind-set, which treats cell phones as nothing more than fancy walkie-talkies; the second is to teach users how to integrate a voice and messaging machine into the rich fabric of all that they do for entertainment. Neither task is easy, especially considering how many of those in the United States still share the same perspective.

Both the infrastructural lag and consumers' unwillingness to increase their monthly phone bills take us back to larger questions such as China's GDP growth, the redistribution of social wealth, and the role of cultural consumption in Chinese society, which is not yet affluent. An equally thorny issue mentioned earlier is music piracy. A Synovate survey says 70 percent of Asian youth who own an MP3 player do not pay for digital music downloads (Synovate 2005). The percentage is even higher in China. Although 45 percent of all respondents reported that they had played music on an MP3 player in the past month (Synovate 2006), Chinese youth, like their American counterparts, are unlikely to give up the habit of buying cheap pirated CDs and to begin to pay for music or video downloads. The task of mobile music marketers will certainly not end with the debuting of 3G handsets.

"HELLO MOTO"

Although the future of MP3 phones is unpredictable, Motorola succeeded in turning itself into a "cool" brand in China by adding entertainment value to the device. The handset maker had the advantage of being the best-known mobile phone brand in China. The Chinese term *dageda* for "mobile phone" was interchangeable with the term for Motorola's 8900 and 9900 models. For a long time, Motorola was to cell phones in China what Kleenex is to tissue paper and Xerox is to copying in the West. But in the mid-1990s, the reputation of the techno-giant fell when it failed to anticipate the worldwide shift to digital cell phones and the Chinese market's drift to the GSM technology that underpins most of the world's mobile phone networks.[15] More mature marketing campaigns have been launched since the late 1990s, but the real turning point took place with the launch of "Moto" campaigns.[16]

A sound-bite turned into a brand concept, the "Moto" idea was first discovered in Taiwan and was tested in China in 2002. It kicked off a mainland "Moto" craze and turned Motorola into a fashion brand overnight. The two-syllable prefix appeared user-friendly for almost any occasion under the sun: MommyMoto, MultiMoto, SohoMoto, 911Moto, MotoMusic, Kara(oke)Moto, and so forth. As the shortest fashion statement in the cell phone world, the chic slogan gave a soul to Motorola, making it a definitive moment in the history of the company. Ultracool lines of Motorola cell phones were produced to live up to the cheeky new language. "Moto" was a perfect solution to the challenge of how to bring the younger generation of white-collar workers and college and high school kids into Motorola's fold. It is a segment for which rival handset makers are all competing. The "new cool" associated with "Moto" offered exactly the kind of antidote that an aging brand was seeking.

"Fashionology" (the intersection of fashion and technology) was a conceptual thread running through the advertising campaign. In one of the most dramatic Moto commercials, a zany lad embarks on a quest for the coolest ring tones for his C289. "There is a soul in every sound," he mutters. Triumphantly shouting "Moto," he jumps from one scraping sound to the next and finally reaches the most dangerous sound on the railway tracks—at his own peril. A roaring train brushes back our hero in the nick of time. A trompe l'oeil fools us into thinking he may be under the wheels. But no, in the next frame he emerges safe and sound with the perfect ring tone captured on his cell. The message we get about the brand is that it is intelligent, crazy, adventurous, and, above all, cool and fun. Combining the Moto sound with a Moto attitude, Motorola was only a tiny step away from becoming the icon of a full-blown entertainment culture.

Following its success in China and Asia, the Moto campaign was launched in the United States and Europe in 2002 and became one of the few advertising campaigns globalized from the reverse direction—from Asia to the West. Global Motospeak has transformed

American Idiot
We Are The Waiting
Baby Please Don't Go
Show Business
Whole Lotta Rosie
Shot Down In Flames
Touch Too Much

500 SONGS, TO GO.

MOTO ROKR

WHAT ROCKS YOUR WORLD?

Ad from MotoRokr campaign. Ogilvy Beijing.

the image of Motorola from a stodgy maker of technological devices to a sleek and stylish creator of communications gear. Outside China, as well, Motorola's promise to create cool musical experiences has given birth to an "emerging artist" platform that showcases new music talents which are a bit edgy and somewhat removed from mainstream pop icons. One such "emerging" music artist who has been made over into a brand endorser for Motorola is the Beijing-born singer Pu Shu, who sang at the gala party for the double launch of E398 (an MP3 smart phone) and MotoMusic (an e-music server).[17] I attended the evening party in July 2004 at the famous 798 Factory, part of an old factory complex that now houses galleries, studios, restaurants, and bookshops in Beijing's avant-garde art district.

LINGLEI YOUTH AND THE PUNK SYNDROME: ETHNOGRAPHIC ENCOUNTERS

I arrived at the 798 Factory with Ye Ying, the editor of Lifestyle Monthly for *The Economic Observer,* to get a feel for the "biggest party of the year." We went late and missed the highlight of the party—Pu Shu's performance of a new song written specifically for E398. When we walked in, the place was littered with empty glasses and discarded hors d'oeuvre plates. Crowds of young people were scattered around drink stands. Those who were lounging on the benches looked bored. An anonymous band was on stage blaring deafening music. The huge exhibition space exuded an air of spent energy. Looking at the nonchalant young crowd lingering at the party, several questions flashed through my mind: What made them embrace an elusive figure like Pu Shu? How can one understand the musical taste of the younger generation without getting a grasp on who they are in the first place? Wouldn't it make more sense to reorient my Cool China Project toward a study of Chinese youth culture than to treat it as a project to discover the emerging musical trends in China? I wondered what "cool" Chinese girls or boys think and do and whether music is the primary driver for an emerging youth culture of "individualism." And finally, is alternative music like hip-hop or rap the default choice for Chinese alternative lifestyle followers?

Chun Shu and Linglei Youth

The Chinese term for "alternative" translates into the word for the "other species" *(linglei)*, as we have seen. But when de-politicized and de-radicalized, the term rings hollow. Since its discovery by Western journalists and marketers, *linglei* has undergone total commodification. Today, the "new edge" has gotten so predictable that it's no longer cool to label oneself as such. It was at the Motorola launch party that I ran into Chun Shu (literally, "Spring Tree"), a *linglei* high school dropout made famous by her controversial tell-all memoir *Beijing Doll (Beijing Wawa)*. Petite Chun Shu, now twenty, came across as an intelligent, precocious, and sensual-looking young woman. She had an air of both defiance and vulnerability. Speaking about her upcoming visit to the States, she said she yearned for an admission to Harvard or Columbia—the "best universities in the U.S."—to resume a student's life. "I love Beida [Peking University], too," she said wistfully, a dream now lost. She enjoyed being rich (through her royalties) and famous (as the cover girl for the *Asia Times*).

Chun Shu's uncool language and uncool aspirations put everybody present at ease but, a minute later, she mutated as our conversation shifted to punk. I asked her to comment on the current popular take on "pseudo-punk," attributing the theory about fake punk to Ye Ying, my journalist companion at the MotoMusic soiree. At first, Chun Shu tried to avoid the topic. Mistaking her reservation for shyness, I pressed her for an answer. She turned to Ye at that instant and gunned her down with a tirade of angry allegations. How on earth did Ye Ying know anything about punk? How could anybody who had such vulgar taste in fashion—Chun Shu now turned our attention to the multicolored sequin-studded skirt Ye wore that evening—and such an obviously uncool spirit comprehend the world of punk? The "pseudo-punk" talk was sheer blasphemy for a punk original like Chun Shu.

The Chun Shu incident was a small indication that the countercultural spirit of punk is not dead in China. Prior to that evening, I had interviewed several music professionals and pop music researchers in Beijing and Guangzhou. Together with a research partner at Ogilvy, I had also held substantial discussions with Ye Ying, who has been an observer of China's punk phenomenon. To go beyond our Beijing focus, we went over blogs from people in other cities that focused on Chinese punk. The general online and offline consensus is that Chinese punk is a fashion accessory for hip kids. It is not the "real thing." When asked about the percentage of "angry youth" *(fenqing)*—a term sometimes interchangeable with Chinese "punk fans"—Xiao Yong, marketing manager at Maitian Records replied, "They are a minority. Besides, although they are considered the avant-garde among the younger generation, the way they express themselves is far from radical" (Xiao Yong 2004). Shanghai and Guangzhou youths are considered too practically minded to appreciate punk. But what about Beijing, where the career of rock rebel Cui Jian took off?

Punk fans and musicians in the capital are nicknamed spiritual "fatsos." The term is a pun on the word "fat guests," which sounds exactly the same as *pangke* ("punk"), only with a tonal difference. Online satirical takes on real punkers versus fatsos help illuminate the current music scene in China:

[Punk] is an opportunistic trend born from the restless upstart mentality characteristics of sons and daughters of the middle class. (Da Zhi 2003)

Deep in their blood, Chinese punkers are neither rebels nor extreme fun seekers. They are "potbellies," an obesity not rooted in real fat genes. "Pang" as in "fat guests" points to a lifestyle of leisure and safe boundaries, a lifestyle marked by insatiable desires for fame and money and besieged by an anxiety that makes them tread carefully [as though] on a high wire. (Yan Jun 2001)

The remark from Yan Jun, the most authoritative Chinese music critic, debunks the myth that equates Chinese punk with a carefree spirit. Yet an element of punk is still found in China, because there is an entire generation of angry young high school students (to which the then-seventeen-year-old Chun Shu once belonged) who live under the oppressive system known as the college entrance examinations *(gaokao)*. Many jump on the bandwagon of punk music to seek solace. A small minority of daredevils reject the rote-memorization required to succeed by choosing the most radical means of rebellion: opting out of the system completely. Together with other like-minded spirits, Chun Shu made "high school dropouts" a new social segment to be reckoned with. *Beijing Doll* became a bestseller, thanks to its blunt exposure of the mental torture an archrebel paid for revolting against the strict norms of society. Youth memoir literature grew quickly in China as a new genre precisely because it struck a chord with repressed, nihilist young minds. These youth, like Chun Shu herself, have developed a strong bond with punk rockers.

Prior to my meeting with Chun Shu, I had discovered the generational logic behind the high school punk phenomenon via a different means of research. I had immersed myself in pop music magazines, which feature special sections with exchanges between fans and magazine editors. Yet it was my encounter with Chun Shu that drove home the crucial link between high school students and the Chinese punk syndrome. Once I was made aware of the connection, I found it everywhere in fan letters written by the high school kids and college freshmen who sent their missives from different parts of China. Below is a sample of typical letters I spotted in the pages of *I Love Rock (Wo ai yaogun yue)* and *Hit Light Music (Ji qing yinyue)*:

> Han Shunyuan (an eighteen-year-old): I became very distressed in the face of the pressure of the entrance exam. That was the burden I shared in common with my peers. Then I discovered Linkin Park. I was drawn to their discontent about reality and their rage against it. I feel empathetic with their music. The college entrance examination is behind it all—it deprives us of a world of precious things . . . Listening to Linkin Park made me feel as if I was listening to myself! (*Ji qing yinyue* 2004, 95)

> Da Li (a college freshman): The last six years of my middle school and high school life were a total misery. F—k it! I shudder at the memory of it. I was real f—king exhausted! My whole life crumbled. I became a f—king hooligan, a f—king madman! That is the Way of Chinese Education. It f—ked me up completely! ("Readers Ring Up" 2004, 61)

> Haozi (a high school senior): Living like this day and night and living under such tremendous pressure is driving me nuts. I feel like killing somebody. I feel like grabbing someone by the collar and punching him hard, once, twice. My reason stopped me from doing that . . . it is too difficult these days. I am exhausted! . . . I have had endless nightmares at night and migraines during the day. I ask myself: am I just surrendering myself to a life sentence imposed by the entrance examination without resistance? . . . I can't stand it any more. I can't! (Ibid.)

These outcries testify to a genuine culture of youth anger in China, but it is a culture that is not totally iconoclastic. Many *fenqing* are ultra-nationalists, for example. As Jack Qiu writes, "Nationalism underlies almost all political discussions in China's cyberspace" (Qiu 2006) and is closely associated with "angry youth." Just how comfortably patriotism sits with the lone-wolf syndrome of youth nonconformism is anybody's guess. But we can be sure that irreverent youth in China, like their counterparts everywhere else in the world, share a resolve to turn the norm upside down. Music that delivers rapture and total disjunction strongly appeals to them. And yet a real punk culture cannot take root or thrive in China precisely because it is just a short-lived phase for most youth, with a high turnover rate of faithful adherents. Once the hurdle of the entrance examination is gotten over, college freshmen tone down their lawless impulses and switch their loyalty from real punk idols to hip Hong Kong and Taiwanese pop singers and other tamer genres. The erstwhile anarchistic young men and women move on quickly. As an *Asia Times'* article on the new radicals in China says, *linglei*s are "like dogs wearing electric collars that know just how far they can stray without getting shocked" (Beech 2004, 37). Most *linglei* originals, like Chun Shu, felt compelled to grow up fast to adapt to society's demands while keeping their loyalty to punk intact. Much less can be expected from their followers—the punk wannabes. Their brand of radicalism exhibits some rough edges—but in their fashion code, not in their musical taste.

DIGITAL PHOTO-NARRATION AND THE "SAFE COOL"

The Beijing punk phenomenon as expressed by Chun Shu shows the importance of treating "punk" as a sociological rather than as a musical phenomenon. Although music is undoubtedly a fertile entry point, it should not be taken as an anchor for our study of Chinese youth culture. Observation of punk in China also teaches us that "age" rather than "musical taste" is the most important demographic index for youth segmentation there. Different age groups develop and define their own cultural preferences and standards of what constitutes "cool" (in musical taste). Although punk's central position in the culture of cool high school kids stands in little doubt, college matriculation often entails an immediate switch of their allegiance away from punk to a mixed genre of musical styles.

"Generational logic" more than "musical taste" drives the pattern of the brand adoption of middle-class youth in China.

Armed with this insight, my research partner and I went out to the "field." After a month's deliberation, we picked five candidates (three men and two women), each belonging to a different age segment (spread between ages sixteen and twenty-three) but sharing a common middle-class background (evidenced by the size of their monthly pocket money).[18] We took care to select candidates who expressed a liking for the following music genres: light pop from Taiwan and Hong Kong; electronic music; Euro-American rock; and Japanese pop, punk, and film music. With one exception, none pledged a single allegiance to a particular genre. Their tastes were not only eclectic but quickly shifting. The only exception was Jian Cui, a twenty-year-old high school dropout, as unique and nonconforming as his friend Chun Shu.[19] He is a music fanatic, an elitist, and thus, understandably, a minority of the minority, representing cultural behaviors that separate the "subculture" groups from the "tribal" culture groups, two extreme poles on the spectrum of Chinese youth culture.

Our project conformed to the rules of typical marketing qualitative research rather than to the protocols for a formal sociological project, which requires at least 2,000 samples to draw credible generalizations. The limits of time and resources also predetermined the nature of this mini–field project. Our goal was modest: to get into the mind—via digital photos—of the chosen candidates, to learn about their likes and dislikes, and to find out what they thought was cool and uncool. Specifically, the assignment of photo-narration aimed to empower our five ethnographic subjects and to motivate them to narrate through their own camera eye how they construct meaning in their specific lifestyle and taste culture. Once the consumer subject is turned into her own ethnographer, she is driven to exhibit and record her innermost thoughts and feelings in vignettes about ordinary days.

Each candidate was asked to take fifty photographs with his or her digital camera during one week for a small payment of 150 yuan (approximately $19). Our working assumption was simple: stories are told not only through the written word but also through the camera eye. A picture contains the seeds of a life story that reveals the moments of truth for the photographer. No single shot in such a photo diary is ever random; each has an emotional logic to trace. We instructed the candidates to capture (1) events and moments in their daily lives that excited them; (2) events, moments, or things that disgusted them; (3) "cool" objects and "cool" people; (4) happy moments and despondent moments; and (5) objects in their own rooms. We asked them to come back and tell us the "story" behind each shot as it flashed over the screen in an Ogilvy conference room. In the meantime, we supplemented the photo-narrative methodology with a creative survey and a three-hour-long in-depth interview conducted with each candidate. The five mini–photo archives that resulted from this project varied in their richness as visual tales. I single out three.

The first archive, from Simon, a design and architecture major aged twenty-one who used to worship the grunge group Nirvana, centers on the motif of "beauty" represented through a variety of shots that highlight the creative spatial relationships among the objects he feels drawn to. He defines beauty in spatial terms. Architecture and natural landscape shots loom large, as well as mundane items in his daily life such as his CDs and memorabilia of what he sees as "cools" (see p. 235). The centerpiece of his archive is what I would dub "a room with a view" (see p. 236), a collage pasted on the wall in his room, which is unmistakably a miniature visual autobiography. It and the shelves adjacent to it lay bare all his hobbies, past and the present, that is, art, music, guitars, and his favorite computer games. Each image or item sets off a story within a story that he eagerly shared with us, stories that told us all about his childhood and young adulthood, growing pains as well as happy memories. At the end of this visual interview, he told us, "You now know me better than anybody else that I know."

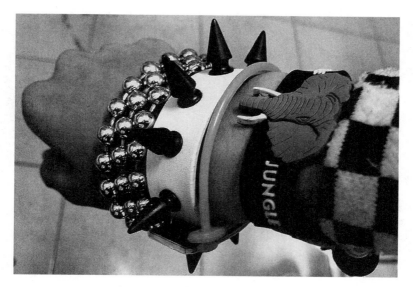

Simon's wristband. Ogilvy Beijing.

Archive number two is a collection of photos that cohere around an "ideal leisure mood," which the photographer Xiao Zhang (aged twenty-three, female) captured with close-up shots of a dragonfly, her beloved collection of old Chinese and foreign comic books, and her boyfriend's pet dog caught in various naughty poses. She travels back through time via those shots into some of the most precious moments in her childhood. It is an elusive mood rather than a particular event that she tried to catch and present. Each photo contains a mnemonic clue revealing a portion of her childhood sensibility around which she hopes to construct an "ideal condition for her future life."

Archive number three was provided by a sixteen-year-old girl whom I dubbed "Miss Cool." Her archive is made up of a hundred shots of cell phones and fashion magazines, many turned into a vast wall and ceiling collage. This candidate was an ideal target for us. She hangs out with her friends all day long, a typical young nomad

who is never home. Her photo collection showcases her colorful peer culture—fun moments collectively produced and consumed, and the hot spots frequented by her group. She and her buddies collaborated on the ceiling collage, and it even became a piece of performance art: she recorded the entire process of its production faithfully, snapping photos as she went along (see p. 239).

Another dozen photos tell us what she likes to wear—Converse shoes and safari motif sweaters. Then there are images of Samsung cell phones covered seamlessly from front to back in stickers (see p. 240). She gives us comparative shots of cell phone decorative art, contrasting cool stickers with ones that look so "ugly" and "uncool" that "you can tell the cell phone owner is a boring gal." Like several other candidates in this project, she loves pets—a squirrel for now, and thirty mice a while ago. Mixed in with the photographs of her squirrel are shots of places that make her depressed: the kitchen and dining room of her parents' home (she hates regular meals and lives on potato chips). Various interesting marketing ideas emerged from this archive. One is *"linglei gongshe"* (*linglei* commune), a tagline she pasted on the front door of the apartment, and another is the sticker culture of high school females.

In addition, all three archives reveal the storytelling potential of collages put up in their own rooms. "A room of one's own" carries special resonance for urban China's single-child generation if we contrast such luxury with the old days, when children shared the same bed with adults in a dingy, tiny apartment and had absolutely no space of their own.

Safe Cool

The five archives testified to the merits of photo-narration as a methodology for fieldwork for marketing investigations. "Music

---

Opposite page: A "room with a view." Ogilvy Beijing.

Xiao Zhang's Chinese and foreign comic book collection. Zhang Yujing.

Ceiling collage. Liu Tianqi.

culture" surprisingly played a relatively minor role in the photo collections. Although MP3 players are a badge of cool for Chinese youth, they featured sparingly and only in two archives. CDs and Sony Walkmans made occasional appearances, but even those images did not dominate. What stands out instead is an emerging pet culture, a different kind of companionship culture than peer culture. The photographs speak volumes about a culture of loneliness specific to the single-child generation, to which marketers have thus far paid scant attention. So much emphasis has been put on the narcissism of global youth that it is easy to ignore that these single children are in constant search of companionship, whether in friends or pets, animate or inanimate objects, and cell phones or other techno-gadgets. Marketing mobile music to the urban single-child generations will be effective if it builds on metaphors of companionship

Miss Cool's cell phone. Liu Tianqi.

and a happy childhood side by side with the conventional emphasis on "self-expression" stressed by transnational marketers.

These are fast-drawn impressions: the photo archives yield more anecdotal insights than solid data. To complement the photo-narrative exercise, the five candidates were asked to choose, from a list of thirty-nine expressions and phrases, those descriptors that best described their emotional, spiritual, mental, and social orientation. First, none of them circled the adjective "cool" *(ku)*, and this conscious evasion was itself interesting. They also bypassed adjectives linked directly to the notion of "cutting edge." As some cool-hunters have already proposed, we may be on the verge of entering a marketing era when the "center" is becoming the new edge, and the uncool will become the new cool (Grossman 2003).

Second, although most of the subjects confessed that they love to "indulge themselves" *(ai zongrong ziji)*, they were all committed to living a "life of purpose." One defined "purpose" as "studying English and becoming an air stewardess"; another as "passing the entrance examination, becoming a financier in the future." Twenty-one-year-old Xiao Li aspired to become "an influential computer software designer." Even Jian Cui, the alternative music fan and iconoclastic high school dropout, said that he is committed "to becoming an *established* researcher on music." Radical-looking college junior Xiao Zhang was most precise in specifying "different purposes for different stages of her life." She wanted to live a colorful life in her twenties so that others would envy her; at thirty, she aimed to become a "well-acknowledged" authority on "professional matters of intelligence"; at forty, she wanted to feel "accomplished as a happy wife and mother."

Third, with one exception, none professed a passion for "going to an extreme" *(xihuan zou jiduan)*. As Jian Cui puts it, "There is no need for that. Too much self-exposure isn't good. I believe in an old Chinese saying, 'Whenever water comes, there is a channel for it.' There are always opportunities for self-realization." Another subject commented, "Those who are content are happy. I don't like big ups and downs." Still another wanted to learn "how to position [himself] right in the middle" for perfect balance. Even the radical-looking female Xiao Zhang professed to frown upon "eccentric vogue" in favor of a "moderate and nuanced fashion sense."

The only person who checked the descriptor "I love to go to an extreme" was the sixteen-year-old "Miss Cool," whom I discovered in the food court of Hua Wei department store at Xidan. She was seen hanging out with a small gang of *linglei* youngsters at the store where fans of Japanese *manga* and idol culture and the Korean fashion tribes aggregate.[20] She stood out among her peers as a sharp punk stylist, wearing green-colored contact lenses, reddish hair sticking out in furious spikes, and more than two dozen bracelets on each of her arms. The long, slender necktie she wore had the distinct look of Japanese fashion. An obvious opinion leader, she was flanked by more than half a dozen peers sitting idly around the table, smoking and chatting. She was impatient, cold, and cool, with a pierced tongue and lower lip. After intensive persuasion, she agreed to participate in the photo-narration project.

On the much anticipated day of her formal interview at Ogilvy, however, "Miss Cool" showed up with bare wrists. Her wicked green contact lenses were now a conventional dark blue. She did not wear any fashion ties. Her tiny tongue stud was also missing. Her androgynous look had disappeared into girlish femininity. She had shed just about everything that would remind us of her punk fashion heritage, except the pierced ring in her lower lip. Dressed in a plain sweater and a pair of blue jeans, she looked completely tame and "ordinary." Not a trace of rebelliousness survived. The testy cold-blooded punk artist who could not wait to get out of my sight at our previous rendezvous had changed into an ultra-friendly, patient, and talkative young lady well versed in all the etiquette that social conventions require. The facility with which she turned herself from a bad girl into a "good" girl carries great analytical value. She knew exactly what separated the "extreme" from the "normal." This "role tailoring" can by no means be equated with a punker's commitment to a constant state of flux moving toward chaos, in Hebdige's terms, or "floating signification," in Barthes's terms (Hebdige 1979, 126). This brand of "cool" can be packaged and then quickly shed. Miss Cool may be too pragmatically minded to remain committed to her radical cause.

An article in the *Asia Times* argues that a Chinese rebel "isn't exactly channeling James Dean or a young Bob Dylan" (Beech 2004,

33). That finding coincides with one of the major viewpoints articulated in the first China Cool Hunt survey conducted by Hill & Knowlton (2004): "Chinese college students seek brands that will help them say 'I am unique' without making them look weird or socially unacceptable" (Smith and Wylie 2004). Although this survey reinforces the conventional wisdom that Chinese youth long for "independence" and "individualism," it also says that 35 percent of respondents name their parents, rather than cool celebrities, as their "idols," and that their outlook on life is built on an optimism characteristic of entrepreneurs at large. All this implies that they know and respect their boundaries well and, indeed, that they will think twice about trespassing them. Translated into ethics and beliefs, this insight highlights a rather uncool connection between the cool-looking youth and the status quo that they are supposedly poised to challenge. Deep in their heart, they are all entrepreneurs.[21] It is that entrepreneurial spirit that has turned the majority of the Me-Generation into pious observers of the "golden mean."[22] Xiao Liu, Xiao Zhang, the middle-school student, and the college students whom we interviewed over the course of two months are all products of this double-faced culture of the single-child generation.

The Hill & Knowlton survey also made clear that international artists lag far behind Asia's own pop singers like Faye Wang and Jay Chou in terms of popularity. "Asian, not Western, musicians are viewed as cool by this generation" (Hill & Knowlton 2004). This finding further reinforces the necessity of a locality-specific definition of "cool" music. Pop singers like Jay Chou, Faye Wong, and Motorola's Pu Shu sell so well precisely because their brand of "safe cool" involves no real iconoclasm.

SUBCULTURES VIS-À-VIS TRIBAL CULTURES

Music is primarily seen as entertainment in China and only to a lesser degree as a vehicle of self-expression. True, urban youth are fascinated with singing contests in the wake of the *Super Girl* craze, the reality show and spin-off of *American Idol*.[23] But that phenomenon is more about television contests than music per se and can be best attributed to the youth fervor for pursuing "fame on an equal footing" (Madden 2005c). Similarly, the music club culture of the nightlife area Sanlitun flourishes because young people use clubs as a networking venue; they party for fun and for a quick accumulation of social capital. Very few go clubbing for a soul-lifting musical experience, much less for alternative music of any kind. There is, of course, a small slice of young music hobbyists who consume counterculture melodies. They constitute a music subculture minority that thrives in Beijing and Chengdu (the capital city of Sichuan province) but has only a tiny presence in Shanghai and Guangzhou. I distinguish music subculture from music tribal culture using the same logic that separates "subculture" from "tribal" cultures.

As we saw in Chapter 5, Maffesoli argues that contemporary consumer society has witnessed an explosion of style cultures, or neo-tribes, that are organized around brand names and role-playing fantasies. Each tribe affiliated with a style niche is fluid in its aggregation and dispersal, with a commitment to a given tribal identity that lasts no longer than the turnover of cool fashion (Maffesoli 1996). In contrast to the subculture gangs, who are impious with a purpose (that is, resisting the status quo) and who play out the politics of in-group solidarity, the optimum strategy of the tribal members is to "tap into a number of lifestyles, adopting whichever one best fits the situation to hand" (Clarke, Doel, et al. 2003, 137). The politics of resistance built into subcultures is thrown to the winds as neo-tribes roam happily from one cool style to the next.

Although no strict dichotomy between subculture and tribal cultures can be neatly drawn, the Chinese music scene can be conceptualized as a spectrum structured on those poles. On one end is a true music subculture, on the other is pop music, which is essentially tribal in nature. Subculture music fans and artists, usually in their late twenties, have elitist musical tastes. They constitute a tightly knit circle in pursuit of a "spirit" *(jingshen)* that "soulless" pop music is considered to be lacking. Whether their heroes are Cui Jian or an emerging electronic music band like Panda Twin, the ethos of the subculture *(ya wenhua)* is characterized by an intense desire for soul bonding. In sharp contrast, the music tribes (teens, late teens, and early to mid-twentysomethings) chase after cool fashions and revel in their skin-deep allegiance to the changing idols on the music BBS (bulletin board systems).

What is the relevance of all this to Motorola and the other cell phone makers? One lesson is the need to clearly define the target segment for wireless music. The conceptual blur between "tribal culture" and "subculture" in China often results in confusion about whom to pick for focus group participants. It would be pointless, for instance, to compare the data culled from Miss Cool (a tribal character) with that from Jian Cui (a subculture pursuer) and try to build consistent consumer insights. Second, there exist in "subculture music" original ideas that can blossom into sustainable trends, a phenomenon encouraged by elite music producers like Zhang Yadong, who eagerly sought ways to break out of underground elitism without making too much of a compromise with the market (Ye Ying 2004). Third, the door of cross-fertilization between "music" and "fashion" *(shishang)* is by no means closed. Last, for transnational marketers genuinely interested in research, a comprehensive understanding of the music culture of Chinese youth can only be brought into full view if we account for the musical taste of soul-searching iconoclasts as well as of the lackadaisical cool-hunting youths who frequent clubs in the Sanlitun area and in its tamer brother, Houhai.

Tapping into the insights of such a diverse musical culture will continue to be seen as a crucial mission for transnational cell phone makers. Whether the new models of music marketing will work depends largely upon the marketers' commitment to pursuing location-sensitive and age-segmented understandings of music fans. Musical taste is not reliable as a sustained marker of personal and social identities even for metropolitan youth in China, and the equation between cool youth and cool music is not a simple one. Underlying that insight is the marketing truth that MTV exemplifies well: there is no single global tween and youth market for music stations. Today MTV has multiplied from a single television channel to thirty different channels, each with its own content and brand images. The research focus, once again, should be placed on the consumers themselves—the single-child generation who set their own agendas and who know how to get what they want with a determination and optimism rarely seen in previous generations. Nobody can hold them hostage for long.

CHAPTER 7

CCTV and the Advertising Media

Branding culminates in placing the product in various forms of media, including ads on television, billboards, the Internet, and so on. Planning and buying media in China share some commonalities with the West. In television, for example, advertisers' decisions about where to place a commercial depend increasingly on Western standards of cost efficiency. But the television media in China is different in one crucial characteristic: it is state owned and state controlled. CCTV (China Central Television) has bested other media outlets in garnering advertising revenues precisely because it is both the government's mouthpiece and a powerful conglomerate.

We can gain insight into CCTV's "monopoly game" by examining its prime-time advertising auctions and by appraising various countermeasures adopted by provincial satellite stations to offset such a monopoly. We will also look at the hottest advertising vehicle in China today—TV dramas. But first I provide a general introduction to China's media environment and the effects of a 1999 landmark policy document.

The mixed impact of state regulations and capital entry on China's media is often noted by observers. But I dispute the conventional wisdom that capital is inherently liberating and that China's policies regarding media are completely disabling. Market-driven media, after all, cannot be equated with democratic media in the

West (Y. Zhao 1998), and their potential to unleash anti-establishment voices in China has been greatly exaggerated. More often than not, the socialist state and the market are related in collusive rather than antithetical terms in the post-1992 Chinese media sector (J. Wang 2004; Gutmann 2005; Y. Zhao 2005).[1]

Some statistics:

- Advertising revenue in 2003[2] was distributed among major media outlets in China as follows: 23.64 percent (television); 22.53 percent (newspapers); 2.37 percent (radio); 11.12 percent (outdoor ads); and 1 percent (the Internet). The total revenue accrued by Chinese television stations during 2003 was $3.1 billion (Zhang Haichao 2004, 21–23).
- The national television penetration rate was 98.2 percent in 2005. The nationwide TV audience amounts to 1.167 billion. There are 368 television stations in China, broadcasting a total of 2,214 channels. Approximately 89 percent of urban households and 40.2 percent of rural households can now receive satellite TV.
- The average TV viewing time per individual per day was 179 minutes in 2003 (about 8 minutes less than in 1998), compared with 230 minutes consumed daily by an average U.S. viewer (Wang Lanzhu 2002, 123; Chinese Gold Eagle TV 2004, 49–56; Zhang Haichao 2004, 21).

Those statistics indicate that television is the most influential advertising medium in China, and it will be our primary focus in this chapter. Urban TV viewers have a plethora of program choices during their average three-hour daily viewing time. Given that the total TV broadcasting time in 2002 translates into 3,000 hours per day across provincial stations, the disproportionate ratio between program supply and spectator demand is astounding (Chinese Gold Eagle TV 2004, 21). Although the number of broadcast hours says little about program quality and the extent of reruns, a quantum leap in broadcasting volume from 2001 to 2002—a 14.5 percent increase that has continued to rise annually—foretells the worsening of the imbalance between the clutter generated by the tube alone and a viewer's maximum capacity for media consumption. In 2005, the average number of channels available to urban households escalated to 42, and in rural China, 33 (CMM Intelligence 2005). Meanwhile, more and more channels are being created as a result of major policy changes that encourage channel proliferation, without a parallel policy incentive to open up the heavily monitored content of television programming. Many media critics hold the bottleneck in stations' ability to provide new content responsible for the increasing homogenization of programs, which in turn disheartens advertisers and curbs the growth of advertising billings.

THE TV CONTENT INDUSTRY: PARTIALLY COMMERCIAL

Discussions in China about deepening media reforms have focused on policy measures aiming to revive the stagnant content sector. The mantra of the regulatory organ SARFT (the State Administration of Radio, Film, and Television) has been "content is king." But despite the post-WTO Western hype regarding the "liberalization of Chinese content," the TV content industry has not made great leaps; on the contrary, it has slid backward since 2001. The Chinese have lagged far behind in this domain while making great progress in other sectors. We may ask where the obstacles lie or, perhaps, where the misleading Western hype went wrong.

To begin, the WTO agreements do not bind China to content liberalization. Chinese authorities associate media with the notion of "cultural security," and policies governing foreign joint ventures keep fluctuating. In 2004, China seemed ready for foreign investment in television show content: Viacom's Nickelodeon division quickly inked a joint venture agreement with Shanghai Media Group (SMG) to co-produce youth and children's programming, and other players like News Corp and Discovery Channel followed suit by negotiating similar partnerships.[3] But the following year saw SARFT scale back earlier promises with stipulations that such productions must be pre-approved and that all content from joint ventures must be "at least two thirds oriented toward Chinese culture" (Madden 2006b). Western media companies must negotiate every nuance of programming with the Chinese authorities. When Nickelodeon's popular children's program "The Kids' Choice Awards" finally came to Shanghai at the end of 2005, the producers were required to make some serious compromises by toning down the unruly aspects of the show.[4] During the same year, SARFT further tightened its control of radio and video joint ventures, forbidding any new foreign-owned television satellite channels from entering the country. And a ban on leasing Chinese radio and TV channels (and channel signals) to foreign media in China and restrictions on joint channel investment and operation with foreign companies placed an indefinite moratorium on Disney and Viacom's co-production plans in the country (SARFT 2005).

Behind these difficulties lay a regulating principle: the Chinese government consistently (and successfully) splits "content" into three categories—that which can be made commercial,[5] that which cannot, and that which is in between. Channels and stations that run financial and economic news, which is considered "safe content," are open to transnational investors. Joint entertainment programming is still off limits. The pacts made between News Corp and the Hunan Media Group, and between Time Warner and CCTV and Shanghai Media, raised hopes that the content market would be wide open before long. But getting government approval is no easy task. Meanwhile, Murdoch and Warner played right into the master scheme of SARFT. Regulators of post-WTO China have not hesitated to give preferential treatment to politically nonsensitive topics such as finance and economy, science and technology, leisure and lifestyle—any ideologically neutral mass-market fare such as game shows and talk shows, sports, and drama. A partial opening is beneficial to the socialist state. It stimulates the growth of domestic Chinese television show content and obtains for China reciprocal broadcasting rights in the West.

Thirty-some foreign satellite channels are allowed to broadcast in China (among them CNN, HBO, CINEMAX, Phoenix Infonews, Bloomberg, Star TV, Euro Sports News, MTV Mandarin, CNBC Asia Pacific, Channel V, TVB8, Discovery, and AXN). Their broadcasting rights are confined to Guangdong province and the foreign diplomatic compounds or to luxury hotels (three stars and above) in urban China. The vast territory outside the Pearl River Delta is out of reach. In addition to these restrictions, all foreign content is subject to rigorous censorship prior to distribution.

The constraints on programming carry important repercussions for Chinese advertising, because the media peddle content to advertisers, whose ultimate goal is to match target segments with media segments. Television, for example, has had a hard time developing sophisticated sponsorship relations with advertisers and taking the lead in attracting advertising dollars unless it has premium programs. Thus one of the major barriers to the growth of Chinese advertising is the only partially commercialized TV content sector. As content regulators let in only certain foreign media and open up only select content for capital entry, China's internal debate on media commodification is focused less on "how to commodify" (a favorite question for Western media analysts of China) than on "*which* subsectors to commercialize." This point is often missed by Western media commentators who celebrate foreign broadcasters' inroads into China as a sign that a communist society has been forced open by the WTO agreement.[6] Not only is such a celebration premature, but it simplifies the complex media strategies Beijing has resorted to in co-opting foreign capital to its own ends.

On the other end of Western misperceptions about China is the myth that Chinese policymaking is incorrigibly opaque. It is true that China's media and cultural policies are intriguingly deceptive, but they have their own logic. Although SARFT's ideological control has prevented a wholesale liberalization in China's cultural industry at large, certain areas are officially designated as "commercializable" *(you yingli xing)*, as we have seen. Some are considered threshold categories to be judged on a case-by-case basis.

Commercializable, nonmonopoly cultural industry subsectors and content service sectors are considered less sensitive to cultural and information security concerns. These include performance, tourism, industrial and cultural exhibitions, technical production and distribution of audiovisual products, sports and the entertainment industry, and higher education and professional education. These various sectors and subsectors are open to domestic and foreign investment. At the same time, national capital invested there is deemed intrusive, and has been ordered to exit by various means such as asset sales and transfers, mergers, close-downs, and declarations of bankruptcy. The government knows that in order to ensure a boom in those sectors that deliver relatively noncontroversial content and services, it has to bring in capital in large volume. The more, the merrier.

Most relevant to advertising, however, are those aspects of the media sector that are or could be commercial, but are part of the monopoly that the Chinese state wants to retain—i.e., on radio and TV broadcasting of news and any other content it considers politically risky or off-limits. Here the government's approach has taken an intriguing turn. Capital entry in these areas is highly contested due to policy fluctuations. State capital has been authorized to monopolize media heavyweights like CCTV and SMG (Shanghai Media Group), but made to exit from medium and small media companies, a policy that is just the opposite of what has been deemed proper for the development of nonmonopoly sectors (and subsectors) over which the government does not want to maintain a monopoly.

This hairsplitting logic of distinguishing safe from risky content and service also prompted a landmark directive in 1999 that dictated the separation of broadcasting and production. Capital is allowed to enter what are considered the "infrastructural subsectors" *(jichu gongye)*, such as service-related value chains in the media industry (cable transmissions, management of printing and publishing, retail businesses, information delivery and distribution networks)—subunits that have little to do with programming and content and are thus deemed "safe" subsectors open for commercial investment.

Painstaking efforts to differentiate content from delivery are also consistent with state logic: identify what can be made commercial and commodify it. Splitting hairs further, the state designates coexisting forbidden areas and free zones within each subsector. When a conflict of interest (between the state and the market) arises, SARFT is called upon to redefine what is and isn't off limits. The regulators' constant redrawing of the boundaries between what can, cannot, and might be made commercial across and within each subsector has baffled Western investors. The Chinese appear to abide by no rules. Impressions of this sort have contributed to the common misconception that Chinese policymakers are "clueless." Yet the central policy has hardly swerved, regardless of micro-instances of occasional relaxation and occasional retrenchment.

DOCUMENT NO. 82: A POLICY MILESTONE

The 1999 media policy that carried far-reaching implications was the famous Document No. 82 "Administrative Guidelines for Strengthening the Construction of Wired Transmissions for Radio and Television," through which major reforms were put in place.[7] Among them were the separation of station (content) and network (delivery) *(wangtai fenying)*, the conglomeration of radio and television groups, the integration of broadcast and cable TV networks at the city and county level for more centralized control, and the theoretical split of TV production units from broadcast units *(zhibo fenli)*.[8] In addition, county TV channels were ordered to phase out. The old four-tier network licensing system was pared down to three tiers (the national, provincial, and municipal). This large-scale restructuring had heavy repercussions for the advertising industry.

First, the exit of county TV stations diminished the media-buying choices of local advertisers and weakened their bargaining power for media buys. Advertisers now face tougher negotiations with provincial TV network for discounts. The emergence of the provincial network as a major player also changed the competition for advertisers seeking national television audiences. As of 2003, for example, provincial satellite stations reached 19 percent of the TV drama audience compared with the 12 percent share held by CCTV (Wu Dong 2003, 18).

Second, the merging of radio and television (both broadcast and cable) networks gave rise to powerful conglomerates, among them the Beijing Radio and TV Group, the Shanghai Media Group, and the Hunan Group. Other provinces and municipalities soon followed suit. By 2005 major broadcasting groups had mushroomed all over China, a phenomenon corresponding to the creation of newspaper groups in the late 1990s. A primary cause of such intense merger movements nationally was the WTO. Beijing has been bracing itself for the imagined foreign onslaught. As soon as China's accession to the WTO appeared inevitable, the country's policymakers began major asset restructuring in all sectors, media included (J. Wang 2005b, 13–18). It is "size" that matters in the wake of the WTO agreements. The Chinese understanding of globalization hasn't gone beyond the notion of scale economy, which underlies policy slogans like "consolidating the big and letting go of the small" *(zuoqiang zuoda)*. Media conglomeration was seen as a countermeasure to infiltration by global media giants like Viacom, Time Warner, and the News Corp. However, these state-orchestrated megamergers have not reconfigured Chinese TV advertising as anticipated.

Theoretically, after asset and resource consolidation, major media groups should be in a better position to develop specialized channels which in turn may generate audience segments primed for paid services. However, as of 2007 or so, Chinese pay TV had not taken off due to the dearth of premium content. Channel reception has been largely free, and as a result, stations rely heavily on advertising income (90 percent of station revenue came from advertisers) to cover operational costs (Xie and Ni 2007). This singular business model has reinforced the dictatorship of program ratings, which has translated into TV stations' preference for reproducing clichéd formulae that guarantee the mass appeal upon which advertisers calculate their advertising expenditure (Zhou, Wang, and Zhu 2002, 19–20). The vicious circle is difficult to break. Program cloning has become the norm (Keane 2002). Incentives for innovation are ruled out by the system. Disappointingly, the megamergers did not reverse the trend of the overdependence of stations on advertising income. On the contrary, the integration of cable and broadcast TV decreased media choices and had a negative impact on advertising volume. The bottleneck in the production of new or more varied program content was all the more evident. Without a parallel provision for opening up and diversifying content platforms, real progress toward media reform cannot be expected.

The Separation of Program Production and Broadcasting

The most important provision of Document No. 82 was its separation of station (production of programs) and network (broadcasting of programs) within the radio and television system—a regulation that brought new life to a sector disadvantaged by restricted content innovation. The separation may also be described as a division between content (stations) and delivery (networks), and it had a huge impact on Chinese advertising. Networks had formerly been inseparable from their stations in their management and financial infrastructure. Because the station was deemed a public cultural institution *(shiye danwei)* and therefore subject to regulations governing national cultural security, commercializing networks had hitherto been off limits. Following the divorce, however, networks were freed up to expand value-added services such as pay TV, VOD (video on demand), distance learning, broadband access, and Internet data services while continuing with television transmissions.

Since the historic separation, local cable operators have been flourishing. As of May 2005, 110 million Chinese households subscribed to cable, making China the top subscription television market in the world (Budde 2005, 2; CMM Intelligence 2005). Many cable transmission companies like Beijing-based Gehua have been active in public offerings. Even for companies not listed on the stock market, the model of the "triple play" (television, telephone, and Internet service) has promised sizable revenue.[9] The charge for cable modem high-speed access was 300 yuan per month in 2003. Although the monthly charge for basic cable TV service rose only to a paltry 15 yuan per month by 2005 (Ai 2003), the sheer number of cable subscribers will add up.[10] Even more auspiciously, by 2005 China was expected to have more than 10 million VOD users. In the meantime, it was said that traffic generated by data communications was doubling each year, yielding estimated annual revenues of 200 billion yuan by 2005 (ibid.). The cable networks are expected to snatch a good slice of that jumbo pie. All these statistics demonstrate the explosive growth that can be anticipated for cable networks for years to come.

Convergence and the Duel between SARFT and MII

A weak link, however, exists in this apparently seamless value chain. The convergence between the Internet and cable businesses has been a focal point of controversy between the MII (Ministry of Information Industry) and SARFT for years.[11] In 1999, an agreement between the two regulatory bodies resulted in a stipulation preventing telecommunication operators and cable operators from crossing over into each other's territory.[12] But new technology made an overlap between the two systems (radio/TV transmission and telecom transmission) inevitable. If cable operators are barred from the telecom business, reducing telecom and Internet access fees through competition between the two will not be possible.[13] The clash of interests between the two regulatory bodies continued well into 2007.[14] On the other hand, convergence is a global trend difficult to ward off for a country whose desire to catch up with international norms is as intense as its regulatory fever. The founding in 2005 of a new national cable monopoly, the China Cable Network (CCN), further upped the ante of cable operators in their bid for a better revenue-sharing arrangement with telecom operators. CCN, whose majority ownership rests with SARFT, owns a 70,000-kilometer-long fiber backbone broadcasting network nationwide. It will consolidate, step by step, the divergent local operators and integrate cable, wireless, terrestrial, and satellite transmissions all under its banner.

Amid all the new opportunities for cable operators, China's move toward digital television (DTV) also occurred. Guangdong, Fujian, Shanxi, Hunan, Shaanxi, Jiangxi, and several other provinces, together with Beijing and Shanghai municipalities, began switching television transmissions from analog to digital platforms in 2005 ("Nation Tunes In" 2005). Cable subscribers are now able to watch DTV programs. According to the statistics, by December 2006 there were twenty-four cities that had finished the overall conversion (China Digital TV Market 2007). This important technological advance owed as much to Document No. 82 as it did to the vision underlying CCN. The commercialization of the cable network driven by that policy document triggered a series of business expansions into other service territories previously closed to it. Convergence and digitalization were two logical scenarios awaiting the cable network once it broke loose from content-driven television stations.

The divorce between "network" and "station" did not mean the end of a relationship, however. One of the basic services provided by the cable network is the transmission of TV programs. A growth-driven network relies heavily on channel leasing and channel broadcasting. It is naturally starved for more channels. This new dynamic in turn puts pressure on television stations to deliver new programs to satisfy cable network demand. Advertisers now have more channels on which to place their products as a result of the accelerating development of the TV programming sector. The automatic feed between an ever-expanding network and a station pressed to deliver more programs proves lucrative for all the players on the value chain.

The No. 82 decree therefore opened the cable network sector to diverse measures of liberalization and market stewardship. Without the policy document, those engaged in content creation for Chinese television programs might not have felt the urgency to seek programming partners abroad and open themselves up partially to foreign investors in 2004 and 2005. Despite their thwarted attempts for the time being, Time Warner's dalliance with CCTV and SMG, and Nickelodeon's alliance with CCTV on programming children's channels represented a turning point in the development of Chinese television content, which was after all made possible because of the television industry's reaction to the separation of production and broadcasting. Even more important, the same policy also helped push the digitalization of Chinese television to the front burner for SARFT (Huang and Ding 2001, 279–285; Chinese Gold Eagle TV 2004, 241–245; Zhongguo dianshi wang 2005). DTV is the ultimate answer to the insatiable demand of broadcasting companies for channel multiplication.[15]

Document No. 82 serves as an excellent entry point for us to investigate the major changes that have redefined the Chinese media market. We have also seen the mutual dependency of the two sectors (media and advertising). Although it is still too early to study the impact of pay TV and DTV on the advertising industry, new formats of advertising may emerge in China to make spot advertisements look outdated. In September 2004, CCTV started airing pay channels "without the interruption of ads." But the station also planned to debut a new channel called "Brands and Consumer Trends" *(pinpai yu shishang),* to be sponsored by big advertisers, and a new automobile channel hawking "added-value services" to the auto-tribe (Li and Yang 2004). New advertising ideas highlighting interactivity will no doubt keep cropping up to counter technology's threat to TV commercials.[16] Meanwhile, even without a technological aid like TiVo, more channel choices have already prompted Chinese TV viewers to grow the habit of channel flipping. Even as early as 1999, statistics revealed channel-switching viewers of Chinese TV to be a high 44.6 percent. In 2000, the rate swung up to 50.4 percent, and to 57.6 percent in 2002 (Chinese Gold Eagle TV 2004, 228). With such fickle audiences, advertisers must find more novel ways to capture their eye. The answer might be product placement in TV dramas and feature films.[17] Or advertisers may soon copy the latest Western trend of integrating campaigns set in fictional gaming universes.[18]

CCTV ADVERTISING AUCTIONS: A MONOPOLY GAME?

We see that advertising is not only bound to the media industry financially but also sensitive to creative innovations made possible by new media technologies. Media, however, is not the only sector accounting for the ebb and flow of the advertising industry. Standing at the intersection between cultural production and commodity production, advertising is also shaped by its structural relationship with the corporate sector. Corporate clients and their media-buying behavior are thus crucial to advertising studies. Similarly, corporate law exerts an influence on advertising practices no less significant than a watershed media policy like Document No. 82.

For example, in May 2000 a proposed new tax law, which capped corporate ad expenditure at 2 percent of the company's annual gross revenue, plunged the advertising industry into a heated debate over the regulatory jurisdiction of the National Tax Bureau—the author of the new edict (Yi Ming 2001). The tax bureau had meddled in advertising regulation in order to curb rampant tax evasion. The 2 percent cap, if implemented, would prevent companies from committing themselves to an oversized ad expenditure, which is exempt from taxation. The proposed cap would deal a blow to corporate advertisers such as pharmaceutical manufacturers, whose annual ad spending runs as high as 30 percent of a company's gross income in the United States. Lifestyle product categories, because of their hefty dependence on advertising, would be badly hurt as well. If the law were implemented, both big advertisers and ad agencies would suffer significant revenue losses.

Not surprisingly, the bureau's proposition, made without prior consultation with the SAIC (the State Administration of Industry and Commerce, which regulates the ad sector), kicked up a storm of protest, and intense negotiations ensued among the different parties involved. In the end, legislation raised the cap from 2 percent of annual gross revenue to 8 percent of a corporation's previous year's sales volume. A large cushion was also added to the bill that allowed newly established enterprises in risky sectors (such as the computer industry) to bargain for a higher allowance for ad spending.[19] The crisis also raised flags about the underrepresentation of the advertising sector in regulatory matters.

More important, the debate over the 2 percent cap on ad expenditures implicated CCTV, China's biggest TV conglomerate. The anti–tax-evasion bill was a double-edged offensive aiming at two targets: corporate advertisers and CCTV. It contained an implicit criticism of CCTV's annual advertising auctions, which crowned a "king bidder" *(biaowang)* every fall. The advertiser with the highest bid for the prime-time segment of the programming was entitled to air its product for *five seconds* every day at 7:30 P.M. (after the news and right before the start of the prime-time programs) in the coming year. A dozen other advertisers also bought the right to show a five-second commercial in the "golden" sixty seconds preceding 7:30. The infamous bidding wars quickly generated a myth: spending big on CCTV prime-time would enable a corporation to boost its sales the following year.[20] The auction started in 1995, but it was not until the late 1990s that print media and policymakers began to unleash criticisms of the "unhealthy phenomenon of the king bidder." The 2 percent cap was thus also the lawmakers' instrument for curbing the disproportionate spending of Chinese corporations on CCTV's prime-time auctions.

Where Have All the King Bidders Gone?

Consider a selected list of the "king bidders" and their bidding prices (Zhang and Liu 2004, 93; Zhao Shuguang 2004, 56–60):

1995	Confucian House Liquor	Yearly bid	$3,750,000 (CCTV suggested starting bids at $1,500,000)
1996	Qinchi Liquor	Yearly	$7,500,000 (CCTV suggested starting bids at $1,725,000)
1997	Qinchi Liquor	Yearly	$40,150,000 (CCTV suggested starting bids at $2,062,500)[21]
2003	Panda Mobile	Unit bid	$13,200,200
2004	Mengniu Dairy	Unit bid	$37,530,000

These figures betray many signs of irrational marketing. The gap between CCTV's asking price and the advertiser's final bid was enormous for 1996 (an increase of 4.6 times) and 1997 (18.7

times). The aggressive bidding was voluntary, and the skyrocketing prices were thus not totally attributable to the domination of monopolistic media.

Other factors contributed to the bidding craze from the mid- to late 1990s as well. Status flaunting (the "face" factor) and excessive optimism regarding the selling power of CCTV prime-time ads played a major role in driving up voluntary overbids. The anomaly—all for the sake of securing a five-second spot—is much more obvious if compared with the quarterly rate for a thirty-second prime-time commercial on U.S. network television, which in 1999 cost only $190,000.[22] It was also apparent that the CEO of Qinchi Liquor was a reckless gambler, in raising the gambit from $7.5 million to $40 million in one year. To be a king bidder for two years in a row was a formula for corporate suicide. Sure enough, Qinchi sank into debt the following year. And the company was not the first king bidder who failed to pay its bills to CCTV. It was, in fact, Qinchi's notorious 1997 bid that triggered a public backlash directed at CCTV and the auction frenzy (Li Weijie 1997; Hu and Yu 1998; Yan Zhigang 1998).

Prime-time ad auctions are a sales method unique to the Chinese media market. It took years before transnational advertisers like Procter & Gamble, Hitachi, and Colgate-Palmolive entered the contest.[23] CCTV has used auctions to set advertising-spot prices for a variety of reasons. One clear reason is that an advertiser's bid often exceeds the real sales value of a media spot. The secret of the auction lay in the voluntary revelation of an advertiser's maximum capacity for ad spending. It also revealed which corporate sector (for instance, liquor) was willing to make the biggest pitch.[24] This auction trend was also propelled by the larger business environment in the mid-1990s. Economic growth has transformed the Chinese market from a sellers' to a buyers' market, and escalating competition for consumers sent corporations in droves to find sensational sales pitches. CCTV was believed to have worked miracles for ambitious domestic corporations. Every evening at 7 o'clock, approximately 300 million television sets are turned on. More than 850 million people are tuning in to Channel-1 simultaneously. The 65 seconds that follow the national news and precede the weather forecast[25]—thirteen spots altogether, with the first one going to the king bidder—naturally became the hottest commodity for competing advertisers. Corporations seeking a year-long "blanket bombing" impact through five-second commercials dreamed big about turning their brands into household names overnight. There were some success stories. Confucian House Liquor—the highest bidder in 1995—achieved record sales of $109 million in 1996. Even Qinchi harvested a good first year, boasting that its market share jumped five times higher than the previous year's after debuting on Channel-1 (Zhao Shuguang 2004, 57). The myth grew rapidly. CCTV's net auction income zoomed from 3.6 million yuan ($450,000) in 1996 to 2.84 billion yuan ($355 million) in 1998. But a slowdown set in after the Qinchi debacle. In 1999, the station's auction income dipped to 2.68 billion ($335 million). It slid further to 1.92 billion ($240,000) in 2000, but gradually recovered to a modest 2.63 billion ($328.7 million) in 2002 (Yu Jianqiang 2004, 212; Zhang and Liu 2004, 94), and ballooned to 6.8 billion yuan ($860 million) in 2006 (Kwok 2006).

The Qinchi factor was not the only reason behind the decline in CCTV's auction revenues after 1998. Media proliferation in China since the mid-1990s has given corporate advertisers more media choices and better bargaining leverage. Another factor driving media prices down has been effective countermeasures adopted by bidding corporations against inflated prime-time rates (Zhang and Liu 2004, 96–97). CCTV reacted to the downward drift by letting go of irrational modes of auctioning such as hidden bids, and opted for approaches that nurture longer-term revenue growth rather than short-term auction gains. This strategic readjustment implied a shift away from overemphasizing the single-spot benefit. Meanwhile incremental pricing reforms at CCTV also allowed advertisers to choose and mix spots. For instance, Mengniu Diary's $37.5 million ad purchase in 2004 was a sum total of scatter buys spread not only across seasons but also across program units and prime-time slots. The "king-bidder" tradition in its old hyperbolic guise came to an end around 1999. A new era of rational media marketing began, with CCTV offering win-win strategies safeguarding the dual interests of corporate clients and media vendors.[26]

"We are selling not only spots, but also services" (Lu Jinzhu 2002, 93). The soft-pedaling by CCTV brought the concept of "media marketing" *(meijie yingxiao)* into the limelight. Bidding zest returned to the annual November auctions. Today CCTV's success is taken as the corporate world's vote of confidence in China's robust economy. Even foreign corporations like P&G and Unilever joined the fray. Combining prime-time spot purchases and TV drama sponsorship, P&G became the biggest winner for the 2005 season, with an outlay totaling more than $46.5 million (Wang Jixin 2004, 104). "King bidder" now took on a new range of meanings. It indicates no more than a savvy mix of expenditures during prime-time TV programming, no longer a single throw of the dice. In 2006 CCTV's auction underwent another major change: re-branded as the "Premium Resources Auction," it dropped its former "prime-time" tag altogether to reflect the inclusion of non–prime-time slots for ratings magnets such as the biennial "Youth Singer" and the 2006 FIFA World Cup (Savage 2005c). The format changes in the auction encouraged more program sponsorship and were no doubt a response to the popularity of competitor Hunan Satellite TV, whose two recent hits—the imported Korean drama *Daejanggeum* (Jewel in the Palace) and the *Idol*-style show *Super Girl*—brought in millions of viewers and big profits for advertisers.[27] Will new challenges from provincial media make CCTV's auction look increasingly outdated and perhaps even overrated? Not yet. The consensus is still that the "CCTV auction is not the only means to grow a brand. But to become a big famous brand, *you have to do it*" (Gu 2002, 89). These words ring true even in 2007.

TV AUDIENCE RESEARCH:
THE ANTI-MONOPOLY LOGIC OF MEDIA MIX

CCTV's 2005 auction raised nearly 5.25 billion yuan ($634 million), 18.9 percent higher than the previous year's yield. The harvest derived in part from the stepped-up engagement of foreign enterprises. P&G outbid domestic advertisers to become the first foreign "king bidder." Unilever, Gillette, Colgate, and KFC all made successful bids, as well.[28] Another important factor contributing to the escalated auction competition was a new SARFT regulation in 2004.

Provisional Measure No. 17 limits advertising to 20 percent of the day's broadcast hours and 15 percent of the hourly programming time between 7:00 and 9:00 P.M. (Xie 2005, 102). The latter stipulation represented a 3 percent cut in prime-time advertising, shortening the total output to eighteen minutes total (that is, nine minutes of commercials for each program aired during those two hours). In addition, advertisements of alcoholic beverages were reduced from seventeen to twelve per day, and from three to two during the prime 7–9 P.M. slots. TV drama advertising suffered further restrictions: drama series shown outside prime-time hours are allowed to broadcast only a single advertising segment capped at 2.5 minutes long (an episode lasts for 45 minutes) (Yuan Fang 2004, 29). If the original intention of the SARFT was to curb advertising clutter, the new measure has led to fewer spots, which has translated into steep rate hikes. Sichuan provincial TV, for instance, raised its ad rates by 30 percent following the announcement of the new regulation (Png 2004). The average rate hike was 22.2 percent for satellite stations, 12 percent for CCTV, and 13.9 percent for municipal TV stations (Xie 2005, 102–103). CCTV capped its auctioned prime-time slots at nine minutes. It left another nine minutes of fringe time for regular TV ad transactions (Zhang Haiying 2004). (Enterprises who fail to win an auctioned slot have to face an equally ferocious competition for the left-over nine minutes.) The curtailing of commercial airtime left advertisers in a crunch.[29]

In part because prime-time spots were in such short supply, CCTV's auction for the 2005 season was a sellout. A more important factor in its success lay in the new availability of media measurement data provided by credible research companies. When Procter & Gamble's representative raised his bidding banner in November 2004, he was betting in confidence on the widely circulated statistics that demonstrated the premium value of CCTV-1.

By November 2004, it was a known fact that the national reach of CCTV-1 was as high as 94.4 percent—the only channel that is received throughout the country, with almost no blind spots.[30] As of the 2007 season, the ratings for the golden minute that follows the evening news and precedes the weather forecast met no rivals in Beijing and in north, central, and northwest China. MindShare, a media subsidiary of the WPP Group, a world leader in marketing communications services, conducted research on twenty-five Chinese cities during 2004. Their statistics further confirmed the market value of the 65 seconds in question. In addition, 29.2 percent of CCTV audiences did not switch channels while they were watching the two programs sandwiched preceding and immediately following the golden minute (MindShare 2004, 27).

Researchers have long been arguing that media exposure rate does not necessarily translate into statistics showing how many persons have actually watched or read ads. But there is no denying that tuning in means increased opportunities for ad exposure.[31] Furthermore, if we accept CCTV's internal data that the CPM (cost per thousand, or the cost of delivering an ad to one thousand people or households) for that channel is as low as 1 yuan (CCTV 2006), it follows that Channel-1 must be the ultimate choice for advertisers.[32] The general principle is to select the media vehicle with the lowest CPM. Conventional wisdom holds that the "vehicle that delivers the largest number of exposed targets at the most efficient cost is a good enough criterion for selecting media" (Sissors and Baron 2002, 51).

A look at TV audience measurement (TAM) highlights the growing internationalization of Chinese media buying and media planning. Since the founding of the TAM company CSM Media Research in 1997 (full name CVSC-SOFRES Media, a joint venture between CCTV-affiliated CTR Market Research and the London-based Taylor Nelson Sofres Group), media research in China has entered a scientific era and become increasingly professionalized. Although ratings *(shoushi lu)*[33] still serve as the basic yardstick of audience measurement, new concepts such as CPP (the cost per rating point), CPM, GRP (gross rating points), and VPVH (viewers per viewing household) have all streamed into the young industry.

CSM is now the largest and most authoritative TAM company in China; its rival, AC Nielsen, lags far behind in coverage and technological development. Utilizing diary panels and planting electronic people meters into households, CSM offers uninterrupted TAM services, monitoring more than 28,000 households and 80,000 persons, viewing data for more than 80 cities and 14 provinces, and measuring over 700 main channels around the clock. It now serves over 20 international ad agencies and broadcasters, 100 television stations, and more than 300 domestic ad agencies (Yu Jianqiang 2004, 155–164; CTR Market Research 2005a).

Cynics may quibble that all the scientific media data prove one thing that requires no TAM technology—the low CPM of a monopoly media conglomerate like CCTV. Yet the monthly CSM media bulletins published in *International Advertising* provide many useful insights for media planners, not least because they validate the cost-efficiency benefit of channel mix. For instance, a CSM measurement study conducted in December 2004 revealed that buying part of CCTV's golden minute is not the sole option for an advertiser. The study ranks each of the top ten media and channels in six major cities, revealing a heterogeneous landscape that casts doubt on the monopoly label many apply to CCTV (CSM 2005, 104). If purchases of ad time in local media are combined wisely, an advertiser with a lower ad budget who is eyeing the Chengdu and Shanghai markets might conceivably bypass CCTV's prime-time auctions by opting for a mix of Chengdu City TV and Sichuan Provincial TV, on the one hand, and of Shanghai Television and Oriental Satellite TV, on the other. Such a hypothetical media selection makes sense, because, as the statistics of CSM show, the top ten most favored channels in Shanghai are all local ones. Reports confirming the strength of Shanghai's local stations (audience share was reportedly 71 percent) over CCTV are readily available (Wang Lanzhu 2002, 230).[34] But the CSM bulletin breaks the shares down into specific channels. When we turn to Chengdu, the ratings gap between the top two CCTV channels and Chengdu and Sichuan stations is surprisingly slim. At least five local and Sichuan provincial channels demonstrate their strength in running close to the three lower-ranked CCTV channels (all scoring below the 5.5 percent mark). The detailed breakdown of channel shares encourages the practice of narrowcasting (see Table 8).

Unintentionally, TAM technology provides us useful tools with which to subvert the myth that media with a monopoly always monopolize. Science is able to destabilize myths by poking holes in them. This is exactly where the true value of the monthly TAM reports lies. They keep CCTV on its toes while empowering the lesser media vehicles that are lying in wait to snatch audiences from the monopoly media giant.

TABLE 8 Reception Ratings of Primary TV Channels in Shanghai and Chengdu, December 2004

Ranking	Program	Channel	Average reception rate (%)
Reception ratings of primary TV channels in Shanghai (December 2004)			
1	News Perspective	Shanghai TV News Catchall	14.1
2	TV Drama (Chinese Style Divorce)	Shanghai TV News Catchall	12.7
3	STV News	Shanghai TV News Catchall	12.0
4	Views from the Audience	Shanghai TV News Catchall	11.3
5	Drama (My Uncle and His Children's Children)	Oriental Satellite Station News & Entertainment Channel	9.1
6	Drama (The Silent Witness)	Shanghai TV News Catchall	8.7
7	Weather Forecast	Shanghai TV News Catchall	8.7
8	Hot Line Calls	Oriental Satellite Station News & Entertainment Channel	8.4
9	Drama (Mother: Episode 1-25)	Shanghai TV News Catchall	8.3
10	Case Focus	Shanghai TV News Catchall	8.2
Reception ratings of primary TV channels in Chengdu, Sichuan province (December 2004)			
1	"The Same Song" New Year Celebration Special	CCTV-3	6.7
2	Drama (Kangding Love Song: Episodes 25–30)	CCTV-1	5.5

TABLE 8 *(continued)*

Ranking	Program	Channel	Average reception rate (%)
3	News Background	Chengdu Station News Catchall-1	5.4
4	Weather Forecast	CCTV-1	4.9
5	Golden 30 Minutes	Sichuan Station-2 (Culture & Tourism Channel)	4.7
6	"The Same Song 2004," Your Favorite Songs	CCTV-3	4.5
7	Real Events: Chen Lixian and Her Daughters	Chengdu Station Public Channel-5	4.4
8	Tonight at 8	Chengdu Station News Catchall-1	4.4
9	18:30 News On Site	Sichuan Station-4	4.3
10	National News Syndicate	CCTV-1	4.2

Source: CSM (CVSC-SOFRES Media) Media Research, "Meiti shuju jingxuan yuebao" (The Monthly Report on Select Media Data), *Guoji guanggao* (International Advertising), no. 3 (March): 104–105.

THE PROVINCIAL SATELLITE NETWORK: THE TALE OF A UNITED FRONT

Just as domination is never total, resistance is never complete (J. Wang 2001b,c). The landscape of Chinese media can never be summed up in a neat tale of the weak fighting the strong, capital against the state, or rationality upsetting myth-making—scenarios that may allow bystanders to make an easy decision about whom to cheer for. CSM, for example, cannot be seen as an oppositional force, because it was formed as a joint venture in which 32.4 percent of the shares are held by state-owned CCTV (Yu Jianqiang

2004, 160). Yet it's not exactly an instrument of the socialist state, either, because the majority stakeholder is semiautonomous CTR Market Research, a firm that claims to have "sorted out" its ambiguous ties with its parent company, CCTV. In most cases, the contests within the Chinese mediascape occur between titans, such as the MII's joust with SARFT, CSM's match with AC Nielsen (Liu Zaixing 2003), or the horizontal body of governance versus its vertical counterparts (*kuai* versus *tiao*) (J. Wang 2005b), and, as we shall see, between CCTV and the provincial networks. Truly marginalized media were gobbled up during the earlier media conglomeration accomplished by administrative fiat (Lee 2000, 12–13). What survived the national integration can only be strong, core media. In all instances, we are not dealing with a commercializing media in the simplistic sense of a capital takeover. Let us not forget that behind CCTV stands Beijing, and behind the provincial networks, the powerful local states. Media organizations in China, because of their importance to cultural security, are androgynous creatures with a capitalist body and a socialist face and soul. I join Yuezhi Zhao in emphasizing that the development of the much-touted media market in China did not result in the atrophy of the state (Y. Zhao 1998, 2005; J. Wang 2001b,c). The media market's growth merely generated new games that are played under dual rules. As media scholar Wu Guoguang says, the "entrepreneurial spirit prevails in mass media, while the party discipline is being maintained" (G. Wu 2000, 60).

Nowhere else does the presence of the Party loom larger than in CCTV. Its strength notwithstanding, the locale-based CSM rating surveys analyzed earlier unveil a media landscape in which audience shares are divided unpredictably between CCTV and local-provincial stations. Those stations have comparative advantages in affluent provinces especially. In the Pearl River Delta, for instance, Guangdong Provincial TV, Guangzhou City TV, and adjacent Hong Kong stations have squeezed CCTV out of the list of the top ten. Poor inland media are more vulnerable to the penetration of CCTV because the latter is considered an authoritative voice in shaping lifestyle choices. But even there, CCTV's rating advantage over local stations may change as modernization creeps deeper into the vast interiors. Coastal media have been preferred advertising vehicles for advertisers because their audiences have stronger purchasing power than their counterparts in less affluent regions of China. But the demography of the preferred media target has shifted as multinationals like P&G and Coca-Cola have been targeting the virgin territory of third- and fourth-tier cities. The reasons behind the maneuver were simple—first-tier cities were oversaturated with fast-moving consumer goods. Nobody can blame a transnational deodorant maker for fantasizing about refreshing the 2.6 billion armpits of China, of which 70 percent belong to rural residents—never minding the fact that Chinese people, especially poor country folks, don't use deodorants.

This shift from the city to the countryside has upped the ante of inland provincial television stations, since advertisers seeking parity with competitors in China should opt for media mix and channel mix to maximize locale-specific ad exposure rather than concentrating on CCTV. The mixed media strategy has already rewritten the rules of the game and carved out a bigger breathing space for local media outlets inland.

"Local TV media," a euphemism for media entities other than those based in first-tier cities, is a complex term to begin with. Prior to 2002, it included county, municipal, and provincial networks, on the one hand, and cable, broadcast, and satellite TV, on the other.[35] Document No. 82 then cleaned up the messy crisscrossing of channel paths and signals by gradually eliminating county networks, combining cable with broadcast transmissions, and thus clearing the playing field for provincial stations.

Rampant Discounts

We may ask how the provincial networks have fared since 2002. To begin to address this thorny question, we need to examine two aberrant media and advertising practices in the kingdom of irregularities: media discounts and landing fees for satellite channels. Both practices have deeply affected the standing of provincial television. In developed countries, substantial bulk discounts are rewards given to big advertisers who commit to buying ads in slack periods as well as in peak seasons (McGann and Russell 1981). In China, however, the proliferation of in-house advertising units in both television stations and large corporations has impaired the "broker" function of ad agencies. For example, big businesses can bypass ad agencies and directly contact an affiliated advertising unit within CCTV. The anomaly has driven a wedge between media and agencies, giving advertisers more bargaining leverage in direct negotiations with media. Discounts have been offered indiscriminately to all clients, big and small. The survival of the fittest media boils down to competition for highest knock-off rates. According to a 2003 survey, CCTV provided a discount of 36.1 percent; provincial stations doubled the offer to 73.5 percent; the twenty-one provincial-capital stations drove it up further to 82.9 percent; and the twenty-five district TV stations elevated the rollback to an infamous 83.4 percent (Xie 2003, 92).

With media so generous in lowering their profit margin to woo advertisers directly, ad agencies struggle to compete. The practice of "zero commission" became rampant, and the system of advertising agencies was thrown into total chaos in the new century.[36] The tiered discounts perpetuate the vicious circle of negative growth to this day, especially for media outlets that fail to absorb the steep knock-offs. The practice has generated an environment benefiting conglomerates like CCTV and rich provincial stations such as Hunan and Anhui Satellites.

Landing Fees

Landing fees are another sore spot for poorer provinces. Theoretically, every satellite station is available to households that own television sets. However, stations have to pay for cross-regional landing. The richer a province or a municipality is, the more expensive the annual access fee. Gehua Cable Company in Beijing, for example, charged 3 million yuan ($363,000) for landing rights that would allow a station outside Beijing to air its programs there (Liu Guoji 2003). Behind-the-door networking and friendship swaps *(youqing luodi)* are the norm, as few stations can afford such skyrocketing prices (Gao Yuan 2002, 91).[37] The threshold is lower in the rest of the country, but its yearly average is $120,000 (Zhao Shuguang 2004, 71), still a substantial burden for smaller and poorer provincial stations in western and central China. Among the twelve channels that gained over 70 percent of national viewer coverage, nine of them belong to CCTV and only three are provincial channels (Shen 2004a, 119). To worsen the trend, Hangzhou City TV *station* started auctioning its own landing rights, raising the bar nearly ten times higher to 2–3 million yuan ($242,000–$363,000). The scheme successfully blocked many stations from entering the city when it hosted the 2006 World Leisure Culture Expo (Yuan 2004; "World Leisure Expo" 2005). It is unclear whether Hangzhou City TV's example will trigger copycat auctions held by other cash-strapped and opportunistic stations in eastern China. In Hangzhou's defense, the inability of cable to air an infinite number of channels was part of the city's decision to weed out smaller provincial stations. Digital TV may conceivably resolve such technological limits. But one may also suspect that the satellite divide or, one may say, the discrimination of wealthier provinces against poorer ones is symptomatic of the inadequate policy provisions by SARFT to ensure media parity.

If there is a culprit here, it may be Document No. 82, which was written in order to provide policy guidelines on how to (partially) commercialize the media market. The separation of production from broadcasting—the backbone of the policy document—gave autonomy to local cable operators, who then cooked up their own schemes for profit making. Not only CCTV but provincial satellite stations now depend on local over-the-air and local cable broadcasters to relay programs and advertising to each target province. Cable networks thus have acquired the power to swap content to suit their own purposes. For some time a high percentage of the advertisements broadcast by central and provincial stations were intercepted and replaced by local ads by local cable companies, a guerrilla tactic that was neutralized by Provisional Measure No. 17, which in 2004 prohibited relay stations from splicing their own ads into television programs.

The Alliance of Provincial Satellite Stations

The lopsided discounts and landing difficulties illustrate a media environment extremely hostile to the survival, let alone the prosperity, of provincial stations. To add insult to injury, provincial television stations are obligated to broadcast CCTV's evening news and weather forecast and what comes in between—the golden sixty-five seconds—thus watching one third of national TV advertising income slide noiselessly into CCTV's pockets. How to earn an entitlement to the enormous advertising pie attached to the golden minute became one of the most urgent issues facing provincial stations in the new century. Their cause was not totally hopeless, considering the statistics on national ratings published in 2002: the rating of provincial television stations in less developed regions reached a 30 percent high; 12 percent and 13 percent, respectively, in provincial capitals and municipalities of developing regions; and an average 17 percent in medium-sized urban centers (Zhao Shuguang 2004, 70). Although individually, each provincial station lagged far behind CCTV and the powerful city stations, united, the twenty-nine provincial stations might be able make advertisers' heads turn.[38]

This theory was put into practice in November 2001, when twelve satellite stations endorsed a "United Service Covenant" promoting media buying across provincial lines (Zhao Shuguang 2004, 74–75). In October 2002, a horizontal alliance called the Advertising Association of Provincial TV Stations came into being. But it was not until a year later that a formal agreement was signed that enabled the twenty-nine stations to air their own commercials—identical across the province—at the same time as the prime-time golden minute. Advertisers buying provincial media for a spot during the 65 seconds no longer need to negotiate province by province. Media mix at the provincial scale became a tangible reality achieved at one stroke: the association settles a unified price with each advertiser, guaranteeing ubiquitous ad exposure at the provincial level, with all stations broadcasting the same commercials between 6:58 and 7:30 P.M. This strategic move offered advertisers a real alternative to CCTV.[39] The golden 65 seconds brought in 198 million yuan ($24.75 million) to the provinces, 40 percent less than what the same period on CCTV auctioned for in 2003 (Zhao Shuguang 2004, 75), as advertisers sought a bargain. The united front was a dramatic turning point for Chinese television, marking the emergence of countermeasures challenging CCTV's monopoly control over national audience share.

Channel Branding: The Diversification of Countermeasures

It may appear that the rise of a provincial conglomerate entails the splintering of China's media market in two, but the Western notion of dichotomy has never worked well in China. As of 2005, the media monopoly of CCTV had not yet been broken. Meanwhile, different anti-monopoly models have emerged, making the "provincial united front" look rather tame.

By 2005 the bedrock principles of branding, positioning and differentiation, had reached the media industry and found many converts. Why would strong provincial stations, each commanding rich resources and a unique selling point of its own, commit themselves to a common body that benefits the weak? Savvy marketing demands a constant search for positioning tactics that make identical products look different. A united front goes against the grain. It did not require much ingenuity for media marketers to emulate what product marketers do best: differentiating themselves from competitors.

Channel branding emerged as a popular measure of media marketing. If a program or a channel appeals to no target audience in particular, it loses its edge over similar programs vying for the same anonymous audience. Forward-looking satellite stations got busy positioning themselves. Hainan TV was one of the earliest to carve out a niche in the cluttered market. Under the name of Tourism Satellite, it spins off programs based on the central theme of "travel" and is waiting eagerly for the arrival of pay TV to reap the harvest. Because Hainan TV's target audiences are high-income white-collar workers who toil longer work hours, prime-time broadcasts on Tourism Satellite were moved up to 9 P.M. and later (Ji Xin 2002a, 84), a sure sign of the professionalization of the station. As the idea of channel branding caught on, satellite stations already well known for quality programming went a step further to define their own niche and audience segment. Hunan Satellite made a pitch to young audiences in 2003 by repositioning its brand at the intersection between entertainment and youth appeal (Yan Feng 2003, 94). Another provincial heavyweight, Anhui Satellite, relies on TV drama as a core brand identity. In 2004 the station launched a new channel, "The First Theater," broadcasting first-run drama series only (He 2004). That move alone differentiated the station from a dozen stations whose revenue came primarily from reruns.

Two final examples of translocal media branding go beyond the cliché formula of simple differentiation. One innovative approach was introduced by Guizhou Satellite. Taking advantage of the national policy of "Developing the West," the station re-branded itself as Golden West Satellite, choosing the "region" as a unique selling point by casting its net beyond Guizhou to other western provinces (Ji Feng 2002a). A similar crossover example is the alliance of four premium channels spearheaded by four acclaimed regional stations (Zhejiang Satellite, Anhui Satellite, Hunan Satellite, and Shandong Satellite). Although the channels are spread far apart in their subject matter—a technological channel, a film channel, an economy channel, and a catchall channel—each of them boasts a strong local rating of 20 percent and higher. The cross-fertilization between the Big Four was said to yield a "golden bull market" *(jinniu shichang)* and was expected to bring in an estimated 40 million yuan ($4.9 million) for prime-time advertising, among other revenue-sharing possibilities (Li Xiumei 2004, 111).

By 2005 Chinese advertisers thus had multiple options for ad placement. The continuous new developments in provincial media marketing have turned media-mixing (between mediums, stations, channels, and programs) into the most cost-effective strategy for advertisers. Bidders will increasingly look beyond the status that comes with advertising on CCTV prime-time and rely instead on the ROI (return on investment) delivered by the precise measurement of reception rates for each channel and spot. In November 2005, CCTV failed to reach its auction target for the season of 2006, its lowest growth in five years (Savage 2005b). It is no surprise that it has had to work much harder than ever before to maintain its comparative advantage. The more commercialized the media environment is, the harder it is for a monopoly to reign supreme.

TV DRAMA AS AN ADVERTISING MEDIUM
AND BRANDED ENTERTAINMENT

Their growing expertise in branding aside, provincial television stations hold another trump card: their broadcasting strength in TV drama. Ad income brought in through new series and reruns was said to amount to 22 billion yuan ($2.7 billion) in 2003 ("Lunli ju" 2005). Watching TV drama in the evenings is a favorite national pastime. Drama and urban soaps brought stations like Hunan TV and Anhui TV into the spotlight very early on. Even in the late 1990s, after outdoor nightlife spread all over the country, watching soap operas at home after dark remained a strong preference for Chinese audiences. Statistics show why the genre is considered the most effective profit-making vehicle for advertising:

- "[As of 2003], amid the 179 minutes devoted to TV viewing daily, 52 minutes were spent on TV drama. During the four months of peak season, which is spread between the New Year, the Chinese spring festival, and summer and winter breaks, daily viewing time of TV dramas exceeded 56 minutes. Audiences in North China watched more TV drama than those in the South, averaging 61 minutes daily" (Shanghai TV Festival 2004, 36, 38).
- "Ad buys for TV drama represent 70 percent of the total ad revenue for a television station" (ibid., 20).
- "1,564 TV drama series were broadcast in 2002, creating revenue of 23.1 billion yuan [$2.8 billion]" (ibid., 83, 145).
- "TV popularity ratings [in 2003] found that 23.4 percent of audiences favored drama; 14.5 percent, entertainment programs; 12 percent, news; 9.3 percent, sports; and 9.2 percent, music and operas" (Liu Yanming 2003, 11).

Such numbers indicate that a client's ad spending rests primarily on the appeal of a station's drama menu. Satellite stations like Anhui TV that have access to quality series gain the upper hand in the competition.

Yet paradoxically, the business of producing TV dramas is generally not lucrative. Nationwide, there are about 36 state-owned production companies (SOEs), 300 independent and SARFT-registered companies (Rinaldi 2006b), and 266 television stations that have in-house content production capacity. It has also been rumored that another 300 guerrilla production boutiques are competitors as well. Despite these impressive numbers, there are only 121 credible, "grade-A TV series production permission certificate holders" (ibid.).[40] The business is risky, to say the least. First of all, the supply exceeds the demand. In 2001, 9,000 new episodes were produced nationally, but the actual transaction volume was kept at 8,000 (Shanghai TV Festival 2004, 26). The rest of the broadcasting time is filled with reruns. Stations' odd preference for recycling dated drama over debuting new series is based on fiscal constraints: poorer stations purchase new series second-hand from stations like CCTV-1 and CCTV-8 rather than buying them directly from production companies. In strict monetary terms, doing the latter requires an expensive production sponsorship of 200,000 yuan ($24,242) per episode. Making 3,000 new episodes (the annual telecast capacity for new drama for a provincial station) would cost a station approximately $72 million, in contrast to $7.27 million if the station buys from elsewhere (ibid., 29). They lose the right to air the series' national debuts to bigger stations like CCTV and Shanghai TV, but having regional premieres is not a bad trade-off.

What happens to the 8,000 new episodes purchased first-hand annually, if reruns are the norm for TV drama? A third are never aired, a third lose money, and only a third bring in ad dollars (Ji Feng 2004, 106). The bigger the supply of new series is, the lower the asking price for each. Slim profit margins impel production companies to substitute quantity (cranking out even larger output) for quality, and a vicious circle ensues. Theoretically, the strict quota for foreign imported drama and the principle of cultural protectionism embodied in state policies should have created an auspicious business environment for domestic TV content producers.[41] But the sector is often both the beneficiary and a victim of conflicting policy mandates from SARFT. After 2002, Document No.

82 led to the integration of cable and broadcast stations, indirectly paring the demand for new drama series from 8,000 down to 5,000 episodes, a drastic 30 percent decrease, cutting total output from 3,800 to 2,200 hours (Liu Yanming 2003, 12). In 2004, another SARFT regulation put a sudden ban on all feature and documentary series concerned with police and crime stories (a subgenre that had been extremely popular the previous year). The entire genre of *she'an ju* (law and order drama) was barred from prime-time broadcasting. This regulation sent stations scrambling for last-minute substitutes and triggered a fall in the prices for cop shows: what had cost 30,000–50,000 yuan dipped to 10,000 yuan per series ("Lunli ju" 2005). TV drama is highly susceptible to SARFT whims as well as fast-shifting popular taste. It is difficult enough to predict which thematic drift will capture more viewers, but even harder to foretell changes in content policies. The sector is shaky, to say the least.[42]

Many industry critics have attributed China's underdeveloped TV programming to a double lack of capital and talent. Time alone can tell if the partial opening of that market to investors (foreign and domestic) will help rejuvenate the sagging sector (J. Wang 2003, 14–17).[43] Meanwhile, advertisers face the dilemma of having to place advertisements in TV drama reruns—now staple fare for provincial stations. Popular series like *Oranges Are Ripe (Juzi hong le)* and *Don't Speak to Strangers (Buyao gen moshengren shuohua)* were relayed to twenty-nine and thirty-one stations, respectively, in 2002 alone (Shanghai TV Festival 2004, 35). Both series debuted on CCTV in early 2002. But the reruns continued well into 2004. When I arrived at Ogilvy in July 2002 for field research, I was able to finish watching the complete reruns of both soap operas by flipping channels. I repeated my viewing experience in the summer of 2004 with another best-seller, *The Big Mansion (Da zhai men)*— a drama of forty episodes that had debuted as early as 2001. My marathon viewing was made possible thanks to two- to three-hour-long reruns of the same best-seller on a number of provincial stations simultaneously during evening hours. There was only one problem: by flipping channels to chase after my desired episodes during advertising breaks, I unintentionally missed all the commercials. Oddly enough, advertisers have shown no qualms about reinvesting in reruns. The 1999 rerun of another crowd pleaser, *The Yongzhen Emperor*, earned CCTV an advertising income larger than the yield of the series' 1998 debut (ibid., 154). Because drama reruns dominate the menu of provincial stations, their strong ratings advantage over CCTV in this category gives local advertisers no reason to discriminate against old best-sellers.[44]

Product Placement

As of 2006, the advertising format for Chinese TV drama is dominated by fifteen- or thirty-second commercials. But "named sponsorship" has become increasingly popular, allowing advertisers to maximize exposure for at least half a year (Shanghai TV Festival 2004, 155). Well-known examples are Wahaha Iced Tea Theater and Coca-Cola Young Idol Theater (Wang Zhenglun 2003, 16). Procter & Gamble's Starry Night Theater (2005) introduced a slightly different formula: sole sponsorship with commercials aired during (rather than at the start and end of) the sponsored drama.

My own stint of speed viewing may serve as a cautionary tale for spot advertisers and named sponsors. If the majority of Chinese viewers are all fervent drama fans like myself, what will prevent them from channel surfing during commercial breaks? A 2006 research report by Horizon Research Consultancy Group confirms my observation: 85.15 percent of audiences surveyed will stop watching when they see a television commercial begin at a station break, and 51.26 percent of them will change channels.[45] The ultimate answer for advertisers seems to lie in branded entertainment (also called product placement, or PP), which is what director Feng

Xiaogang did in his best-seller movies *Cell Phone* and *A World without Thieves* (see Chapter 6).

While ad placement in films is quite common, product placement in Chinese TV drama is a nascent category, because creative financing through branded content is still a new concept for producers and marketers. Scholar and observer of Chinese creative industries Michael Keane credits the satirical series *Stories from an Editorial Office (Bianjibu de gushi)* (1991) as the earliest example of product placement in the post-Mao era (Keane 2001). But the format didn't catch on in China as it did in the United States, where an average program had a ratio of 36 seconds of brand appearances for every 100 seconds of network advertising time. Late-night talk shows did even better (or worse, depending upon one's sympathy with that format): the *Tonight Show with Jay Leno* averaged 93 seconds for every 100 seconds of network ad time (Kerwin 2006). The ubiquity of the practice and its reputed creative deficit prompted a taunt from Joseph Jaffe, the author of *Life after the 30-Second Spot:* product placement is "a bubble that has already burst" (Jaffe 2005).

No such problem exists with product placement in China, where branded content, with the exception of Volkswagen and BMW, has not yet been incorporated into media and marketing expenditure, according to Larry Rinaldi, founder and marketing director of the Beijing-based ONA (Office of New Advertising) and former chief operating officer of JoyMedia, a company specializing in TV program production and distribution. ONA is one of a small handful of product placement agencies in Beijing. Rinaldi, its founder, is a visionary marketer and a PP evangelist who sees a future of $10 million in PP spending if the category takes off. Asked where the barriers lie, he attributes them to the inertia of China's TV entertainment industry:

Broadcasters/production companies [have] worked the only business model they knew . . . Creative financing was unnecessary, if not impossible, so product placement became an afterthought. It was a furtive business, handled by PR departments and assorted production personnel, and even mothers-in-law of stars . . . for a quick buck. Most of it was, and continues to be, simple celebrity placements gratuitously created and poorly executed. (Rinaldi 2005)

What agencies like ONA hope to achieve is to evolve the PP that is done fortuitously (for example, in foregrounds, backgrounds, and some props) into character or scene integrals or "cross-promotions like Hostess-cupcakes promoting Twinkees with green filling for Shrek or Samsung's Matrix Push" (Rinaldi 2006a). Rinaldi is optimistic about his cause, because like Jaffe in his observations of the United States, he considers the demise of the fifteen- and thirty-second spots inevitable in China.

Effective reach and creative advertising formats are probably only the tip of the iceberg.[46] The future of TV drama in China will rely in part on content innovation (branded content included) and in part on the emergence of new business models driven by daring provincial stations. The latter may be able to change the patterns of transactions of domestic production companies (which usually sell exclusive rights to CCTV and Shanghai stations) and perhaps make deals with foreign investors (who have thus far been largely barred from the TV programming sector). In the end, improvements on both fronts also depend upon policy breakthroughs and on home-grown initiatives to incubate "innovative content" (Keane 2005). In all likelihood, groundbreaking regulation from SARFT in April 2006 already heralded the coming of a creative era for the TV drama industry. After May 1, 2006, production companies were no longer required to submit their scripts for preproduction approval by SARFT, which had formerly regulated thematic choice and balance (SARFT 2006). Even though content deregulation in China is never complete, a partial opening may give rise to surging demands for quality content, inevitably raising the bar of excellence.[47] A semi-independent TV drama industry may flourish as a result and challenge the monopoly position of CCTV, which also owns China's largest in-house drama-production centers. The enabling role of state policies should never be underestimated, even while we critique the constraints imposed by them (J. Wang 2001b).[48]

The Chinese media landscape in 2007 defies any simple application of the monopoly or anti-monopoly thesis, since the state-market relationship is never an antithetical one. A growing consensus supports this more nuanced view (Ma 2000, 28; Y. Zhao 2005; Fung 2006). If anything, we have seen that regulations like Document No. 82 and Provisional Measure No. 17 created a ripple effect that has had enabling as well as restraining consequences. An excessive emphasis on market forces as an instrument with which to crush the authoritarian state often results in a complete dismissal of the empowering aspects of state media policies in China, an analytical imbalance I hope this chapter has helped to remedy.

Ethan Gutmann, a former American businessman in China, has condemned what he sees as U.S. corporations' voluntary capitulation to the Communist state. His *Losing New China: A Story of American Commerce, Desire, and Betrayal* (2004) lists companies (Cisco, Nortel, and Sun Microsystems) who in his opinion were morally complicit in helping the Chinese government with surveillance technology in return for lucrative market entry deals. In a speech given in January 2005 at the National Press Club in Washington, D.C., he reiterated the central theme of his book: The "Chinese Communist Party could not have controlled this radical new means of communication [the Internet] without overwhelming technical assistance from North American corporations" (Gutmann 2005). Although Gutmann's book is marred by evangelistic fervor and replete with condescending assumptions about what America must do to "save" China, it is useful pedagogically because in it he lays bare the collusive relationship between foreign capital and the authoritarian state. Capital does not always emancipate the oppressed, precisely because it eagerly colludes with the power that is present.

The cycle of state policies that promote opening of (in this case) the market, then retrenchment, followed by readjusted partial opening is characteristic of Chinese socialism. Given the complex role of capital influx in Chinese media, neither the liberal view (the market stands in opposition to authoritarian state power) nor the Marxist view (capital accumulation impedes media pluralism) provides a satisfying framework for assessing Chinese media reform. I have shown how problematic the liberal view is. It remains to be said that the Marxist view has blind spots, too. Characterized by Raymond Williams's and the Frankfurt School's antimarket positions, the Western Marxist view oddly has come to buttress the ideology of the ultra-leftists in the Chinese Communist Party who want to take ideological control by holding content hostage as in the old days. It suffices to say that the Marxist approach is most powerful in critiquing the Western liberal-capitalist media that are part of full-scale commercialization (Lee 2000, 27–28). But the Chinese problem is not of the same order. China suffers from the double ills of authoritarianism *and* rampant commercialization, and thus neither the Marxist nor the liberal approach provides a fully critical treatment. If neither the Chinese state nor the market should be taken as the primary driver of creative media content, where should hopes be placed? I return to this topic in the Conclusion.

Critiquing the idea that the state and the market are in opposition to each other has been only one focus of this chapter. Mapping out the complex media environment has been another. Using "media-buying" as an entry point, we could see in CCTV's annual advertising auction the structural dependency among the media, advertising, and the corporate sectors, as their interests simultaneously converge and conflict. A look at "king bidders" allowed us to scrutinize popular assumptions about the media monopoly in

China and to take note of the countermeasures spearheaded by provincial TV media. Audiences and content (especially TV drama) have played large roles in the pushing and shoving between competing stations, as have state media policies. Heretical as it sounds, we need to acknowledge the enabling, as well as the constraining, effect of the Chinese state policies pertaining to the opening of the television market.

One final note: Until the day arrives when the content of Chinese television programming is delivered from both political and total market control and until excessive reruns are replaced by quality series like *A Beijinger in New York* (1993), *The Romance of Three Kingdoms* (1994), and the now-banned *Marching toward the Republic (Zouxiang gonghe)* (2003), Chinese advertisers' and media architects' visions of what pay TV and digital TV might bring them will remain a mere fancy.

Conclusion:
Countdown to the Olympics

Today old paradigms like positioning are under attack. A new generation of marketers in the United States claim that consumers have tuned out commercial messages and now desire only one-on-one interactions with a brand through personally meaningful, gratifying, and memorable experiences. The emphasis of this new school is placed on seeing the consumer as a self-empowering agent, fully engaged in authentic, interactive dialogues with the brand, with or without the mediation of marketers. Experiential marketing has burst onto the scene.[1] And the rise of the "prosumers"—techno-enthusiasts or do-it-yourself amateurs who take an active role in producing goods and services—is pushing corporate America to re-examine earlier concepts such as "brand essence" and "brand positioning."[2] These older tools smack of product-centric mass marketing no matter how instrumental they were to the integration of consumer insights into the elaborate process of branding and advertising. In China, as we have seen, positioning is still only an emerging paradigm and will remain dominant for some time. But in a parallel development, one can also spot the burgeoning of buzz marketing—a big trend in experiential marketing.[3] On the eve of the Beijing Olympics, we can spot several key indicators of what the future may hold.

The year 2008 is Nirvana for the Chinese advertising industry,

288

and not just because of the Olympics. Several trends are maturing and converging to make the year an extraordinary one for Chinese admen and -women. Global communications solutions for Chinese brands are gathering momentum: the West-East (WE) Marketing Group is establishing its credibility in building brands in and out of China and facilitating crossover alliances between Chinese ad agencies and global partners; Chinese sports marketing will be building its interface with branded entertainment; and viral marketers are beginning to form a critical mass and starting to deliver rich-media ads over P2P (peer-to-peer) networks. "Creativity" is the name of the game, and the buzzword is spreading across digital platforms like Creative Commons China—a local chapter of the global icommons movement launched in Beijing in March 2006. It is correct to think that the Beijing Olympics is the torch that will light the biggest bonfire for the Chinese, but the field is already primed for a convergence of all the forces crucial to the debut of a "new China" on the Olympian stage.

WE: WEST MEETS EAST

In 2006, when China, in order to fulfill its WTO agreement, opened the door to advertising agencies of sole foreign ownership, it thereby removed the barrier that had prevented the entry of medium-sized international ad boutiques. The changes provoked a crisis that was rooted in the longtime unequal power relationship between domestic and transnational ad agencies. Prior to the Chinese WTO agreement, international 4As paid little attention to clients who did not spend more than 30 million yuan ($3.8 million) per transaction on advertising. But the new WTO stipulation changed the agency-client configuration. Choosy fish get no food in the overcrowded pond. International 4A agencies are now picking up even tiny clients who spend less than 3 million per year ("Guangzhou shi guanggao" 2006, 71). The old order of the food chain—the 4As monopolizing domestic biggies and transnational clients, while domestic agencies nibble on medium and small Chinese clients—is breaking down. Big fish are swarming into the small fishes' waters, with both fighting for a limited supply of minnows. The situation is more precarious for domestic ad companies. Survival is difficult if they are counting solely on domestic Chinese clients.

The food-chain crisis is one problem plaguing corporate China. An equally pressing concern is embodied in the perpetual anguished question: "Do we have our *own* name brands?" Only 4 of China's brands have made it to the Fortune 500 list, compared with 249 American brands, 46 French, and 45 Japanese (Chen and Tong 2006, 24). Will the Chinese catch up? For every China brand enthusiast, there is a skeptic (Roberts, Balfour, et al. 2004). Nothing is new in this debate except that in 2007 the Chinese government started to speed up the transformation of what are termed "made-at-home brands," into national brands, intended for the international market, by investing 700 million yuan ($90 million) in an initiative called "Exporting Chinese Brands" (Chen Xutong 2006). Some industry critics argue that Chinese companies' typically paltry investment in R&D gives multinationals the edge. Others consider Chinese manufacturers' lack of attention to IP (intellectual property) issues an equally serious handicap for their long march overseas. For example, when many Chinese companies took belated action to register in foreign countries, they found their names already usurped by other firms. About half of the fifty most famous Chinese brands suffered the same problem (Chen and Tong 2006). Lenovo had to give up the name "Legend" because of the oversight. The R&D deficiencies and IP culture lag are problems difficult to resolve without large-scale governmental interventions. But there may be solutions that can go hand in hand with state initiatives (like the Exporting Chinese Brands project) without participants finding themselves being led by the nose by Beijing.

Enter the WE Marketing Group, which kills two birds with one stone. Founder Viveca Chan (former head of Grey China) takes a different approach to solving the problems just outlined. She seeks answers to two questions: First, how can Chinese domestic agencies make themselves better known to a global pool of clients and avoid the difficulties they face in trying to survive on domestic accounts alone? The second question is a response to the plaintive "national brand" query. Instead of whining about the global anonymity of Chinese manufacturers and their labels, why can't we ask instead whether there are practical means of making Chinese brands more visible overseas? The barrier confronting both Chinese ad agencies and Chinese manufacturers, according to Chan, is the same: a communications gap crying out for a communications solution. The WE Marketing Group was created to fill in the communications void: it provides a platform that integrates local Chinese resources with global ones by "allowing [domestic] brands the flexibility to move into global markets and at the same time providing a path for international brands looking for a foothold [local agency] in China" (Murphy 2005).

At least fourteen domestic agencies have already signed on, including outdoor media group Dahe, Guangzhou-based Dark Horse, Apex (a Chengdu-based event organizer behind the *Super Girl* phenomenon), and Pingcheng (the agency for the cell phone brand "Bird").[4] The global platform for the WE Group is provided by Worldwide Partners, a Denver-based international community of independent ad agencies, with whom WE has established a strategic joint venture. Conceptually, WE is all about synergy-making, with the goal of pooling local and global resources, expertise, and client relationships into a loosely knit but win-win alliance. Viveca Chan says, "If a Chinese corporation finds WE, [it has] already found the international platform to exhibit itself" (V. Chan 2005, 27). Launched in October 2005, WE instantly galvanized all three sectors in China—advertising, media, and the corporate sector. A recent catch has been Yahoo China, an old client of Grey, which gave the WE team an integrated brand communications and creative services account ("Yahoo China" 2006). Everyone is watching to see how fast Chan's vision will materialize, and she has had critics. A legitimate question concerns the measurement of success: how do we know if the model is actually working? The year 2008 is pivotal for WE, since the Group has set a two-year timetable to break even. But achieving financial stability is only a partial answer. The sustainability and evaluation of the model remain open questions.

These reservations aside, WE Marketing Group has broken loose from the one-agency one-house structure to form a "third zone" *(zhongjian didai)*, sitting between domestic Chinese agencies and transnational 4As but not conflated with either. "WE" is not a hybrid in a straightforward sense. On the one hand, its Chinese name, *Weihan*, "Empowering China" leaves the impression that this group is led by Chinese nationalists promoting the cause of "localization" in resistance to the globalizing trends in advertising. Yet on the other hand, the main architects behind WE are all veteran 4A internationalists (Chan herself was born in Hong Kong, then under British control). In other words, this advocacy group for domestic Chinese brands and domestic agencies is led not by localists but by those who have had genuine transnational identities and experiences (Chen Gang 2005, 28). Wu Xiaobo, the CEO of Pingcheng and a close collaborator of Chan's, comments that the WE Group adds "an intriguing footnote to the diversification of globalization that drives international advertising today" (Wu Xiaobo 2005). The group offers an alternative to localism and globalism because it is driven by centrifugal, internationalist aspirations while representing a "self-conscious breakthrough of Chinese advertising professionals, precipitated by the encirclement of powerful 4A rivals" (Lu and Li 2005, 48). The allusion to the crisis triggered by the WTO is unmistakable, and so is the promise of this experiment to break down the boundaries between the local and the global and create a new synergy. WE began by helping second-tier mainland brands gain global exposure on a previously unimaginable scale, thus edging China a step closer toward "Brand China," the Saatchi & Saatchi vision of turning the nation itself into a brand.

SPORTS MARKETING AND ENTERTAINMENT MARKETING

The defining moment for "Brand China" will surely arrive in the summer of 2008, when Beijing hosts the Olympics. Many companies—both domestic and multinational—have already started thrashing out their marketing plans for the Games. China Mobile, an Olympic sponsor, is the world's largest mobile operator in terms of subscribers and the world's fourth most valuable brand (after Microsoft, GE, and Coca-Cola). It has primed itself for the Olympics by divvying up its creative roster among several agencies (Savage 2006). Nike made a similar move. It tuned up competition with arch-rival Adidas—another sponsor of the Games—by ending its eight-year partnership with J.W. Thompson Shanghai and switching to Wieden & Kennedy, another TNAA (Savage 2005d). The prized account was awarded to Wieden after it made the best pitch for a project featuring new sports favorite Liu Xiang, who became a national hero shining even brighter than basketball star Yao Ming after winning China's first Olympic gold medal in track and field at the 2004 Athens Games. Coca-Cola was not far behind in signing Liu for a 2006 spring festival commercial. The heart-warming ad plays on the homesickness of a lonely athlete who gets stuck in Paris on Chinese New Year's Eve, missing his mom's dumplings and drinking Coke alone in a French Chinese restaurant. He is magically transported back home to Beijing by two animated characters in the nick of time, and joins his family for a traditional dumpling feast. Meanwhile, Adidas kicked off its marketing campaign by unveiling 1,000 T-shirts carrying images of the Beijing Olympics' "Five Friendlies," mascots that embody the characteristics of popular Chinese animals such as the fish, panda, Tibetan antelope, and swallow (Hargrave-Silk 2005). Lenovo, now a worldwide sponsor of the Olympic Games and the official computing partner for the 2006 Winter Games and the 2008 Beijing Games, has tied the knot with Coke to roll out a limited edition of a commemorative laptop carrying the Olympics logo on the case.

But whether businesses are official sponsors or not, they are turning to Olympic marketing to generate goodwill and perhaps even good profits. The impact of Olympic sponsorship on brand image and sales has been well documented. According to a 1998 research report, 88 percent of TV viewers in the United States think that "having commercials is a fair price to see Olympics for free." Eighty-five percent of them regard Olympic sponsors as "industry leaders," 78 percent of them notice which companies sponsor the Olympics on television, and 44 percent feel that "I'm personally contributing to the Olympics by buying brands that are advertised during the TV coverage" (Hart, Schiavone, and Stipp 1998).

The Chinese have even greater expectations for the Beijing Olympics. Big domestic brands are counting on following in the footsteps of Samsung and Matsushita, which were made into global brands via the Olympic Games hosted on their home turf. Even corporations that can't afford official sponsorships are dreaming big about turning into heavyweight brands overnight, thanks to the media campaign launched by CCTV to promote the efficacy of Olympic advertising. CCTV has exclusive rights to broadcast the 2008 Olympics and expects advertisers to outbid each other for commercial spots.[5] On the question of whether the Beijing Olympics will create global brands for China, Bruce Oltchick, formerly of Star TV, offers an insightful perspective: "Several answers are part of the puzzle. Most importantly, what are the global entitlements that a [Beijing] Olympics sponsor gets? My sense is that most of the entitlements are domestic. What would be really interesting is to see whether China's brands sponsor the 2012 Olympics—outside of

China. That would help the 'China, Inc.' create global brands"
(Oltchick 2006). The road to becoming an Olympic-sized brand
will no doubt take more than one cycle of the Games. But there is
no other race that the Chinese would rather run and win.

Sports marketing, however, is not going to monopolize the cash
flow. In 2005, a marketing trend of equal importance emerged
when Hunan Satellite TV beat the ratings of CCTV with two hits—
the reality show *Super Girl* and the Korean drama *Daejanggeum*—
unleashing a singing-contest frenzy on the one hand and a metropolitan craze for Korean cuisine and Korean tonic medicinal culture
on the other.[6] Hunan's success turned "entertainment programming" into a buzzword. Such programming may seem mundane in
the West, but in China, where news programs and chop-suey
amusement shows dominate the tube, Hunan's experiment with
recreational television was a refreshing change. The trend is catching on quickly in advertising as well. Since 2005 entertainment
marketing has produced some of the most exciting ad campaigns in
China.

The most celebrated branded entertainment in 2005 was a series
of sixty-second nonsense films *(wangluo dianying)* designed to
brand the Chinese search engine baidu.com.[7] The commercials, created by a Guangzhou-based boutique, Xiezuo Advertising, were
built on concepts that made the innovative BMW films such a successful formula to woo media-savvy Western consumers. (Grouped
under the title "The Hire" and initially viewable only on the Web,
these product-placement films, each eight minutes long, featured a
Driver played by Clive Owen who exhibits deft car racing skills in a
BMW vehicle.)

The decision to make Baidu's films much shorter completely
blurs the boundary between content and commercial. They won a
gold award at the Twelfth Chinese Ad Festival, further boosting
Baidu's position as the "first-choice search engine" for the Chinese.[8]
The series is made up of four commercials dramatizing a simple

pitch: Baidu is the best Chinese search engine because it better understands the nuances of the Chinese language. "Better" than whom? Google's name is never mentioned, but the short films suck its blood in dark humor. The satirical bite hinges on punctuation marks, or, more precisely, the semantic transformations that caesuras bring to a sentence written in unpunctuated vernacular Chinese.

One film is based on a simple building block: *wo zhidao ni bu zhidao*, literally, "I know you not know." The sentence multiplies indefinitely, depending upon how adventurous one gets. Playing on the verb "know how" *(zhidao)* and its negation "don't know how" *(buzhidao)*, the short Baidu commercial stages a hilarious linguistic contest between a Western foreigner whose Chinese vocabulary is limited to three syllables—*wo zhi dao* ("I knew")—and his smart challenger Tang Bohu, a legendary Don Juan type and famous poet-painter during the Ming Dynasty (1368–1644). Tang shows his dumbfounded rival just how fast he can change the meaning of the growing sentence by pausing at different junctures.

> *wo zhidao ni bu zhidao* (I know you not know) → *wo zhidao, ni buzhidao* (I knew but you didn't)
>
> (I know you not know) → *wo zhidao nibuzhidao* (I knew that you didn't know)
>
> → *ni bu zhidao, wo zhidao ni bu zhidao*
> (You didn't know that I knew you didn't knew.)
>
> → *wo zhidao. ni buzhidao wo zhidao. ni buzhidao.* (I knew. You didn't know I knew. You didn't know.)

The campaign was touted for its nonsense humor à la the director-actor Stephen Chow, a genre that some critics rightly assert will forever elude 4A company executives.[9] In the Baidu series, Tang Bohu's tongue twisters are such a hit that he ends up charming the foreigner's Chinese girlfriend and makes the Westerner (an allusion to Google) literally spit blood. More important than trumping Google, the nonsense comedy and its sequels turned Internet short-short movies into the hottest new advertising medium, prompting Chen Gelei, the mastermind behind the campaign, to ask, "Will commercials evolve into short-form digital entertainment?" (Chen Gelei 2005, 37). The key term is "digital entertainment," and the pull is the pleasure principle. We see this formula picked up again by Ford Motor Company in a 2005 campaign to launch its Focus in China. The "Motion Life" campaign presents eight three-minute short films made by famed Sixth-Generation directors (who began in the 1990s to make edgy, anti-romantic movies in the cinema verité tradition, some produced underground and some as joint ventures, and who include Wang Xiaoshuai, Zhang Yuan, and Jia Zhangke). The films debuted on the English Web site of Ford in China (www.ford.com.cn/focus) and also played on Web portals sina.com and sohu.com.[10] The premise underlying the campaign was entertainment marketing, and the target segment for the Focus in China was believed to be fervent movie fans and young pleasure seekers (Wang Jing 2006).

Is the combo of entertainment marketing and product placement a better formula for success than sports marketing? The competition is such that neither formula working by itself can sustain the attention of Chinese audiences for long. To rise above the clutter of copycats, the real winner will be the one who knows how to turn "sports into entertainment and entertainment into a sporty contest" (Wang Runjue 2005, 72), in short, the ability to create synergy between the two marketing prototypes.[11] Some initial efforts have already been made in this direction. In 2005, Motorola's wireless service brand "M-Zone" held a competition in street break dancing, itself a cool athletic form. An even more innovative attempt was made by TCL's Island PC game console. Claiming that it was the only console used by the Chinese team participating in the 2004 Electronic Games French Cup, TCL was able to attach a "fighter jet" image to Island, and the association itself was said to raise the adrenalin level of its navigators and enhance the whole experience of gaming as a sporting affair (ibid., 73). Across all product spectrums, the merging of athletic drive and the pleasure-seeking impulse has tremendous appeal for twenty- and thirtysomethings.

DYNOMEDIA AND SOCIAL NETWORKING

Those belonging to Generation X or Y share one more characteristic in common: they can smell a marketing come-on from miles away. Marketer-led advertising campaigns are becoming less and less effective in grabbing the attention of these consumers. Baidu.com's nonsense movie series generated a huge fanfare precisely because it was entirely dependent on word of mouth. The search engine didn't spend a single penny on advertising or send a press release to mainstream media as Ford had for M-Life. Nor did it announce or post the four films on its own home page. Chen Gelei and his co-conspirator designed a viral campaign from start to finish. To kick it off, they asked Baidu employees to send emails to friends and a handful of Internet domains to create linked pages. Within a month, 100,000 Netizens had viewed the four short movies. By the end of 2005, approximately 20 million hits were reported (Chen Gelei 2005, 35), backing up the hypothesis that China has untapped niche markets out of which may grow the Long Tail economy.

Chris Anderson's Long Tail theory, now guerrilla marketing gospel, has circulated widely on Chinese blogs. Some have applied Anderson's analysis to the *Super Girl* sensation, suggesting that Chinese marketers turn the traditional marketing principle of 20/80 on its head.[12] Viral experiments in unleashing the long-tail effect in China were seen sporadically as the new millennium began. But it was not until the summer of 2006 that the Chinese had their first domestic viral marketing company, DynoMedia, based on the peer-to-peer social network model.[13]

The company delivers nonintrusive rich-media content and coupons to consumers over a large umbrella of P2P networks across various devices and platforms and across viral communications applications (such as instant messaging, e-mail, mobile SMS/MMS, podcasting, and P2P software). Its main target is China's 40 million P2P Internet users and its 150 million mobile subscribers, who will be able to send to the DynoMedia Web site user-created, open, or rights-flexible content that includes videos, reviews, ratings, and exchanges in discussion forums. The company strives to kill two birds with one stone, building an open platform for consumers and creating a fast channel for marketers to set up their social networks, as Nike did with Joga, an invitation-only social network for soccer enthusiasts. Founded by MIT graduates, DynoMedia consists of a team of technology entrepreneurs and media/advertising experts. A distinctive feature of their platform is using coupons as a medium of communication between advertisers and consumers. Coupon categories include "fashion and cool trends," "food," "digital communications," "leisure and travel," and "home decorations and furniture." For instance, by clicking on a coupon posted on DynoMedia's site for McDonald's fried chicken legs, a user can not only redeem the coupon but access rich-media content linked thematically to the product. These are context-sensitive coupon services embedded in the branded TV drama programs distributed by DynoMedia over the Internet.[14] Before or after the show, the audience will receive free coupons, and when they click on them, a digital coupon will download into the designated local folder.[15]

DynoMedia's content is diverse. For McDonald's, offerings include commercials and funny videos shot by customers who have something unique to say about the McDonald's experience or fast food culture. Take tourism as another example. Coupons from a tourist agency promoting Lijiang (an attraction in Yunnan) are matched with documentaries on the heritage town made by independent filmmakers, with music, art, and even travelogues and digital photo albums centered on the Lijiang motif submitted by users from DynoMedia P2P networks. Content providers come from the growing creative class in metropolitan China. Some of them are young underground filmmakers and freelancers seeking maximal exposure of their work through viral channels. They can choose to share their work as open content or charge a small fee. The flexible digital-rights architecture is another distinctive characteristic of DynoMedia. The end-user, of course, is welcome to send both the coupon and the rich-media content to his or her network of friends. By publishing, sharing, redistributing, and reformatting funny videos and targeted ads across viral platforms, DynoMedia achieves a unique four-in-one positioning: it is a high-tech service brand, a viral marketing and social networking platform, an open content provider, and an e-commerce network builder.

The company's self-adaptive profiling engine offers advertisers segmentation-on-demand and well-integrated online/offline metrics services to track consumer usage of the site, enabling a company or agency to test the market, launch campaigns, and measure ROI (return on investment) accurately. Service charges are determined by CPM, cost-per-click (CPC), coupon redemption rates, media "watch-through" rates, and "pass-along" referral rates. Dyno-Media has a Chinese media partner, CRD 360, a cutting-edge television and digital entertainment company based in Beijing. When quizzed about the difference between their model of content provision and the models usually found on other P2P social networks, Han Cheng, the main architect behind the DynoMedia venture, explained that other social networks are littered with pirated content, but DynoMedia only provides legal content. "Our business conduct will always comply with MIT and MIT Sloan professional standards," he says.

It remains to be seen if this viral business model will be attractive enough for end-users to engage in building the DynoMedia community site with devotion. Will they contribute their own creative materials while being targeted with advertising up front? The answer is as yet unknown, but it seems clear that social network media and Web 2.0 technology are engendering more and more business concepts that integrate grassroots creative communications with commercial communications in China.

CREATIVE CULTURE AND CREATIVE COMMONS

The mention of Web 2.0, a vision of collaborative online communities enabled by the second generation of software tools and services, brings us to the Creative Commons movement (CC).[16] CC mirrors DynoMedia in its flexible digital-rights management and stresses "open content" and user-generated creativity—two key concepts that set the tone for the communications culture of the digital generation. CC is part of the iCommons movement and is made up of a network of participants who include artists, Internet users, cyberactivists, lawyers, scientists, and scholars in more than forty countries and legal jurisdictions. It is a nonprofit organization dedicated to creating a commons of creative work that is easier to share and build upon. CC challenges the stringent copyright regime of "all rights reserved" by providing creators with flexible copyright licenses free of charge. The licenses (more than six major choices) cover a "spectrum of possibilities between full copyright—*all rights reserved*—and the public domain—*no rights reserved*" (Creative Commons site). CC promotes a voluntary, "some rights reserved" digital copyright approach, enabling content providers to mark their work as either free or in graded levels of increasing restriction for copying, modifying, or distributing for users online. The end goal is an ambitious global digital commons to which individual end-users can import their own work and access others' work without intervention by third parties. Christiane Asschenfeldt, former iCommons executive director, explains that "Creative Commons mirrors the structure of the Internet itself: it is merely a tool, used to ever surprising ends by the intelligence of individuals" (Asschenfeldt 2005).

CC's emphasis on end-users and the advancement of the "right to share" is exactly what DynoMedia is aiming for. Although CC is concerned with licensing creative works and liberating the intellectual property regime, and DynoMedia is concerned with viral marketing, they both use P2P networks as a medium for distributing shared creative ideas. The development of these and similar digital platforms bears special significance for China, where the content industry is reined in by the state and "creative freedom" is a loaded concept. Precisely because it is harder to monitor the spread of viral content online, Chinese digital networks are a breeding ground for creative expression that tests the boundaries of the norm. In the Western context, Creative Commons challenges the restrictive corporate copyright culture dubbed the "permission culture" by Lawrence Lessig (Lessig 2004).[17] The Chinese don't have a hegemonic IP culture in the same sense meant by Lessig, but open-content platforms like CC and DynoMedia will stimulate the growth and dissemination of creative ideas and generate a trickling-up effect beneficial to all grassroots creators.

The local chapter of ccChina is still in its infancy, but its influence on Chinese society may turn out to be multifaceted. Project leader Wang Chunyan believes that ccChina will help "promote a new copyright culture, widely disseminate Chinese creative knowledge and culture, and offer a reasonable path for protecting intellectual property" (Wang Chunyan 2005; see also http://creativecommons.net.cn). CC's emphasis on a "win-win" solution for all will eventually prompt it to develop commercial licensing. Although this is a point of contention within the global iCommons community, ccChina is interested in holding CC promotional events in collaboration with viral marketing platforms like DynoMedia. If such cooperation materializes, it may facilitate an experimental convergence of marketing and grassroots creativity in China.

Imagine that every end-user of interactive digital media is a potential prosumer, generating content voluntarily for brands while leveraging his or her stakeholder status to better monitor corporate conduct. Although a prosumer culture is as yet a hardly known luxury in China, the new participatory culture is already in full swing in the United States, prompting media scholar Henry Jenkins to speculate on the ways in which American prosumers are changing how business is conducted. His take is an upbeat one: not only are communities of prosumers bringing "greater collective bargaining power" that liberates the public sphere and contributes to the decentralization of media environments, but they are also holding big media and other business conglomerates accountable for corporate citizenship (Jenkins 2006, 249).

If grassroots efforts like the ones Jenkins describes will hold corporate greed and misconduct in check in the future, we might ask about the place of academic critics—the scourge of corporate conscience—in this dawning new reality. Jenkins does not address this question; I am aware of no one who has yet anticipated what kind of critical concerns will emerge from the convergence of corporate media and grassroots media.

What does a corporate–grassroots "alliance" mean in the Chinese context, where big media is state media and where the corporate sector is inseparable from the state sector? The best recipe for China—if we care about alternative spaces at all—will have to differ from the "convergence culture" described in Jenkins's and information law professor Yochai Benkler's books.[18] China will be better served if grassroots media run parallel to corporate (state) media and *never* converge. The potential alliance between ccChina and DynoMedia hypothesized earlier is not the same as the convergence that has taken place in the United States between *Survivor*'s fan communities (grass roots) and CBS (corporate). DynoMedia is a fascinating model precisely because it isn't "corporate (state) media" per se. It strives to become a social media platform brokering the relationship between commercial networks and social networks.

This look at "convergence culture" indicates that we need to scrutinize the traveling theories originating in the West with care. Analyses of what is taking place in Western post-affluent societies may not be applicable for developing countries—and may never be. We may also ask whether a Chinese creative digital culture (if not a prosumer culture) might ever contribute to progressive change from the bottom up in a sustainable manner. It is too early to tell. The critical mass for the Web-based "producer-creator" blend will be slow in emerging in China, given that the primary media for the Chinese at present are televisions and mobile phones, not digital media. For those waiting to see a Chinese equivalent of the Long Tail emerge soon, the news is equally mixed. It is technology that drives demand down the Tail. Other than the Internet, a range of new communication tools that provide low-cost distribution need to be put in place in China so that an average consumer can gain instant access to content, goods, and services and complete transactions in an instantaneous fashion. The Net is not the immediate answer, because it is a luxury for the majority of Chinese consumers— the 700 million peasant consumers. Although it is probably more appropriate to think of Generations X and Y as consumer prospects for the "niche markets" understood in Anderson's terms, it makes no sense to exclude hundreds of millions of peasants from the picture simply because their medium of choice is not the Web. If scale economy is what drives Anderson's vision, the aggregate market should extend beyond the "niches" to incorporate all kinds of "small" markets. The sheer numbers of Chinese peasants can create a sales miracle that Coca-Cola and P&G are counting on. And there is no other medium more powerful than the mobile phone to reach that consumer mass.

My speculations about the Chinese Long Tail and the digital divide in the country carry one more implicit message: anyone who overlooks the gaps in disposable income between developing countries and post-affluent societies will forever chase after mirror images of Euro-America in Shanghai and fail to crack the "China puzzle." When an observer thinks in terms of a global (the West)–local (China) dichotomy, it is easy to equate Shanghai and Beijing with the "local" and forget about the rest of China. Not only transnational marketers in China but scholars in international advertising and transnational media studies must be careful not to look at the developing world from an exclusively Euro-American standpoint. This book has shown where Western thinking about branding, marketing, and advertising has worked in China, where it hasn't, and, more important, where it has opened up opportunities for cross-fertilization. Ultimately the best way to grasp China's marketing and advertising culture is to see it from a vantage point that celebrates "synergy" and "difference" simultaneously, while giving the latter more elbow room and respect.

WHERE CONSUMER MEETS TECHNOLOGY
AND THEORY MEETS METHOD

My final comments have been saved for readers interested in gaining critical, theoretical, and methodological insights. Since theory is inextricably linked to methodology, this book's experiment with method already has implications for theory in two ways.

First, an industry-bound approach shows what research opportunities there are if academics stop theorizing about the consumer from their perch in the ivory tower. In the humanities, advertisements are often studied in relation to interpretation alone and seen as finished texts waiting to be decoded by experts trained in sophisticated intertextual readings. Although such work is instructive regarding the psychosocial formation of cultural values, the consumers reconstructed in these interpretative frameworks end up being imagined entities, rather than the target consumers who share little in common with the academic interpreter in taste and behaviors. This book, through company fieldwork, stresses the importance of production-centered methodology in gaining access to the target consumers' points of view. A focus on advertising as an industry and on advertisements as products branded by a team also lays bare the intertwined perspectives of the two most important agents of pop culture—marketers and consumers—working in tandem. The nexus of marketers' and consumers' points of view acts as a needed conduit between the trade literature and pop culture scholarship, resulting in a hybrid perspective not available in the pedagogy of either business or cultural studies.[19]

Second, industry fieldwork not only yields rich empirical details but also opens up new conceptual windows. Once the consumer is seen as an end-user active in the production and transmission of creative content (rather than as a passive interpreter of producers' content), then the marketer and the academic, and the lay reader, can break away from the confines of the classic view that frames the "China question" only in terms of the (authoritarian) state versus the (free) market.[20] The consumer, I argue, can become an agent who drives a wedge into binary thinking and, in the process, changes the ways in which we conceptualize social change in China.

I question the conventional wisdom that transnational capital can liberate Chinese society from state authoritarianism. I argue instead that the Chinese state and transnational capital have a complicitous relationship with each other, rather than being in opposition, with the implication that neither the state nor the market should be seen as the primary agent of change for a better China. But even this counterargument is not much different from either/or thinking, because the "neither/nor" perspective falls into the same trap of dualism. An escape from the binary circle has to come from elsewhere.

My two summers of fieldwork at Ogilvy brought about a sharpened understanding of media as a field of study adjacent to advertising, and, with it, an awareness of the possibilities provided by new media technologies to bail us out of our conceptual stalemate.[21] Once we make a connection between the "consumer as end-user" and "new media technology," it becomes possible to ask: what agent of change might emerge in China if it is neither the state nor the market? The answer could be the technologically enabled young consumers in China. I should probably avoid painting an excessively romantic picture of "liberated" Chinese end-users earnestly engaged in decentralizing big media capitalism, because they themselves are busy making money, too. How successful the urban Generations X and Y are in balancing their desire to be both entrepreneurial and creative at the same time is anybody's guess. I anticipate that the launch of HiPiHi (haipishi), a Chinese 3D virtual world commercially released in fall 2007, will provide us a few clues. Like their counterparts in Second Life, HiPiHi residents are "creating, inhabiting, and governing a new world of their own design" (HiPiHi 2007). There are some notable differences, however, between the American vision and the Chinese one. Linden Lab, the U.S. company that runs Second Life, is not selling advertising space all over the game except on private islands where big corporations like IBM and Toyota buy their own land and sell their own goods. But HiPiHi may open the flood gates to advertisers, since its managers have already allowed billboards on the side of the road and into some areas of the public domain. Such a laissez-faire attitude could imply that players, whose age averages fifteen to twenty-five, will not be morally or legally discouraged from selling or renting advertising space to big companies. Many are striving to become the mainland Anshe Chung, the first millionaire in Second Life, who made a fortune by reselling and leasing virtual real estate she owned.

Perhaps the user behavior generated by greed will feed right back into the creative drive and perhaps not. It is too early to tell, and there is no reason to believe that the virtual economy in HiPiHi cannot be a creative economy at the same time. Regardless of the caveats that come with emerging technologies, new media is an enabler that gives Chinese users the opportunity to test the limits of state and market control through viral effect. The exposure of the SARS epidemic via instant messaging, the sprouting of spoofs, and the challenges posed by Chinese cyberfeminists to gender mores all point to new forms of empowerment that should be taken into consideration by scholars in multiple disciplines who examine state and market relations in China.

Technology is an instrument available to the ruler as well as the ruled, of course, so the liberating potential of new media should not be overrated. China's firewalls and the legions of Chinese Internet police are sufficient reminders that the hype about new media freeing "Red China" is just another fallacy to counter. I suggest that future studies of the Chinese state and market will not be effective unless they address four conceptual categories together: the twin issues of "media technology" and "consumer as end-user" and their impact on both the "government" and the "marketplace." The current disciplinary divides in the China field between the studies of governance, media, marketing, and communications technology should be torn down to make way for more border-crossing traffic. In the same spirit, to encourage further research, future milestones should be set up on multiple fronts, leading us to a wealth of new trajectories: for example, audience fieldwork in the media and advertising sectors needs to be undertaken; studies of news media need to be complemented by studies of entertainment media; and user studies of mobile media (which serve a large number of rural subscribers in China) need to be given priority to catch up with the attention now given to digital media research.

If pop cultural studies can meet marketing research halfway, what are the implications for the two dominant disciplinary approaches to Western advertising—that of cultural studies in the humanities disciplines and marketing studies in business schools? The contrast between these two approaches provides an interesting context for the theoretical ground opened up in this book. Tang Ruitao, as we saw in the Introduction, describes the fundamental essence of Chinese culture not as desire but as the need for safety—a need we saw among Chinese consumers making choices about fast-moving consumer goods (Tang Ruitao 2005, 118). Yet numerous advertising campaigns launched by transnational agencies in China have gone in the opposite direction: they mistake Chinese consumers for their Western counterparts by overselling them lifestyle aspirations in ad campaigns while underrating the importance of safety appeal. This observation brings an irony to light: inasmuch as Western marketing practice is rooted in the trope of "desire," it shares an epistemological common ground with cultural criticism, whose mission is to debunk marketing and consumerism. The practice of advertising in the West and the critique of it are thus two sides of the same coin—both marketing speak and critical theory on consumption are built on the Freudian discourse of the libido.

For example, Jean Baudrillard's work, which has inspired many younger critics of consumer culture, offers a typical Freudian connection. Under the theoretician's scrutiny, an advertisement for Airborne, specialists in armchairs and seating, reveals an "ideological discourse of the phallic phantasy of violence" (Baudrillard 1996, 182). He describes the encounter of the consumer with the material object as a moment of a "reassuring regression into objects calculated to buttress the images of the Father and the Mother" (ibid., 204). Many of his followers read into the phantasmagoric advertising images a sign of nostalgia for "lost referentials," or a longing for the phantom original whose absence motivates the desires for it (Baudrillard 1994; Ivy 1995; Wernick 1997). The list of academic authors writing about "excess" in the name of desire, the fetish, the gift economy, and magic is long. An entire corpus of critical literature on advertising in cultural studies and its adjacent fields utilizes the psychoanalytic lingo of repression, (consumption as) obsessional rituals, anxiety and guilt, sublimation, transference, and the conflicted unconscious to account for the "infantilizing" mechanism of advertising and the symbolic meaning of the consumer's encounter with the "object of desire."

But *whose* meaning is it? Western advertising scholarship and visual studies rely heavily on Freud and Lacan, and to some degree, Marx, but they largely ignore research on consumer insights and consumer behaviors, with the result that consumers are muted in theoretical discourses that purport to speak for them and their emotions. Those who are given a hearing are often not the target consumers. Although now and then a critic may acknowledge that target marketing (as opposed to mass marketing) elicits an "incoherent plurality" of audience responses, the same critic insists on reading into ads a unified ideological pitch and reception (Wernick 1997, 210).

The ethnographic turn in cultural studies, with which this book is aligned, does not leave behind the cardinal question raised by anthropologists and cultural critics regarding the meaning of material culture and material consumption. Rather, the onus of the analytical burden is shifted from "what meaning is it?" to "whose meaning is it?"

If cultural studies literature writes the target consumer—together with her insights and behaviors—out of sight, business literature does the opposite. Journals run by marketing academics take model building of the target consumer as a primary mission. Aggregate panel data are gathered with meticulous care to explain loyalty maintenance of the target segment, their purchasing behaviors, belief systems, knowledge structures, and brand memory composites and patterns of advertisement recall. The measurement of the effect of advertising and the testing of advertising messages are all dependent upon the sampling of target consumers. A different kind of abstraction arises from these cognitive models and empirical findings: consumers are categorized into subsegments of "long loyals, rotators, deal selectives, etc." (McQueen et al. 1993), and their likes and dislikes are often reduced to attitudinal correlates of behavioral regularities across product categories. Even when the topic switches to international advertising, the burning question is not about local sensibilities but about "whether and how far to standardize" (Editorial 2002, 291) and how to develop "cross-culturally equivalent measures of advertising processes and effects" (Ewing, Caruana, and Zinkhan 2002, 338). A notable example is Marieke de Mooij's application of Hofstede's five dimensions of national culture to international marketing (de Mooij 1998).[22] Her framework is marred by two assumptions: first, that national values are "stable," and second, that European nation-states are representative of nation-states around the globe. Difference is contained in neat formulae. And target consumers are dehumanized into national segments.

Similarly, the MBA literature on the science of brand management is as obsessive about categorical thinking as the consumer-focused research. The standard questions are: How is brand equity defined and managed? How does a manager measure, maintain, and upgrade a brand's performance? Although I learned a great deal from this literature, which is filled with practical tips about successful (or failed) marketing campaigns, I often had to rescue myself from the diagrammatic thinking imbued in those works by turning back to David Ogilvy's *Ogilvy on Advertising* and James Twitchell's *Twenty Ads That Shook the World*. For nearly a decade, I traveled back and forth between the brilliant semiotic epiphanies (provided by critics in the humanities) and the scientific modeling of the best branding practices (built by marketing specialists in business schools), wondering whether there were ways of negotiating the methodological distance between them. And more important, I wondered whether there were better methods of reconciling semiotics and academic marketing theory. In the end, I found that reconciliation was neither the point nor even the ideal goal, because I remain critical of both methodologies. The answer lies, I believe, in opening up advertising studies to multiple entry points. One such entry explored in this book is the study of advertising as a practice, both in terms of doing industry fieldwork and in terms of bringing together marketers', consumers', and advertisers' perspectives in a discussion of Chinese and transnational advertising.

Advertising can be a multidisciplinary site of scholarship that taps into the expertise of practitioners on the ground without compromising the humanist's critical vocation. A new generation of scholars, who have grown up in a branded culture, will no doubt greet fieldwork in culture industries with less suspicion than the baby boomers' generation. These younger scholars will perhaps undertake more methodological experiments in the field of advertising research. I believe that it is under their watch that a paradigm shift in consumer culture studies will occur as the practice of "being critical" takes on new meaning.

NOTES

REFERENCES

ACKNOWLEDGMENTS

INDEX

Notes

INTRODUCTION

1. Throughout this book, two different currencies—U.S. dollars and Chinese yuan—are used in various places. Because dollar equivalents are not always possible given the fluctuation of exchange rates, I use the yuan in contexts that require precision. Dollar equivalents are provided in contexts that call for a comparative reading of Chinese statistics.
2. A remark by Zhao in her 2003 article illustrates the fallacy of dichotomous thinking in our analysis of China's global integration. She says, "The language of 'openness' and the focus on the WTO accession proper as the new beginning for the Chinese communication industry obscures the important fact that the Chinese communication system had always been 'open' to varying degrees even before the reform period." She gave many examples indicating that even Mao's China was not closed to foreign interaction. That history "is important to visit," she says, because "it is precisely its suppression that helps to sustain an ahistorical 'isolationist' versus 'openness' dichotomy" in our view of China (Y. Zhao 2003, 60).
3. Most famous among these designer artists were Zhang Guangyu, Liang Dingming, and Zheng Mantuo.
4. A conventional view in cultural studies is opposed to what I argue in this book and to my "production-centered" approach to branding and advertising. Cultural studies critics of the Frankfurt School tradition are used to pitting (manipulative) producers against (deceived) consumers. In that dichotomous view, producers play down rather than privilege the consumers. My conception of a "production-centered" approach differs from both ideologically oriented and text-centered approaches.

5. The "Acquire" segment is made up of consumers whose focus is on the physical attributes of the luxury product. They are preoccupied with the meaning of exclusivity attached to this mode of consumption. "Repertoire" customers, in contrast, care deeply about their emotional relationship with the luxury brand. It is the experience of shopping and the process of building the intimate relationship with the brand in question that take precedence over the mere acquisition of the product itself.

6. In the United States, there were only an estimated 2.7 million American consumers with liquid assets of $1 million or more, according to Greg Furman's report. See Furman (2005).

7. Three such examples are "The Quick Expansion of Luxury Goods in China" (*Economic Information Daily*, May 30, 2005); "The Slogans of Global Luxury Brands Traveled to China" in *Guoji guanggao*, no. 7 (2005), see http://jjckb.xinhuanet.com/www/Article/200553092221-1.shtml; and "Chinese People Are Going to Top Luxury Consumption" in *Daily Economic News* (October 21, 2005), http://www.nbd.com.cn/luxury, accessed February 2006.

8. According to the press, Inna Iranyi (Shorex's marketing director) said during the FT Summit, "The abundance of freshly made money in China has left well-to-do Chinese consumers overwhelmed with the selection of expensive and luxurious goods . . . The luxury industry market in China is forecast to grow by 8 per cent . . . China will become the second largest luxury market in the world by 2008." See Iain Marlow and Miao Qing, "Luxurious Lifestyle Catches On," *Shanghai Star*, May 26, 2005. Reprinted from *China Daily*, http://app1.chinadaily.com.cn/star/2005/0526/ls17-1.html. Accessed December 2005.

9. The fanfare surrounding China's "blue collar" segment was set off after HorizonKey (Lingdian) Research published its survey report "Lanse de chuntian: Zhongguo lanling qunti shenghuo fangshi ji xiaofei tezhe yanjiu" (The Blue Spring: The Lifestyle and Consumption Characteristics of China's Blue Collar) in 2004. http://www.horizonkey.com/showsoft.asp?soft_id=190. Accessed December 2005.

10. Dabao Lotion's success demonstrates the lucrative potential of the segment. A cosmetic brand targeting low-end users of both sexes, Dabao achieved a record high 34 percent market share in 1998, surpassing many of its more glamorous rivals. See "Lanling dingwei: Da Bao

chenggong de weiyi mijue" (Positioning the Blue Collar: The Sole Secret for Da Bao's Success) (2004) in *Chenggong yingxiao* (Successful Marketing), no. 7 (July), http://finance.sina.com.cn/salesconduct/20040707/1710856493.shtml. Accessed July 2005.

11. Horizon Research is a full-service market research company in China. Founded in 1992, Horizon's experience covers the full range of consumer and B-to-B (business-to-business) markets, with emphasis on diverse product categories such as automobiles, IT/electronics, telecommunications, financial services, real estate, household appliances, fast-moving consumer goods, media, and logistics. Its fields of marketing research encompass consumer usage and attitude; marketing segmentation and target consumers; consumer needs; corporate image; brand equity and brand evaluation; product concept development and testing, and so on. The CEO's estimate that the white-collar segment makes up 20 percent of China's population, however, is an exaggeration. For a detailed discussion of the percentage of the Chinese "middle class" (6–8 percent), see Chapter 5.

12. See "Shichang da cankao" (2003), 132.

13. The "four olds" refer to old Chinese feudal customs, culture, habits, and ideas. Gifting is not only a custom and a habit but part of the Chinese cultural unconscious.

14. Statistics for Generations X and Y are difficult to calculate and vary within the statistical literature. After careful study and consultation with a population studies specialist at People's University in Beijing, Shi Song, a research affiliate of MIT's comparative media studies program, came up with the following figures, which are more reliable than most of the statistics culled from the Internet and from Chinese marketing literature. His calculation is based on the statistics provided by the Chinese Population and Development Research Center (2007, 177, 181). Generation X occupied approximately 19.8 percent (259 million) of the total Chinese population in 2005; and Generation Y, approximately 14.6 percent (191 million). Among Generations X and Y, there are approximately 111.9 to 142 million single children—8.56 to 10.71 percent of the total population. According to these figures, the oldest generation (the Cultural Revolution generation) is steadily declining. Lu Taihong's statistics are therefore not completely accurate.

15. Gilmore and Dumont make an insightful observation that the second-generation higher-quality counterfeit goods are being sold at the same

price as the "genuine article." I have also noticed the rise of that phenomenon in first-tier cities. I doubt, however, that counterfeit goods, though they strike the younger generation as cool, can be turned into mainstream luxury goods. See Gilmore and Dumont (2003), 6.

16. An example of the pro-Western school is Zheng Xueyi's article "Weihe Zhongguo de pinpai he shijie de pinpai you zheme da de chaju?" (Why Is There Such a Huge Difference between Chinese Brands and Global Brands?) See International Advertising Editorial Board (2005), 13.

17. I owe this to an insight from Edward Bell, head of strategic planning at Ogilvy Beijing.

18. For a detailed discussion of the Chinese encounter with and application of Western cultural and literary theories during the early period of the reform era, see J. Wang (1996).

19. Ogilvy excels in demonstrating its thought leadership, a tradition started by David Ogilvy himself. The agency partnered up with the World Economic Forum and *Fortune* Global Forum. It also launched digital seminars across Asia under the Verge banner for clients and the industry, according to a source in *Media* (December 14, 2005). In the Mandarin-speaking world, Shannon Chuang and her team in Taiwan and the PRC have coedited several books sharing the Ogilvy experience with the public. Among them are a series called *Ogilvy Viewpoints (Guandian)* (Beijing: Qiye guanli chubanshe, 2000).

20. In the United States, consumers definitely understand the difference between name brands, store brands, and generic goods; in China, consumers may not know how to classify them. A powerful domestic brand (such as Lenovo and Haier) may be known as *mingpai* or *pinpai,* or simply as *paizi.*

21. Books published in Chinese on CIS have attributed its origin to IBM in the 1950s. But a close look at the literature indicates that it was primarily the VI (visual identity) and specifically, corporate design—the logo of IBM, by Eliot Noyes and his team—that attracted the attention of his Chinese promoters. It is not clear, to me at least, whether the invention of MI and BI systems can also be credited to IBM and to the United States. A typical example of such literature is *Zhongguo CI jiaocheng* (The Curriculum of Chinese CI), ed. Mei Yu (Beijing: Gaige chubanshe, 1999), 20–21.

22. Aaker and Joachimsthaler's *Brand Leadership* (Pinpai lingdao) was published by state-run Xinhua Bookstore in 2001.

23. In marketing terms, "digital individualism" can be defined as the habit of end-users to seek "Lovemark relationship with brands" via new media technology. See Love (2001), 111.

24. Statistics show that the slow development of online advertising has also been seen in Europe, where consumers spend an average of 20 percent of their time on the Internet, but the adspend of European companies on Internet media only amounts to 3–4 percent of the total for all advertising. See Dobson (2005).

25. For the percentage in Europe, see the preceding note. For the U.S. percentage, see Wendy Davis, "Merrill Lynch: Online Ad Spend to Surpass $16B," OMMA (Online Media, Marketing and Advertising), May 9, 2006, http://publications.mediapost.com/index.cfm?fuseaction=Articles.san&s=43135&Nid=20221&p=305145. Accessed June 2006.

26. The capacity of SMS-related services for generating substantive revenue is hardly surprising. In 2002, 90 billion text messages were sent in China—a 379 percent increase over the previous year. See Zhao Shuguang and Zhang Zhi'an (2004), 126–127.

27. The figure 64 percent was quoted for the third quarter of 2003 for sina.com. The ratio between sohu.com's Internet advertising stream and its offline transactions was roughly 40 percent to 60 percent as of 2004. See Zhao and Zhang (2004), 127–134.

28. "Record Online Ad Spend," ClickZ Network, http://blog.searchenginewatch.com/blog/060531-173738. Accessed June 2006.

29. See http://game.5617.com/moshou/index.aspx for "World of Warcraft," and http://mland.sdo.com/new/home/index.asp for "Mland." "Birdman" is available on http://www.pepsi.com.cn/blueonlinetv.asp?id=9. The Coke WoW commercial is available on http://icoke.sina.com.cn/moshou/tvc.html. Accessed May 2006.

30. Compared with the Coke commercial, the mental age of Pepsi's target seems a grade lower. As business blogger Bill Bishop comments, Pepsi's strategic decision to invest in Magic Land seems highly questionable, because it is "a game for female[s]." He asks, "Doesn't Shanda [M-Land's dealer in China] know only 1/5 game players are girls?" See Bishop (2005).

31. You can watch Hu Ge's spoof on YouTube. http://www.youtube.com/watch?v=AQZAcT1xaKk&search=Mantou. Accessed April 2006. For the Chinese debate on the Hu Ge incident, see a Sina blog: http://blog.sina.com.cn/lm/html/2006-02-14/316.html. Accessed June 2006.

32. See their performances on http://video.google.com/videoplay?docid= -6440135875935340811 and http://youtube.com/watch?v=BpWvXQ _Fj78&mode=related&search=. Accessed May 2006.

33. See http://www.life365.com/member/login.html. According to China-Circle, when a user selects an Espoir (a cosmetics brand) background for her homepage, not only does she download the advertisement made by Espoir, but she also advertises and endorses that brand for every friend she invites to her blogs and photo collection.

34. In 2005, city-based single children occupied 40.45 percent of the national single-child population; township-based single children amounted to 18.36 percent; their counterparts in rural China, 41.18 percent. Presumably only the city-based and township-based single children—approximately 60 percent of 111.9 to 142 million (see note 14 above)—have the luxury of logging on to the Internet.

1. LOCAL CONTENT

1. De Mooij argues in all her works that converging income levels will not result in converging value patterns across borders. Instead, using Hofstede's 5-D model of culture, she insists that patterns of national culture provide a better explanation of differences in consumer behavior across borders than income. It follows that cultural diversity should influence marketing and advertising, and she debunks the paradigm of international marketing and global branding. Her work reflects the European partiality for cultural specificities. The 5-D model distinguishes five dimensions of national culture: strong or weak power distance, individualism versus collectivism, masculine cultures versus feminine cultures, strong or weak uncertainty avoidance, and long-term or short-orientation.

2. See the Nike commercial at http://www.asianmediawatch.net/nike/. Accessed June 2005.

3. See "Heineken Counts on Stout Growth after Guinness Deal," http://www.cee-foodindustry.com/news/news-ng.asp?n=57560-heineken-counts-on. Accessed July 2005. I am fortunate to have access to Ilya Vedrashko's views on international advertising, because he quit the industry to come to MIT as a graduate student in comparative media studies. In spring 2005, Ilya took my course "Advertising and Popular Culture,"

which provided ample opportunities for us to exchange our views on advertising.

4. In 1995 Beijing published China's *Advertising Law,* stipulating the implementation of the agency system with the understanding that commissions should be calculated in the range of 10–15 percent of the media spending by a client. But in reality, most agencies received only 2–8 percent commissions. The situation worsened with the trend of zero commission fees. Competition for clients grew so intense that agencies were willing to sacrifice their own commissions to please clients. As Chapter 7 demonstrates, media discounts for advertisers early in the twenty-first century were as high as 80–90 percent. Therefore clients could go directly to media for discounts, bypassing agencies completely. Zero commission was used as an incentive by agencies to attract clients. How did agencies make money if they returned their commissions to their clients? Chinese media has an informal "kickback" system *(fandian):* if media-buying bills accumulated by an agency exceed 20 million yuan, the kickback rate from the media is 5 percent (1 million yuan); if media buys exceed 100 million yuan, the kickback is 10 percent. Agencies can thus accumulate media buys from big clients (through the lure of zero commission) up to a quantitative ceiling to gather their 5–10 percent kickback fees. Often, the earnings for the agency are so lucrative that they can kick back 1 percent to their clients in addition to charging zero commission. It is well known that some 4A agencies participate in the practice of zero commission. See Kou Fei (2003), 239–244.

5. The second- and third-tier cities will follow the same joint venture model that characterized transnational ad agencies' initial forays into the big metropolises—tier-one cities—during the 1980s and 1990s. The joint venture model in the advertising sector usually drives a cooperative rather than a confrontational relationship between TNAAs and their domestic partners.

6. The emphasis on "talent" used to dominate Chinese advertising discourse in the late 1990s.

7. The controversy over Ogilvy's account with Yu Congrong is well known within the ad industry. The product advertised is a kidney tonic. The television commercial named "Water Pistol" associates the weakened kidney function of men with a water pistol that cannot shoot. After it

was aired, sales of the product reportedly dipped. However, the commercial also won an award for Ogilvy at an Asia-Pacific ad festival. For a sample analysis of the Yu Congrong case, see Fu Dingwei, Mao Xiaoming, et al. (2002), 159–166. In 2003, Toyota published a print ad in the Chinese magazine AUTO Fan, featuring a stone lion saluting and another lion kowtowing to a Prado Land Cruiser. The tagline says, "You have to respect Prado." In Mandarin Chinese, Prado is translated into the word "ba dao" which means "supremacy" and "rule by force." That image incensed the Chinese. Consumer critics posted scathing messages online until Toyota apologized. Chinese Netizens also did a spoof of the ad, showing two huge angry-looking lions smashing the Prado SUV, complete with a tagline saying "Prado, we will crash you!" See the ad at http://ad-rag.com/107456.php (accessed June 2005). For a Chinese discussion of the incident, see Gui Shihe and Liu Yinglei (2004), 113–114.

8. In 2003, the big news in the ad industry was the exodus of local clients from Bates Shanghai. The new ad boutique Star Beauty to which they defected turned out to be a local company set up by top Chinese executives who had formerly serviced those same clients for their old employer Bates Shanghai. The message was clear: as far as the local clients are concerned, it matters little if an agency is an international 4A as long as the client has absolute trust in who is managing the brand. See Onicek (2003).

9. One of the most powerful core competencies of transnational agencies lies in the capital resources they can mobilize for "regional office development and national coverage." See Mitchell, Rupp, et al. (2004), 188. That is why the logic of scale economy has such a strong appeal for domestic strategists. As the Chinese market opens up tier by tier, its sheer size is a mixed blessing for local agencies. On the one hand, they can claim regional dominance; on the other hand, they can never stray too far away from their home base because they are short on capital for branching out. The transnationals, in contrast, can pace their expansion to multiple regional markets.

10. These brand manuals also include the title for each division executive (including account executive, account director, account manager, art director, copy director, creative director, production executive, which all come with abbreviations to match); the format for client, account,

and creative briefings; formats for contact reports and status reports; and normative tips for positioning and creative strategies (Zhu Haisong 2002).

11. In Feng's words, it is essential to grasp the mode of thinking embedded in Mandarin Chinese. For him, writing copy in Chinese is not enough; the adman has to respect the mother tongue and get into the logic of the language. He has written a book entitled *Dictionary on the Grammar of Chinese Advertising Language,* published by Beijing's China Youth Publications Company.

12. This was the typical reaction I received when showing this commercial to academic crowds who did not understand that commercials are made for a targeted audience (in this case, the Shanghainese). Yet the opinions of nontarget segments do not matter to advertisers. Their typical response was "Oh, but Hengxin Square looks just like any other metropolitan locale, it is not convincingly Shanghai." The insistence on performing a hermeneutic reading of advertisements (made by studio-bound critics) is revealing. It shows that the humanities researchers are locked into the problematic approach of treating advertisements as mere texts rather than as products resulting from the complex process of branding. Consumer segmentation is the first and most important step of branding. For details, see Chapters 2 and 5.

13. The manufacturer behind Libo has stakes in Singapore, Thailand, and the Netherlands, as well as Shanghai. See Gao Tao (2005).

14. The Library of Congress online collection of Coca-Cola's commercials includes works as early as 1954 through 1999. For more recent Coke commercials in the United States, see http://www.coca-cola.com/usa/tvcommercials/index.html (accessed July 2005). For a much-talked-about Chinese Coke commercial centered on a popular computer game, see http://icoke.sina.com.cn/moshou/tvc.html (accessed in July 2005).

15. The most stringent entry rule for the Guangzhou 4As is the stipulation for the annual gross revenue of an agency applicant—$2.5 million as of 2003. The minimum cap has deterred many domestic agencies. The agency candidate must also be a full-service agency striving to obtain three major clients with billings from each reaching at least $1.3 million.

16. The one Naobaijin commercial I watched several times in 2002 during my visit in Beijing was centered on a big parade. I was not alone in ap-

preciating the creative idea lying behind it. See Lao Han (2002), 133–134.

17. Lord Guan is Guang Yu, a third-century hero whose military fame rose during the Eastern Han Dynasty. He was the sworn brother of warlord Liu Bei and known for his loyalty, courage, and justice. He was later deified in several religious sects and worshipped as a patron god of law and the God of War.

18. In the 1970s, Leo Burnett aired Marlboro's signature cowboy commercial in Hong Kong. But sales fell far behind other brands, and Marlboro barely made it into the top ten cigarette brands. The agency researched to find an answer, and discovered that cowboys signified to the pragmatically minded Hong Kongese a loser who could not afford to dress well and whose spirit was considered too downbeat to be inspirational. Leo Burnett then transformed the cowboy into a handsome, well-mannered, and neatly dressed ranch owner who, escorted by a bevy of assistants and secretaries, hopped onto a private jet to fly to his ranch. There he enjoyed a luxurious party with relatives and close friends. Thanks to the image makeover, in the 1980s, Marlboro became the top cigarette brand in Hong Kong. See Wong Xiangdong (2002), 99. I discuss the spider-web distribution channel, a strategy of Wahaha, and the public relations successes of Coca-Cola in Chapter 3. For details about the distribution channel strength of Bird, see Chapter 6. Also see Michael Keane (2007), chap. 10.

19. A quote from the spokesman for Blue Flames: "Our creatives are all purebreds—local [Chinese] copywriters, local [Chinese] art director . . . and mind you, our business has never relied on foreign capital for a single day since its inception." See Yuan Ying and Tian Bin (2003), 29.

20. Buick is proud of its Chinese tagline in a television commercial aired in Shanghai. "Water Drips" associates the purity of the essence of Buick in the metaphor of the best-quality oil that tolerates not a single drop of water *(bu rongxu you renhe shuifen)*. See Meng Xiangsheng (2002), 156.

21. The "I'm lovin' it" campaign was launched in 2003. It has a Chinese version that also uses hip-hop music and images of with-it youngsters to broaden the Golden Arches' popularity.

22. Although there is ample literature on the localization of McDonald's menus in different parts of the world, what the chain has done in China pales in comparison with KFC's approach. McDonald's may be selling

rice burgers in Bangkok, lamb burgers in India, vegan burgers in the Netherlands, teriyaki burgers in Japan, frankfurters in Germany, and poached egg burgers in Uruguay. But local reception is often lukewarm. My point is that those local variety menus still betray inside-the-box thinking. In the twenty-first century, product adaptation calls for more than variations of the same motif.

2. POSITIONING THE NEW MODERN GIRL

1. I was informed by Jaime FlorCruz, the bureau chief of CNN in China, of the Beck's ad campaign.
2. For a detailed discussion about the complicit relationship between the socialist state and capital, see Jing Wang (2001b).
3. For the interview of Mu Zimei by Danwei TV 7, see http://www.danwei .org/danwei_tv/danwei_tv_7_mu_zimei_interview.php. The *New York Times* published an article about her written by Jim Yardley, titled "Internet Sex Column Thrills, and Inflames, China," on November 30, 2003.
4. The trio was recently joined by Hong Huang, a media mogul and director Chen Kaige's ex-wife. She started a tongue-in-cheek blog soon after the controversy evolving around Hu Ge's spoof of Chen's *The Promise* broke out—an event analyzed in the Introduction. Her blog is known as representing a different brand of cyberfeminism. Cerebral, witty, and satirical in turn, http://blog.sina.com.cn/honghuang exhibits a hooligan style of blogging attributed especially to Chinese female intellectuals. You can access an interview of Hong in English by Beijing-based Danwei TV on YouTube: http://www.youtube.com/watch?v= 7shR9VMIaBE.
5. What is "brand equity"? The value of a brand or assets that make a brand strong. Brand value, like all values in capitalist societies, has a price tag. The concept of brand equity gained currency in corporate America after the mid-1980s. It spawned numerous conferences and publications, not to mention myriad seminars taught in business schools worldwide, including in the PRC. An American invention, "brand equity" has achieved scientific valence since the 1980s as commercial researchers developed and sold methods for tracing and optimizing brand value in quantifiable terms. Some industry critics are still debating the utility of this concept, but it has undoubtedly replaced the

earlier term "brand image" (brought forth by David Ogilvy in the 1950s) as the leading theoretical paradigm of branding and marketing. David Aaker divides brand equity into four dimensions: brand awareness, perceived quality, brand associations, and brand loyalty (Aaker 1991). Others have extrapolated a wide variety of definitions from Aaker's basic formula, but they all cohere more or less on the point of measurability and the balance of tangible assets with intangible ones. The bottom line is the profit principle, ROI (return on investment), and stock return. The 360 Degree Brand Stewardship approach has six equity items. Accompanying each category is a question that helps the client and agency measure the health of a brand. (1) Product: How does the product performance support the brand? (2) Image: Is the brand image strong and engaging? (3) Visual: Does the brand project a clear, consistent, and differentiating presence in the market? (4) Customer: How strong is the brand's customer franchise? (5) Channel: How well is the brand leveraged in the trade environment? (6) Goodwill: Is the brand endorsed both by influential individuals and by the communities in which it is present? (Ogilvy 2000).

6. The "360 Degree" approach has been written about extensively by Ogilvy executives and published in both English and Chinese. Shenan Chuang, group chairman of Ogilvy, penned *Aomei you qing* (Ogilvy & Mather E-motives) (2000); T. B. Song and et al. published *Guandian* (Viewpoint) in two separate volumes, two collections of short essays and articles culled from an internal publication. Mark Blair et al.'s *The 360 Degree Brand in Asia* (2003) is well known in the industry.

7. A regular focus group meeting lasts for three hours, during which a panel of consumers engages in conversations with a planner-interviewer who comes in with a collage of images and a set of interview questionnaires. The marketing company researcher is often present as well. She observes the interviews in an adjacent room equipped with listening-in equipment. The best conversations I witnessed were spontaneous and structured at the same time.

8. Verbal methods for brand audits usually take the form of sample questionnaires, such as: "What springs to your mind when you hear the brand name? What specific feelings and emotions did you experience in connection with using it? What personal memories or associations does this brand bring to mind? How does the brand make you feel about yourself? What kind of people do you think are behind the brand, and

what do you think they think of you? What does this brand do for you that other brands cannot? What aspects of your own behavior or way of thinking reinforce what the brand does for you? How do the moods of the brand differ from those of its leading competitors? These routine questions are intermingled with creative questions, such as, If you imagined a brand to be a person, what would she be like?

9. I should note that as a market research company, Oracle was more indulgent in its analysis of the factors that led to C&B's weak image. Ogilvy's mission was more action oriented. They ask the question "where are we" in order to move on to the next big question, "where do we want to be." Ogilvy's internal document is usually short and pithy, in contrast to the elaborate, lengthy reports done by Oracle.

10. The profile for the new freedom seeker in Ogilvy's recommendation includes other features such as "she is natural, positive, and honest about her feelings, a girl of personality and spirits and she wants a free expression of them. She can say No to the things she does not believe. She is *not* a bad, rebellious girl and unaccepted by society, nor a mission impossible girl, nor a successful white-collar career-driven woman, nor a feminist. She actually enjoys all the delightful little things a girl is entitled to. We see her . . . laughing loudly when she is happy, you can even hear her merry laughter on the Internet, cheering over the World Cup match without knowing who is kicking the ball."

11. In the early 1990s, Kotex in Korea was steadily losing its mind share and market share to Procter & Gamble's Whisper. By positioning itself a product for the ideal modern woman, Whisper had by default repositioned Kotex into a "middle aged housewife next door" (Ogilvy 2000). To shed this image, KC Korea rebounded with a marketing objective aimed at replacing Whisper as the brand of choice for teens and young women. Drawing on consumer insights, Ogilvy in Korea tossed out the Red Dot idea and developed a White Dot campaign so potent that it turned "White" into a subbrand.

12. I wish to acknowledge Winnie Wong's contribution to my rethinking of the complexities of consumer participation in the production cycle.

13. Alvin Toffler coined the term "prosumer" in his work *The Third Wave* (1980), predicting the blurring of the role of the consumer and the producer in the digital age. The notion of "prosumer" also refers to the blend of "consumer" and "professional"—a consumer who thinks of him/herself as a semi-professional and who feels passionate about the

digital media technology he or she uses for creative pursuits. The creativity generated by these advanced amateurs or semiprofessionals is associated with "user-generated content," which enables them to partner up with corporate biggies or compete with them. The "prosumer" in this book refers to both shades of meaning.

14. For instance, I have little doubt that the MIT brand name helped me a great deal in securing an opportunity to work at Ogilvy and to conduct my research there.

15. At times, Servaes and Lie's position falls into the localist one, thus reinforcing the dichotomy in question. But their desire and analytical effort to highlight the conceptual links between the local and the global is unmistakable. One of their most salient arguments in redressing the analytical bias of communications studies is the view that "global media may be the largest in terms of coverage, however their size shrinks significantly if measured in terms of viewing rate" (2001).

3. THE SYNERGY BUZZ AND JV BRANDS

1. Terms such as *hudong hezuo* (proactive cooperation) or *shuangxiang shentou* (mutual penetration) between local and global ad agencies are common in advertising trade magazines and books. Another good example can be found in Yu Mingyang (2002), 41.

2. Zong accused Danone of making a number of deals in China that have undermined the Wahaha-Danone joint venture. He says these include: (1) in 2000, Danone bought 92 percent of Wahaha's biggest rival, Guangdong Robust Group, which Wahaha says cost it market share and the loss of 49 million yuan in profits that year; (2) the French company has bought stakes in at least seven leading Chinese food and dairy companies, so that, according to Zong, Danone has a 45.2 percent stake in the Shanghai-based Bright Dairy and Food Company, and a 22 percent stake in Beijing-based Huiyuan Juice Holdings Company; (3) last December, Danone also set up a joint venture with Mengniu Dairy Company, China's largest liquid milk producer, in which it owns 49 percent of the stake. See Lu Yuliang (2007).

3. The general sentiment is that even if Danone seized the Wahaha brand, it would face retaliation in the China market. The French company would have a huge PR problem in a market where nationalist sentiment can be reactivated at any time by hostile media and/or angry consumers.

4. These insights were conveyed to me by Bruce Oltchick in an email dated February 10, 2004. Oltchick is the former executive vice president of Star Group and a former vice president of Asia Grey.

5. Zong now asserts that he did not realize when the JV was first set up that Wahaha's majority stakeholder position would be endangered by Danone's incremental acquisition strategies of buying out other partners from the initial Danone-Wahaha joint venture. He says that he only belatedly came to realize that Danone had quietly consolidated its own shares in the JV to 51 percent.

6. In 2002 Zong failed to disclose that Danone did own 51 percent of Future, which constitutes, after all, only an insignificant percentage of the entire portfolio of the JV.

7. Danone's legal troubles in emerging markes were about to boil over in spring 2007. Ironically, its Indian partner, the Wadia Group (a food and fabric conglomerate), threatened to sue the French company for "stealing its bestselling Tiger biscuit brand by licensing it outside India without its knowledge." A war of words ensued in the same fashion as had taken place between Danone and Wahaha, except in this case, the role of the accused fell on Danone. See O'Connor (2007). Many speculated that it would not work to Danone's advantage to take on both legal cases simultaneously. Most people wanted Danone's threat to sue Wahaha to be resolved through an out-of-court settlement.

8. In 2001, Wahaha and Sohu joined online to launch a forum spun off from a joint event titled "The Future Cola Ten Biggest News Stories of 2001."

9. Its Bottled Water series, for instance, drew on celebrity appeal; the company signed up pop singers Jing Gangshan, Mao Ning, and Wang Lihong to deliver sentimental one-liners such as "only you in my eyes," "only you in my heart," "loving you is loving myself." These commercials successfully spoke to the target segment—young consumers in the twentysomething age bracket, many of whom are pop music fans.

10. In his book, Ong Xiangdong discusses a third strategy, "endorsement" *(danbao)*. In this brand architecture, an endorser brand, usually a well-respected and established brand (such as Ralph Lauren), lends its name to an endorsed brand (such as Polo Jeans). The ambiguous relationship between Kotex and C&B in the 2002 re-launch campaign could also be interpreted in terms of the endorsement logic. A clearer example is the endorsement C&B gave to the new subbrand Blue Strip. Sometimes an endorsement can be a first step in a gradual name change or a calcu-

lated move toward a co-brand strategy. Given the strength of safety appeal in China, endorsement can be seen as a viable option among other brand architectures.

11. History can provide even better perspectives on current events if we return to the details about Danone's competition with Nestlé for a partnership with Meilinzhengguanghe. Nestlé didn't respond favorably to two non-negotiable requests from Zhang Li: that Meilin continue to own the Zhengguanghe brand name and that the foreign investor's share not exceed 50 percent (Nanfang Zhoumo 2000, 11). Negotiations stalled, Nestlé failed both "national pride" tests, and Danone moved into the vacuum. Back in the early 2000s, insistence on brand independence and management autonomy was a crucial point of reference for joint venture partnerships in China.

12. "Synergy making" is not, however, Danone's signature marketing strategy. The French conglomerate does not follow the "synergy" paradigm in the crackers category in Asia, for instance. There, only international biscuit brands are marketed, and ones that could be locally acquired are not included. The inconsistent application of the French company's transnational brand strategies only underscores the uniqueness of its partnership with Wahaha and Meilinzhengguanghe. Danone obliged Chinese conglomerates by resorting to an acquisition strategy that provided the backbone for an evolving Chinese discourse on "synergy."

13. According to a survey conducted in Yunnan (a rural province in the southwest), the average expenditure of a peasant on a snack or a drink ranges between six cents and thirty-six cents. A can of Coke costs thirty cents. A bottle of Future costs approximately twenty-four cents.

14. Building a sound distribution network in China today involves more than just building good public relations with neighborhood committees of the Chinese Communist Party, an earlier feat that author Charles Decker credited as one of P&G's successful product-sampling strategies in the PRC. See Decker (1998), 155–156.

15. Roughly speaking, the major achievements of the Chinese government are found in the domain of social policies that pertain to the leveling of the gaps between the country's rich and poor. China's antipoverty programs are well established. The implementation of the *San Nong* policies, in particular, benefits the rural population and has pushed the development of agriculture *(nongye),* the welfare of peasants *(nongmin),* and the enrichment of villages *(nong cun)* to the top of Beijing's agenda.

Financial policies aimed at redistributing social wealth have been stipulated. Although they sound like anathema to neoliberal economists, these policies are meant to benefit poor provinces and rural China. There are other public policies implemented in the last two years aimed at addressing the long-standing Chinese problems of unequal development between the coastal areas and interior China. They include the "develop the West [of China]" policy, the allocation of central and local government education subsidies for the children of poor households in rural China, the readjustment of low-income wages region by region, and the establishment of a medical insurance program in rural areas in which the central and local governments will subsidize up to 80 percent of the medical expenses of a rural patient.

16. Joseph Nye is the proponent of the concept of "soft power." He elaborates it in his *Soft Power: The Means to Success in World Politics* (2004). International politics or the strength of a nation-state used to be played out on the battlefield. But Nye argues that the foundations of power have been shifting away from the emphasis on "coercion" to an attraction that is cultivated through "relations with allies, economic assistance and cultural exchanges with other countries." Adaptors of his theory tend to use "soft power" as a descriptive rather than critical term, emphasizing the content rather than the means of achieving it. For instance, many East Asianists point to *anime* and *manga* in Japan as examples of soft power.

17. For more details on the conceptualization of "peaceful emergence" and the internal debates within the Chinese Communist Party, see Wang Jisi (2006).

18. I have had many opportunities to discuss "The Beijing Consensus" with (1) China enthusiasts who know little about China and (2) with Chinese academics in the United States who assume that they are authorities in speaking for China and for Chinese people. The second group's rejection of Ramos grew primarily from academic elitism. The first group did not appreciate Ramos because his critique of Western images of China—seen either as a threat to liberal values or as a country about to disintegrate into autonomous regions—went over their head. More precisely, Ramos's critique of dichotomous (and logocentric) views of China runs counter to their habitual thinking about China and about knowledge production in general. Many readers, no matter how sophisticated, are reluctant to acknowledge the

blurred boundaries between the "state" and "society," the "public" and the "private," a way of managing life and space characteristic of contemporary China. To many, the notion that "marketization" does not necessarily lead to "liberalization" makes little sense. It is worth noting that there is also a critical mass of scholars in China who appreciate the spirit and content of Ramos's work, although they do not necessarily endorse every single argument put forward in his white paper. I was impressed by Ramos's intuitive understanding of China's dilemmas and its positioning. For those interested in my critique of Western binary thinking about China, see the final section of Chapter 7.

19. Ramos's new treatise is entitled "Brand China." I don't have a copy of it, but even without reading it, I think the title of the sequel indicates that he now realizes the significance of country branding implicit in his ideas in his earlier work.

4. STORYTELLING AND CORPORATE BRANDING

1. America and Europe were designated early targets for Haier, because Zhang was intent on entering advanced markets first and less competitive underdeveloped markets later. By 2003 Haier had succeeded in capturing 35 percent of the small refrigerator market in the United States and 20 percent of the total market. See "Electronics Giant Eyes Top Spot in the World," http://joongangdaily.joins.com/200403/05. Accessed April 2004.

2. Donald N. Sull's book is *Made in China: What Western Managers Can Learn from Trailblazing Chinese Entrepreneurs* (Boston: Harvard Business School Press, 2005).

3. The other two books favored by Zhang are the *Tao Te Ching* and Confucius's *Analects*.

4. In Zhang's words, "if we don't feel the crisis, we are *in* crisis; only when we feel it constantly can we resolve it; living in crisis helps us prevent crises from happening" (Liu, Zhao, and Zhang. 2001, 29). This brings to mind the necessity of waging unending struggles preached by Mao Zedong.

5. How did Little Prodigy come to be invented? Summer is known to be a slow season for washing machine manufacturers, but the reason for this was unknown to Haier's marketing researchers. It makes little sense that Chinese people would do less laundry in sweltering weather.

Persistent research led to the discovery that customers were wary of using a regular-sized machine, whose large washing capacity entailed a bigger water and electricity bill in the summer months. Haier thus invented Little Prodigy, which weighed only 33 pounds. The lesson for Haier? "There are no slow-season markets, only slow-season thinking" (Ge 2003a, 17).

6. In the last few years, its stock option program has been extended to include midlevel managers.

7. The Chinese word *zuoren* is difficult to translate, because it has two shades of meaning—"people-handling" and "diplomatic know-how."

8. See Technorati, http://www.technorati.com/about/. Accessed August 15, 2006.

9. Corporate America has warmed up to "business blogging," which uses marketers, employees, spokespeople, customers, and even company CEOs to build brand traffic and to keep tabs on what's happening in the industry on a day-to-day basis. Innovative blogging strategies can also help businesses spy on competitors and determine where the whole sector is going. A helpful guide to blog marketing is Jeremy Wright's *Blog Marketing* (2006). A powerful blog-tracking tool is the multilingual Technorati. The idea of building interactive relationships with your prized customers is of course not new, but blogging takes it to a new level of intimacy and authenticity.

10. Today, 2 million (out of 5 million Chinese bloggers) have BlogChina user accounts.

11. The young Parisian girl did fulfill her promise, but stood with her back facing the public in the third advertisement, showing her bare buttocks.

12. Books written in defense of Liu Chuanzhi came out quickly in the wake of these two rounds of online debates. *Lianxiang ju* (The Saga of Lenovo) (2005) by Chi Yuzhou and *Legends of Lianxiang* by Ling Zhijun (2005) are two such examples.

13. The BMW short films grouped under the title "The Hire" are a series of eight product-placement Internet films showcasing the carmaker's sport sedans, luxury and executive sedans, SUVs, and other models. The short films debuted in 2001 and 2002, directed by internationally known auteurs like Ang Lee, John Woo, and Wong Kar Wai, starring Clive Owen as the Driver paired with other famous stars. "The Hire" quickly set an example for branded content as a marketing ploy.

14. The cartoon series took up 15 percent of Haier's advertising budget,

while 26 percent was spent on television commercials and 30 percent on outdoor ads. See Feng Guoying and Zhu Haisong (2004), 14.

15. The Ford commercials were broadcast on major network programs, including "Good Morning America," "Lost," "Desperate Housewives," and "CSI," as well as during the World Series and the NFL season.

5. BOURGEOIS BOHEMIANS IN CHINA?

1. www.associatedcontent.com/article/56421/conspicuous_consumption _the_crude_oil.html.

2. The catchphrase the "Three Represents" was coined by Jiang Zemin, former Party general secretary and former Chinese president. In a series of speeches going back to 2000, he promoted the "Three Represents" theory: the Chinese Communist Party (CCP) must always represent the development trends of advanced productive forces, the progressive orientation of an advanced culture, and the fundamental interests of the majority of Chinese people. He delivered the same message on the eightieth anniversary of the CCP on July 1, 2001, which caught the attention of China watchers because he simultaneously urged that entrepreneurs and other business elites be allowed to join the Party.

3. Members of the Visual Tribe very rarely read books. Instead they indulge in visual reading, meaning they decipher images in films, on television, and on the Internet every day. Their world is dominated by the pictorial and the visual. "International Freemen/women" (IFs) are well-to-do Chinese who can speak more than one foreign language, have the leisure and money for frequent international travel, and are cultural ambassadors whose sense of fashion is bicultural or even international—the three prerequisites for IF membership, according to the founder of the tribe, Liu Keya, a well-known personal speech coach (in English) and a taste trainer. See "IF lai le, qianwan buyao zaiti Bobo" ("The IFs Have Come. Don't You Ever Mention Bobos Anymore!"), www.sqdaily.com/20030114/ca24225.htm. January 14, 2003.

4. *San nong* was first raised as a policy slogan by Wen Tiejun, an agricultural economist and the dean of the School of Rural and Agricultural Development at the People's University in Beijing. "San" means "three"; the word "nong" is embedded in the three Chinese expressions for "village," "agriculture," and "peasants." Shortly after solving the *san nong* problem was recognized as a priority by the Chinese gov-

ernment, Wen established a contemporary James Yen Rural Reconstruction College in Hebei province. Founded in July 2003, the institute follows the Yen model of "release not relief" and carries on Yen's ideas of popular education and rural reconstruction through community development in rural villages. Wen and a team of volunteers and college students work to train and nurture migrant elites from among the rural migrants themselves, in order to send them back to their own villages to promote self-governance and rural cooperatives.

5. In the U.S. context, the term "bourgeois" is considered a cut above "middle class." But in the Chinese context, the two terms are interchangeable. Furthermore, the living conditions and income of the Chinese "middle class" are much better than those of the vast majority of Chinese people, who have only reached the *xiaokang* level (see next note). Roughly speaking, the social stratification in the Chinese context thus comprises the nouveau riche on the top, the "middle class" in the mid-tier, factory workers a grade lower, and peasants at the bottom. Seen in this context, being a member of the Chinese middle class conveys the impression that a person is well-off. This shade of meaning is largely absent in the American perception of what the middle class stands for. Americans also speak of the "upper-middle class," which Chinese usually do not. An excellent study of the differences in the conceptualization of the middle classes between China and Europe and the study of stratification within the Chinese middle class can be found in Goodman (2008).

6. "*Xiaokang* society" was a catchphrase used by former president Jiang Zemin at the Communist Party's 16th National Congress, held in Beijing in November 2002. He said that Chinese people will enjoy an all-around *xiaokang* life by 2020. By then, he said, their per capita GDP would be around $3,000. There has been a general consensus in the PRC that the fundamental key to achieving the goal of a *xiaokang* society lies in the solution of the "Three Nong" problems (peasant, village, and agriculture). Sociologist Lu Xueyi expounds the significance of *xiaokang* socialism as follows: it indicates that (1) the government will place a greater emphasis on social justice and social well-being than on GDP and sheer economic growth; (2) the government will pay greater attention to the social index rather than to the economic index of a "prosperous society." The social index for comprehensive *xiaokang* includes the employment ratio for the tertiary sector, level of

336 · Notes to Page 194

food and electricity consumption, ratio of doctors per thousand households, floor space per household, and so on. According to Lu Xueyi,
comprehensive *xiaokang* requires that rural labor not exceed 15 percent, the rural population not exceed 50 percent, and the college entrance ratio not go below 20 percent of those eligible for college education. See Wang Xiu and Xia Jinbiao (2002).

7. Published in China in 1998, Fussell's *Gediao* (the Chinese translation
of "class") was still going strong when bobo fever arrived in China in
2002. Many regarded it as a companion to *Bobos in Paradise*. Just like
the latter, *Class* was turned by Chinese cultural missionaries into an instrument that promotes a leap of faith: if the Chinese learn how to
dress, eat, drink, and consume in a classy manner, they will acquire a
classy social status.

8. Shi Tao, the Chinese translator of Fussell's *Class*, missed all the book's
ironies regarding the bourgeoisie and their taste, which Shi earnestly
promotes in his preface to his translation. In that preface, Shi illustrates the logic that taste determines class: "A person's taste in life
and his 'style' determines his social status. And tastes can only be expressed through one's daily lifestyle. 'Taste' is a more standard and
more effective means of determining one's social class. Taste and
class are something that can be nurtured and acquired . . . Through
self-cultivation and the elevation of one's taste, a person who is not
rich can attain a higher social status" (Shi 1998a). What kind of taste
are we then supposed to follow? Shi Tao cited Roland Barthes as a role
model. "Barthes spoke of his ideal life: he said, 'Have just a little bit of
money, not too much; have some power, but not too much. Have a lot
of leisure.' What did Barthes do with his leisure? Read, write, social-
ize with friends, drink (red wine), listen to music, travel a lot, etc. In
a word, live a life of taste" (ibid.). In defense of "taste," Shi labels
his critics a "marginalized social group" who fail to understand that
"in a pluralistic society, people have the right to choose their values."
He goes on to declare that the "laboring masses" are entitled to a life
of taste and that "living tastefully" is "no longer a privilege of the
wealthy" (ibid.). Shi Tao bounced questions back at his attackers:
"Why would some people find [social stratification] an intolerable reality? Why would a book that tries to instruct commoners how to position their social status and better their lifestyles be treated like something misguided?"

9. "One-upsmanship" refers to in-your-face kinds of display consumption. Ownership of luxury items and showing off in public lie at the core of "one-upsmanship." In contrast, "one-downsmanship," a landmark of the American bobos culture, is less about ownership of commodities and more about connecting to the universe, perfecting oneself, and expressing oneself—an organic notion of consumption in the new century.

10. The Chinese term *hou* is rich with implications. Other than "post," it also means "behind" and "back." Thus the name of the tower contains within itself a literal description of its physical location—it is situated right *behind* SOHO. Its print and outdoor advertisements contain some of the most creative copy ever written in contemporary China; they display an excellent positioning strategy for being number two. One of the tower's billboard ads says, "Before the post-modern Time debuted, there was nothing wrong about modern times," a clever jab at SOHO Modern. See Hu Jin and E Bo (2003), 26.

11. DINKs are a major target segment in the real estate market.

12. Hebdige's subculture paradigm was couched in the critical tradition of the Birmingham Centre for Contemporary Cultural Studies. Unlike the Frankfurt School's outright dismissal of mass culture, Birmingham School critics like Hebdige and Richard Hoggart (the Centre's first director) treated subjects of media and pop culture seriously and found within them real possibilities of resistance to the status quo. Their celebratory stance toward mass culture invited rebuttals by devout followers of the Frankfurt School. The Centre has made methodological contributions to cultural studies as theorists associated with it explore an interdisciplinary approach to the study of culture, incorporating theoretical paradigms as diverse as structuralism, Marxism, feminism, critical race studies, as well as more traditional methodologies such as sociology and ethnography.

13. In a similar vein, Maffesoli's theory on the neo-tribe can also lead us to reevaluate Bourdieu's social theory of the "habitus." "The schemes of the habitus, the primary forms of classification, owe their specific efficacy to the fact that they function below the level of consciousness and language, beyond the reach of introspective scrutiny or control by the will" (Bourdieu 1984, 466). "Life-styles are thus the systematic products of habitus . . . all the practices and products of a given agent are objectively harmonized among themselves, without any deliberate

pursuit of coherence, and objectively orchestrated, without any conscious concentration, with those of all members of the same class" (ibid., 172–173). If each class is believed to occupy its own specific habitus, and our habits are thus unconsciously differentiated and motivated, then a person is unlikely to switch from one norm to the next effortlessly and to exchange identity labels with total abandon. Lifestyle, in other words, is never simply a matter of free choice, but is habitus bound, according to Bourdieu. Can we reconcile Bourdieu's structuralist impulse with Maffesoli's assertion that "sociality is structurally deceptive, unknowable" (Maffesoli, 1996, 5)?

14. Yuichi Washida at Hakuhodo Foresight has been perhaps one of the first marketers to deliberate on the generational demography of *xin xinrenlei*. His elaboration on the difference of the usage of the term *shin shinjinrui* in Japan vis-à-vis Taiwan is very useful. According to Washida, there are two kinds of references for *shin shinjinrui*: "the generation among 25–35 years old in Taiwan; the second reference is to the generation under 25 years old in Japan." In Taiwan, this term is used (in its Chinese form) as almost the same as "Generations X and Y." In Japan, "Generations X and Y are called by two different names, *shin jinrei* (neo-tribe) and the "second-baby-boomers' generation." Many people also call the second baby boomers *dankai junior*, because they are the sons and daughters of the first baby boomers' generation. Therefore, in Japan, *shin shinjinrui* is a rather new term for the *post*-second baby boomers, early twentysomethings and teens. A well-known TV news program began to use this word in Japan, and it gradually spread.

15. This is taken from an email conversation that Washida and I shared. January 6, 2004.

16. The information was culled from an Ogilvy Beijing PowerPoint presentation on the launch of San Miguel Light given in the summer of 2002.

17. Ogilvy Interactive Asia displayed the Sammy ad campaign at http://our-work.com/version1_2/files/web_sites/sammy_site/sammy_explan.htm. Accessed June 2005.

6. HELLO MOTO: YOUTH CULTURE AND MUSIC MARKETING

1. Statistics about China's single-child population varies from source to source. According to the figures given by the National Population and Family Planning Commission of China, there were more than 100

million single children in the mid-2000s. See China Population.com. September 13, 2006. http://www.chinapop.gov.cn/rkxx/rkxw/ t20060913_152918774.html, accessed May 2007. However, other statistics indicate that the number ranges from 111.9 to 142 million. See Introduction, note 14. A note of caution should be given here. Not all of these single children can afford the kind of brand consumption described in this chapter. Although the finding seems counterintuitive, the percentage of single children in rural China is as high as 40 percent of the total single-child population. See Introduction at note 34 and note 34 itself. If we subscribe to the statistics, it means that only 67–85 million single children—potential consumers—live in urban China, as of 2006.

2. Although Feng Xiaogang is not the first director to take advantage of product placement, he alone has the flair to merge a product seamlessly into the plot, and turn cinema into advertising. *The Big Shot's Funeral* (*Dawanr,* 2002), a BMW-sponsored film and Feng Xiaogang's first attempt at product placement, is an ingenious parody of the practice itself. It takes an ad-savvy Chinese audience to identify which brand names are advertised in that film. In comparison, *Shouji* is much more straightforward about what Feng is selling: Motorola cell phones and China Mobile. How can we fail to notice the Motorola A760 when the credits of the film are run on its screen? How can we miss the satellite mapping function and the M-Zone service of China Mobile since the movie ends with those features? There was nothing subtle about the placement of these two big products or services. No wonder BMW, the film's other major sponsor, was upstaged.

3. Feng Xiaogang is the first mainland Chinese director to adopt the marketing model of celebrate-the-new-year films *(hesui pian),* a genre that originated in Hong Kong. He gave the Hong Kong model a new twist by highlighting the comic aspects of those "end-of-the-year" films, which proved to be highly successful. By catering to the taste of the mass audience, which is especially in the mood for light-hearted entertainment as the year draws to an end, Feng turned each *hesui pian* into a box-office hit. Yomi Braester wrote about this marketing practice in his "Chinese Cinema in the Age of Commercials Advertisement: The Filmmaker as a Cultural Broker," a paper presented at the *China Quarterly* Special Issue Workshop on Art and Culture in Contemporary China, held at Harvard University, October 15–16, 2004.

4. Motorola alone contributed a handsome 4 million yuan, trailed by

BMW's 1.2 million and China Mobile's 800,000, according to Yan Feng in his article on the film published in *Xiaoshou shichang* (China Marketing), no. 4 (2004): 72–76. But these were not the only funds gathered. The producers were rolling in cash from minor commercial sponsors as well. In fact, in the first ten minutes of the film, if you were alert enough, you could spot more than half a dozen product ads, not all of which were related to cars and cell phones. There were several precedents for movie marketing by handset makers. Ericsson invested in *Tomb Raider* (Paramount, 2001) and Samsung in *The Matrix* (Warner Brothers, 1999). *Heroic Duo* (*Shuang xiong*, produced by Benny Chan Muk-Sing, 2003) leisurely shoots a fifteen-second-long sequence of its male lead Zheng Yinjiang composing a text message to his girlfriend on his Nokia 6180.

Product placement alone, however, did not work miracles for *Shouji*. What made the film a major event for the Chinese film industry was not, in fact, its product placement but the underreported multimedia and cross-sectoral marketing phenomena that the film triggered. China Mobile, for instance, piggybacked on the film's anticipated success by releasing a new SMS game named *Shouji*, days before the movie debuted. "Enter our SMS game, experience life's dramas," its tagline promised. Another underrated marketing effort was the contract signed between the film producers and Guomei Electric Appliance Company, which gave the latter the exclusive right to play *Shouji* trailers simultaneously on all the TV sets displayed on the floor of their 130 or so chain stores around the country. If *Shouji* scored by ushering Motorola into the limelight, it scored even bigger by inaugurating an unprecedented model of multimedia and multisectoral marketing.

5. The site address is www.motomusic.com.cn.

6. Some literature reported a sales volume of 10.26 million units in 2005 (Madden 2006a), which is expected to grow to 45 million by 2010. See "2005 nian Zhongguo yinyue shouji xiaoshou liang" (The 2005 Sales Volume of Music Handsets in China), CBiNews, http://www.cbinews.com/inc/showcontent.jsp?articleid=38782. Accessed September 2006.

7. iPod users in China, for example, use the gadget primarily to import music from their own collection of pirated music onto the device.

8. The limits of a Beijing-based, location-specific study are obvious. However, while Shanghai and Guangzhou can claim a vibrant commercial

culture and brand culture, Beijing is the cradle of avant-garde music and art, a place where cultures on the margin have a chance to flourish. From the days of Cui Jian and the Chinese rock group Tang Dynasty, music trends in the capital are the barometers of the larger Chinese rock music scene.

9. WAP, Wireless Application Protocol, is a secure specification that allows users to access and interact with information instantly via hand-held wireless devices such as mobile phones, pagers, two-way radios, and smart phones.

10. The dire situation for domestic handset makers was best captured by the scenario described by Quinn Taw: "In China, the high-end brands do well and the low-end models do shockingly well, but it's the middle ground inhabited by TCL and its domestic peers which gets badly squeezed." See Shaw (2005), 20.

11. Fierce advertising battles came to a head in 2002. Panda made a successful bid of $2 million for a fifteen-second spot that aired in 2003 for two months on CCTV. Although TCL topped all of them, latecomer Samsung caught up with a stunning investment of $290 million—5 percent of its sales of electronic appliances, according to Li Guangdou (2004), 12.

12. In 2001, TCL launched the first Chinese WAP phone TCL999D series, and with it, a new brand culture called the "Diamond Culture." This was no mere metaphor. The handset shell is inlaid with sparkling diamonds or precious stones to accentuate the brand's premium image. In the press conference that unveiled the 999D series, a company spokesman harped on the link between the so-called precious stone culture in China and the brand symbolism of auspiciousness, nobility, and enduring commitment. TCL 999D was a hot sell.

Korean-style flip-over lids and decorative wallpapers became the norm. Together with those trends, streamlined shell shapes and changeable face covers (in different colors) have ushered the cellular phone into a new era of design marketing, which quickly became inseparable from celebrity endorsements. Each brand now owns its own celebrity. The list runs on and on: Maggy Cheung for Konka, Jin Shanxi (a Korean actress) for TCL, Zhao Wei (singer-star best known as the female lead in Stephen Chow's *Shaolin Soccer*) for Xiaxin, Zhang Ziyi (best known for her performance in *Crouching Tiger, Hidden Dragon*) for Southern High-Tech, and CoCo (singer Li Wen) for Bird.

13. China was expected to launch 3G networks before the 2008 Beijing Olympics. China Mobile, China Telecom, and China Netcom are running trials on 3G licenses in different parts of the country. The results of the trials will influence the Chinese government's decision on when to issue the licenses. The new technology will enable international visitors to the Olympic Games and media companies to transmit video and other mobile data about the Games faster than the current system allows. China has been developing its home-grown 3G standard—TD-SCDMA—to give the advantage to local vendors who can then avoid paying royalties to foreign companies that hold the patents for other 3G technologies. The rolling out of 3G has been held off by the government to give the domestic standard time to mature. But TD-SCDMA suffered a lackluster performance during trials conducted in several Chinese cities. And Beijing is running out of time to get 3G networks up and running before the 2008 Olympics as planned. The latest news is that 3G licenses will be allocated sometime in 2007. Meanwhile, rumors ran that Chinese telecommunication operators would likely build 3G mobile networks that combine one of the main international 3G technologies (such as W-CDMA or CDMA2000) with China's home-grown standard. If the rumor is true, operators would need dual-mode handsets capable of supporting two 3G networks. Handsets that support hybrid 3G networks do not exist yet and "would not necessarily be easy to produce." See Lemon (2006). See also Miao Su (2007).

14. These are internal statistics from Ogilvy & Mather that were available in 2004.

15. GSM (Global System for Mobile communications) is the world's most popular mobile phone standard. Although it originated in Europe, GSM networks are now operational in 120 countries around the globe. In 1998, GSM networks took off in China. Nokia, having quickly developed large-scale manufacturing facilities for complete GSM networks, achieved a strong position in the Chinese market.

16. In late 1999 and early 2000, a more mature marketing plan was unveiled. Motorola differentiated its target market into four segments, each served by a corresponding cell phone model: Accompli *(Tiantuo)* for techno-types; Timeport *(Shisuo)* for time management types; V (V Series) for image-conscious types; and Talkabout *(Xinyu)* for socialites. Underlying the logic of segmentation is the long overdue recognition that a cell phone should be promoted not as a simple technological gadget, but as a commodity product with a variety of identities and

personalities. Motorola thus began a new advertising campaign that sold lifestyles characteristic of each segment designated above. This four-pronged approach, a Motorola global brand strategy, signaled that the company had moved from technology-driven branding to consumer-relationship branding.

17. A mainland pop singer, Pu Shu has won six trophies at the annual Pepsi Music Chart Awards. He was also the only mainland Chinese singer who was given the title of "most popular artist" at the third MTV Asia Music Awards in 2004.

18. The size of monthly allowance varies from region to region, individual to individual. It is extremely difficult to make reliable statistical generalizations. The five participants in my Cool China Project had pocket money ranging from 500 to 2,000 yuan ($62–$250) per month. The figures do not mean much, however, because they can always request more from one of their six parents whenever the need arises. CTR market research agencies and the China Youth Research Center recently released a youth lifestyles survey of youngsters aged thirteen to eighteen years old living in Beijing, Shanghai, Guangzhou, Shenyang, Nanjing, Wuhan, Chengdu, Xi'an, and other cities. According to the survey, urban youth spend an average of 82 yuan (about $10) monthly on online games. See "Ba chengshi diaocha" (A Survey of Eight Cities), October 5, 2006, http://www.youth.cn/xw/yw/200610/t20061006_422951.htm. Accessed November 2006.

19. Jian Cui's pseudonym is the reverse of rock singer Cui Jian's name. Our naming strategy aimed at reminding people of his admiration for music subculture. Cui Jian is, of course, his hero.

20. "Idol culture" is a Japanese pop culture phenomenon that began in the 1970s and spread into other parts of Asia. It revolves around a celebrity who achieves fame largely by virtue of his or her cute looks. These "idols" are primarily performers in their late teens and early twenties. The phenomenon goes hand in hand with the idol-manufacturing industry that absorbs young people into its system of production by molding them into marketable personalities. It is a practice especially prevalent in the music performance sector. See Aoyagi (2005).

21. Many have commented that the teens in the United States are noted for being marketing-savvy as well. They are known to be more entrepreneurial than Generation X. See Sutherland and Thompson (2001), 152–153.

22. In Greek philosophy, "golden mean" refers to the felicitous middle be-

tween excess and deficiency. The Chinese are known to prefer a middle-of-the-road approach, a Confucian legacy that can be traced back to one of the Four Classics of Confucius, *Doctrine of the Golden Mean.*

23. Hunan Satellite TV rolled out a Chinese knock-off of the *American Idol* in 2005 for Chinese TV, setting off a national *Super Girl* craze. Fans and Chinese TV audience got to vote for their idol via text messages. It was said that the *Super Girl* show triggered nationwide online discussions on issues ranging from democracy to standards of beauty.

7. CCTV AND THE ADVERTISING MEDIA

1. For a detailed discussion of the significance of the year 1992 in post-Mao China, see J. Wang (2001b), 69. For a detailed discussion of the relations between foreign capital and the socialist Chinese state, see J. Wang (2004).

2. The growth rate of Chinese advertising in 2003 was 19.44 percent compared with a rate of 13.62 percent in 2002. The total 2003 advertising turnover was $13 billion, accounting for 0.92 percent of China's GDP (compared with $128 billion in the United States, with the U.S. advertising-to-GDP ratio at approximately 2.3 percent in 2002) ("Ad Sector" 2004; Nelson 2004; Zhang Haichao 2004, 10; CTR Market Research 2005b).

3. In October of 2004, SARFT and the Ministry of Commerce jointly released a new regulation on the establishment of joint ventures of radio and TV programming (news not included). Foreign media companies are allowed to have no more than a 49 percent share in the joint venture. And at least two thirds of the programs produced have to contain Chinese content. Viacom hoped to gain approval for creating another JV company with Beijing TV, but a 2005 policy stipulated that foreign media are allowed to set up only one such joint venture.

4. For instance, there was no voting on a favorite burp. Nor would children judge which movie character was the best at breaking wind. See Barboza (2006).

5. Because China is a socialist country, "commercialization" carries a meaning different from that in the modern West. In the Chinese context, "commercialization" means the "diversification of state capital" of state-owned enterprises. Specifically, it means that the government will open up such an enterprise for domestic and international investors to a degree. As I point out in this chapter, the threshold for capital

infusion varies from sector to sector and from subsector to subsector within a given sector. Therefore, commercialization in China is not the same as "privatization." In a similar manner, "commercial content" is nuanced. But the degree to which a particular type of commercial content is open to foreign investment varies. For instance, advertising content is relatively more open than film content. The news subsector is the least open for domestic and foreign investment. The logic about which sectors can be made commercial is elucidated in the following pages.

6. Media scholar Yuezhi Zhao wrote in "When the Tide Goes Out, the Rocks Are Revealed" about the Western mainstream view that holds "that China's WTO entry and the opening of its media system to foreign owners will inevitably undermine the CCP's authoritarian control and facilitate press freedom" (Y. Zhao 2004). Whether the activities of transnational media corporations in China will have an inherently democratizing impact on Chinese media is indeed a question widely discussed online and offline by commentators of different persuasions. Numerous articles have been published since China's entry to the WTO in anticipation of the impending changes in regulations on Chinese TV media. Optimism ran high in 2001, but in 2002 the optimists found themselves filled with deep reservations. A typical latter view is seen in Guo Zhenzhi (2003). In contrast to such pessimism (that is, that the status quo in Chinese media has not changed much at all in the post-WTO era) are mainstream views that emphasize the long-term impact of capital to liberalize the sector. For instance, according to Doris Leung, as more and more foreign media giants enter China, international standards of how to run media industry will take root in the country. In the same view, as the media market becomes more open and mature, the Chinese state will not be able to control it as tightly as it used to. See her "WTO and the Future of Chinese Media," *Global Beat,* http://jmsc.hku.hk/newmedia/WTO_media.htm.

7. This important policy document has been analyzed in trade magazines and books on media reform published in Chinese ever since 1999. China Broadcasting and Television Yearbook Committee, ed., *Zhongguo guangbo dianshi nianjian 2000* (The 2000 Yearbook of Chinese Broadcasting and Television) (Beijing: China Broadcast and TV Yearbook Publishers Co., 2000).

8. The separation of production from broadcasting within the radio and TV sector was only partially implemented as of 2005. It was a countermeasure that big stations like CCTV supported in the hopes that they

could gain more comparative advantages over local stations, whose small-scale operations could not afford such a systemic separation. The hidden agenda was to commercialize the content of sports and entertainment programs by drawing in "social production forces" (that is, production resources and capital from outside the station) so that programming could be gradually specialized and professionalized. But because of infrastructural barriers, the shortage of capital, the lack of professional programming skills, and the immaturity of China's content production market outside the state-run system, it has been difficult for TV stations to separate broadcasting rights from programming rights. Reality was a far cry from the theory. In a survey conducted by Huang Shengmin and Ding Junjie, most station managers said that their experimentation with the policy was limited to a few select programs (rather than entire channels). The managers auctioned the rights of production for these programs' categories to content producers. (News programs were off limits for the experiment.) But in a system that has a hard time differentiating the "public" from the "private," the overlap of rights remained a problem. See Huang and Ding (2001), 30–32.

9. The prospects of such an auspicious asset expansion for cable transmissions companies grew even rosier as MII (the Ministry of Information Industry) reportedly considered softening its stance on the investment of foreign capital in the cable sector. The recommendation was to divide cable transmissions into two platforms: Platform A was to cover cable operators broadcasting TV programs (which would remain closed to foreign investors) and Platform B for operators who had the capacity to offer value-added telecom services such as voice and data communication. Foreign investment was said to be allowed for operators classified under Platform B. See Budde (2005), 4. As of mid-2007, the two ministries are still at odds with each other about convergence. It remains to be seen "whether the two [MII and SARFT] can set aside their vested interests and work together." See Chan and Ip (2007).

10. Calculated on the basis of the number of users and charges, the annual revenue for Chinese basic cable TV service was expected to reach RMB 30 billion by 2005, an increase of 275 percent from 2001. See Ai Mai (2003).

11. In a major policy statement made in 2001, the MII gave the green light for the convergence of the two sectors while SARFT rejected it. At stake is whether fixed-line telecom operators such as China Telecom

and China Unicom will be allowed to offer cable television over their broadband networks owned by the MII and whether cable TV companies owned by SARFT should be able to deliver Internet and voice services over the cable network overseen by SARFT (Budde 2005, 6).

12. I am referring to the "Directive on Reinforcing the Management and Construction of Radio and TV Cable Networks" published by the General Office of the State Council in 1999. It was a gentlemen's agreement between MII and SARFT.

13. According to reports, Chinese Netizens prefer to connect with the Internet via cable TV networks. Those currently accessing the Internet through telecom services will switch sides if the convergence between the two sectors takes place. The technology enabled by cable TV networks is more advanced. Connection speed is "ten times faster, and the charges will be only a fraction of that of telecom networks." See "China's Cable TV Networks Could Outcompete China Telecom's Networks," www.chinaonline.com/industry/telecom/NewsArchive/cs-protected/2000. Accessed May 2003.

14. In May 2005, SARFT gave the Shanghai Media Group the first license for IPTV (Internet Protocol Television), enabling broadband users to access TV broadcasting services on their computers or TV sets with a set-top box. It was not a coincidence that this pathbreaking SARFT initiative was unveiled only a month and a half after China Telecom and China Netcom (two crown jewels owned by the MII) showcased their IPTV services at the annual exhibition of the China Cable Broadcasting Network (CCBN). See "China's IPTV License Opens Door for Broadcasters, Telcos," *Yahoo Asia,* May 17, 2005, http://asia.tech.yahoo.com/050517/4/213dq.html. Accessed June 2005.

15. The contradiction between SARFT's interest in developing DTV and the telecom sector's interest in developing IPTV is another point of contention between the two regulatory bodies. The irony is that SARFT has been given the mandate of promoting DTV, but at the same time it controls the licensing for IPTV (because video programs are considered "content"), which is in direct competition with DTV. According to current regulations, video programs can only come from legal broadcasters. Yet several telecom operators have already entered the IPTV market through collaboration with local TV broadcasters. The cooperation of iCCTV with telecom operators to provide IPTV services is a good example.

16. The biggest threat thus far is TiVo. TiVo, Inc., puts convenience and

control in the hands of consumers via the digital video recorder (DVR) it pioneered. Among its many features, the device screens out commercials if the viewer desires. TiVo was introduced in Shanghai in 2007. Those who will be able to afford it will be people in China's most affluent class, the most important target for transnational corporations in the country. For a brief account of the impact of TiVo on spot advertising, see "The TiVo Story" (http://www.tivo.com/5.1.asp) and "On Tivo and Advertising" (http://george.hotelling.net/90percent/geekery/on_tivo_and_advertising.php). Both sites accessed July 2005.

17. See Chapter 6 for a discussion of mobile phone advertising in feature films in China. Following Motorola's example, Nokia also placed its phones in Feng Xiaogang's 2004 *A World without Thieves (Tianxia wuzei).*

18. Three different kinds of gaming-related advertising are gaining popularity in the United States: in-game advertising, which works just like traditional advertising, except that it exists in the virtual world. Then there is immersive in-game advertising, which is interactive with players. Typically, a client pays an agency or game developer to develop a "level" of game play with a key sponsor's product in mind. The third type is called advergames—whole games developed from scratch with a marketing message and product-specific themes in mind. Advergames are the virtual world counterpart of branded entertainment. For more details, see Jones and Martin (2007). The first video game advertising agency, Massive, was launched in New York City in 2005. Considering how quickly the Chinese catch up with Western marketing trends, it is only a matter of time before advergames are introduced into China.

19. The selective sectors eligible for the 8 percent cap include medicine, food, electrical appliances, and telecommunications. For risky sectors like investment and advanced technology, within the first five years of the business's start, the tax bureau will examine its request for pretax advertising spending on a case-by-case basis. Depending on the results of such assessments, the bureau will allow either no cap or a higher percentage cap on ad expenditure for the company involved.

20. To compare this practice with Super Bowl advertising, the difference lies in CCTV's marketing emphasis on sales vis-à-vis the Super Bowl's on product branding.

21. These statistics are culled from Shou Peipei (1996).

22. According to Optimum Media, in the third quarter of 1999, a thirty-

second commercial on U.S. network television cost $190,000 in prime time but $21,960 in daytime. See http://www.newspaperadvertising .com/articles/art5.html. Accessed May 2005.

23. Industry speculations about why foreign companies were slow in joining CCTV's annual auction centered on two possible reasons. First, the auction is held in early November, when most foreign investors do not yet have their next year's advertising schedule. Second, most foreign advertisers do not engage in the auction, because they buy media on the basis of quantitative media measurement. Not until the early 2000s could CCTV provide statistics to support its claim that prime-time advertising is worth the investment.

24. The fact that the first few "king bidders" were all liquor makers indicates that the Chinese liquor sector was the most impulsive and aggressive sector for voluntary bids during the early years of CCTV auctions. After China's accession to the WTO, the tariffs for spirits were lowered from 65 percent to 10 percent, easing the entry of wine, beer, and other Western liquor brands from abroad. The battlefield for Chinese liquor manufacturers is increasingly confined to the medium and lower end of the liquor market. It is a huge market, nonetheless, which can accommodate many players, who line up for well-segmented regional and local targets. Probably because of the low-cost and high-return nature of the domestic liquor industry, big liquor makers like Wu Liang Liquor and Gu Yue Long Shan have been able to allow sub-brands to proliferate rather recklessly in order to cater to different tastes specific to different targets. The sector, as a whole, is characterized by the "more is more" and "big is more" marketing strategy (the more sub-brands the better), which also explains the sector's drift toward the sensationalism that the "king bidder" phenomenon promised. For a more detailed analysis of domestic liquors, see Wang Xiangdong (2002), 182–187.

25. In 2005, the sixty-five-second segment placed after the news broadcast was reduced to sixty seconds. The number of spots during that segment was changed from thirteen to twelve. But the length of each spot remains five seconds. See CCTV Advertising Department, "Huangjin duanwei guanggao zhaobio zhengce tiaozheng shuoming" (Explanations for the Policy Shift for the Prime-Time Auction), *Guanggao ren* (Ad Men), no. 11 (November 2004): 20–21.

26. More than a few adjustments were made. In 1999, the station changed its seasonal units to two-month units, which allowed media segments to coincide more with the selling cycles of electrical appliance makers,

in particular. The splintering of media units into months and an off-season (that is, July and August) also helped smaller enterprises to enter the otherwise unaffordable prime-time ring. During that same year, CCTV marketers began touring major tier-one and tier-two cities, introducing their newly unveiled service-oriented plans to local enterprises. Length adjustments for prime-time spots were also made in 2003—the three five-second spots before the national news broadcast gave way to four fifteen-second spots, and premium spots aired right after "Focus Interviews" *(Jiaodian fangtan)* were decreased from four fifteen-second spots to three. These measures not only took into account the needs of branding, which favored fifteen seconds over five seconds, but also put into practice the fundamental market principle that fewer (spot) supplies could stimulate fiercer competitions and drive up media prices (Zhang and Liu 2004, 98–99). Compared with the "king-bidder" phenomenon, this approach to spurring the growth of ad spending is much more rational in the long run.

An equally noteworthy strategy was CCTV's emphasis on "added value" for prime-time advertising clients. The media packet for the station's most favored clients incorporates free advertising on other CCTV-owned media and preferential transactions with the station's long-term strategic partners, such as national financial news media and outdoor and public transportation ad-dealers in several cities (Ji Feng 2002b, 86), adding up to an integrated media mix that rival provincial and local media stations cannot match.

27. Drawn by the fanfare surrounding the Korean drama, I bought a collection of one series' shows and watched all seventy episodes. The success of the drama was attributed to several intertwining factors: historical palace dramas are a favorite genre of Chinese audiences; the sound tracks were dubbed in Mandarin, making those viewers forget that they were watching a foreign show; and it was a drama about imperial gourmet food and herbal medicine, and how the two can be fruitfully combined to promote the eater's health while not compromising flavor. The theme of *shibu* ("food as medicine"), a unique tradition shared by the Chinese and the Koreans, had never been treated in a TV drama before. The appeal was natural. Added to all those ingredients is the tear-jerker formula: a story about a young woman who struggles through endless misfortunes but prevails in the end. There was also, of course, a love story and a love triangle, which spiced up the odyssey of an ordi-

nary girl's bid for the title of the emperor's doctor in a time when women were forbidden to treat male patients. The Koreans knew how to cash in on the *Daejanggeum* fever in China and Taiwan. They kept intact the fictional palace site where the drama was filmed and turned it into a tourist attraction for mainland Chinese, Taiwanese, and other Asian tourists. Within China, the drama triggered a passion for Korean food, clothes, music, and, of course, ginseng, an ingredient used indulgently by the imperial cooks in the drama.

28. Foreign companies spent a total of 753.3 million yuan ($94 million) in CCTV's 2005 auction, compared with less than $21.7 million invested by Procter & Gamble the previous year. See Zhang Lu, "P&G Becomes CCTV Bidding King." *China Daily*, November 20, 2005. http:// www.chinadaily.com.cn/english/doc/2004-11/20. Accessed May 2005.

29. Meanwhile, because of pricing hype, many weak provincial channels failed to fill up the eighteen-minute quota.

30. This observation was borne out by the statistics on the breakdown of national audience shares for the evening news (CCTV's golden goose) among different age groups: 13.5 percent for viewers aged 25–34; 18.1 percent for ages 35–44; 20.5 percent for ages 45–54; and 31.3 percent for ages 55–64. See CTR Market Research (2004), 23.

31. The MindShare research indicates that 68.4 percent of viewers gained their knowledge about a certain famed (and heavily recalled) brand by watching its commercials aired on CCTV-1 (MindShare 2004, 27).

32. CCTV statistics may not be far-fetched, since we know that Chinese television has the lowest mean CPM (cost per thousand) score, 18, followed by newspapers' 24. See Hung, Gu, et al. (2005).

33. Ratings are the basic means of measuring the size of an audience. Ratings are derived from the number of households watching a program divided by the total number of TV households in a population. See McGann and Russell (1981), 93.

34. The most popular local stations in Shanghai are Shanghai City TV, the Oriental Pearl Station, and Shanghai Cable TV.

35. Document No. 82 did not immediately disable county TV stations. It took a few years for them to be phased out.

36. The discussion of "zero commission" was particularly heated in the first few years of the new millennium. For a typical discussion, see Zhao Nannan (2002). See also Chapter 1, note 4, above.

37. As of 2003, only two stations—Shanghai and Sichuan TV—could af-

ford to pay the 100 percent landing fees in other provinces. However, Beijing TV (BTV) and Sichuan TV made a deal involving "friendship swaps," allowing each station to land without fees in Sichuan and Beijing respectively.

38. The city stations in question include Nanjing, Beijing, Shanghai, Shenyang, Kunming, Suzhou, and Hangzhou.

39. I have explored the implications of the trans-boundary logic embodied in the "provincial united front" in an edited volume on space and pop culture. I noted that trans-areal media networks mushroomed as the principle of scale economy gained a life of its own. Since the new millennium, many such border-crossing alliances have been made. The Provincial United Front is one such example. For details of the phenomenon, see *Locating China: Space, Place, and Popular Culture* (J. Wang 2005b, 16–18).

40. To earn the grade A designation, a production company must have had the experience of completing and airing six TV shows or three TV series in the previous two years.

41. According to a SARFT regulation announced in June 2000, broadcasting time for foreign TV drama cannot exceed 25 percent daily. In addition, it cannot exceed 15 percent of prime-time broadcast (from 6 P.M. to 10 P.M.) See Shanghai TV Festival (2004), 216.

42. Thematically, Chinese TV drama has been dominated by historical romances (including *Romance of the Three Kingdoms,* the *Kangxi Emperor, Dream of the Red Chamber,* and other Qing dynasty palace dramas), traditional knight-errant kung-fu drama, modern-day urban drama focused on relationships, and crime stories. Whenever a topic catches on with the national audience, copycats mushroom and exhaust interest in the theme. For instance, in 2000 alone, three productions on Ji Xiaolan and two on Zheng Chenggong were made. Both were famous historical heroes well known to the public.

43. The entry of domestic capital into publicly owned media industries is also a highly problematic area that is vulnerable to policy fluctuations. As we have seen, the content industry has not been liberalized by the state. Which sub-sectors within the media can be commodified is an important agenda item for SARFT. Because China's commitment to the WTO binds it to liberalizing its retail and distribution sectors, the "media and cultural industries" allowed to go public are specifically defined as publishing, audiovisual production, film distribution, and

information transmission. Domestic companies specializing in these potentially commercial sectors (or in more clearly commercial ones such as real estate) are highly sought by content sectors, which are unable to go commercial, for joint venture formation and asset investment and transfusion in preparation for public listing. On the surface, the IPO pipeline is bulging. On closer scrutiny, though, only a limited amount of domestic "social capital" has been permitted to enter the media sector.

44. National statistics about TV drama ratings in 2002 show that provincial satellite channels captured 61 percent of the audience share, leading CCTV by 22 percent. See Shanghai TV Festival (2004), 48.

45. The Horizon Report "TV Program Consumption Habits" was commissioned by the product placement agency ONA and conducted in April 2006. It covers Beijing, Changsha, Chengdu, Xiamen, Xinxiang, Qujing, Shaoxing, Zhuji, Anqing, and other second- and third-tier cities. The analysis covered 2,018 valid samples.

46. "Effective reach" is a media marketing term referring to the percentage of the target audience exposed at the frequency level desired by the media planner.

47. Thematic taboos on extramarital affairs and historical parodies *(xishuo lishi)* were added to old taboos such as cop and crime drama.

48. Another example of the enabling function of policymaking in the PRC is the policy of the Double Leisure Day *(shuang xiu ri)* implemented in the mid-1990s. On the impact of the forty-hour workweek policy on the rise of urban Chinese leisure culture, see J. Wang (2001b,c).

CONCLUSION

1. More and more books on experiential marketing (XM) have been published in the United States. Max Lenderman's *Experience the Message* (2006) is a good introduction. Erik Hauser's XM Forum is an important resource for XM. See http://www.experientialforum.com/adboard .php. Accessed in September 2006.

2. See footnote 13 in Chapter 2 for a detailed definition of "prosumers." Those proactive consumers are talking back to the "mass-produced, Wal-Mart world—to take power back, prove that they can make the products that they want to consume, have fun doing so, and, just maybe, make a few dollars." See Roth (2005). The informal economy

contributed by prosumers is a subject of Alvin and Heidi Tofflers' book *Revolutionary Wealth: How It Will Be Created and How It Will Change Our Lives* (2006).

3. Experiential marketing takes advantage of new media technology to spread the brand message. The Internet is the best incubator for buzzes. Buzzes can also be circulated in the traditional word of mouth (WOM) fashion. But more often than not, they take the form of technologically enabled WOMs that use P2P networks such as blogging communities for viral transmission.

4. An excellent interview of Wu Xiaobo, the CEO of Pingcheng, can be found in http://www.baoye.net/bencandy.php?fid=308&id=9570. The interview both showcases Wu Xiaobo's cutting-edge thinking about the globalization of Chinese advertising and provides an excellent analysis of the trends of Chinese advertising in the last twenty-five years from an insider's point of view.

5. Examples of successful sports marketing on CCTV are already plentiful. During the World Series in 2002, anonymous local brands were made famous overnight within fairly reasonable media budgets. The two-week Series reaped an astounding audience—the frequency of audience tune-ins was approximately 8.5 billion—turning CCTV into the hottest Chinese medium for sports events. Shen Tianlan (2004b), 111.

6. The *Super Girl* phenomenon in China was briefly treated in Chapter 7. The show stirred up a controversy leading to further restrictions announced by SARFT in March 2006. According to the new regulation, contestants have to be at least eighteen years old. Broadcasters are prohibited from awarding prizes to winners. Contestants are not allowed to behave erratically—no more dancing on stage. They are also forbidden to wear unconventional hairstyle and clothing. Furthermore, judges are not allowed to embarrass contestants on air. And broadcasters are banned from copying the format of the existing *Super Girl* shows. The government eventually canceled *Super Girl* in early fall 2007. For details on *Daejanggeum*, see Chapter 7, note 27.

7. You can watch the film at two sites: http://www.youtube.com/watch?v=j-5G98g3-DI, accessed June 2007, or http://daodao.org/article.asp?id=112, accessed in August 2006.

8. According to the 2006 CNNIC *China Search Engine Market Research Report,* Baidu owned the largest market share in China at 62.1 percent, up 14.2 percent points, compared with Google, whose shares dropped

from 33.3 percent to 25.3 percent. See Interfax China, http://www .interfax.cn/showfeature.asp?aid=17250&slug=IT%20SURVEY. Accessed September 2006.

9. Stephen Chow is a Hong Kong–born film maker and actor. His performance style is called "Mo-Lei-To," "makes no sense." His nonsense comedies have starred small backalley heroes and heroines. With the making of his best-selling movie *Kung Fu Hustle,* he learned the tricks of appealing to global youth audiences. He is particularly interested in glorifying underdogs and in catering to local Chinese sensibilities. His classics include *Shaolin Soccer* and *From Beijing with Love* (a parody of the James Bond movie). He is known for his critiques of the conventional norms of social propriety. Extremely rich in wordplay, Cantonese slang, and folk and burlesque humor, his films have broken box office records in the Greater China region. He is the single most popular director-actor in Chinese-speaking countries. More important, Chow is the source of inspiration for contemporary Chinese parodies. He holds the key to understanding "Chinese humor."

10. The campaign's full title is *Motion Life Focus (donggan shenghua jiaoju Fukesi).* The other five directors were Liu Hao, Xiaojiang, Sun Xiaoru, Li Hong, and Jiang Lifen. The site www.ford.com.cn/focus, where the films were originally posted (July 2005), was pulled down. Through other linked pages, I was able to watch fragments of two films, Meng Jinghui's *Watermelon* and Li Hong's *Xiaoxiao fu dan* (Incubation). But they are not consistently available online. For the news release, see http://auto.sina.com.cn/z/jjfkswstpqmqd/index.shtml. Accessed August 2006.

11. Some industry critics say that NBA games and the World Cup are already no different from entertainment programs in the eyes of Chinese generations X and Y members. Athletes like hurdler and Olympic gold medalist Liu Xiang and Houston Rockets basketball star Yao Ming are treated like movie stars, and if they can sing a song or two to entertain the masses, that is even better.

12. These critics recommend that marketers "leave the top 20 percent of elite consumers behind" and "speak to the 80 percent of those on the long tail." See Zhang Binwu (2005), 30–32. In traditional marketing, the top 20 percent of consumers are valued the most by marketers because they are seen to account for 80 percent of sales volume.

13. Please see the company web site www.ucantv.com.

14. All these TV programs have legal rights and are authorized to operate the digital coupon services under the CCTV licenses.

15. Coupons are grouped into two sets: free-for-all coupons and with-restrictions coupons. DynoMedia distributes the former to mass audiences but selectively pushes the latter to targeted segments. Free-for-all coupons are mainly for restaurants and fast-food chains. With-restriction coupons usually have a higher value for consumers in electronics, cosmetics, and automobiles.

16. Web 2.0 is a term coined by Tim O'Reilly in 2004. It refers to a vision of the Web in which documents are broken up into "microcontent" units that can be distributed over dozens of domains. It also refers to the second generation of software tools that enables end-users to aggregate and remix these microcontent bits and build collaborative Web-based communities such as wikis and social networking ones. The best definition of Web 2.0 I have seen is provided by Richard MacManus and Joshua Porter (2005).

17. To quote Lessig, "Creators get to create only with the permission of the powerful, or of creators from the past" (Lessig 2004, 8).

18. I am referring to Benkler's *The Wealth of Networks: How Social Production Transforms Markets and Freedom* (2006). Benkler's thesis coincides with that of Jenkins.

19. The cross-fertilization of marketing research and cultural studies is made more urgent because the advertising industry has tapped into the resources offered by critical semiology, psychology, sociology, cultural anthropology, psychoanalysis, and communication studies. The reverse flow of expertise can only benefit studies of youth culture and popular culture in academia.

20. Here the "producer" can refer to any of the following—business corporations, the government, or any authorities that produce commercial, political, or social messages and disseminate them from the top down.

21. Every good advertising trade magazine in China today incorporates columns on media as well as marketing and advertising.

22. On Geert H. Hofstede's 5-D dimensions of national cultures, see Chapter 1, note 1, above. See also his *Cultures and Organizations: Software of the Mind* (1991).

References

Aaker, David A. 1991. *Managing Brand Equity*. New York: Free Press.

Aaker, David A., and Erich Joachimsthaler. 2000. *Brand Leadership*. New York: Free Press.

"Ad Sector Competition Heats Up." 2004. *Chinese Business Weekly*, September 21. http://www.china.org.cn/english/BAT/107668.htm. Accessed May 20, 2005.

Adorno, Theodor W., and Max Horkheimer. 1972. *Dialectics of Enlightenment*. Trans. John Cumming. New York: Seabury Press.

Ai Mai. 2003. "High-speed Growth Expected in Cable TV Network Industry." http://www.tdctrade.com/report/indprof/indprof_030306.htm, March 24. Accessed May 2005.

Aitchison, Jim. 2002. *How Asia Advertises*. Singapore: John Wiley & Sons.

Allison, Anne. 2006. *Millennial Monsters: Japanese Toys and the Millennial Imagination*. Berkeley: University of California Press.

Anderson, Chris. 2004. "The Long Tail." *Wired*, no. 12.10 (October). http://www.wired.com/wired/archive/12.10/tail.html. Accessed June 2006.

———. 2006. *The Long Tail: Why the Future of Business Is Selling Less of More*. New York: Hyperion.

Anderson, Michael H. 1984. *Madison Avenue in Asia: Politics and Transnational Advertising*. Rutherford, NJ: Fairleigh Dickinson University Press.

Anholt, Simon, and Jeremy Hildreth. 2005. *Brand America: The Mother of All Brands*. London: Cyan Communications.

Aoyagi, Hiroshi. 2005. *Islands of Eight Million Smiles: Idol Performance and Symbolic Production in Contemporary Japan.* Cambridge: Harvard University Asia Center.

Appadurai, Ajun. 1986. *The Social Life of Things.* Cambridge: Cambridge University Press.

"Asia Television Commercials Videotape: Films for the Humanities and Sciences." 1999. Princeton, NJ: Films Media Group.

Asschenfeldt, Christiane. 2005. "iCommons Summit: 2005." San Francisco: Creative Commons.

Baker, Stephen, and Heather Green. 2005. "Blogs Will Change Your Business." http://www.businessweek.com/magazine/content/05_18/b3931001_mz001.htm. Accessed May 2006.

Barboza, David. 2006. "Viacom Testing Limits of Youth TV in China." *International Herald Tribune,* January 10. http://www.iht.com/articles/2005/12/28/business/nick.php. Accessed May 2007.

Barthes, Roland. 1972. *Mythologies.* New York: Hill & Wang.

Baudrillard, Jean. 1994. *Simulacra and Simulation.* Trans. Sheila Faria Glaser. Ann Arbor: University of Michigan Press.

———. 1996. *The System of Objects.* London: Verso.

Beck, Lindsay. 2007. "China Ex-Food and Drug Safety Chief Sentenced to Death." Reuters. May 29. http://www.reuters.com/article/worldNews/idUSPEK4362920070529?pageNumber=1. Accessed June 2007.

Beech, Hannah. 2004. "The New Radicals." *Asia Times,* February 2, 32–38.

Bell, Edward. 2006. Email exchange.

Benkler, Yochai. 2006. *The Wealth of Networks: How Social Production Transforms Markets and Freedom.* New Haven: Yale University Press.

Bishop, Bill. 2005. "Coke, Pepsi, World of Warcraft, Magical Land, The9 and Shanda." http://bbb.typepad.com/billsdue/2005/04/coke_pepsi_worl.html. April 21. Accessed January 2006.

Blackett, Tom. 2004. "What Is a Brand?" In *Brands and Branding,* ed. Rita Clifton and John Simmons, 13–25. Princeton, NJ: Bloomberg Press.

Blair, Mark, Richard Armstrong, and Mike Murphy. 2003. *The 360 Degree Brand in Asia: Creating More Effective Marketing Communications.* Singapore: John Wiley & Sons.

Bluethinker. 2004. Sina.com, January 31. http://tech.sina.com.cn/it/2004-02-02/1316287002.shtml. Accessed May 2006.

Blustein, Paul. 2006. "Senators Deride U.S. Position on China." *Washington Post,* May 19. http://www.washingtonpost.com. Accessed June 2006.

"Bobo guoji: Chengshi jingying de lixiang jiayuan" (Bobo International: The Ideal Abode for City Elite). 2003. http://jrnb.rednet.com.cn, November 19. Accessed 2003.

Bourdieu, Pierre. 1984. *Distinction: A Social Critique of the Judgment of Taste.* Trans. Richard Nice. Cambridge, MA: Harvard University Press.

Brooks, David. 2000. *Bobos in Paradise: The New Upper Class and How They Got There.* New York: Simon & Schuster.

"Bubo zu de xin chonger: Aerkate OT715" (The New Pet Toy for Bobos: Alcatel OT715). 2002. http://topdigital.vip.sina.com/ . . . /products/ 200208. Accessed 2004.

"Bubo zu shangji da gonglue zhi luntan yu dianping" (Commentaries on the Symposium of "A Marketing Offence Targeting Bobos"). 2003. http://finance.sina.com.cn/roll/20030416, April 16. Accessed 2003.

Budde, Paul. 2005. "China—Broadcasting—Cable, Pay, and Interactive TV." Paul Budde Communication Pty Ltd. http://www.budde.com.au/ Reports/Contents/China-Broadcasting-Cable-Pay-and-Interactive-TV-3543.html, March 5. Accessed June 2005.

Cai Yugao and Zhu Liyi. 2005. "Shui duozou le tamen de fuyu ganjue: Jiedu Changjiang Sanjiaozhou jumin shouru yu xiaofei de kunhuo" (Who Took Away Their Sense of Affluence? Deciphering the Income and Consumption Bottleneck of Those Residents Living in the Yangtzu River Delta). *Guoji guanggao* (International Advertising), no. 7 (July): 56–57.

Cantrell, Amanda. 2006. "Lenovo's Big Blues." CNN.com, May 19. http://money.cnn.com/2006/05/19/technology/lenovo_story/index.htm. Accessed May 2006.

Cartier, Carolyn. 2001. *Globalizing South China.* Oxford: Blackwell.

CCTV. 2006. "Meiti baojia" (Media Price). Meiti kanli wang (Media Price Net). http://www.mtklw.com.cn/User/mAnalyse-2524.jhtml. Accessed June 2006.

Chan, Jeanette, and Bianca Ip. 2007. "Viewpoint: Departments Pull in Different Directions on Media Integration." *Financial Times,* May 22. http://www.ft.com/cms/s/d548c88a-0871-11dc-b11e-000b5df10621.html. Accessed May 2007.

Chan, Joseph Man. 1997. "National Responses and Accessibility to Star

TV in Asia." In *Media in Global Context: A Reader*, ed. Annabelle Sreberny-Mohammadi, Dwayne Winseck, et al., 94–106. London: Arnold.

Chan, Viveca (Yinan). 2005. "Zhongguo guanggao de Zhongguo liliang" (The Chinese Power of Chinese Advertising). *Guanggao daguan* (Advertising Panorama), no. 12 (December): 24–27.

Chang, Leslie, and Peter Wonacott. 2003. "Cracking China's Market—Adapting to Chinese Customs, Cultural Changes, Companies from U.S., Europe Find Profit." *Wall Street Journal*, January 9, B1, 1–6.

"Changcheng dichan shouci yi da shoubi jianzheng 'guoji Shenzhen'" (The Great Wall Estate Validates "International Shenzhen" in Grand Style). 2003. http://www.soufun.com, December 25. Accessed 2003.

Chen Beiai. 1997. *Zhongwai guanggao shi* (The History of Chinese and Foreign Advertising). Beijing: Zhongguo wujia chubanshe.

Chen Gang. 2005. "Zhongjian didan zhi huyan luanyu" (Babbles about the Third Zone). *Guanggao daguan* (Advertising Panorama), no. 12 (December): 28–29.

Chen Gelei. 2005. "Baidu Tang Bohu: Zhongguo guanggao zouxiang shuzi yule xiaodianying de dianji zhi zuo" (Tang Bohu on Baidu.com: The Foundation Stone for the Movement of Digital Entertainment Media in Chinese Advertising). *Guoji guanggao* (International Advertising), no. 12 (December): 34–38.

Chen Jianfu and Zhou Wei. 2002. "Wahaha de xin tonghua" (The New Fairy Tale of Wahaha). *Jingji ribao* (Economic Daily), August 27. http://www.people.com.cn/GB/jinji/33/172/20020827/808874.html. Accessed June 2006.

Chen Peiai and Tong Wenjuan. 2006. "Quefa jingzheng li, tanhe minzu pinpai?" (We Lack Competitive Edge, How Can We Even Talk about National Brands?). *Guanggao daguan* (Advertising Panorama), no. 2 (February): 24–26.

Chen Subai. 2005. "Jiegou Zhongguo chengshi hexin jiating haizi xiaofei" (Deconstructing Children's Consumption in Chinese Urban Nuclear Families). *Guoji guanggao* (International Advertising), no. 6 (June): 67–70.

Chen Xutong, ed. 2006. "Zhongguo you 'minzu pinpai' ma?" (Does China Have "National Brands"?). *Guanggao daguan* (Advertising Panorama), no. 2 (February): 22–51.

Chi Shuangming. 2004. *Caizhi yingxiong Zhang Ruimin* (A Hero of Riches and Intelligence: Zhang Ruimin). Beijing: Zhongguo shangye chubanshe.

Chi Yuzhou. 2005. *Lianxiang ju* (The Saga of Lenovo). Beijing: Zhongguo Broadcast and Television Publishers.

"China Bans Blasphemous Nike Commercial." 2004. *Asian Media Watch.* http://www.asianmediawatch.net/nike. Accessed March 2005.

"China Digital TV Market Operation Report, 2006-2007." 2007. *Research and Markets,* February 2007. http://www.researchandmarkets.com/reportinfo.asp?report_id=452701. Accessed May 2007.

China Online. 2001. "WTO and Policy Forum." http://www.chinaonline.com:80/industry, December 4. Accessed January 2002.

"China Playing Hard-to-Get." 2007. Bangkok.com. May 12. http://www.bangkokpost.com/120507_Business/12May2007_focus01.php. Accessed May 2007.

China's Commerce Ministry. 2007. "Shangwu bu yu Baojie dacheng 'wancun qianxiang shichang gongcheng' hezuo yixiang" (Commerce Ministry Reached Cooperative Agreement with P&G about the "Ten Thousand Village Project"), April 26. http://news.xinhuanet.com/politics/2007-04/26/content_6030977.htm. Accessed June 2007.

Chinese Gold Eagle TV Art Festival Committee and CSM, eds. 2004. *Zhongguo dianshi shichang baogao: 2003–2004* (China TV Report). Beijing Broadcasting College. Beijing: Huaxia chubanshe.

Chinese Population and Development Research Center. 2007. *Renkou yu jihua shengyu changyong shuju shouce: 2006* (The 2006 Statistics Manual on Chinese Population and Childbirth Planning). Beijing: Zhongguo renkou chubanshe.

"Chinese Women Score Lowest Brand Loyalty." 2005. *Media,* September 23, 10.

Clarke, David B., Marcus A. Doel, et al. 2003. *The Consumption Reader.* London: Routledge.

CMM Intelligence. 2005. "The 2005 China Media Yearbook." http://www.cmmintelligence.com/. Accessed May 2005.

"Coca-Cola Moves into China's Bottled Tea Market." 2001. http://www.china.org.cn. Accessed July 2001.

Cody, Edward. 2005. "In Chinese Cyberspace, a Blossoming Passion." *Washington Post,* July 19, A15.

Condry, Ian. 2006. *Hip Hop Japan: Rap and the Paths of Cultural Globalization.* Durham, NC: Duke University Press.

Creative Commons. http://creativecommons.org. Accessed July 2006.

CSM Media Research. 2005. "Meiti shuju jingxuan yuebao" (The Monthly Report on Select Media Data). *Guoji guanggao* (International Advertising), no. 3 (March): 104–105.

CTR Market Research. 2004. "Zhaobiao duan guanggao de shida chuanbo jiazhi" (The Ten Broadcasting Values of Auctioned Slots). *Guanggao ren* (AdMan), no. 11 (November).

———. 2005a. "SVSC-SOFRES Media (CSM) Profile." http://www.ctrchina.cn/en/inve/csm.html. Accessed May 2005.

———. 2005b. "U.S. Advertising Market Shows Strong Growth in 2004." http://www.ctrchina.cn/en/articles/19.html. Accessed May 20, 2005.

Curran, James. 1990. "The New Revisionism in Mass Communication Research: A Reappraisal." *European Journal of Communication* 5 (2/3): 135–164.

Da Zhi. 2003. "Zhongguo de pangke, wubing shenying" (Chinese Punk: Fussing about Being Sick). http://www.scream-records.net/community/cmmunity043-punk.htm. Accessed August 2004.

de Lussanet, Michelle. 2003. "Limits to Growth for New Mobile Services." Forrester. http://www.forrester.com/ER/Research/Report/Summary/0,1338,15598,00.html. Accessed June 2006.

de Mooij, Marieke. 1998. *Global Marketing and Advertising: Understanding Cultural Paradoxes.* Thousand Oaks: Sage Publications.

———. 2003. *Consumer Behavior and Culture: Consequences for Global Marketing and Advertising.* London: Sage Publications.

Decker, Charles. 1998. *Winning with the P&G 99: 99 Principles and Practices of Procter & Gamble's Success.* New York: Pocket Books.

Deng Gang. 2001. "Chinese Cartoon to Land in US." *People's Daily,* May 28. http://english.people.com.cn/english/200105/28/eng20010528_71242.html. Accessed May 2006.

"Difang xing pijiu" (Local Beers). 2004. *Chenggong yingxiao* (Successful Marketing), July. http://cmarketing.hexun.com/. Accessed June 2005.

Dobson, Chris. 2005. "China's Online World Ready for Great Leap in Ad Opportunities." *Media,* November 18, 17.

Doctoroff, Thomas. 2005. *Billions: Selling to the New Chinese Consumer.* New York: St. Martin's Press.

Duncan. 2005. "Number of blogs now exceeds 50 million worldwide."

The Blog Herald. http://www.blogherald.com/2005/04/14/number-of-blogs-now-exceeds-50-million-worldwide/. Accessed May 2006.

Eckert, Tracy, Juanita Haron, et al. 2004. "Taking Global Brands to Local Success: Marketing Western Snack Foods in China." In *Kellogg on China*, ed. Anuradha Dayal-Gulati and Angela Y. Lee, 161–173. Evanston, IL: Northwestern University Press.

Editorial. 2002. *International Journal of Advertising* 21, no. 3: 291–292.

Einhorn, Bruce, and Alysha Webb. 2001. "Legend Thinks Out of the Box." *Business Week*, June 25. http://www.businessweek.com/magazine/content/01_26/b3738144.htm. Accessed May 2006.

Ewing, Michael T., Albert Caruana, and George M. Zinkhan. 2002. "On the Cross-National Generalisability and Equivalence of Advertising Response Scales Developed in the USA." *International Journal of Advertising* 21, no. 3: 345–366.

Fang Jun. 2007. "Ni tongqing Zou Qinghou ma?" (Are You Sympathetic with Zong Qinghou?). April 16. http://www.mindmeters.com/showlog.asp?log_id=5117. Accessed June 2007.

"Fang Lingdian diaochu Dongshizhang Yuan Yue" (An Interview with the CEO of Horizon Research Co.). 2004. *Chenggong yingxiao* (Successful Marketing), no. 7 (July). http://finance.sina.com.cn/x/20040707/1809856558.shtml. Accessed December 2005.

Farquhar, Judith. 2001. "For Your Reading Pleasure: Self-Health Information in 1990s Beijing." In *Chinese Popular Culture and the State*, ed. Jing Wang, a special issue of *positions: east asia cultures critique* 9, no. 1 (Spring): 105–130.

Feldwick, Paul. 1999. "Brand Equity: Do We Really Need It?" In *How to Use Advertising to Build Strong Brands*, ed. John Philip Jones, 69–96. Thousand Oaks, CA: Sage Publications.

———. 2002. *What Is Brand Equity, Anyway?* Oxfordshire, UK: World Advertising Research Center.

Feng Guoying and Zhu Haisong. 2004. *Haier Brothers* (Behind Haier). Guanzhou: Guangdong jingji chubanshe.

Feng Xindong. 2005. "Jianchi yuanchuang Zhongguo xin guanggao" (Insist on Creative Originality for New Chinese Advertisements). *Guoji guanggao* (International Advertising), no. 1 (January): 107–109.

"FM365 huigui Lianxiang zao 'xuecang'" (FM365 Was Frozen after Its Return to Lianxiang). 2004. *Shantou Info*. http://info.st.gd.cn/ShowNews.php?id=177149.

Fu Dingwei, Mao Xiaoming, et al., eds. 2002. *Kuaguo gongsi Zhongguo gonglue* (The Invasion Strategies of Transnational Agencies in China). Beijing: Jixie gongye chubanshe.

Fu Hu. 2004. "Guoji 4A liu nian toushi: Chengzhang, tongku, beipan" (A Close Examination of Six Years of International 4As). *Guoji guanggao* (International Advertising), no. 1 (January): 51–54.

Fung, Anthony. 2006. "Think Globally, Act Locally: China's Rendezvous with MTV." *Global Media and Communication* 2, no. 1 (April): 71–88.

Furman, Greg. 2005. "Exceeding All Expectations." *Media*, September 23, 26–27.

Fussell, Paul. 1992. *Class: A Guide through the American Status System.* New York: Touchstone Books.

Gabriel, Yiannis. 2000. *Storytelling in Organizations: Facts, Fictions, and Fantasies.* Oxford: Oxford University Press.

Gao Tao. 2005. "Libo pijiu de Shanghai gonglue" (The Strategy of Shanghai's Libo Beer). www.globrand.com/2004/12/05. Accessed June 2005.

Gao Yuan. 2002. "Shengji weishi fazhan xin zhanlue: Quyu weishi fuchu shuimian" (The New Development Strategies of Provincial Satellite Stations: The Rise of Regional Satellite [Alliance]). *Guoji guanggao* (International Advertising), no. 11 (November): 90–91.

Garner, Jonathan. 2005. *The Rise of the Chinese Consumer: Theory and Evidence.* Hoboken, NJ: John Wiley and Sons.

Ge Huaisha, ed. 2003a. *Jingyan: Zhongguo shichang zhumin pingpai chenggong anli tudian* (Experiences: Case Studies of Successful Chinese Market Brands). Vol. 1. Changchun: Jilin daxue chubanshe.

———. 2003b. *Jingyan: Zhongguo shichang zhumin pingpai chenggong anli tudian* (Experiences: Case Studies of Successful Chinese Market Brands), Vol. 2. Changchun: Jilin daxue chubanshe.

Gerth, Karl. 2003. *China Made: Consumer Culture and the Creation of the Nation.* Cambridge, MA: Harvard University Asia Center.

Gilmore, Fiona, and Serge Dumont. 2003. *Brand Warriors China: Creating Sustainable Brand Capital.* London: Profile Books.

Gobé, Marc, and Sergio Zyman. 2001. *Emotional Branding: The New Paradigm for Connecting Brands to People.* New York: Watson-Guptill Publications.

Goldman, Robert. 1992. *Reading Ads Socially.* London: Routledge.

Goodman, David S. G. 2008. "Why China Has No Middle Class: Captains of Industry, Cadres and Professionals." In *The New Rich in China: Future Rulers, Present Lives,* by David Goodman et al. London: Routledge.

Grossman, Lev. 2003. "The Quest for Cool." http://www.time.com/time/ covers/1101030908/xopener.html. Accessed August 2004.

Gu Yue. 2002. "Deng yan kan zhaobiao" (A Close Look at the Auction). *Guoji guanggao* (International Advertising), no. 10 (October): 88–89.

Guang Xuan. 2005. "2004 nian Zhongguo guanggao ye tongji shuju fenxi" (An Analysis of Statistics of the Chinese Advertising Industry in 2004). *Xiandai guanggao* (Modern Advertising), no. 7 (July): 15–17.

———. 2006. "2005 nian Zhonogguo guanggao ye tongji shuju baogao" (2005 Statistics Report on China's Advertising Industry). *Xiandai guanggao* (Modern Advertising), no. 4 (April): 38-40.

Guangzhou Editing Department of *International Advertising.* 2004. "Guanggao xianzai chuyu shenme shidai?" (What Critical Juncture Has Our Advertising Arrived At?). *Guoji guanggao* (International Advertising), no. 1 (January): 12–13.

"Guangzhou shi guanggao ye diyi kuai mudi ma?" (Is Guangzhou the First Graveyard in Chinese Advertising Industry?). 2006. *Guoji guanggao* (International Advertising), no. 5 (May): 64–71.

Gui Shihe and Liu Yinglei. 2004. "Dang chuangyi yu bentu wenhua xiang zhuang: cong Fengtian guanggao shijian shuoqi" (When Originality Collides with Local Culture). *Xiandai guanggao* (Modern Advertising), no. 1 (January).

Guo Changyang et al. 2002. *Zhongguo zhumin qiye yingxiao anli pinxi* (Case Analyses of Marketing Campaigns for China's Famous Corporations). Guangzhou: Guangdong jingji chubanshe.

Guo Jin. 2005. "2005 nian Zhongguo guanggao ye de bianju" (The Changing Scene of Chinese Advertising in 2005). *Guoji guanggao* (International Advertising), no. 1 (January): 15–19.

Guo Zhenzhi. 2003. "Playing the Game by the Rules? TV Regulation and China's Entry into WTO." Special Issue, "Chinese Media after China's Entry into WTO," no. 4. See http://www.euricom.si/ Pub1004.html.

"Guochan shouji lirun baojiang xipai jiandi" (Bottoming Out: The Sudden Drop of Profits for Domestic Cell Phone Makers). 2005. *Guoji guanggao* (International Advertising), no. 9 (September): 132.

Guoji guanggao and IAI International Ad Research, eds. 2004. "2003 nian Zhongguo da guanggao gongsi jiben qingkuang diaocha" (A Basic Survey of the Big Ad Agencies in China in 2003). *Guoji guanggao* (International Advertising), no. 7 (July): 12–21.

Guoke. 2003. "Xin xin renlei ji duo xin" (How Trendy Is the Neo-Neo-Tribe). http://campus.etang.com/html/life/heter/daily/life-heter-daily-0192.htm. Accessed April 3, 2004.

Gutmann, Ethan. 2005. "Ethan Gutmann's Speech at the First English Jiuping Forum." *The Epoch Times,* Janurary 7. http://english.epochtimes.com/news/5-1-7/25560.html. Accessed June 2005.

Haier. 2007a. http://www.ehaier.com/jsp/category/more_newstone.jsp?col=2&categoryid=KT. Accessed May 2007.

———. 2007b. http://haier.com/abouthaier/corporateprofile/index.asp. Accessed June 2007.

"Haier Goals." 2005. *New York Times Magazine,* November 20, 38.

"Haier Rises through Reform and Opening Up." 2001. *People's Daily* (English edition), August 8.

"Haier's Purpose." 2004. *The Economist,* May 18. http://www.economist.com/business. Accessed May 2006.

"'Haier xiongdi' jiang fengxing milaoshu de jiaxiang" ("The Haier Brothers" Will Travel to the Homeland of Mickey Mouse). 2001. http://www.people.com.cn/GB/wenyu/64/128/20010526/475180.html. Accessed April 2004.

Hall, Stuart. 1991. "The Local and the Global: Globalization and Ethnicity." In *Culture, Globalization, and the World-System: Contemporary Conditions for the Representation of Identity,* ed. Anthony D. King, 19–39. Binghamton: State University of New York.

Hardt, Michael, and A. Negri. 2000. *Empire.* Cambridge, MA: Harvard University Press.

Hargrave-Silk, Atifa. 2005. "Adidas Kicks Off Olympics Marketing." *Media,* December 2, 8.

Hart, Heather, Nicholas Schiavone, and Horst Stipp. 1998. "The Value of Olympic Sponsorship." *Admap,* September. http://www.warc.com/Search/IndexSearch/Browse.asp. Accessed July 2004.

He Qingkai. 2004. "'Diyi juchang': Xianqi shoushi xin fengbao" ("The First Theater": Arousing a New Reception Craze). *Guoji guanggao* (International Advertising), no. 12 (December): 120.

Hebdige, Dick. 1979. *Subculture: The Meaning of Style.* London: Routledge.

Hill & Knowlton. 2004. "China Cool Hunt" Survey. April. http:// www.hillandknowlton.com/netcoms/index/media_room/press_ releases/7. Accessed 2004.

HiPiHi. 2007. http://www.hipihi.com/index_english.html. Accessed June 2007.

Hofstede, Geert H. 1991. *Cultures and Organizations: Software of the Mind.* New York: McGraw-Hill.

Howard, Teresa. 2006. "Bill Ford Takes Chamois to Namesake Automaker's Image." *USA Today,* April 16. http:// www.usatoday.com/money/advertising/adtrack/2006-04-16-ford-track_x.htm. Accessed May 2006.

Howe, Neil, William Strauss, et al. 2000. *Millennials Rising: The Next Great Generation.* New York: Vintage.

Hu Jin. 2005. "Shun xi lan gushi" (The Story about the Blue Strip). *Guoji guanggao* (International Advertising), no. 4 (April): 23–25.

Hu Jin and E Bo. 2003. "Hou Xiandai Cheng kungang Xiandai Cheng yilu zhaoyao" (Postmodern Tower Piggybacked on Soho Modern and Swaggered Along). *Guoji guanggao* (International Advertising), no. 2 (February).

Hu Jing. 2005. "Saatchi & Saatchi: shishang wu shi buke wei" (Saatchi & Saatchi: Nothing Is Impossible). *Guoji guanggao* (International Advertising), no. 9 (September): 9, 116.

Hu Yanping and Yu Yang. 1998. "Qinchi moshi zhongjie le ma?" (Was This the End to the Qinchi Model?). *Beijing qingnian bao* (Beijing Youth Daily), June 28, 3.

Huang Shengmin. 2003. "2001–2002 nian: Zhongguo guanggao ye fazhan baogao" (The Report on the Development of Chinese Advertising Industry between 2001 and 2002). In *Zhongguo wenhua chanye fazhan baogao: 2003* (The 2003 Blue Book on the Development of Chinese Cultural Industry), ed. Jiang Lansheng, Xie Shengwu, et al., 164–181. Beijing: Shehui kexue wenxian chubanshe.

Huang Shengmin and Chen Subai. 2004. "2002–2003: Zhongguo guanggao ye fazhan baogao" (The Report on the Development of Chinese Advertising Industry between 2002 and 2003). In *Zhongguo wenhua chanye fazhan baogao: 2004* (The 2004 Blue Book on the Development of Chinese Cultural Industry), ed. Jiang Lansheng,

Xie Shengwu, et al., 177–192. Beijing: Shehui kexue wenxian chubanshe.

Huang Shengmin and Ding Junjie, eds. 2001. *Zhongguo guangdian meijie jituanhua yanjiu* (Research on the Integration of China's Broadcasting Media). Beijing: Zhongguo wujia chubanshe.

Huang Shengmin and Yang Xuerui. 2005. "Suipian hua lailin, pinpai yu meijie zouxiang hechu?" (The Arrival of Fragmentation: What Should Brands and Media Do?) *Guoji guanggao* (International Advertising), no. 9 (September): 25–29.

Huang Yan and Ye Chao. 2001. "Libo guanggao dingwei yibo sanzhe" (The Brand Positioning of Libo: Setbacks). *Guanggao daguan* (Advertising Panorama), 72.

Huang Zongkai. 2003. "Dianxing wenti tuchu" (Typical Problems Emerged). *Guoji guanggao* (International Advertising), no. 1 (January): 12–14.

Hung, Kineta, Flora Gu, et al. 2005. "Improving Media Decisions in China: A Targetability and Cost-Benefit Analysis." *Journal of Advertising* 34, no. 1 (April). http://www.backchannelmedia.com/newsletter/articles/1325/IMPROVING-MEDIA-DECISIONS-IN-CHINA-A-Targetability-and-Cost-Benefit-Analysis. Accessed August 2007.

International Advertising Editorial Board. 2005. "Guanyu Zhongguo youwu pinpai de shenceng lunshuo) (A Deep Analysis of Whether China Has Brands or Not). *Guoji guanggao* (International Advertising), no. 5 (May): 11–14.

"Interview with Zong Qinghou." 2007. *Sina.com.* April 8. http://finance.sina.com.cn/chanjing/b/20070408/17483482198.shtml. Accessed May 2007.

Ivy, Marilyn. 1995. *Discourses of the Vanishing: Modernity, Phantasm, Japan.* Chicago: University of Chicago Press.

Jaffe, Joseph. 2005. *Life after the 30-Second Spot.* Hoboken, NJ: John Wiley & Sons.

Jenkins, Henry. 2004. "Understanding Emotional Capital: A proposed initiative of Coca-Cola and faculty and students from the MIT Comparative Media Studies Program." MIT Comparative Media Studies Program.

———. 2006. *Convergence Culture.* New York: New York University Press.

Jhally, Sut. 1990. *The Codes of Advertising.* London: Routledge.

Ji Feng. 2002a. "Xibu huangjin weishi daodi neng zou duoyuan?"(How

Far Can the Golden Satellite of West China Travel?). *Guoji guanggao* (International Advertising), no. 9 (September): 93–94.

———. 2002b. "Yangshi zhaobiao, jinnian zenmo bian?" (CCTV Auctions Ad-Spots: New Changes This Year). *Guoji guanggao* (International Advertising), no. 10 (October): 86–87.

———. 2004. "Yangshi yu longduan dianshi ju youzhi ziyuan" (CCTV Hopes to Monopolize the Resource for Quality TV Drama). *Guoji guanggao* (International Advertising), no. 9 (September): 105–106.

Ji qing yinyue (Hit Light Music). 2004. (June): 95.

Ji Xin. 2002a. "Luyou weishi duoyuan chayihua shengcun" (The Mode of Existence Dependent on Diversification). *Guoji guanggao* (International Advertising), no. 10 (October): 83–85.

———. 2002b. "Nokia qiangpao" (Nokia Made a Running Lead). *Guoji Guanggao* (International Advertising), no. 11: 56–58.

———. 2003. "Jiangxi weishi" (Jiangxi Satellite TV). *Guoji guanggao* (International Advertising), no. 3 (March): 93–95.

Jiang Ruxiang. 2003. *Chaju: Zhongguo yiliu qiye li shijie yiliu qiye you duoyuan* (Distance: The Gaps between First-Class Chinese Businesses and World-Class Businesses). Beijing: China Machine Press.

Jiang Wei. 2005. "Zhongguo wangluo guanggao fazhan taishi fenxi" (Analysis of the Trends of China's Internet Advertisements). *Xiandai guanggao* (Modern Advertising), no. 11 (November): 18–20.

"JianLibao 2006 nian lizheng chongfan yinliao diyi jituan" (JianLibao Struggled to Regain Its Number One Status in the Beverage Industry in 2006). 2006. *Zhongguo shipin chanye wang* (Chinese Food Industry Portal). February 15. http://cbi.clii.com.cn/corporation/show.asp?ShowID=526. Accessed June 2007.

"Jiedu zhongguo lanling" (Decoding the Chinese Blue Collar). 2004. *Chenggong yingxiao* (Successful Marketing), no. 7 (July). http://finance.sina.com.cn/x/20040707/1703856485.shtml. Accessed December 2005.

Jin Ke. 2003. "Baojie jiangjia, wushi wufei" (P&G's Discount Tactics Are Neither Right nor Wrong). *Guoji guanggao* (International Advertising), no. 7 (July): 47–49.

Jones, George, and Andy Martin. 2007. "Game for Entry in a Fantasy World?" *Digital Media* (Hong Kong), March, 40–42.

Jones, John Philip. 2000. "Introduction: The Vicissitudes of International

Advertising." In *International Advertising: Realities and Myths*, ed. John Philip Jones, 1–10. London: Sage Publications.

Kang Ning. 2005. "Baipishu: Zhongguo chengzhen danwei nuxing jiuye renshu" (White Paper: The Number of Employed Women in Chinese Cities and Townships). *Xinhua net.* August 24. http:// news.xinhuanet.com/newscenter/2005-08/24/content_3395664.htm. Accessed June 2007.

Keane, Michael. 2001. "Television drama in China: Engineering Souls for the Market." In *Global Goes Local: Popular Culture in Asia*, ed. Richard King and Tim Craig, 176–202. Vancouver: University of British Columbia Press.

———. 2002. "Send in the Clones: Television Formats and Content Creation in the People's Republic of China." In *Media in China: Consumption, Content, and Crisis*, ed. Stephanie Hemelryk Donald, Michael Keane, and Yin Hong, 80–90. London: RoutledgeCurzon.

———. 2005. "Television Drama in China: Remaking the Market." *Media International Australia*, no. 115: 82–93.

———. 2007. *Created in China: The Great New Leap Forward*. London: RoutledgeCurzon.

Keane, Michael, and Stephanie Hemelryk Donald. 2002. "Responses to Crisis: Convergence, Content Industries and Media Governance." In *Media in China: Consumption, Content and Crisis*, ed. Stephanie Donald, Michael Keane, and Yin Hong, 200–211. London: RoutledgeCurzon.

Kellner, Douglas. 1995. *Media Culture: Cultural Studies, Identity and Politics between the Modern and the Postmodern*. London: Routledge.

Kerwin, Ann Marie. 2006. "When Clutter Creeps into the Programs." *Advertising Age*, April 25. http://www.adage.com. Accessed June 2006.

Khalfan, Jameel. 2006. "Paper 1." Paper written for 21F036 "Advertising and Popular Culture: East Asian Perspective." March 1. Massachusetts Institute of Technology.

Klein, Naomi. 1999. *No Logo*. New York: Picador.

Kotler, Philip, Donald H. Haider, and Irving Rein. 2002. *Marketing Places*. New York: Free Press.

Kou Fei. 2003. *Guanggao Zhongguo* (Advertising in China: 1979–2003). Beijing: Zhongoguo gongshang chubanshe.

Kwok, Vivian Wai-yin. 2006. "Hot Bidding For China TV Ads." *Forbes.com*. November 20. http://www.forbes.com/markets/2006/11/

20/cctv-advertising-television-markets-emerge-cx_vk_1120markets20.html. Accessed May 2007.

Lannon, Judie. 1999. "Brands and Their Symbols." In *How to Use Advertising to Build Strong Brands,* ed. John Philip Jones, 37–53. Thousand Oaks, CA: Sage Publications.

Lao Han. 2002. "Xi kan Naobaijin guanggao gaixuan yizhe" (Pleased to See the Change of Course of Naobaijin Commercials). *Guoji guanggao* (International Advertising), no. 8 (August): 133–134.

———. 2005. "Aomei jiang minsu jinxing daodi: Zhongguo yidong hesui guanggao chuangyi xitan" (Ogilvy Went All the Way with Folk Art: An Analysis of the Creative Idea behind the New Year Festival TVCs by China Mobile). *Guoji guanggao* (International Advertising), no. 2 (February): 36–38.

Lears, Jackson. 1995. *Fables of Abundance: A Cultural History of Advertising in America.* New York: Basic Books.

Lee, Chin-chuan. 2000. "Chinese Communication: Prisms, Trajectories, and Modes of Understanding." In *Power, Money, and Media,* ed. Chin-chuan Lee, 3–44. Evanston, IL: Northwestern University Press.

Leiss, William, Stephen Kline, et al., eds. 1997. *Social Communication in Advertising.* 2nd ed. London: Routledge.

Lemon, Sumner. 2006. "Chinese Operators to Build Hybrid 3G Networks." *InfoWorld,* November 17. http://www.infoworld.com/article/06/11/17/HNhybrid3gnetworks_1.html. Accessed May 2007.

Lenovo. 2006. "Lenovo Reports Fourth Quarter and Full Year 2005/06 Results." http://www.lenovo.com/news/us//en/2006/05/results.html. Accessed May 2007.

———. 2007. http://lenovo.com/news/us//en/2007/05/4QFY06-07.html. Accessed June 2007.

"Lenovo Posts 16.2% Rise in Profit." 2004. *China Online.* http://www.chinaonline/topstories. Accessed December 2004.

Leonard, Mark. 2005. "China's Long and Winding Road." *Financial Times,* July 9–10.

Lessig, Lawrence. 2004. *Free Culture.* New York: Penguin.

Li Chunlin. 2004. "Zhongchan jieceng Zhongguo shehui zhide guanzhu de renqun" (The Middle Class: A Chinese Social Group Worthy of Our Attention). In *2004: Zhongguo shehui xingshi fenxi yu yuce* (2004: Analysis and Forecast on China's Social Development), ed. Ru Xin, Lu Xueyi, and Li Peilin, 51–63. Beijing: Sheke wenxian chubanshe.

Li Conghua et al. 1998. *China: The Consumer Revolution.* Singapore: John Wiley & Sons.

Li Guangdou. 2004. "Xinxin ren lei shuzihua lianpu" (The Digitalized Face of the Neo-Neo-Tribe). *Xiaoshou shichang* (China Marketing), no. 2, 8–15.

Li Guoqing. 2005. "Wu Litou, jianke, jian wenhua" (Nonsense, Tramps, and Tramp Culture). *Xin zhoukan* (New Weekly), no. 206 (July 1): 24–27.

Li Lin and Yang Linxiang. 2004. "Fufei pindao kaibo: Yangshi shao de yiba xuhua" (The Start of Pay TV: A Deceptive Measure of CCTV's). *Guoji guanggao* (International Advertising), no. 10 (October): 100–101.

Li Weijie. 1997. "Biandi jiujing bu fuhe Zhongguo guoqing" (Alcohol Is Spreading All over the Country: A Condition That Ill-Suits China). *Beijing qingnian bao* (Beijing Youth Daily), February 12.

Li Xiumei. 2004. "Sitai lianhe qidong 'Zhongguo meijie jinniu shichang.'" (Four Stations Launched the 'Golden Bull Market' of Chinese Media). *Guanggao ren* (AdMan), no. 4 (April): 108–111.

Lin Jingxin. 2003. "Xiaohu xing bailing gongyu wangluo xingxiao tuiguang fangan" (The Marketing Case of a Small-Sized White-Collar Apartment Complex). http://house.focus.cn/newshtml/51716.html, September 23.

Lin Lingdong. 2000. "Danone (France) Purchases Meilingzhengguanghe in the Blink of an Eye." *China Pulse: SinoFile's Weekly Selection of Important Information on Chinese Society and Economy* 3, no. 47 (December 11–18): 7–10.

Lin Sanzho. 2004. "Zhongguo shichang pijiu pinpai baogao" (The Report on the Beer Brands in Chinese Market). *Shijie shangye pinglun* (World Business Forum). http://cmo.icxo.com/htmlnews/2004/12/13/506069.htm. Accessed June 2005.

Lin Zimin. 2003. "C xingxiao" (C-Marketing). *Guoji guanggao* (International Advertising), no. 1 (January): 64–66.

Lindstrom, Martin. 2001. "Country of Origin as a Branding Statement." *ClickZ Network,* January 25. http://www.clickz.com. Accessed June 2006.

Lindstrom, Martin, and Patricia B. Seybold. 2003. *Brand Child.* London: Kogan Page.

Ling Zhijun. 2005. *Lianxiang fengyun* (Legends about Lianxiang). Beijing: Zhongxin chubanshe.

Liu Botao. 2003. "JianLibao DiWuJi tupo wuyi yuan" (JianLibao's Fifth Season Broke through Sales of Five Billion Yuan). China E-Marketing World Wide Web. http://Emkt.com.cn, February 19.

Liu Chuanzhi. 2001. "Legend Holdings Ltd.: 2001/2002 Fiscal Year Interim Results Announcement." Beijing: Lianxiang Group.

Liu Guoji. 2003. "Pindao luodi de linglei siwei" (The Alternative Thinking to Channel Landing). *Guoji guanggao* (International Advertising), no. 4 (April): 11.

Liu Haiming, Zhao Peng, and Zhang Rongda. 2001. *People's Daily*, August 7. http://www.people.com.cn. Accessed May 2004.

Liu Juanjuan. 2006. "Li Delei xipai zhuanxiang" (CEO Li Delei Changed Course). http://it.sohu.com/20050503/n243545524.shtml. Accessed June 2007.

Liu Lijun. 2001. "Winning Strategy in China." Ultra China.com, May 25, 1–6.

Liu Lin and Zhang Jiansong. 2006. "Zhongguo yingxiao: 2005 nian dashi ji" (Chinese Marketing: The Chronicle of Events in 2005). *Guoji guanggao* (International Advertising), no. 3 (March): 66–72.

Liu Wei, Wang Weiqun, et al. 2003. "Bubo zu shangji da gonglue" (A Marketing Offensive Targeting Bobos). *Chenggong yingxiao* (Successful Marketing), no. 4. http://www.cmarketing.com.cn.

Liu Yanming. 2003. "Zhongguo dianshi ju: xianzhuang he jidai jiejue de wenti" (Chinese TV Drama: The Present Condition and Problems Awaiting Solutions). *Guoji guanggao* (International Advertising), no. 6 (June): 11–15.

Liu Yinghua. 2005. "Zhang Ruimin cheng Haier guojihua zhi wancheng yiban" (Zhang Ruimin says the Internationalization of Haier Was Only Half Completed). *Guoji guanggao* (International Advertising), no. 9 (September): 23–24.

Liu Zaixing. 2003. "Niersen duihan Yanshi-Suofurui" (Nielsen versus CCTV-CSM). In "Sports and TV," a special issue of *Meijie* (Media), 38–41.

Longyuan huquan. Undated Internet post. "Zouchu liuxing xianxiang de xin xinrenlei" (The Neo-Neo-Tribe That Transcends Fads). http://www.54youth.com.cn/gb/paper107/zt/xyzt/hz7.htm. Accessed April 1, 2004.

Love, Tim. 2001. "Think Like the Sun: The Secret to Building Global Lovemark Brands." In *Inside the Minds: Leading Advertisers*. Bedford, MA: Aspatore Books.

Lu Changsheng. 2004. "Tisheng bentu guanggao gongsi hexin jinzhengli de fenxi" (An Analysis of Raising the Bar of the Core Competitive Advantages of Domestic Agencies). *Guoji guanggao* (International Advertising), no. 10 (October): 118–121.

Lu Jinzhu. 2002. "Yangshi guanggao zuihou yizhao" (The Last Trump Card of CCTV Advertising). *Guoji guanggao* (International Advertising), no. 11 (November): 92–93.

Lu Shaofeng and Li Wen. 2005. "Guoji hua Beijing xia Zhongguo guanggao zizhu yundong de yiyi jiedu" (An Interpretation of the Meaning of a Chinese Movement for Autonomy in the Climate of the Internationalization of Chinese Advertising). *Guanggao daguan* (Advertising Panorama), no. 12 (December): 45–48.

Lu Taihong. 2005. *Zhongguo xiaofeizhe xingwei baogao* (Chinese Consumer Behavior). Beijing: Zhongguo shehui kexue chubanshe.

Lu Xueyi. 2004. "Tiaozheng chengxiang guanxi, jiejuehao nongcun nongmin wenti" (Adjusting Rural-Urban Relationships and Resolving Problems Occurred in Villages and in the Lives of Peasants). In *2005: Zhongguo shehui xingshi fenxi yu yuce* (Analysis and Forecast on China's Social Development 2005), ed. Ru Xin, Lu Xueyi, et al., 175–186. Beijing: Shehui kexue wenxian chubanshe.

Lu Xun. 1926. "Wei Bannong tiji 'He Dian' hou zuo" (Afterthoughts on My Preface for *He Dian* [Bannong's Edition]). In *Huagai ji xubian* (Sequel to the Huagai Collection), Vol. 3, *Lu Xun quan ji* (The complete works of Lu Xun), 284–288. 16 volumes. 1973. Beijing: Renmin wenxue chubanshe.

Lu Yuliang. 2007. "Fight between Beverage Giants Spills Out in Public." *Xinhua.net*. April 14. http://news.xinhuanet.com/english/2007-04/14/content_5975960.htm. Accessed June 2007.

"Lunli ju huole shoushi lu jiang le" (Family Drama Was in and the Reception Rating Went Down). 2005. *Guoji guanggao* (International Advertising), no. 2 (February): 102.

"Luxury? What It Means in China." 2005. http://in.rediff.com/money/2005/feb/07guest1.htm, February 7. Accessed March 2005.

Ma, Eric Kit-Wai. 2000. "Rethinking Media Studies: The Case of China." In *De-Westernizing Media Studies*, ed. James Curran and Myung-Jin Park, 21–34. London: Routledge.

MacManus, Richard, and Joshua Porter. 2005. "Web 2.0 for Designers."

Digital Web Magazine, May 4. http://www.digital-web.com/articles/ web_2_for_designers/. Accessed May 2007.

Madden, Normandy. 2005a. "Coke Brings Fantasy to Life." *AdAge China,* July 4. http://adage.com/china/article.php?article_id=46112. Accessed August 2006.

———. 2005b. "Real Winner of Super Girl is Mengniu Dairy." *AdAge China,* October 10. http://adage.com/china/article.php?article_id= 46903. Accessed August 2006.

———. 2005c. "Western Marketers Make Music in China." *AdAge China.* June 6. http://adage.com/china/article.php?article_id=45844. Accessed September 2006.

———. 2006a. "Can Motorola Attract the Youth Market through Music?" http://adage.com/china/article.php?article_id=110324, July 12. Accessed September 2006.

———. 2006b. "China's TV Market." *AdAge China.* http://www.adage.com. Accessed June 2006.

———. 2007. "Q&A with AsiaVision's Kenny Bloom." *AdAge China.* June 15. http://adage.com/china/article.php?article_id=117119.

Maffesoli, Michel. 1996. *The Time of the Tribes: The Decline of Individualism in Mass Society.* London: Sage Publications.

Manalansan, Martin F., IV. 2003. *Global Divas: Filipino Gay Men in the Diaspora.* Durham, NC: Duke University Press.

Manning, Anita, and Calum MacLeod. 2007. "China Denies Role in Pet Food Recall." *USA Today.* April 2. http://www.usatoday.com/news/ world/2007-04-02-china-pet-food_N.htm. Accessed June 2007.

Mao Shijie. 2004. "Gongsi bushi jia" (Our Company Is Not Home). Blog—RexSong.com, March 11. http://www.rexsong.com/blog/article.asp?id=226. Accessed May 2006.

Marchand, Roland. 1985. *Advertising the American Dream: Making Way for Modernity, 1920–1940.* Berkeley: University of California Press.

Martin, J. 1990. "Deconstructing Organizational Taboos: The Suppression of Gender Conflict in Organizations." *Organizational Science,* 1: 1–22.

Mattelart, Armand. 1991. *Advertising International: The Privatization of Public Space.* Trans. Michael Chanan. London: Routledge.

McFall, Liz. 2002. "Advertising, Persuasion, and the Culture/Economy Dualism." In *Cultural Economy,* ed. Paul du Gay and Michael Pryke, 148–165. London: Sage Publications.

———. 2004. *Advertising: A Cultural Economy*. London: Sage Publications.

McGann, Anthony F., and J. Thomas Russell. 1981. *Advertising Media: A Managerial Approach*. Homewood, IL: Richard D. Irwin.

McQueen, Josh, Carol Foley, and John Deighton. 1993. "Decomposing a Brand's Consumer Franchise into Buyer Types." In *Brand Equity and Advertising*, ed. David A. Aaker and Alexander L. Biel, 235–245. Hillsdale, NJ: Lawrence Erlbaum Associates.

Meng Xiangsheng. 2002. *2001 Zhongguo niandu zuijia guanggao anli* (Case Studies of the Best Advertising Campaigns in 2001). Beijing: Zhongguo jingji chubanshe.

Miao Su. 2007. "Midi jiekai zaiji, wu da xuanyi kaoyan Zhongguo 3G" (The Mystery Was About to Be Unveiled: Five Trials Facing China's 3G). *Zhongguo jingji wang* (China Economy Net), May 3. http://intl.ce.cn/specials/zxxx/200703/05/t20070305_10578422.shtml. Accessed May 2007.

Miao Wei, Lu Xiaoxun, et al. 2002. "Bobo zu yu 'xin wenhua yundong'" (The Bobos and the "New Culture Movement"). *Shenghuo zhoukan* (Life Weekly), no. 47 (November 25). http://www.lifeweek.com.cn/2003-04-08/000013313.html. Accessed April 2004.

Miller, Paula M. 2006. "Wahaha: The Chinese Beverage Company's Expansion Is No Laughing Matter." *China Business Review*. http://www.chinabusinessreview.com/public/0409/company_profile.html. Accessed June 2006.

MindShare. 2004. 'Yangshi zhaobiao duan de meijie jiazhi pinggu" (An Assessment of the Media Value of the Auctioned Segments on CCTV). *Guanggao ren* (AdMan), no. 11 (November): 26–27.

Mitchell, Khristian, Scott Rupp, et al. 2004. "The Challenge of Winning Local Clients for Multinational Advertising Agencies." In *Kellogg on China*, ed. Anuradha Dayal-Gulati and Angela Y. Lee. Evanston, IL: Northwestern University Press.

Moeran, Brian. 1996. *A Japanese Advertising Agency: An Anthropology of Media and Markets*. Honolulu: University of Hawaii Press.

Mooney, Paul. 2003. "Bobos in Shangri-La." *Newsweek* (Atlantic Edition), March 3.

Morley, David. 1997. "Theoretical Orthodoxies: Textualism, Constructivism, and the 'New Ethnography' in Cultural Studies." In *Cultural Studies in Question*, ed. Majorie Ferguson and Peter Golding. London: Sage Publications.

Morrissey, Brian. 2003. "MTV, Motorola Ink $75M Marketing Pact." http://www.clickz.com/showPage.html?page=2109581, March 13.

Motorola. 2004a. "Motorola and Apple Bring iTunes Music Player to Motorola's Next-Generation Mobile Phone." http://www.motorola.com/mediacenter/news/detail. Accessed August 17, 2004.

———. 2004b. "Orchestrating a World of Personalized Music." http://www.motorola.com.cn/en/news/2004/07/0712_01.asp. Accessed August 2004.

Movius, Lisa. 2005. "Luxury Execs Eye Potential of China." *Women's Wear Daily*, June 13. http://www.movius.us/articles/wwd-ft.html. Accessed December 2005.

Mu Hong and Li Wenlong, eds. 2005. *Guanggao anli: quan an* (Cases of Advertising: The Whole Portfolio). Beijing: People's University.

Murphy, James. 2005. "WE to Target Second-Tier Mainland Brands." *Media,* November 18: 8.

Nanfang zhoumo (Southern Weekend). 2000. December 7, 11.

"Nation Tunes in to Digital TV Era." 2005. *China Daily,* March 21. http://www.china.org.cn/english/null/123347.htm. Accessed June 2005.

National Bureau of Statistics. 2004. "2004 nian Zhongguo nongcun pinkun zhuangkuang jiance gongbao" (The 2004 Public Report on Poverty in Chinese Villages). China Population and Development Research Center. http://www.cpirc.org.cn/tjsj/tjsj_gb_detail.asp?id=4669. Accessed September 2006.

Nelson, Jon P. 2004. "Advertising Bans in the United States." In *EH.Net Encyclopedia of Economic and Business History,* ed. Robert Whaples. http://www.eh.net/encyclopedia. Accessed June 2005.

Nie Yanmei. 2002. "Shijie guanggao de weilai zai Zhongguo" (The Future of World Advertisment Is in China). *Guoji guanggao* (International Advertising) 11: 118.

Nie Yanmei, Ma Xiaoying, et al. 2003. "Kuaguo guanggao gongsi de bentu hua celue tantao" (An Examination of the Localization Strategies of Transnational Advertising Agencies). *Guoji guanggao* (International Advertising), no. 9 (September): 12–25.

Nussbaum, Bruce. 2005. "Is Ford Innovative?" *Business Week,* October 31. http://www.businessweek.com/innovate/NussbaumOnDesign/archives/2005/10/is_ford_innovat.html. Accessed May 2006.

Nye, Joseph S., Jr. 2004. *Soft Power: The Means to Success in World Politics.* New York: Public Affairs.

Oakes, Tim, and Louisa Schein. 2006. *Translocal China: Linkages, Identities, and the Reimagining of Space.* London: Routledge.

O'Connor, Ashling. 2007. "Danone Faces Lawsuit over Biscuit Brand." *Times Online.* April 19. http://business.timesonline.co.uk/tol/business/law/article1674156.ece. Accessed June 2007.

Ogilvy. 2000. "Aomei 360 du pinpai guanli jichu peixun" (Ogilvy 360 Degree Brand Stewardship Basic Training).

Ogilvy, David. 1955. "About Ogilvy China." http://www.ogilvy.com.cn/about_ogilvy_china/main.html. Accessed December 2002.

———. 1985. *Olgivy on Advertising.* New York: Vintage Books.

Ogilvy & Mather. 2003. "PRD Patriot's Paradox." Hong Kong General Chamber of Commerce. http://www.chamber.org.hk/info/the_bulletin/feb2004/brands.asp. Accessed July 2004.

Ogilvy & Mather Asia Pacific. 1999. "Simmering Within: Asian Mothers and Their Expectations." Internal document.

Ogilvy Guangzhou. 2002. "Shen Li dazao xinshengdai pijiu pinpai" (San Miguel Light Pitches a New-Generation Beer Brand). *Guoji guanggao* (International Advertising), no. 9 (September): 36–37.

Ohmann, Richard. 1996. "Knowing/Creating Wants." In *Making and Selling Culture,* ed. Richard Ohmann, 224–238. Hanover, NH: Wesleyan University Press.

Oltchick, Bruce. 2004. Email exchange. February 10.

———. 2006. Email exchange. October 22.

Ong, Janet. 2007. "Lenovo Profit May Rise 11% on Job Cuts, Market Share (Update2)." *Bloomberg.com.* February 1. http://www.bloomberg.com/apps/news?pid=20601087&sid=aTgbGu6oSkPA&refer=home. Accessed May 2007.

Ong, Xiangdong. 2002. *Bentu pinpai zhanlue* (Local Brand Strategies). Hangzhou: Zhejiang renmin chubanshe.

Onicek. 2003. "Bentu kehu xuyao de shi shenmo—you Dabisi fengbo yinfa de sikao" (What Do Local Clients Want? Thinking about the Bates Incident). *Xiandai guanggao* (Modern Advertising), no. 10 (October): 38–40.

Opoku, Robert Ankomah. 2005. "Let's get more serious in branding our nation Ghana." Ghana Home Page, January 11. http://www.ghanaweb.com/GhanaHomePage/NewsArchive/artikel.php?ID=73152. Accessed June 2006.

Ouyang Ming, Zhang Hongxia, et al. 2002/2003. "Does Nationalist Appeal Affect Chinese University Students' Product Evaluation? A Conjoint Analysis." *Asian Journal of Marketing* 9, no.1. http://www.mis.org.sg/homepage/ajm.htm. Accessed August 2005.

Owen, Stewart. 1993. "The Landor Image Power Survey: A Global Assessment of Brand Strength." In *Brand Equity and Advertising*, ed. David A. Aaker and Alexander L. Biel, 11–30. Hillsdale, NJ: Lawrence Erlbaum Associates.

"P&G Tries to Reach Out to the Masses." 2003. *Times News Network*, July 2. http://economictimes.indiatimes.com.

Park, Albert. 2007. Classroom comment during 21F036, "Advertising and Popular Culture," taught at MIT by Jing Wang.

Paterson, Thane. 2004. "The Branding of China." *Business Week*, November 10. http://www.businessweek.com/bwdaily/dnflash/nov2004/nf20041110_0338_db053.htm. Accessed December 2004.

Patton, Dominique. 2006. "Coca-Cola Gains Control of Kerry Beverages." Beverage.com. August 31. http://www.beveragedaily.com/news/ng.asp?n=70238-coca-cola-kerry-beverages-bottling-china. Accessed May 2007.

Paul, Anthony. 2002. "Asia's Businessman of the Year." *Fortune*. http://www.legend-holdings.com/eng/index2.html. Accessed April 2004.

Png, Ivan. 2004. "Tweaking TV Ads Rules a New Way to Compete." *The Straits Times*, January 27.

Prystay, Cris. 2002. "As China's Women Change, Marketers Notice: Procter & Gamble, Like Others, Tries to Appeal to Evolving Sensibilities." *Wall Street Journal*, May 30, A11.

Qiu, Jack Linchuan. 2006. "The Changing Web of Chinese Nationalism." *Global Media and Communication* 2, no. 1 (April): 125–128.

Qu Jianmin. 2004. "Waizi guanggao ke konggu, bentu ziyuan jidai zhenghe" (Foreign-Owned Agencies Can Hold Majority Stakes, Domestic Resources Await Integration). *Guoji guanggao* (International Advertising), no. 6 (June): 11.

Rainey, Mary T. 2001. "Change or Be Changed." In *Inside the Minds: Leading Advertisers*, 11–32. Bedford, MA: Aspatore Books.

Ramos, Joshua Cooper. 2004. "The Beijing Consensus." London: Foreign Policy Center.

Ransdell, Eric. 2002. "The Monternet." http://www.thefeature.com/article?articleid=15322, July 3. Accessed August 2004.

"Readers Ring Up" (Duzhe "lingling"). 2004. *Wo ai yaogun* (I Love Rock), May 30, 60–63.

Richards, Thomas. 1990. *Commodity Culture of Victorian England.* Stanford, CA: Stanford University Press.

Ries, Al, and Jack Trout. 2001 [1981]. *Positioning: The Battle for Your Mind.* New York: McGraw-Hill.

Rinaldi, Larry. 2005. "Has the time come for product placement in China?" *AdAge China.* http://www.adage.com/china/article.php?article_id=48666. Accessed June 2006.

———. 2006a. Email interview exchange with Jing Wang. June 29.

———. 2006b. Email interview exchange with Jing Wang. July 3.

Roberts, Dexter. 2006. "China's Online Ad Boom." *Business Week,* May 24.

Roberts, Dexter, Frederik Balfour, et al. 2004. "China's Power Brands." *Business Week,* November 8. http://www.businessweek.com/magazine/content/04_45/b3907003.htm. Accessed May 2006.

Roberts, Kevin. 1998. "Brand China." http://www.saatchikevin.com/talkingit/shanghai.html. Accessed March 2002.

Rosenkranz, Eric. 2001. "Rallying the Troops." In *Inside the Minds: Leading Advertisers,* 33–65. Bedford, MA: Aspatore Books.

Roth, Daniel. 2005. "The Amazing Rise of the Do-It-Yourself Economy." *CNNMoney.com.* May 30. http://money.cnn.com/magazines/fortune/fortune_archive/2005/05/30/8261236/index.htm. Accessed May 2007.

Rowdy Swallow (Liumang yan). 2005. "Tamen shuo, tamen xihuan zheyang de nuren" (They say they don't like those women.) BlogChina, November 6. http://liumangyan.blogchina.com/3433473.html. Accessed June 2006.

Sahlins, M. 1976. *Culture and Practical Reason.* Chicago: University of Chicago Press.

SARFT. 2005. "Guangbo dianshi xitong defang waishi gongzuo guanli guiding" (Regulations on the Administration of Domestic and Foreign Affairs in the Radio, Film, and TV Sectors), July 6. http://www.sarft.gov.cn/manage/publishfile/35/3030.html. Accessed June 2006.

———. 2006. "SARFT guanyu yinfa 'dianshiju paishe zhizuo beian gongshi guanli zhanxing banfa' de tongzhi" (Regarding the Notice on the Temporary Measures of Administering TV Drama Production), April 11. http://www.gov.cn/zwgk/2006-04/11/content_250700.htm. Accessed June 2006.

Savage, Mike. 2005a. "Can Reality Live up to the China Net Hype?" *Media*, December 2, 3.

———. 2005b. "CCTV Expands Line-up for '06 Airtime Auction." *Media*, September 23, 5.

———. 2005c. "CCTV Auction Results Could Curb Rate Hikes." *Media*, December 2, 10.

———. 2005d. "Nike Turns Up Heat for China Market." *Media*, December 5, 3.

———. 2006. "China Mobile Splits Creative Roster." *Media*, July 4, 1.

Schiller, Dan. 1996. *Theorizing Communication: A History*. New York: Oxford University Press.

Servaes Jan, ed. 2003. *Walking on the Other Side of the Information Highway: Communication, Culture, and Development in the 21st Century*. Penang, Malaysia: Southbound.

Servaes, Jan, and Rico Lie. 2001. "Media versus globalization and localization." *Media Development*, March. http://www.wacc.org.uk/wacc/publications/media_development/archive/2001_3/media_versus_globalisation_and_localisation. Accessed September 2006.

Shameen, Assif. 2001. "The Deal: AOL and Legend Going online in China." *Asiaweek*, June 22. http://www.asiaweek.com. Accessed May 2006.

Shandwick, Weber. 2005. "Italy, U.S. and Australia Rank Highest as Country Brands—Thailand Is Only Asian Country in Top 10." *Circle of Asia*, November 15. http://www.circleofasia.com/News.asp?nID= 89. Accessed June 2006.

"Shanghai Leads the Nation in Per Capita Disposable Income." 2007. *People's Daily Online*. May 16. http://english.people.com.cn/200705/16/eng20070516_375144.html. Accessed June 2007.

Shanghai TV Festival and CSM. 2004. *Zhongguo dianshi ju shichang baogao* (China TV Drama Report: 2003–2004). Beijing: Huaxia chubanshe.

Shaw, Sharon Desker. 2005. "Re-energised Rivals Draw Blood from TCL." *Media*, November 4.

Shen Tianlan. 2004a. "Huigu yu qianzhan: Zhongguo dianshi meiti guanggao shichang jingzheng geju toushi" (Retrospect and Forward Looking: An Analysis of the Advertising Market Competition in Chinese TV Media). *Guanggao ren* (AdMan), no. 4: 118–121.

———. 2004b. "Yadian aoyun, Yangshi dacan" (The Athens Olympics: A Feast at CCTV). *Guanggao daobao* (Advertising Guide), no. 5 (May).

Shi Tao. 1998a. "Dengji, gediao: xinde shehui huati" (Class and Taste: A New Social Topic). http://www.guofeng-net.com. Accessed April 1, 2004.

———. 1998b. *Gediao* (Lifestyles). Beijing: Zhongguo sheke chubanshe.

"Shichang da cankao" (Market References).

———. 2003. *Guoji guanggao* (International Advertising), no. 9 (September): 135.

———. 2005. *Guoji guanggao* (International Advertising), no. 9 (September): 132.

Shou, Peipei. 1996. "Biao wang heyi tianjia" (Why Did the "Bidding-King" Offer Sky-Rocketing Bids?). *Beijing qingnian bao* (Beijing Youth Daily), November 15.

Siewert, Patrick T. 2002."Remarks at the 8th Annual International Conference on 'the Future of Asia'," May 22. http://www2.coca-cola.com/presscenter.

Simons, Craig. 2003. "Marketing to the Masses." *Far Eastern Economic Review,* September 4. http://www.feer.com. Accessed 2004.

Sissors, Jack Z., and Roger B. Baron. 2002. *Advertising Media Planning.* Chicago: McGraw-Hill.

Sister Lotus (Furong jiejue). 2005. "Furong yulu" (Quotes from Sister Lotus). http://joke.myrice.com/arts/xhqy/xhqyyl/15016517.html. Accessed June 2006.

Smith, Jeff, and Jean Wylie. 2004. "China's Youth Define 'Cool.'" *The China Business Review.* http://www.chinabusinessreview.com/public/0407/smith.html. Accessed August 2004.

Stalnaker, Stan. 2002. *Hub Culture: The Next Wave of Urban Consumers.* Singapore: John Wiley & Sons.

Stark, Myra. 2003. "Storytelling." *Ideas from Trends: Saatchi & Saatchi.* http://www.saatchikevin.com/workingit/myra_stark_2003ideastrends. Accessed April 2004.

Stockdale, Mark. 1999. "Are All Consumers Equal?" In *How to Use Advertising to Build Strong Brands,* ed. John Philip Jones, 211–223. Thousand Oaks, CA: Sage Publications.

Su Yong and Chen Xiaoping. 2003. *Pingpai tongjian* (Comprehensive Research on Brands). Shanghai: Renmin chubanshe.

Sull, Donald N. 2005. *Made in China: What Western Managers Can Learn from Trailblazing Chinese Entrepreneurs*. Boston: Harvard Business School Press.

Sun Jian. 2002a. *Haier de qiye wenhua* (The Enterprise Culture of Haier). Beijing: Qiye guanli chubanshe.

————. 2002b. *Haier de qiye zhanlue* (The Battle Strategies of Haier). Beijing: Qiye guanli chubanshe.

"Sun New Media Launches FM 365." 2005. *PrimeZone*. http://www.primezone.com/newsroom/news.html?d=87940. Accessed May 2006.

Sun Tzu. 2003. *The Art of War*. Trans. Lionel Giles. Ed. Dallas Galvin. New York: Barnes & Noble.

Sutherland, Anne, and Beth Thompson. 2001. *Kidfluence*. New York: McGraw-Hill.

Swyngedouw, Erik. 1997. "Neither Global nor Local: 'Glocalization' and the Politics of Scale." In *Spaces of Globalisation*, ed. Kevin R. Cox, 137–166. New York: Guilford Press.

Synovate. 2005. "Synovate Survey Reveals 70% of Asians Don't Pay for Digital Music Downloads." http://www.synovate.com/current/news/article/2005/10/synovate-survey-reveals-70-of-asians-don-t-pay-for-digital-music-downloads.html, October 3. Accessed June 2006.

————. 2006. "Survey Finds That Digital Music Matters." http://www.synovate.com/current/news/article/2006/05/survey-finds-that-digital-music-matters.html, May 10. Accessed June 2006.

Tang Ruitao. 2005. "Dui xiaofei dazhong de xinli tansuo" (A Psychological Probe into the Consumer Public). *Guoji guanggao* (International Advertising), no. 7 (July): 118–21.

Tang Yong. 2005. "I Never Said That Haier and Lenovo Are Not Brands." http://english.people.com.cn/200502/27. Accessed May 2006.

Taylor, Peter J. 2003. "What's Modern about the Modern World-System?" In *The Consumption Reader*, ed. David B. Clarke, Marcus A. Doel, and Kate M. L. Housiaux. London: Routledge.

Thomas, Mike. 2005. "Ford Launches Corporate Ad Campaign." Ford Motor Company. http://media.ford.com/newsroom/feature_display.cfm?release=21864. Accessed May 2006.

Toffler, Alvin. 1980. *The Third Wave*. New York: William Morrow.

Toffler, Alvin, and Heidi Toffler. 2006. *Revolutionary Wealth: How It Will Be Created and How It Will Change Our Lives*. New York: Knopf.

Travis, Daryl. 2000. *Emotional Branding: How Successful Brands Gain the Irrational Edge*. New York: Crown Business.

Twitchell, James B. 2000. *Twenty Ads That Shook the World*. New York: Crown Publications.

"2003 Zhongguo guanggao ye niandu shida guanggao gongsi jingli ren" (The Ten Best Managers in Chinese Advertising Industry in 2003). 2004. *Xiandai guanggao* (Modern Advertising), no. 1 (January): 19–21.

Usui, Yoshito. 2002. *Crayon Shinchan*, vol. 1. Trans. Sahe Kawahara. Originally published in Japanese in 1992 by Futabasha Publishers in Tokyo. Fremont, CA: ComicsOne Corporation.

Veblen, Thorstein. 1994. *The Theory of the Leisure Class: An Economic Study in the Evolution of Institutions*. New York: Dover Press.

Vedrashko, Ilya. 2005. Email exchange. May 7.

Von Hippel, Eric. 2006. *Democratizing Innovation*. Cambridge, MA: MIT Press.

Wang Bin. 2005. "Furong jiejie, Liumang Yan deng wangluo nu xieshou ziliao zhaopian ji" (The Collection of Materials and Photos on Sister Lotus and Rowdy Swallow). Babeijiu Entertainment Online, June 15. http://www.babeijiu.com/bbj17/254/31480942a.htm. Accessed June 2006.

Wang Chunyan. 2005. "Creative Commons China." Internal document shared with the International Advisory Board of Creative Commons China which I chair.

Wang Jing. 2006. "Xinrui dianying, kaiqi qiche yingxiao xin shidai" (Avant-garde Cinema Opened Up a New Era of Automobile Marketing). *Guoji guanggao* (International Advertising), no. 3 (March): 26–28.

Wang, Jing. 1996. *High Culture Fever: Politics, Aesthetics, and Ideology in Deng's China*. Berkeley: University of California Press.

———. 2001a. "Chinese Popular Culture and the State." In *Chinese Popular Culture and the State*, ed. Jing Wang, a special issue of *positions: east asia cultures critique* 9, no. 1 (Spring).

———. 2001b. "Culture as Leisure and Culture as Capital." In "Chinese Popular Culture and the State," a special issue of *positions: east asia cultures critique* 9, no. 1: 69–104.

————. 2001c. "The State Question in Chinese Popular Cultural Studies." *Inter-Asia Cultural Studies* 2, no. 1: 35–52.

————. 2003. "Framing Chinese Advertising: Some Industry Perspectives on the Production of Culture." *Continuum: Journal of Media and Cultural Studies* 17, no. 3 (September): 247–260.

————. 2004. "The Global Reach of a New Discourse: How Far Can 'Creative Industries' Travel?" *International Journal of Cultural Studies* 7, no. 1 (March): 9–19.

————, ed. 2005a. *Locating China: Space, Place, and Popular Culture.* London: Routledge.

————. 2005b. "The Politics and Production of Scales in China: How Does Geography Matter to Studies of Local, Popular Culture?" In *Locating China: Space, Place, and Popular Culture,* ed. Jing Wang, 1–30, "China in Transition" series, ed. David S. G. Goodman. London: Routledge.

Wang Jisi. 2006. "Peaceful Rise: A Discourse in China." A talk given at the Cold War Studies Centre, London School of Economics–Peking University Public Lecture Series. May 8.

Wang Jixin. 2004. "2005 yangshi zhaobiao huobao" (The Explosive Climaxes of CCTV's 2005 Auction). *Guoji guanggao* (International Advertising), no. 12 (December): 103–104.

Wang Lanzhu, ed. 2002. *Jiaoju shoushi lu* (The Focus on Reception Ratings). Beijing: Beijing Broadcasting College.

Wang Runjue. 2005. "Zuo yule, you tiyu: chengzhang kuaile zhe" (Entertainment on the Left and Sports on the Right: The Pleasure Is Growing). *Guanggao daguan* (Advertising Panorama), no. 9 (September): 72–75.

Wang Xiangdong. 2002. *Bentu pinpai zhanlue* (The Strategies of Local Brands). Hangzhou: Zhejiang chubanshe.

Wang Xiu and Xia Jinbiao. 2002. "Quanmian jianshe xiaokang shehui: shehui zhibiao nanyu jingji zhibiao" (Building a Comprehensive *xiaokang* Society: Social Index Is More Difficult [to Achieve] Than the Economic Index). *sina.com,* November 15. http://finance.sina.com.cn/g/20021115/1748279148/shtml. Accessed February 2004.

Wang Yang and Kang Yiren. 2002. *Haier shi hai: Zhang Ruimin de guanli yishu* (Haier Is an Ocean: Zhang Ruimin's Art of Management). Beijing: Minzhu yu jianshe chubanshe.

Wang Yukun. 2004. "Zhongguo xiandai shangye shi shang yongyuan de tong: Suoni yu Lianxiang de renxing guancha" (The Eternal Wound in the History of Corporate China, A Comparative Analysis of Commercial Humanism—Sony vs. Lenovo). Blogchina.com, January 16. http://www.blogchina.com/new/display/21412.html. Accessed May 2006.

Wang Zhenglun. 2003. "Dianshi ju cuire guanggao toufang" (TV Drama Drove Feverish Ad Spending). *Guoji guanggao* (International Advertising), no. 6 (June): 16–17.

Wang Zhidong. 2007. "An Interview with Zong Qinghou." *Sina.com,* May 9. http://chanye.finance.sina.com.cn/2007-05-09/320502.shtml. Accessed May 2007.

Wang Zho and Qiu Xiaoli. 2004. "Zhongguo lanling jiating xiaofei shilu—shihe wode pinpai zai nail?" (A True Tale about a Chinese Blue-Collar Family—Where Is Our Brand?) *Chenggong yingxiao* (Successful Marketing), no. 7 (July). http://finance.sina.com.cn/roll/20040707/2001856666.shtml. Accessed July 2005.

Washida, Yuichi. 2003. "Collaborative Structure between Japanese High-Tech Manufacturers and Consumers." *Journal of Consumer Marketing* 22, no. 1: 25–34.

———. 2004. Email exchange.

———. 2005. Email exchange.

Watson, James, ed. 1997. *Golden Arches East: McDonald's in East Asia.* Stanford, CA: Stanford University Press.

Weinzierl, Rupert, and David Muggleton. 2003. "What is 'Post-subcultural Studies' Anyway?" In *The Post-Subcultures Reader,* ed. David Muggleton and Rupert Weinzierl, 6–9. Oxford: Berg.

Wen Jing and Zhang Mo. 2007. "Wahaha Daneng jiufen an: Pinpai zhi zheng? Minzu chanye zhi jie?" (The Dispute between Wahaha and Danone: A Fight over the Brand Name? or A Calamity of [Chinese] National Industry?" *Xinhuanet.com,* April 17. http://mnc.people.com.cn/BIG5/54849/59580/5623763.html. Accessed May 2007.

Wernick, Andrew. 1991. *Promotional Culture: Advertising, Ideology and Symbolic Expression.* London: Sage Publications.

———. 1997. "Resort to Nostalgia: Mountains, Memories, and Myths of Time." In *Buy This Book: Studies in Advertising and Consumption,* ed. Mica Nova, Andrew Blake, et al., 207–223. London: Routledge.

Wertime, Kent. 2005. "Search Marketing Is the Future, But Give Consumers Control." *Media,* December 2, 17.

White, Amy. 2005. "Motorola Backs Creative Festival." *Media,* December 2, 13.

White, Roderick. 2000. "International Advertising: How Far Can It Fly?" In *International Advertising: Realities and Myths,* ed. John Philip Jones, 29–40. London: Sage Publications.

Williamson, Judith. 1978. *Decoding Advertisements: Ideology and Meaning in Advertising.* London: Routledge.

Wong, Alayne. 2007. *Asia/Pacific Mobile Consumer Services Survey, 2006.* IDC. http://www.idc.com/. Accessed June 2007.

Wong Xiangdong. 2002. *Bentu pinpai zhanlue* (Brand Strategy in China). Hangzhou: Zhejiang renmin chubanshe.

"World Leisure Expo: Hangzhou China." 2005. http://www.wl-expo.com/funcms/zwlm/index.html. Accessed July 2005.

Wright, Jeremy. 2006. *Blog Marketing.* New York: McGraw-Hill.

Wu Dong. 2003. "Zhongguo dianshiju shoushi fenxi" (An Analysis of the Reception of TV Drama in China). *Guoji guanggao* (International Advertising), no. 6 (June): 18–20.

Wu, Guoguang. 2000. "One Head, Many Mouths: Diversifying Press Structures in Reform China." In *Power, Money, and Media,* ed. Chinchuan Lee, 45–67. Evanston, IL: Northwestern University Press.

Wu Jing. 2002. "Wahaha shiwu nian pandian" (Taking Stock of Wahaha: Fifteen Years). *Guoji guanggao* (International Advertising), no. 11 (November): 22–24.

Wu Xiaobo. 2003. "Dianxing wenti tuchu" (Typical Problems Emerged). *Guoji guanggao* (International Advertising), no. 1 (January): 12–14.

———. 2005. "Cong konglong dao long" (From the Dinosaur to the Dragon). *Guanggao daguan* (Advertising Panorama), no. 12 (December): 12.

Wuming. 2004. "Haier, Lianxiang, Huawei: Zhongguo mofansheng zhengzai zaoyu nanti" (Haier, Lenovo, and Hua Wei: The Chinese Models Are in a Fix). In *Shiqu Lianxiang* (Losing Lenovo), ed. Wang Kukun et al., 325–329. Beijing: Shijie zhishi chubanshe.

Xiao Tong. 2005. "Jiqing zaoyu jihui" (When Passion Meets Opportunities). *Guoji guanggao* (International Advertising), no. 2 (February): 58–59.

Xiao Yong. 2004. Interview by author. Beijing, June 9.

Xiao Zhiying. 2002. "Chayi hua pinpai yingxiao de sikao" (Reflections on the Marketing Notion of Brand Differentiation). *Guoji guanggao* (International Advertising), no. 10: 55.

Xie, Ying. 2003. "Jiedu Yangshi xinwen pindao 2.5 fenzhong guanggao shi chang" (An Analysis of the 2.5 Minute Advertising Segment in the New CCTV News Channel). *Guoji guanggao* (International Advertising), no. 7 (July): 92–93.

———. 2005. "Jiu fenzhong biange" (The Nine-Minutes Revolution). *Guoji guanggao* (International Advertising), no. 3 (March): 102–103.

Xie Yungeng and Ni Woyu. 2007. "2006 Zhongguo dianshi baogao: II" (A Report on the 2006 Chinese TV Industry). *Zhongguo xinwen chuban wang* (Chinse News Publication Net). January 30. http://www.media365.com.cn/2007-01/30/content_34208.htm. Accessed May 2007.

"Xin xinrenlei de 'ku' shenghuo" (The "Cool" Life of a Neo-Neo-Tribe). 2003. http://www.xiayidai.com.cn/qczx/ssx/xxrl. Accessed April 3, 2004.

Xinhua News. 2005a. "Per Capita GDP in Yangtze River Delta Passes 4,000 US dollars." *People's Daily Online,* April 4. http://english.people.com.cn/200504/04/eng20050404_179424.html. Accessed May 2007.

———. 2005b. "Top Statistician on China's Economic Figures after National Census." *People's Daily Online,* December 22. http://english.people.com.cn/200512/22/eng20051222_230128.html. Accessed May 2007.

Xu Baiyi. 1991. *Marketing to China: One Billion New Customers.* Lincolnwood, IL: NTC Business Books.

Xu Chun. 2003. "Quanqiu hua de huanxiang yu guanggao chuangyi de minzu hua" (Globalization as an Imaginary and the Nationalization of Advertising Creativity). *Guanggao ren* (AdMan), no. 6 (June): 91–93.

Yahoo. 2005. "Yahu miaoshu zhong de zhongchan zhe tupu" (The Portrait of the Middle Class by Yahoo). *Guoji guanggao* (International Advertising), no. 3 (March): 46.

"Yahoo China Taps WE Marketing." 2006. *Media and Communications,* September 1. http://media.resonance.com.sg/mailer010906.htm. Accessed September 2006.

Yan Feng. 2003. "Hunan weishi: Guanggao yeji gantou zhishang" (Hunan Satellite TV: The Steady Increase of Its Advertising Revenue). *Guoji guanggao* (International Advertising), no. 9 (September): 94–95.

Yan Guoxiang and Fang Zheng. 2002. "Minzu pinpai zhi si" (The Death of National Brands). *Xiandai guanggao* (Modern Advertising), no. 3 (March): 62–63.

Yan Jun. 2001. "Zhongguo de pangke yu pangke" (Chinese Punk and "Fatsos"). http://www.scream-records.net/community/cmmunity042-punk.html. Accessed August 2004.

Yan Zhigang. 1998. "Qinchi sunshang le meiyu du" (Qinchi Damaged Its Reputation). *Beijing qingnian bao* (Beijing Youth Daily), September 16, 6.

Yang Haijun. 2005. "Chaoji nusheng: li pingpai you duoyuan?" (Super Girl: How Far Is It Becoming a Brand?). *Guanggao daguan* (Advertising Panorama), no. 9 (September): 30–32.

Yang Huishu and Huang Gang. 2004. "Lanling jieceng xiaofei pinpai quefa" (The Shortage of Blue-Collar Brands). People.com, March 9. http://www.people.com.cn/GB/paper53/11492/1036830.html. Accessed December 2005.

Yang Keming. 2003. *Haier binfa* (Haier's Art of War). Beijing: Zhongguo jingji chubanshe.

Yang Wen. 2001. "Zaitan 4C" (More on 4C). *Xiandai guanggao* (Modern Advertising), no. 11 (November): 16–19.

Yang Youzhong. 2002. "Zhongguo pinpai zhuru zheng" (The Dwarf Syndrome of Chinese Brands). *Guoji guanggao* (International Advertising), no. 3 (March): 10–11.

Yardley, Jim. 2003. "Internet Sex Column Thrills, and Inflames, China." *New York Times,* November 30. http://www.chinadaily.com.cn/en/doc/2003-12/01/content_286293.htm. Accessed May 2006.

Ye Maozhong. 2003. *Chuangyi jiushi quanli* (Creativity Is Power). Beijing: Jixie gongye chubanshe.

Ye Ying. 2003. "Logo de liliang" (The Power of Logo). *Sanlian shenghuo zhoukan* (Life Weekly), March 24.

———. 2004. "Zhang Yadong: Jixu yingyue shiyan" (Zhang Yadong Continues His Experiment with Music). "Lifestyle Monthly" in *The Economic Observer,* April 16, 4.

Yi, Jeannie J., and Shawn X. Ye. 2003. *The Haier Way: The Making of a Chinese Business Leader and a Global Brand.* Dumont, NJ: Homa & Sekey Books.

Yi Ming. 2001. "Xin shuifa de libi kao" (On the Pros and Cons of the New Tax Policy). *Guoji guanggao* (International Advertising), no. 1 (January): 94–95.

"Yidong Bobo zu, Liangxiang zhaoyang E100 xuanchu xin jingying linian" (Mobilizing the Bobo Tribe: Legend's Zhaoyang Notebook E100 Promoted the Concept of the New Elite). 2003. http://www.sina.com.cn, November 19.

Yu Hong and Deng Zhengqiang. 2000. *Zhongguo dangdai guanggao shi* (The History of Contemporary Chinese Advertising). Changsha, Hunan: Kexue jishu chubanshe.

Yu Jianqiang. 2004. *Meijie zhanlue guangli anli fenxi* (Media Management Strategies: Case Studies). "Media Management" series, ed. Guo Qingguang and Meng Jian. Beijing: Huaxia chubanshe.

Yu Jinjin. 2005. "Guojia tongji ju zhengshi guonei zhongchan jieceng shuju queshi cunzai" (National Bureau of Statistics Confirmed the Existence of the Statistical Data for Defining the Chinese Middle Class). Xinhua Net, January 25. http://news.xinhuanet.com/video/2005-01/25/content_2504048.htm. Accessed June 2006.

Yu Mingyang. 2002. "Guanggao gongsi shichang jingzheng li de quanmian tisheng" (The Overall Intensification of the Capacity of Market Competition of Chinese Advertising Companies). In Qiao Jun et al., eds., *Zhongguo guangao hangye jingzheng li yanjiu* (Studies on the Competitive Capacity of the Chinese Advertising Sector). Chengdu: Xinan caijing daxue chubanshe.

Yu Ruidong. 2002. "Liuxing jujiao: wo xing wo ku, xin xin renlei" (Trend Focus: I do what is cool, neo neo-tribe). China News Service. http://www.chinanews.com.cn/2002-04-25/90/6.html.

Yuan Fang. 2004. "Jiedu xilie guangdian ling" (Reading the Series of SARFT Regulations). *Guanggao ren* (AdMan), no. 11 (November): 29.

Yuan Fang and Wu Qi. 2005. "2004 nian Zhongguo pinpai chengzhang jiance baogao" (The Assessment Report on the Growth of the Chinese brands in 2004). *Guoji guanggao*, no. 4 (April): 12-20.

Yuan Ying and Tian Bin. 2003. "Lanse huoyan de shutu tonggui" (Blue Flames: All Roads Lead to Rome). *Guoji guanggao* (International Advertising), no. 8 (August): 29.

Yudice, George. 2003. *The Expediency of Culture: Users of Culture in the Global Era.* Durham, NC: Duke University Press.

"Zai Zhongguo, an guize jinzheng" (Play Chinese Rules in China). 2005. *Guoji guanggao* (International Advertising), no. 1 (January): 23.

Zang Zhongtang and Cheng Tao. 2005. "Bodao qudao jingbing jianzheng, Ximenzi Bodao lianmeng mingcun shiwang" (Bird's Retrenchment on Channel Policies, Siemens-Bird Alliance in Tatters).

Nanfang zhoumo (Nanfang Weekend), March 3. http://
www.nanfangdaily.com.cn/zm/20050303/jj/it/200503030043.asp.
Accessed June 2005.

Zhang Binwu. 2005. "Changwei: yingxiao yu fei chenmo de daduoshu"
(The Long Tail: Marketing and the Great Non-Silent Majority).
Guanggao daguan (Advertising Panorama), no. 9 (September): 43–
45.

Zhang Haichao. 2004. "Pandian 2003 Zhongguo dianshi guanggao"
(Taking Stock of the Gains of the 2003 Chinese TV Advertising Market). *Guanggao ren* (AdMan), no. 4 (April): 9–30.

Zhang Haiying. 2004. "Guanggao zhaobiao zhengce de pingjia" (An Assessment of the Policy Regarding Advertising Auctions). *Guanggao
ren* (AdMan), no. 4: 21.

Zhang Liming. 2005. "Guonei zhongchan jieceng dingyi de maodun"
(The Contradictions about the Definition for the Chinese Middle
Class). *Guoji guanggao* (International Advertising), no. 3 (March): 44.

Zhang Ruimin. 2003. "Haier shi hai" (Haier Is an Ocean). In *Jingyan:
Zhongguo shichang zhumin pinpai chenggong anli tudian* (Experi-
ences: Case Studies of Successful Chinese Market Brands), ed. Ge
Huaisha. Vol. 1. Changchun: Jilin daxue chubanshe.

Zhang Zhian and Liu Jianneng. 2004. *Meijie yingxiao anli fenxi* (Case
Studies of Media Marketing). "Media Management" Series, ed. Guo
Qingguang and Meng Jian. Beijing: Huaxia chubanshe.

Zhao Nannan. 2002. "'Ling daili' jiaosha Zhongguo guanggao ye"
("Zero Commission" Is Killing Chinese Advertising Industry). *Guoji
guanggao* (International Advertising), no. 6 (June): 10–12.

Zhao Shen. 2001. *Zhongguo jindai guanggao wenhua* (Modern Chinese
Advertising Culture). Changchun, Jilin: Kexue jishu chubanshe.

Zhao Shuguang. 2004. *Meijie jingjixue anli fenxi* (Case Studies of Media
Economy). "Media Management" series, ed. Guo Qingguang and
Meng Jian. Beijing: Huaxia chubanshe.

Zhao Shuguang and Zhang Zhi'an. 2004. *Meijie ziben shichang: Anli
fenxi* (Media Capital Market: Case Analysis). Beijing: Huaxia
chubanshe.

Zhao, Yuezhi. 1998. *Media, Market, and Democracy in China*. Urbana,
IL: University of Illinois Press.

———. 2000. "From Commercialization to Conglomeration: The Transformation of the Chinese Press within the Orbit of the Party State."
Journal of Communication (Spring): 3–25.

———. 2003. "Transnational Capital, the Chinese State, and China's Communication Industries in a Fractured Society." *Javnost—The Public* 10, no. 4: 53–74.

———. 2004. "When the Tide Goes Out, the Rocks Are Revealed." *New Internationalist,* no. 371, September. http://www.newint.org/issue371/tide.htm.

———. 2005. "The Media Matrix: China's Integration with Global Capitalism." In *The Empire Reloaded: Social Register,* ed. Leo Panitch and Colin Leys, 197–217. London: Merlin Press.

"Zhongguo Bubo zu: dangdai bei faxian de dushi buluo" (Chinese Bobos: An Urban Tribe Waiting to Be Discovered). 2002. http://www.sina.com.cn, December 12. Accessed 2004.

Zhongguo dianshi wang (China TV Net). 2005. "Tebie guanzhu: Jiaoju Zhongguo youxian, guanzhu wangluo fazhan" (Special Report: A Focus on China Cable and Network Development). TV.cn, March 24. http://www.tv.cn/gbdsxx/jctj/1111647188.html. Accessed May 2005.

Zhongguo guanggao ye qunian jingying e" (Total Billing of Chinese Advertising Industry Last Year). 2007. *Xinhua.net,* May 29. http://news.xinhuanet.com/fortune/2007-05/29/content_6169497.htm. Accessed May 2007.

Zhou Yen, Wang Ying, and Zhu Miao. 2002. "Shuzihua zhi yang: Wangtai lihe yu biaozhun zhizheng" (The Itch for Digitalization: The Marriage and Divorce of Station and Network and the Fight for Standards). *Meijie* (Media), (October): 14–22.

Zhu Haisong. 2002. *Guoji 4A guanggao gongsi jiben caozuo liucheng* (The Basic Operating Manuals on "Traffic" for International 4A Companies). Guangzhou: Guangdong jingji chubanshe.

Zhu Qingfang. 2004. "Jumin shenghuo he xiaofei jiegou de bianhua" (The Changes in the Structure of Livelihood and Consumption). In *2005: Zhongguo shehui xingshi fenxi yu yuce* (Analysis and Forecast on China's Social Development 2005), ed. Ru Xin, Lu Xueyi, et al., 81–92. Beijing: Shehui kexue wenxian chubanshe.

Zong Qinghou 2007. "Wahaha yu Daneng jiufen de shishi zhenxiang" (The Truth Behind the Wahaha-Danone Dispute). *Sina.com,* April 13. http://finance.sina.com.cn/chanjing/b/20070413/10043499496.shtml. Accessed June 2007.

Acknowledgments

Brand New China testifies to a change in my scholarly pursuits. In 2001, I relocated to MIT and began research that explores the cross-fertilization between academia and the advertising industry. Many people and institutions have helped to make this adventure a possibility.

The Chiang Ching-kuo Foundation for International Scholarly Exchange (USA) supported this project during the initial stages of its conceptualization. Combined with a sabbatical from MIT, the CCK grant enabled me to take a leave between 2003 and 2004 to get my writing started. In subsequent years Lindsay Waters, my editor at Harvard University Press, was instrumental in bringing me to the finishing line earlier than I expected. The production team at the Press—Elizabeth Gilbert, Phoebe Kosman, and Lisa Clark—all played pivotal roles in helping me to prepare the manuscript. Lisa and I spent a memorable evening together, selecting the cover design. Elizabeth was a creative and tireless coordinator and an incredibly engaging editor.

I was fortunate to be able to work at Ogilvy Beijing, a branch of the transnational advertising agency, for two long summers in 2002 and 2004. The opportunity fell into my lap thanks to Jamie A. FlorCruz, CNN bureau chief in China. Jamie introduced me to his basketball buddy Scott Kronick, the head of public relations at Ogilvy, who kindly took me in. Lola Zhang (former senior planner at the agency) mentored me on branding, and together with Vivian Liu (account manager), we had numerous working lunches, brainstorming sessions on campaign concepts, and shopping sprees at supermarkets as part of our marketing assignments. I am also very grateful to other Ogilvy coworkers in Beijing, among them my good-humored Australian boss, Edward Bell (head of strategic planning); wise and gentle Raymond Tao (vice president); fun-loving Liang Li (former planner); Mickey Chak (group planning partner); Sarah Xu, Linda Li, and Samuel Liu in the Knowledge Center; and of course T. B. Song, chairman of Ogilvy & Mather Greater China. I also owe a great deal to Lisa Li, marketing manager at Kimberly-Clark in Beijing, for her numerous insights on marketing from the advertisers' viewpoint.

This book is dedicated to an old friend, Bruce Oltchick, former executive vice president of advertising sales at Star TV Hong Kong and former vice president of Grey Asia. Bruce was one of my first (and best) students at Middlebury College, where I first started teaching. Although he is likely to disagree, I consider him one of the smartest admen I have known. He insists on addressing me as "Wang laoshi" (Teacher Wang), even though our teacher-student relationship has reversed since I began my research on Chinese advertising. He read several chapters of this book, raised provocative questions, sent me useful articles, and called me often from abroad to debate important issues. His adventurous spirit, intellect, generous friendship, and unusual sense of humor are greatly cherished. I am fortunate to have remained connected to him and his father, Merrill Oltchick, for twenty-six years.

Other friends from whom I learned a lot include veteran adman Larry Rinaldi, marketing director of ONA (Office of New Advertising) and former chief operating officer of JoyMedia Group in

Beijing, who shed light on product placement in China for me, and my young friend Ye Ying (at the *Economic Observer* in Beijing), who chatted with me enthusiastically about trends in Chinese youth culture and creative culture. Tara Tranguch at Wireless Marketing provided me with valuable data pertaining to Asia's mobile phone market; she and I had many good conversations in Beijing about the development of Chinese new media. Shi Song, a research affiliate of MIT's comparative media studies program, volunteered wonderful assistance and helped me sort out the complicated statistics on China's Generations X and Y. Together with population specialist Professor Zhou Yun at People's University in Beijing, he brought the data sets up to date with scientific precision. Bao Yaming at the Shanghai Academy of the Social Sciences found the commercial for Libo Beer analyzed in Chapter 1. Wang Xiaoming at Shanghai University introduced me to Lindsay Waters. I had useful exchanges regarding the Asian neo-neo-tribes and Japanese advertising with Yuichi Washida, research director at Hakuhodo and also a research affiliate of the comparative media studies program at MIT. Colleagues Yuezhi Zhao, Michael Keane, Stephanie Donald, Anthony Fung, and Jack Qiu are fellow travelers in the emerging field of Chinese media. I would like to thank Yuezhi Zhao particularly for her sharp critical reading of the manuscript. Generous comments from Michael Keane, Michael Dutton, and two other anonymous readers also helped me to tighten my writing.

I have built a personal library on Chinese advertising and marketing thanks to resources provided by Longzhimei (Dragon Media), a specialty bookstore on advertising in China. Their staff in the Beijing office has offered me patient, warm support and has taken meticulous care of my orders year after year. It is no exaggeration to say that without Longzhimei, this book could not have been written. I am also grateful to the staff at *International Marketing (Guoji Guanggao)*, the leading industry magazine on Chinese advertising, for letting me subscribe to the magazine directly from abroad. The annual research funds that came with the S. C. Fang Chair at MIT have made it possible for me to conduct the costly advertising research that was necessary for this project. I thank Mr. Kenneth Fang for his confidence in me and support of my work.

My colleagues at MIT, among them Ian Condry, Kurt Fendt, and Edward Turk at the department of foreign languages and literatures (FL&L) and William Uricchio and Henry Jenkins in the comparative media studies program (CMS), contributed valuable thinking on the subject of advertising and new media. I also owe my former dean, Philip Khoury, many warm thanks for his strong support and wise professional counseling whenever it was needed. Winnie Wong, a graduate student in MIT's history, theory, and criticism program, is an inspiring interlocutor on matters of cultural theory. She read several chapters and offered smart and inspirational remarks. It is students like her that make teaching exciting and challenging.

I am also indebted to my former student Helen J. Tang, who came to my rescue by consolidating the reference list on short notice. Helen also did the indexing and proofreading for me. Doug Purdy at CMS has helped me build the video collection of television commercials at MIT. Staff members Christine Phillips, KC Cortinovis, and Jeffrey Pearlin at FL&L have helped in logistical terms—Christine and KC printed numerous versions of the manuscript and Jeff helped solve the many computer-related technical problems I encountered.

One of the daunting tasks in publishing this book was to acquire permission to use the illustrations. Dealing with conglomerates like Coca-Cola Atlanta was impossible, but I was able to clear up most Chinese rights issues surprisingly quickly during a short visit to Beijing in January 2007. My special thanks go to Chunyan Wang of

Creative Commons China and her enthusiastic friends (Dr. Li Xu at Qinghua University, Fang Jie, Fu Yulin, Wang Qiuyang, and Huang Aiping), who helped me connect with Zhu Mingping at Taihu Advertising Company in Suzhou. The company owns the image of the perfectly aligned fork and chopsticks on the jacket—"when East meets West"—an outdoor ad made for Bifengfang Food Court. The copywriter for the original wording in this ad was Liu Wenzheng, and the art designer, Chen Huipin. I was delighted to spot this exquisitely designed advertisement, because its double-edged imagery conveys perfectly what this book is all about.

Qin Li at Ye Maozhong Advertising Company, Mickey Chak, Raymond Tao, Vivian Liu, and Sarah Xu at Ogilvy Beijing, Lisa Li at Kimberly-Clark, and Victor Liang at Baidu.com helped me clear up various other rights issues. My colleague Chen Tong at MIT, Professors Gao Xudong from Qinghua University and Li Yuan from Xi'an Jiotung University introduced me to Haier and repeatedly offered me help in negotiating with the company to release an image. My friend Cui Zien (novelist and internationally known film maker) at the Beijing Film Academy helped me to reconnect with Zhang Yujing, one of the five young people who participated in my Ogilvy research on youth culture and cool music (see Chapter 6); Ye Ying at the *Economic Observer* helped me find Liu Tianqi (Miss Cool in that chapter) rather miraculously. Zhang and Liu were very generous in granting me the permission to publish their photographs.

A writing career is a lonely one, but I am blessed with many friendships. Don DeSander shared many exciting discoveries I made about ideas and life; Tani Barlow is a fellow traveler in many regards and a sympathetic sister; Benjamin White's spiritual presence and patience are a great comfort. Lawrence Gunselman and Justin Life are two young friends whose creativity and friendship have brought me much joy. I also thank Leo Ching, Cui Zien, Dai

Jinhua, Jane Dunphy, Su-hui Hsieh, Liang Li, Lisa Li, Lin Chun, Vivian Liu, Larry Rinaldi, Hsiao-wei Rupprecht, Heidi Sarkozy, Lea Wakeman, Wang Chunyan, Yuichi Washida, Wen Tiejun, Sarah Xu, Ye Ying, and Lola Zhang for the generosity of their hearts. And although she is long gone, my daughter, Candy R. Wei, is entwined into the very fabric of my being.

Over the years, I have received numerous encouraging responses and stimulating inquiries from young scholars and students in various disciplines. Their moral support matters a great deal. I particularly thank all the students at MIT who have taken my course "Advertising and Popular Culture." They are my best teachers in new media practices. I cheer the young minds who are the ultimate avant-garde.

An earlier version of Chapter 5, now revised, appeared in "Bourgeois Bohemians in China? Neo-Tribes and the Urban Imaginary," *The China Quarterly,* no. 183 (September 2005), 532–548, © The China Quarterly, 2005. An excerpt from an earlier draft of Chapter 6 was published in *Global Media and Communication* under the title "Youth Culture, Music, and Cell Phone Branding in China," vol. 1 (2), copyright © Sage Publications 2005, and is used here in revised form by permission of Sage Publications Ltd.

Index

Aaker, David, 25, 123, 326n5
AC Nielsen, 267, 271
Adornian critique, 101
advertising agencies. *See* 4As; advertising industry; TNAAs
advertising industry, 4, 23, 41, 43, 45, 99, 109, 169, 254, 259, 260, 288, 356n19
advertising medium, 5, 27, 30, 85, 297; TV, 247–248; TV drama, 278. *See also* billboard
advertising theorists. *See* Aaker, David; Ogilvy, David; Ong Xiangdong; Ries, Al; Trout, Jack
alternative, 72; music, 215–216, 217, 228, 241, 244; youth, 201, 228. *See also* Chun Shu; *linglei*
American Idol, 29, 175, 244, 344n23. *See also Super Girl*
Anderson, Chris, 14, 298, 304, 355n12
Anhui Satellite TV, 273, 277, 278, 279
AOL Time Warner, 168, 171, 254, 258
Apollo *(Taiyang shen)*, 26
Apple, 214

Art of War, 155–156. *See also* Sun Tzu
Association of Accredited Advertising Companies. *See* 4As

baby boomers, 19, 20, 338n14
Back Dormitory Boys, 31–32
baidu.com, 295–296, 298, 354n8
Bates, 45, 48, 49–50, 51, 322. *See also* Libo Beer
Baudrillard, Jean, 309
Beck's, 64, 68, 69, 76; ad campaign, 70–71
Beijing Consensus, 134, 139, 141, 331n18. *See also* Brand China; Ramos, Joshua Cooper
Bell, Edward, 12, 318
bentu, 58–59, 64, 108, 124. *See also* localization
billboard, 8, 50, 80, 168–172, 209, 247, 307, 337n10
Bird (Ningbo Bird), 15, 62, 64, 113, 211, 218, 219, 291, 341n12
blog, 100, 101, 164; Lenovo story, 165–166; marketing, 101, 333n9
bloggers. *See* Bluethinker; Hong Huang; Mao Shijie; Rowdy Swallow; Sister Lotus; Wang Yukun